CReating **I**ndependence *throu*

Helping Teachers Teach and Learners Learn

Project CRISS®

4th Edition

Carol Santa, Ph.D.
Lynn Havens
Debra Franciosi, Ed.D.
Bonnie Valdes

Carol Santa, Ph.D. **Lynn Havens** **Debra Franciosi, Ed.D.** **Bonnie Valdes**

If you have any questions or would like additional staff development, please contact:

40 Second Street East, Suite 249
Kalispell, Montana 59901
406-758-6440 (direct)
877-502-7477 (toll free)
406-758-6444 (fax)

info@projectcriss.com
www.projectcriss.com

Copyright © 2012 by Lifelong Learning, Inc. (dba Project CRISS), Kalispell, Montana. Copyright © 1988, 1996, 2004 by Kendall Hunt Publishing Company, Dubuque, Iowa.

ISBN 978-0-7575-9455-7

Cover design:	Leslie Clayborn, Clayborn Graphics
Book layout and design:	Brittany Romo and Charles R. Deese
Front cover photos:	Heidi Long (top and bottom), iStock (second photo), Leslie Clayborn (third photo)
Back cover photo:	Heidi Long

CRISS-trained educators have permission to use the online reproducibles that accompany this volume (with students in their school(s) and classrooms).

All rights reserved. No part of this publication may be reproduced, stored in a retrieval system, or transmitted, in any form or by any means, electronic, mechanical, photocopying, recording, or otherwise, without the prior written permission of the copyright owner.

www.kendallhunt.com

Kendall Hunt Publishing Company has the exclusive rights to reproduce this work and to publicly display this work.

Printed in the United States of America
10 9 8 7 6 5 4 3 2   15 14 13 12

ACKNOWLEDGMENTS

Revising this Project CRISS training manual has truly been a labor of love as we so strongly believe in the principles elaborated upon in this book. This work is a collaborative effort. The four of us spent countless hours head-to-head and phone-to-phone debating and reviewing the components of the third edition along with the exciting new Frameworks and strategies developed since its publication. This fourth edition product arose not only from our collaboration, but depended heavily on the experience and knowledge shared with us by hundreds of educators across the country—especially by our CRISS trainers. Although we cannot mention everyone, we would like to thank and recognize our Master Level Trainers and Project CRISS Advisory Board members, without whose support we would not have this program. They are:

Carol Avery	**Chuck Kobliska**
Judy Bramlett	**Evelyn Maycumber**
Peggy Clark	**Jeff Means**
Cheryl Conn	**Donald Meints**
Maureen Danner	**Ken Miller**
Anna Deese	**Linda Moehring**
Maureen Dombrowski	**Nancy Rice**
Kit Granat	**Marg Stewart**
Ray Jones	**Elmer Whitcraft**

In addition, we want to acknowledge the help, support, and tireless energy of the Project CRISS office staff: Stacy Liebig, Jenny Martin, and Darlene Treweek.

CONTENTS

Chapter 1 **Teaching for Understanding** 1

The Elements of Metacognition 3
    Background Knowledge 3
    Purpose Setting 3
    Author's Craft 4
    Active Persistence and Transformation 4
        Writing 4
        Discussion 4
        Visualizing 4
        Organizing 5
    Reflection 5
The Frameworks for Teaching and Learning 7
    The Framework for Teaching 9
        PLAN for Instruction 9
        PREPARE for Student Learning 11
        ENGAGE with Content and Transform Information 13
        REFLECT on Teaching and Learning 15
    Modeling and Guided Practice 15
    The Framework for Learning 17
Summary 19
Research Base 21

Chapter 2 **Text Complexity: Identifying the Author's Craft and Design** 23

Section 1: Examining Text Complexity 24
    Quantitative Measures of Text Difficulty 24
    Qualitative Measures Defining Considerate Text 25
    Common Writing Patterns 27
    Student and Text Variables 28
    Content Domain Variables 30
    Student Knowledge of Text Structure 32
Section 2: Tools for Examining Text 33
    Content Textbook Assessment Rubric 33
    Sample Subject-Specific Rubrics 37
Summary 39
Research Base 41

Chapter 3   Analyzing & Applying Basic Patterns & Structures   43

Analyzing Author's Craft and Perspective   46
    Analyzing Author's Craft   46
    Analyzing the Author's Perspective   47
Main Idea—Detail Organizers   50
    Power Thinking   50
        Power Writing   53
    Selective Underlining and Highlighting   54
    Concept Maps   55
        Pre- and Post-Reading Concept Maps   58
Comparison Organizers   58
    Venn Diagrams   58
        V-Diagram   61
        Contrast and Compare Chart   62
        Differences and Similarities Chart   63
        Triangular Comparison Diagram   63
Pattern Organizers   64
    Sequence Organizers   64
    Pattern Puzzles   66
Summary   68
Research Base   69

Chapter 4   Discussion: The Conversation of Learning   71

Small Group Discussion Strategies   75
    Think-Pair-Share   75
    Mind Streaming   76
        Paired Verbal Fluency   76
    ABC Brainstorming   77
    Three-Minute Pause   78
    Concentric Circle Discussions   79
    Fishbowl   79
    Socratic Circles   80
    Read-and-Say-Something   81
    Read and Explain   81
    Discussion Web   82
    Sticky-Note Discussions   84
        React to the Fact   86
    Carousel Brainstorming   86
    Seed Discussions   87
    Roles Within Cooperative Teams   89
Questioning Strategies   94
    Authentic Questions   95
    Question-Answer Relationships   97
        Question Starters   100
    Higher Level Thinking Questions   102
    Questioning the Author (QtA)   105
Summary   108
Research Base   109

Chapter 5   Active Strategies for Learning   111

Pre/Post Strategies   112
    Know—Want to Learn—Learned Plus: K-W-L +   112
    Anticipation Guides   117
Visualizing Strategies   119
    Mental Imagery   120
    Picture Notes   121
        Review a Book in an Hour   123
Paraphrasing Strategies   123
    In My Own Words   123
Summarizing Strategies   124
    Summarizing Nonfiction Text   125
    Read-Recall-Check-Organize-Summarize   127
    Magnet Summaries   127
    One-Sentence Summaries   129
Combined Strategies   131
    Reciprocal Teaching   132
Summary   133
Research Base   134

Chapter 6   Organizing for Learning: Two-Column Notes, Frames, and Story Plans   135

Two-Column Notes   137
    Main Idea—Detail Notes   137
        The 12 Minute Study   139
        Fact-Reason   140
        Fact-Opinion   140
        Main Events—Significance   141
        Three-Column Notes   141
    Conclusion-Support Notes   142
        Conclusion-Support-Interpretation Notes   143
        Advantages-Disadvantages   145
        Proposition-Support   146
        Hypothesis-Evidence   148
    Problem-Solution Notes   149
        Problem-Solution Graphic Structure   152
        Problem-Analysis Notes   153
        Cause-Effect (or Because-Effect)   153
        History-Change Frame   153
    Process Notes   154
        Problem-Solving Organizer   157
Other Organizing Formats   158
    Content Frames   158
    Story Plans   161
Summary   166
Research Base   167

Chapter 7   **Informal Writing to Learn**   **169**

     Free-Write Entries   170
        Stop-and-Think   171
     Double-Entry Reflective Journals   174
     Dialogue Journals   176
     Pre- and Post-Reading Entries   178
     Observation Entries   180
     You Ought to Be in Pictures   181
        Walking Through a Painting   184
     Perspective Entries   184
     Explanation Entries   186
Managing and Evaluating Journals and Learning Logs   189
Summary   190
Research Base   191

Chapter 8   **Formal Writing to Learn: Writing Reports and Essays**   **193**

     Writing Templates   195
     Spool Papers   200
     RAFT   206
        Multi-Genre Report   212
     The Essay Examination   213
Summary   216
Research Base   218

Chapter 9   Vocabulary   219

Research Principles   220
Organizing for Vocabulary Instruction   222
    Identifying Words Worthy of Rich Instruction   222
    Academic Word Walls   223
    Vocabulary Learning Logs   224
Survival Word Attack Skills   225
    Figuring Out New Words from Context   226
    Morphemic Analysis   228
Building Personal Definitions   231
    Rate Your Knowledge   231
        Vocabulary Knowledge Chart   232
    Student-Friendly Explanations   233
Graphic Organizers and Charts   235
    Concept of Definition Map   235
    Vocabulary Maps   238
        Vocabulary Flash Cards   240
    Frayer Model   240
    Semantic Feature Analysis   244
Active Processing Through Writing and Discussion   245
    Word Elaboration   246
    Sentence and Word Expansion   247
    Word Combining   249
        Possible Sentences   250
Summary   251
Research Base   252

Chapter 10   Program Implementation   253

Quality of Project CRISS Implementation   254
    The Five Star School   254
Impact of Project CRISS on Instruction   255
    Framework for Teaching Inventory   255
    Level of Use Matrix   256
    CRISS Framework for Teaching   256
    Teacher Journals and Portfolios   258
    Administrator Support and Observations   258
Student Implementation   259
    District/School-Specific Questions   259
    Framework for Learning Inventory   260
    Informal Research Studies   260
    Quantitative Research   260
Summary   261
Research Base   262

Chapter 11 Project CRISS: A Story of Teachers and Students as Researchers 263

Teacher Research 264
- High School Mathematics 265
- High School Science 265
- High School History and Science 265
- High School History 266
- The Role of Reflection 266

Student Research 267
- Fourth Grade Social Studies 267
- High School Language Arts 268
- Eighth Grade Mathematics 271

Framework for Learning Research 272
- Seventh Grade Montana History 272
- Longitudinal Research 276

Summary 278
Research Base 279

Chapter 12 Beyond the CRISS Workshop 281

Electronic Resources 282
Resources for the Classroom 283
- Project CRISS for Students I 283
- Project CRISS for Students II 284
- Project CRISS Classroom Presentation Materials 284
- Project CRISS Reference Guide for Teachers 284
- CRISS Learning Posters 285
- CRISS at a Glance Poster/Desk Mat 285
- CRISS at a Glance for Students 285

Resources for the School/District 286
- CRISS for Administrators 286
- CRISS Cornerstones 286
- Reading in the Content Area with Dr. Carol Santa 286
- Project CRISS Certified Trainer Materials 286

Reaching out to Parents 287
- CRISS for Parents 287
- Project CRISS for Homeschool Parents 287

Research Base 288

References Cited 289

Index 297

Teaching for Understanding

1

TEACHING FOR UNDERSTANDING

- Elements of Metacognition
  - Background Knowledge
  - Purpose Setting
  - Author's Craft
  - Active Persistence & Transformation
  - Reflection

- Frameworks for Teaching & Learning
  - Framework for Teaching
  - Framework for Learning
  - Modeling & Guided Practice

We teach based on who we are and what we believe. Our personal philosophies about how children learn make us the kind of teachers we are. Usually, we don't make time to think about how our personal theories permeate every aspect of our teaching. Yet, taking the time is important because our own personalities, our own instructional theories, and our understanding of what is important in our own particular discipline define how we teach.

Project CRISS (CReating Independence through Student-owned Strategies) has helped us to uncover what we believe about teaching and to modify our philosophies based on our own growth as professionals. It has been and will be our professional journey.

We began this journey more than twenty-five years ago because our students did not have sufficient knowledge about how to learn, and consequently remained dependent on us to do the learning for them. This awareness launched us into a continuous process of self-examination. Perhaps our teaching models were wrong. At the time, the most prevalent teaching model in our high school was the lecture → read → answer the questions → take a test paradigm. Teachers taught like they were taught. This flat, boring methodology derailed our vitality and curiosity. Even more damaging, it was degrading to our students! Such a passive, teacher-directed paradigm also conflicted with common sense and our growing knowledge of theoretical principles about how students read, write, study, and learn. We had to change the situation.

As developers of Project CRISS, we became teacher-scholars. We read professional research, conducted our own classroom research, and presented at conferences. We started teacher support groups in our schools where we took time to talk about our discoveries with other colleagues. We became a professional learning community of knowledge-seekers and investigators, unwilling to stagnate in our professional lives. As scholars, we puzzled about the progress of our students, asked hard questions, and studied the latest research. We developed a philosophy of learning and teaching to guide our practice, basing it on our own experiences and on wisdom gathered from researchers, practitioners, and most importantly, our students. Now, over twenty-five years later, our CRISS community of teacher-learners continues to nourish our scholarly lives.

We found the literature on reading comprehension and learning to be vast and sometimes confusing. Given the richness and complexities of this field, we pulled together fundamental premises, the big ideas about what is essential to teaching and learning, and created Project CRISS as a means to support teachers in their quest to develop students who are independent, lifelong learners.

▲ ▲ ▲

CRISS represents a merging of work from cognitive psychology, social learning theory, and neurological research about how our brains learn (Fisher, Frey & Lapp, 2009; Kintsch, 2009). Kintsch argues that learning represents a construction of knowledge where the reader builds a representation of meaning. CRISS is not simply a collection of discrete strategies lacking cohesiveness; it is a means for students to build knowledge and to examine the how and why of their learning processes to help them comprehend and learn more effectively. As teachers, we ask ourselves, *do our teaching methodologies reflect what we know about accepted theories of how students read, learn, and remember information?* And, more importantly, *do students have a deep understanding of these principles as a backdrop for evaluating and planning their own learning?*

A foundational element of Project CRISS is the concept of metacognition. Guiding students to become strategic, metacognitive learners is the fundamental goal of CRISS. It is the key to learning independence, and it rests on a rich history of research and practice.

Over the past thirty years, scientists and practitioners have attained basic and applied knowledge about human learning (Bransford, Brown & Cocking, 2000; Kintsch, 2009). In reviewing the literature, a central principle underlying much of the research is metacognition. Metacognition is a term used to refer "to the knowledge and control we have of our own cognitive strategies" (Baker, 2002), where "knowledge" refers to one's understanding of oneself as a learner, including our knowledge of learning expectations and the strategies needed to accomplish learning tasks. "Control" refers to the construction of a plan for learning and monitoring whether or not one is successful with that plan. Being metacognitive involves evaluating and remediating comprehension and learning difficulties that arise. Since understanding is essential to success in subject area learning, students must learn to recognize when they understand content and when they need more information. They also need to know how to repair gaps in their comprehension and how to use strategies to extend their understanding beyond the information presented.

The central goal of this project is to develop expert, executive learners: Students who achieve well in school have a heightened awareness of the state of their learning and have a repertoire of self-regulatory behaviors. They know when they understand, and they can employ a variety of strategies to attain meaning (Duke & Pearson, 2002). In other words, successful learners have a deep understanding of what it means to be metacognitive. Teachers and their students also need to understand that being metacognitive involves some important sub-processes or elements.

THE ELEMENTS OF METACOGNITION

Metacognition
- Background Knowledge
- Purpose Setting
- Author's Craft
- Active Persistence and Transformation
    ✓ Writing
    ✓ Discussing
    ✓ Visualizing
    ✓ Organizing
- Reflection

Background Knowledge

Metacognitive readers prepare for learning by understanding how their background knowledge influences their comprehension. Integrating new information with prior knowledge lies at the heart of metacognition and comprehension. Activating background knowledge opens channels in the brain that allow new information to latch onto existing understandings. The more knowledge a learner brings to a learning situation, the more that learner can take away and comprehend. This conclusion is not only documented by many research studies (Kintsch, 2009; Pearson & Fielding, 1991; Pressley, 2000), but by neurological research—particularly that on selective attention (Jensen, 2005). We are far more likely to attend to information when we have some previous knowledge or mental priming about the topic. We have trouble paying attention to something we know nothing about.

Purpose Setting

Metacognitive learners have a purpose for every learning task, whether it's reading a text, listening to a lecture, or watching a media presentation. Having a clear purpose allows learners to focus their attention and disregard extraneous information. A key facet to being a metacognitive learner is understanding the power of purpose. Reading or listening for *specific* information influences what one recalls (Pickert & Anderson, 1977; Narvaez, 2002).

Author's Craft

Metacognitive learners have an awareness of the Author's Craft and how texts differ according to content areas. When students know how authors structure their writing, they can more readily understand and remember what they read. Good readers and writers know how text structure aids comprehension. They recognize poetic forms as well as the structure of a scientific research article or a word problem in mathematics. Strong research supports the idea that knowledge of expository and narrative text structures plays an important role in comprehension (Kintsch, 2009; Goldman & Rakestraw, 2000).

Active Persistence and Transformation

Metacognitive learners actively and persistently engage in their learning. It takes effort to go beyond the written word and build personal representations of text. When the going gets tough, metacognitive learners don't give up; they energetically puzzle through challenging content using a variety of strategies and tools. Research in cognitive psychology documents this activity principle: Learning happens when students build representations of meaning by transforming information through discussion, writing, visualizing, and organizing (Duke & Pearson, 2002; Keene & Zimmermann, 2007; Kintsch, 2009; Wilkinson & Son, 2011). Just passively reading, viewing, or listening isn't enough.

Writing

Few students think about how writing is a way of knowing, and we must help them recognize why it is integral to all learning (Graham & Hebert, 2010). It is a powerful metacognitive tool that allows us to construct our own meaning; it lets us know what we know. We cannot write about something we do not understand. When we can explain concepts in writing to ourselves and to others, we can claim knowledge as our own. The process forces us to actively persist after—and make choices about—meaning, and it helps each of us make personal sense out of what we read. In addition, writing provides vital personal processing time that allows neural connections to solidify and imprint after each new learning experience (Jensen, 2005). The power of writing as a metacognitive tool cannot be overstated.

Discussion

Learning is an active, constructive process and a social, interpersonal process. Work in brain research highlights the importance of students interacting with one another. Students create meaning by transforming information and by building their own connections. Discussion is essential to these constructive processes. We live in a social world and learn by interacting with others (Anders & Spitler, 2007). By pooling our understandings, we develop deeper meaning. Teachers who use a one-sided lecture method as their primary mode of teaching not only discount key principles drawn from cognitive and social psychology, but also run counter to what we know about how the brain functions. Discussion is critical because we are biologically wired for communicating with one another (Jensen, 2005).

Visualizing

When readers construct mental pictures about what they are reading, their comprehension improves (Gambrell & Koskinen, 2002). Creating mental images during and after reading aids metacognition. That is, visualization helps learners know whether or not they are understanding (Zoss, 2009). It also brings student misconceptions to the surface. In addition, representing visualized images with pictures and symbols leads to active engagement through transformation.

Organizing

Our short-term memories have limitations; the average adult can remember from five to nine discrete units of new information at once (Miller, 1956) However, our ability to remember increases dramatically when we organize information by clustering discrete bits into categories, by developing hierarchical relationships, and by converting information into charts, notes, and concept maps (Kintsch, 2009). The more organized the information is, the better it is remembered.

Reflection

For students to become effective metacognitive learners, they must have time during and after a learning experience to evaluate their learning (Baker, 2008). They need to recognize both what they did to be successful, and how to modify their learning approaches to become more effective. Writing (learning log entries—see Chapter 7) and discussion (process conferences) provide outlets for reflection. Helping students use the elements of metacognition as the basis of this self-examination fosters understanding of what it takes to be a successful, independent learner.

During or at the end of a lesson or learning plan, guide reflective discussion by using the questions relating to one or more of the following topics based on the CRISS Framework for Learning. Pose questions that relate to the specific components of metacognition emphasized during the lesson. Focus on the strategy(ies) used to activate each metacognitive element.

- **Metacognition**: *How did you evaluate your comprehension? How did the strategy(ies) you used (writing, discussion, visualizing, organizing) work for you? What could you do better next time—use the same strategy(ies) more effectively, modify or adapt the strategy(ies), and/or use a different strategy(ies)?*

- **Background knowledge**: *What did you do in order to think about what you already knew? How did the strategy(ies) you used (writing, discussion, visualizing, organizing) work for you? What could you do better next time—use the same strategy(ies) more effectively, modify or adapt the strategy(ies), and/or use a different strategy(ies)?*

- **Purpose setting**: *Did you have clear purposes? If so, how did you use them to help you learn? If not, what could you have done to determine the purpose for this learning activity (reading, listening, viewing, or hands-on)?*

- **Author's craft**: *What internal and external text structures were present, and how did you identify them? How did you use the features you identified to help you learn?*

- **Active persistence**: *How were you actively engaged? How did the strategy(ies) you used (writing, discussion, visualizing, organizing) work for you? What could you do better next time—use the same strategy(ies) more effectively, modify or adapt the strategy(ies), and/or use a different strategy(ies)?*

- **Transformation**: *What were the different ways you transformed information? How did the strategy(ies) you used (writing, discussion, visualizing, organizing) work for you? What could you do better next time—use the same strategy(ies) more effectively, modify or adapt the strategy(ies), and/or use a different strategy(ies)?*

- **Strategy**: *How did this strategy work for you? Why do you think it (worked/didn't work) for you? How could you use it more effectively next time? How could you use (modify or adapt) the strategy for a different purpose in your Framework for Learning? How could you use or modify the strategy for use in a Framework for Learning for another class?*

In this manual, you will find sample reflective process conference questions in a shaded box at the end of the "Introduction, Modeling, and Reflection" section for each strategy (see page 50 for a sample). These or similar strategy-specific questions should be asked of students during a lesson, after they have successfully learned and applied the strategy. When students have this opportunity to share what works and what doesn't and when they can hear how others used and/or adapted a strategy, they will be more likely to try the strategy again and eventually "own" it.

▲ ▲ ▲

Why is being metacognitive so essential to becoming a mature, lifelong learner and so fundamental to Project CRISS? When students are metacognitive, they…

- are in charge of their own learning.
- know how to construct meaning by sorting through the author's words to fit with their own background experiences and knowledge.
- set learning goals, know how to use a variety of strategies to meet these goals, and can revise their plans to reach their goals effectively.
- know how to reread, to self-question, and to organize information.
- constantly assess their own learning progress. *Do I understand this point? Should I write this idea down? Is the author making this clear, or do I need additional information?*

The conceptualization of the good reader as metacognitive–a goal-directed, active strategist–sets the stage for the strategic instruction offered in this project. Project CRISS helps students understand how to set their own goals for learning and, through teacher modeling and guidance, how to use a variety of comprehension strategies for learning content. More importantly, students learn how to dig beneath the application of strategies to examine their effectiveness based on the metacognitive elements. When students own metacognition, they truly become independent learners.

As part of daily content instruction, we must help students experience what it means to be metacognitive. They need to understand the how and why of metacognition as a foundation that underlies the active process of comprehension. To help students grapple with the concept, we define it as having two central components. The first is awareness of one's learning processes, and the second is having and using a toolbox of strategies to facilitate learning. Through modeling and reflection, we help students understand why these components are so critical to their success as learners. Vignette I (below) is an example of how to introduce the concept of metacognition to middle and high schools students. For a lesson that models how to incorporate metacognitive teaching, see Vignette II on page 19.

Vignette I:
Helping Students Understand Metacognition

The teacher explains, *Metacognition is a term you are going to hear a lot about in this class. By the end of this school year, I hope you will all be metacognitive learners. Let me begin with a brief explanation of what metacognition means, and then I want to share with you how it works for me.*

Being metacognitive involves becoming aware of how your learning is progressing. You can think about metacognition as having two parts. The first part is self-awareness about learning. Each of us has a device in our heads that watches over our learning. If we are metacognitive learners, this device continually whispers in our ears as we read, write, talk, and listen. It badgers us with questions and suggestions about understanding. How is it going?

Do you understand? Be metacognitive. Don't give up. Keep trying. Ask yourself questions to see if you are getting it.

Students having trouble in school haven't turned on this monitoring device. They don't know when they aren't understanding. They think the job of monitoring their learning belongs to someone outside of themselves, such as a teacher or parent. The first step toward becoming metacognitive is taking responsibility for evaluating your own learning progress. You, as the learner, are the only one who can do it. So turn on that monitoring device in your head. Let it badger your brain!

The teacher further explains, *Being aware of whether or not you understand leads to the second part of being metacognitive—the decisions you make about how to fix your comprehension if you aren't getting it. Not only do successful learners keep track of whether or not they are learning, but they also know strategies to go after meaning. In fact, metacognitive learners use a variety of learning strategies to ensure their understanding and learning.*

Next, the teacher models her use of metacognition with a reading selection from one of the course texts. As she reads, she stops after each paragraph and asks herself if she "gets it." She might start with, *Yes, this seems clear,* but, finally, she identifies a lack of comprehension, *No, I don't get it; I'm confused. I don't understand what the author is trying to say about . . . I need to reread this and figure out what I am not understanding. What questions do I have? I'll read the next paragraph to see if the author does a better job of explaining it. If it still isn't clear, I am going to talk with someone about what I'm not understanding.*

Turning to the class, she continues, *Did you notice that when I determined the text wasn't making sense, I knew a few strategies I could try—asking myself questions, rereading, reading ahead, and talking with someone—to help me understand? Metacognition involves this two-part process—self-monitoring understanding and, when needed, applying strategies for fixing-up comprehension.*

So, while learning the content of this course, you will also learn how to become metacognitive, strategic learners. In other words, I am going to teach you how to turn up the volume on those monitoring devices in your heads, and I will show you how to use learning strategies to succeed with the content in this class. My two goals for you are you to (1) learn the content of my course, and (2) learn how to learn so you won't have to rely on anyone but yourself to be successful.

THE FRAMEWORKS FOR TEACHING AND LEARNING

The concept of metacognition forms the basis of both the teaching and the learning frameworks which define Project CRISS. Liang and Dole (2006) describe an instructional framework as "a set of principles or ideas to organize instruction." While they only talk about frameworks in the context of teaching, we have expanded their idea of frameworks to include student learning. In both of our contexts, frameworks encompass the big ideas about teaching and learning. Frameworks are not scripts or simple process steps; they are the fundamental principles guiding instructional and learning decisions.

Our intention in casting Project CRISS as two frameworks—a Framework for Learning and a Framework for Teaching—is to make the theoretical underpinnings of Project CRISS more cohesive and accessible to you and your students. We use the teaching framework to plan instruction and to guide students to internalization of the learning framework. We think of these two frameworks as the flipsides of the same metacognitive coin—with one side focusing on the teacher's instructional role and the other on the student's role as the learner. It makes sense, given their mutual metacognitive foundation, that the frameworks are practically identical. They include the same steps: PREPARE, ENGAGE, and REFLECT. The only surface difference between the two is that the Framework for Teaching begins with an additional step: PLAN (see online reproducibles for Chapter

1 for a Framework for Teaching template). Conceptualizing this rich and vibrant field of literacy learning as two frameworks brings order to the myriad of ideas and theories about what it takes to make a difference in the learning lives of young people. As we describe them, you will see why these frameworks are so central to every aspect of this project.

CRISS Framework for Teaching: The CRISS Strategic Learning Plan (P-PER)	CRISS Framework for Learning: The Ingredients of Metacognition (PER)
PLAN *for instruction* • Determine Enduring Understandings • Create Assessments • Assess Student Needs • Select a variety of Content Materials	
PREPARE *for student learning* • Elicit Background Knowledge • Set Purposes for Student Learning • Determine Author's Craft Instruction	**PREPARE** *for student learning* • Think about Background Knowledge • Determine Purposes for Learning • Identify the Author's Craft
ENGAGE *with Content & Transform Information* • Identify Processes to Facilitate Involvement and Active Persistence • Identify and Facilitate Learning Activities with Writing, Discussion, Visualization, and Organization	**ENGAGE** *with Content & Transform Information* • Be Involved and Actively Persistent • Write, Discuss, Visualize, and Organize
REFLECT *on Teaching & Learning* • Facilitate Student Process and Content Discussions • Evaluate Student Learning • Analyze and Evaluate Planning & Instruction, including Modeling	**REFLECT** *on Teaching and Learning* • Evaluate the Effectiveness of Learning Processes • Assess Content Learning

Although the recursive nature of these frameworks cannot be shown effectively in a linear diagram, it is important to note here that throughout the PER stages, a learner will be moving back and forth through the steps. And further, for each learning activity within a lesson (different reading selections, labs, field trip, lectures, etc.) students will activate different PER processes as needed in a continual cycle of connecting with background knowledge, revisiting purposes, actively engaging in various learning activities, and reflecting on the effectiveness of the current processes and adjusting accordingly. Likewise, the teacher will move through the P-PER stages of the Framework for Teaching in a gradual release of responsibility cycle that may include incorporating new or different content.

The Framework for Teaching

The CRISS Framework for Teaching provides a process for planning lessons, executing instruction, and evaluating teaching. Readers familiar with Wiggins and McTighe's *Understanding by Design* (2005) will recognize elements of their work in our framework. Wiggins and McTighe offer a template for lesson planning that incorporates identification of enduring understandings and learning goals. Our Framework for Teaching acknowledges their work and expands it, adding important instructional elements. It includes guided practice and independent application of learning strategies tied to content understandings and explicit instruction in metacognitive processes. Basically, we have filled in their skeleton planning piece with learning strategies that help students reach the enduring understandings.

Incorporating CRISS strategies as part of an overall Framework for Teaching also fits with research on the ineffectiveness of teaching strategies for strategies' sake (McKeown, Beck, & Blake, 2009). This study, described more fully in Chapter 3, provides evidence for teaching students how to use strategies important for learning content. For example, becoming competent about taking notes in itself isn't particularly useful unless note taking leads to deeper learning. Learning strategies must always be nested within important content. With this said, let's now take a more detailed look at the elements comprising the Framework for Teaching.

PLAN for Instruction

Planning for instruction involves several components: identifying content and process enduring understandings, figuring out what assessments to use, determining student needs, and specifying content materials.

▸ Determine Enduring Understandings

The first part of the framework focuses on what we want students to learn and remember from a lesson or a series of lessons comprising a unit of study. We begin this process by identifying the big ideas, or Content Enduring Understandings, students are to take away from the lesson or unit. These are the concepts and ideas we hope our students will remember long after a specific lesson or sequence of lessons. Usually, they are tied to district curriculum and to state and/or national standards.

Things to consider when drafting Content Enduring Understandings:
- How do these understandings relate to the content standards?
- To what extent do they reside at the heart of your discipline? Are you stressing the central organizing ideas of a content domain rather than superficial details?
- Does this content really merit study? Is it worth the time it will take to teach to mastery?
- Is this the content you want your students to remember five or ten years after they have taken your class?

After determining the content understandings, we post them—in student-friendly language—to inform students about the overall purpose for a lesson or a particular sequence of lessons. These understandings are usually written as statements. To help students focus on the most important concepts, we often create questions related to the enduring understandings (in Wiggins and McTighe [2005] called "essential questions"). This is particularly important when addressing standards as part of enduring understandings, because the standards may not explicitly connect to the school or district curriculum.

In addition to content understandings, we identify metacognitive process understandings—the reading, learning, and writing skills we hope students will learn and begin to own.

Things to consider when drafting Process Enduring Understandings:
- What do students already know about metacognition?
- How do these process understandings relate to the Framework for Learning?
  - ✓ What will students learn about tapping into their own background knowledge and about setting goals or purposes for reading and learning?
  - ✓ What will students learn about being active, engaged learners?
- How do these process goals help students reach the content understandings?
  - ✓ What will students learn about the process of . . . solving a mathematical problem, conducting a scientific investigation, identifying an author's perspective, etc.?
- What learning strategies will support these process understandings?
- How will these process understandings help students make the CRISS Framework for Learning their own?

▸ Create Assessments

Our next step in this planning phase focuses on assessment. What formative and summative assessment evidence is needed to document whether or not students have attained the identified content and process enduring understandings? If the assessment targets aren't clear, students will have difficulty hitting them. Identify what is important for students to accomplish and how those skills and knowledge will be assessed. For example, in mathematics, students deserve sample problem sets that will be on the assessment so they have a clear idea of what they need to accomplish. If the assessment is an essay, let them know the topic before beginning the unit. Post topics or questions in an accessible location and refer to them throughout the lesson. Students can use essay topics as overall purposes for learning.

Posting topics is even more effective when students know the criteria and have a rubric for scoring the essay or project. Engage students in analyzing examples or models so they develop a vision of what the product or performance looks like when it's done well. Ask students what they think constitutes quality in a product or a performance, and then, with students, develop scoring criteria, rubrics, and benchmarks. Do this throughout the lesson in order to share accountability for assessment with students (Stiggins, Arter, Chappuis, & Chappuis, 2007).

Things to consider when developing content assessments:
- Do my assessments reflect the deep understandings?
- How will I ensure students know assessment information before beginning the unit of study?
- How will I involve students in developing the assessment criteria?
- How will my students learn from these assessments (especially formative assessments)?
- Are assessments engaging and practical? For example, will students be able to use a variety of technology applications?

Things to consider when developing process assessments:
- How will I involve students in examining their own learning as they progress through the unit?
- How will I use writing and discussion as tools for self-reflection?

▸ Assess Student Needs

Before we select materials for a unit of study and/or before we begin our instruction, we must identify our students' abilities with regard to both the content and process understandings.

Things to consider when evaluating student needs:
- What basic information do my students need to succeed with the content of this unit, and how can I assess whether or not they have it?

- What familiarity do my students have with the strategies I plan to use? How much modeling will I have to do? Can students help with the modeling? Can students succeed if they work in groups? Can students use the strategies without additional instruction?
- Can all students reach the content understandings by using traditional classroom materials, or do I need to supplement for lower ability and English Language Learners and provide enrichment materials for higher ability students?

▸ Select Content Materials

Identify the materials—written selections, videos, lectures, labs, and other hands-on activities—students will use to attain the enduring content and process understandings.

Things to consider when selecting learning materials:
- Do materials provide sufficient content richness to help students attain the deep understandings of the lesson?
- Are materials considerate (with helpful text structures and learning guide tools—see page 33)?
- Are materials on varying levels of difficulty so all students can succeed?
- Are materials engaging? Have I included online materials or appropriate fiction selections along with the more traditional content materials?

PREPARE for Student Learning

Once you have completed the planning portion of the framework, think about how to prepare students for learning. This process involves making decisions about strategies for activating background knowledge, for setting purposes, and for analyzing the Author's Craft.

▸ Elicit Background Knowledge

Before students begin a lesson, plan ways to help them integrate their background knowledge with new information. Find out what students already know about a topic and figure out what to do if students know very little.

Sometimes we become frustrated by the lack of student background knowledge. Remember, everyone has background knowledge and experiences. Our challenge is to elicit enough background sharing for students to make some kind of meaningful connection—and sometimes this means looking for broader connections. For example, not all students will have knowledge of the Boston Tea Party or taxation without representation, but all students have experienced being treated unfairly. Bringing out their feelings and sharing class experiences of unfair treatment will help students engage with and understand the text material dealing with the Boston Tea Party. It's not a question of your students not having appropriate background knowledge—the issue is: Are you asking the right questions to activate their background knowledge?

Help students recognize that their comprehension of new material is completely related to their background knowledge. If they know little about the featured topic, the text will be more challenging than one on a familiar topic. Likewise, their approaches to learning need to differ according to their background about the upcoming information.

Taking time for students to talk about what they know (or think they know) about an upcoming topic also helps to repair possible misconceptions. Frequently, students have incorrect background knowledge that can become a powerful impediment to learning. Eliciting their prior knowledge about a topic helps bring to light misunderstandings, simplistic knowledge, or flawed interpretations. Once recognized, students can repair misconceptions with accurate information and start to see how their preconceived inaccuracies can impede their grasp of new information.

Things to consider with background knowledge:
- Do students have a foundation in the core concepts, or is a broader tack needed to set the stage for all new learning?
- How will I help students recognize what they already know about the enduring understandings?
- How can I help students build connections to what they already know?
- Will time be needed for extensive scaffolding through video, lecture, hands-on activities, and/or readings, or will a simple visual image or question be enough?
- Will I need to pre-teach key vocabulary so students have a sufficient knowledge base to integrate new information?
- Ask students questions about process to shift metacognitive understanding about background knowledge to them:
    Why is it important to consider your background knowledge before reading?
    Why is getting in touch with your background knowledge essential to being a metacognitive learner?

▶ Set Purposes

Help students define a clear purpose for reading, listening, or viewing. Establishing purposes provides them with a benchmark for checking their understanding. Link purposes to the assessment and the enduring understanding you want students to achieve. What information should be the focus of their attention? Do the materials provide effective purpose setting guides, or does something need to be created?

Things to consider with purpose setting:
- With challenging content, set explicit purposes for students.
    After reading this selection, you should be able to . . .
    After viewing the video, you should be able to identify . . . , and you should be able to evaluate the best process for . . .
- Coach students to prime their own background knowledge and to build their own goals for reading:
    Page through the assignment and think about what you already know about the content. What might you learn? Make some predictions.
- Preview vocabulary to direct purpose setting.
    Here are key words from this reading/lecture/video. What do you know about them? Based on these words, predict what this text is about.
- Stress questions about process to shift metacognitive understanding about purpose setting to students.
    Why is it important to know your purpose before reading?
    What clues does the author provide about purpose?
    How does the author signal important information?

▶ Analyze Author's Craft

Another aspect of preparing students for learning content is to guide their examination of how the content is presented. How well is it written? Will some or most students have difficulty understanding how the author presents information? How much help will students need?

In Chapter 2, we discuss in detail how the content domain, text features, and the author's ability to write clearly influence a reader's comprehension. In planning instruction, we need to be aware of the potential difficulties students might face with an assignment and help them attend to the author's style of writing whether it is in printed or electronic form (see Chapter 3). If an author has not presented important ideas clearly, students will need our help in figuring out how to extract essential information. Through our guidance, students learn ways to examine text according to content domains and how to get inside an author's head to determine style of presentation. When students realize how authors structure their writing, they can more readily understand and remember what they read. When preparing students for reading an assignment, consider the following questions:

Things to consider with analyze author's craft:
- If the text is poorly written and complex, is there a tool or process students can apply to facilitate comprehension?
- What tools are provided within the text?
- Are students familiar with the genre in this discipline, or will they need instruction in the nature of this particular structure (e.g. scientific journal article)?
- Is information on a website user friendly, well organized, and authored by a non-commercial and reputable expert?

ENGAGE with Content and Transform Information

Moving beyond the traditional model of passive learning means students must actively engage with content and transform information. At this stage of the lesson, plan ways for students to be actively persistent while reading, listening, and viewing. Many learners don't know what it means to be actively persistent. They think learning means glossing through a text or passively viewing a video. Students too often lose focus, become distracted, and let their minds drift away. Therefore, give careful thought about ways to engage students to become actively persistent during reading, listening, or viewing. This manual is filled with energizing strategies such as Read-and-Say-Something (page 81), Read and Explain (page 81), Sticky-Note Discussions (page 84), and various ways to read and write questions (pages 94-107). As you plan instruction, select strategies appropriate to your content and to the goals of your lesson.

Transforming information is essential if students are going to make content their own. Some engagement and transformation of content occurs during reading, listening, and viewing, but we also want to deepen students' understanding after they have some familiarity with the information. Create opportunities for students to extend their understandings through writing, talking, visualizing, and reorganizing information.

Transforming concepts drives understanding deeper because the learner must reconceptualize information from words into images, charts, or notes. Converting information to other forms helps learners take ownership of content—they are no longer using an author's or lecturer's words; they are identifying relationships and teasing out meaning for themselves. It also facilitates driving new information into long-term memory. The processing learners do as they categorize and organize speeds the creation of neural connections that allows them to hook new learning to prior knowledge. Encourage students to transform information multiple times by using a variety of discussing, writing, visualizing, and organizing strategies.

Keep in mind how important it is to model what transformation looks and feels like. Plan to model strategic approaches and help students recognize why being actively persistent is essential to their learning. Knowledge and information don't simply float into our heads. Learning takes work! Learners need to discuss, write, visualize, and organize.

▸ Create Writing Opportunities

Incorporate writing throughout your lesson plan. Help students recognize how writing forces organization. As we write, we begin to see clusters of information and hierarchies of ideas. Writing also encourages active involvement in learning. It is impossible to remain passive as a writer. Because writing is such a powerful vehicle for learning, it is integrated into every component of Project CRISS—before, during, and after a reading or learning experience (see Chapters 7 and 8).

Things to consider:
- What informal writing strategies will help students attain deeper understanding of content?
- How can I incorporate reflective writing to help my students be metacognitive?
- What kinds of brief and more extended writing opportunities can I provide for my students?
- How can I make sure students transform ideas through their writing rather than copying someone else's writing?

▸ Facilitate Discussions

Plan time for students to talk about what they are learning. Conversations among communities of learners are an important part of Project CRISS. Through a variety of discussion strategies, show students how to lead effective discussions and then provide opportunities for them to examine why these approaches lead to deeper conceptual understandings. Discussion helps them transform content to make it their own. Students intuitively know the power of talk and how discussion helps them sort through what they know and what they don't understand. Extend this knowledge by helping them recognize why discussion is essential to learning. It is their talk, not the teacher's talk, that is important.

This manual offers a rich assortment of discussion strategies (see Chapter 4). Select those that work for your content domain and will help students grapple with the essential understandings of your lessons.

Things to consider:
- What are some strategies to use to help students understand what it means to have an effective discussion?
- What discussion strategies keep students focused on the topic at hand?
- How can I shift responsibility for discussion to students?
- How can I include student-to-student discussion throughout the lesson?

▸ Encourage Visualization

If the material is conducive to imagery, plan how you might engage students in creating mental pictures as they read, view, or listen. Students might also sketch their visualizations into pictures, symbols, or diagrams. For more information on mental imagery and Picture Notes see Chapter 5.

Things to consider:
- How can I help students create mental images while reading or viewing in order to deepen their understanding?
- Would having students draw their visualizations lead to deeper comprehension?
- How can I help students evaluate the effectiveness of visualization and transforming information into pictures?

▸ Elicit Organizational Plans

After students have read or viewed content, they need to organize information so it can be practiced and reviewed for in-depth understanding. We offer many options (see Chapters 3, 5, and 6). Project CRISS students explore multiple ways to organize information for understanding and retention. They learn how to do Power Thinking (page 50), Selective Underlining (page 54), Main Idea—Detail Notes (page 137), Concept Mapping (page 55), Picture Notes (page 121), and lots more!

Choose organizing strategies that reflect the uniqueness of your content domain and those that lead students to succeed with your assessments. This is where your deep understanding of the content area discipline is vital, because the types of thinking required dictate the strategies used.

Things to consider:
- What organizing strategies reflect the academic content and will lead students to understanding the big ideas?
- What is the content structure—hierarchical, sequential, comparative, or descriptive? Would it be more effective to use an organizing strategy with a similar structure, or one based on the reader's purpose?
- What organizing tools and strategies will help students deeply process the content?

REFLECT on Teaching and Learning

The final stage of the Framework for Teaching gets at both the teacher's analysis of instruction and the student's analysis of learning.

Things to consider when analyzing the lesson from the teacher perspective:
- What could I do next time to improve student learning—different learning materials? Different strategies?
- If students weren't successful with a strategy, did I model enough? Did the strategy effectively match my purpose?
- What additional modeling is needed for students to take full ownership of the Framework for Learning?

Things to consider when analyzing the lesson from the students' perspective:
- *How did I help you prepare for this lesson? How did it work for you? What could I do to help you prepare more effectively for the next lesson?*
- *How did I help you engage with and transform the materials? Was it enough? What could I do to help you engage and transform more effectively for the next lesson?*

Modeling and Guided Practice

Implicit within the Framework for Teaching is teacher modeling and guided practice. When introducing a new strategy, we take the stage. We show, tell, model, demonstrate, and explain how to use the strategy effectively with our content (reading materials—paper or online, videos, lectures, labs, etc.). During this modeling stage, focus on the content and the purposes for learning and explain why you base strategy selection on these two components. As the student learns how to apply a strategy or skill, there is a gradual release of responsibility from teacher to student. Teacher modeling and guided practice leads to pronounced effects on student achievement. It even improves student performance on standardized reading tests of comprehension when incorporated over weeks and months of instruction (Duffy, 2002). Improvement in student learning doesn't happen in a day.

Strategy instruction includes three steps:

1. The first step involves an *introduction*, where the teacher explains what the strategy is and why students should use it to improve their learning. If students do not know why they are performing an activity, they rarely repeat the behavior on their own (Duffy, 2002).

2. The second step is *modeling* the procedures for doing the strategy. During this step, the teacher demonstrates or asks students to show how they do a particular task. The teacher explicitly discusses, models, and thinks-aloud during this stage. After students watch and listen to their teacher and other students demonstrate a strategy, they have opportunities to

practice the strategy on their own or in a small group situation with guidance and feedback from the teacher (or their peers). Throughout, the teacher encourages students to talk about the strategy and its applications.

3. The third step is ***reflection***. If our goal is for students to own the strategy, they need to talk (process conference) or write (journal entry) about how the strategy worked and how they adapted it or could adapt it for different content-specific purposes.

NOTE: *Steps 1, 2 and 3 may be repeated multiple times before students eventually reach the independent stage.*

This process of gradual release of responsibility is often described to students as, "I do. We do. You do." The end goal is always focused on students becoming metacognitive, independent learners.

When we think back on our own teaching experiences, we realize that when lessons don't work as well as planned, the underlying factor usually has to do with insufficient modeling. We simply did not model enough for students to negotiate the task on their own. With second language learners, teacher modeling becomes an even more important issue. Students new to English face more obstacles to comprehension and need far more scaffolding support than native English speakers.

Not all strategies will need the same degree of support and modeling. While some, such as Think-Pair-Share (page 75) require little modeling, others, such as Conclusion—Support Notes (page 142), may need multiple demonstrations. In order to teach the more difficult strategy applications, begin with content familiar to all students—school information, music, TV shows. This allows students to focus their learning on the process, rather than trying to learn content and process at the same time. If your students require more practice, consider using course material they have already studied before moving into current course material. As students begin to take ownership, have them demonstrate and reflect upon the newly-learned process.

Because we know how important this three-step process is for strategy instruction, we have built it into our explanation of each strategy under the following heading (see page 81 for a model).

Introduction, Modeling, and Reflection

Numbered instructional steps follow this heading and provide guidance for introducing and modeling the strategy. Frequently, we provide modeling ideas and student examples. After the numbered steps, you will find a shaded box in which we provide reflection prompts to use with your students during a process conference.

Following this section you will find the heading:

Support and Extensions

Bulleted ideas provided in this section include applications and adaptations of the strategy for different ability (or age) groups and for content-specific use. Where appropriate, we include teacher and student examples.

Inherent in this entire Framework for Teaching discussion is respect for learning content and respect for our students. Always keep in mind that Project CRISS is not a collection of discrete learning strategies. By casting our instructional plans into a Framework for Teaching, we keep important content at the forefront. Strategies are not add-ons to a lesson; they are integral for students to attain deep understanding of essential concepts in our courses of study. Providing students with the big ideas or content understandings not only focuses our teaching, but it helps students establish purposes for learning. When they know what they are about to learn up front, they are able to monitor how well their learning is progressing—particularly when they also have information about the assessment. Moreover, providing assessment information helps to alleviate student anxiety about testing performance—they know what to expect.

Being straight about what is on the docket and scaffolding learning so students know how to succeed on assessments serves to build relationships with students. We take away fear of failure. Our students aren't alone struggling to figure out what we want and/or how to accomplish a task. We show them the way by helping them know how to succeed. We honor who they are, what they need, and what they can be. We sit by their side, guiding and cheering them on to success.

The Framework for Learning

Given that we have already described in depth what metacognition involves from the teacher's perspective, we will only briefly talk about becoming metacognitive from the learner's perspective. The Framework for Teaching and the delivery of instruction through modeling and guided practice are designed to help students internalize the Framework for Learning. It is not enough for us to understand what it means to be a metacognitive learner—students must own this learning framework as a foundation for becoming lifelong learners. If we introduce strategies such as K-W-L+ (see page 112) or Questioning the Author (page 105) without emphasizing how they activate the metacognitive processes, students will look upon these approaches as discrete activities—things one might do just to get through an assignment—rather than as part of an overall approach to learning. They need the backdrop of the Framework for Learning to understand and employ strategies. By teasing out the components of metacognition, students can begin to wrap their arms around what it means to be a strategic learner and apply these principles across the content areas.

The Framework for Learning: Questions to Consider chart (next page, also available in the online reproducibles for Chapter 1) contains questions students can use to apply the framework.

The Framework for Learning: Questions to Consider

PREPARE for Learning

DETERMINE BACKGROUND KNOWLEDGE.
- *After previewing the assignment (headings, pictures, graphs, questions, etc.), what do I think I know about the topic? What questions do I have?*
- *Where did my background knowledge come from? How do I know it is reliable?*

SET PURPOSES
- *What is my purpose for reading/listening/viewing? What are the learning goals?*
- *If the teacher or author doesn't provide any guidance, how will I determine my purpose for learning?*

ANALYZE AUTHOR'S CRAFT
- *What organizing features of the text will help me learn this content?*
- *If the text is poorly written and complex, what can I do to figure out what the author is trying to say?*
- *What structures are specific to this discipline, and how can I use them to help me learn?*

ENGAGE with Content and TRANSFORM Information

WRITE
- *How will I use writing to help me understand and learn the information?*

DISCUSS
- *How will I use discussion to attain deeper understanding?*

VISUALIZE
- *How will visualizing information help me be more actively engaged?*
- *How can transforming information into pictures or diagrams help me learn?*

ORGANIZE
- *Given the content and my purposes for learning, what strategies will work best to organize this information?*
- *How can I transform or organize the author's/speaker's words to make the information my own?*

REFLECT on Learning

- *How has my understanding changed or developed throughout this lesson?*
- *In what ways was I metacognitive? Did I remember to check to see if I understood what I was learning? What did I do when I was not getting it?*
- *How did I prepare myself for this learning experience?*
- *How did I stay engaged? Did my attention drift to other things while reading/listening/viewing? What did I do to get back on task?*
- *How did I transform or organize the information after I read or listened to the content? Were these transforming strategies helpful?*
- *Did the teacher do enough modeling, or could I have used more help?*

Summary

Conceptualizing Project CRISS as two frameworks helps both teachers and students begin to attain a deeper understanding of what this project is really about. The frameworks provide a philosophical and theoretical stage for guiding our day-to-day classroom experiences. Our focus is to help students become confident learners who have internalized the dimensions of metacognition. Attaining this deeper level of understanding happens gradually in classrooms where students learn rich content through guided application of learning strategies. The CRISS Framework for Teaching is a powerful tool for planning instruction that incorporates the CRISS Framework for Learning. Through multiple exposures to the Framework for Learning and with a healthy dose of teacher guidance and modeling, students will learn the framework components and gain ownership of the process. This ownership is the ultimate goal of Project CRISS.

With this overview, we now move on to the practical applications of Project CRISS. As you turn the pages of this book, think about how these ideas can be adapted to your own teaching and content domain. Choose those that make the most sense for you. Be selective. Revise them to fit your content, whether you are doing a science lab in biology, a hands-on activity in geometry, a field trip for civics, or a short story in American lit. Take what we offer. Shape it. Mold it. Then, turn knowledge about how to learn over to your students. Give them control so they leave your classroom with the self-confidence and tools to go forth in their lives as lifelong learners.

Vignette II: A Model of Metacognitive Teaching

Carmen, a history/English teacher, asks her students to read the first stanza of "The Star-Spangled Banner".

> O say, can you see, by the dawn's early light,
> What so proudly we hail'd at the twilight's last gleaming.
> Whose broad stripes and bright starts, thro' the perilous fight,
> O'er the ramparts we watched, were so gallantly streaming?
> And the rockets' red glare, the bombs bursting in air,
> Gave proof thro' the night that our flag was still there.
> O say, does that star–spangled banner yet wave
> O'er the land of the free and the home of the brave?

Carmen decides not to tell the students her own ideas about the song. She wants her students to feel comfortable developing their own interpretations. She uses a CRISS strategy called Free-Write Entries (see page 170).

Carmen begins by reading the first stanza of the song aloud. She asks her students how many times they have heard and sung this song. Then she says, *Read the stanza through several times. Write down any thoughts, questions, and personal stories the song triggers. Anything you write down will be correct. Don't give up. Remember, there are no wrong answers. As you write, think about the strategies you use as a reader to create meaning for yourself.*

Her students begin to read and write. Carmen models by writing her own journal entry while they work. To explore what's happening, let's focus on one student. Derrick reads the song several times and begins to write in his journal.

> *Who wrote this song?*
> *What was going on when the song was written?*
> *What does ramparts mean?*
> *Why were bombs bursting in air?*
> *Was a war going on at the time the composer wrote this song?*
> *I wonder why there is a question mark at the end of the last line.*

Does the composer think freedom is in jeopardy?

After about ten minutes, Carmen asks her students to discuss their ideas with a partner. Derrick talks with Matt. They share comments and ask each other questions. Together they begin to make meaning. When conversations begin to run their course, Carmen asks each student to write about what the song means. *What is your personal response to the song?* Derrick writes the following in his journal:

This song reminds me of what happens in times of war. Rockets are glaring, and bombs are bursting in the air. I see pictures in my head of the U.S. flag at half mast because a local soldier was killed overseas. His Humvee ran over an explosive. Around town, there are American flags everywhere. The flag means honor, freedom. I guess you can't take it for granted—have to work for freedom.

Then they talk as a whole group. Carmen asks volunteers to share their entries. Each student offers his or her own interpretation. Together, they build a variety of meanings.

Carmen then asks her students to write a process entry about the strategies they used to derive meaning from the song, *What did you do to make meaning from the song?*

Derrick writes: *I read through the stanza once, but I didn't understand it very much. I have heard this song many times, and I guess I never thought about what the words meant. I had lots of questions. Then I went back and reread. I thought about what each phase might mean. It helped talking with Matt. He had some different ideas. We both talked about some of the videos of war we've seen online and on TV. Wounded soldiers were given flags as they returned to the states. There were a ton of flags. Both of us thought the song was about war and how the flag stood for freedom.*

Derrick is an example of an active, self-regulated reader who energetically attacked the problem of making sense from his reading. After the first reading, he knew that he did not understand. He created meaning by bringing his own life into the words of the author. Through his conversation with Matt, he begins to think through and elaborate on his ideas.

Next, Carmen asks, *What did I do as a teacher to help you read and interpret this song? How did I help you use your own background knowledge? What did I do to help you become more actively involved in the lesson? I could have read the song to you, asked you questions about it, and then given my own interpretation. Instead, I did something quite different. I want to know what you think.*

Students talk while Carmen summarizes their comments:
- *I liked it when you told us that everything we wrote or talked about was right. That made me feel OK about writing about my own ideas. We had different ideas about the song.*
- *I got more out of the song when you made us write about what we were thinking. I wouldn't have come up with the same ideas if you had told us the real meaning—your meaning—first.*
- *I made mind pictures while I was reading—I saw bombs bursting and the flag.*
- *It helped to talk about our ideas with someone else.*
- *Talking about the song and writing questions has made me really curious. I want to know when and why "The Star-Spangled Banner" was written.*

Finally, Carmen leads a discussion about how students have uncovered what it means to be a metacognitive, strategic learner. She says, *Connecting with your background knowledge, talking, writing, creating mental pictures—all of these processes are part of succeeding as a learner. None of you were passive. Instead you actively persisted after meaning. If you didn't understand something, you figured out ways to make meaning. You continually checked your comprehension.* They also discuss why talking and writing about learning helps them become more aware of the strategies that work. Carmen explains, *The* how *of learning is just as important as what* they learned.

CHAPTER 1 RESEARCH BASE

Research Conclusion	Reference
Learning is an active process and learning represents construction. Learners are not just receiving knowledge, but actively building representations of meaning.	Kintsch, 2009
Proficient readers are metacognitive. They have knowledge and control of their own cognitive strategies.	Baker, 2002
Students who achieve well in school have an awareness of their own learning and can employ a variety of strategies to attain meaning.	Duke & Pearson, 2002
Integrating new information with prior knowledge lies at the heart of metacognition and comprehension. This conclusion is not only documented by research in cognitive psychology, but by neurological research—particularly that on selective attention.	Kintsch, 2009; Pearson & Fielding, 1991; Pressley, 2000; Jensen, 2005
Effective learners have clear purposes or goals in mind as they read.	Pichert & Anderson, 1977; Narvaez, 2002
Knowledge of expository and narrative text structures plays an important and positive role in comprehension.	Kintsch, 2009; Goldman & Rakestraw, 2000
Learning involves building representations of meaning by transforming information through writing, discussing, visualizing, and organizing.	Duke & Pearson, 2002; Keene & Zimmermann, 2007; Kintsch, 2009
One learns by interacting with others. Discussion is critical because we are biologically wired to communicate with one another.	Anders & Spitler, 2007; Jensen, 2005
Writing about text leads to improved understanding. When students respond to text by writing personal reactions and by analyzing and interpreting the text, they have a better understanding of text material.	Graham & Hebert, 2010
When readers construct mental pictures about what they are reading, their comprehension improves.	Gambrell & Koskinen, 2002; Zoss, 2009
Memory and learning increase when learners organize information by clustering discrete bits into categories, by developing hierarchical relationships, and by converting information into charts, notes, and concept maps. The more organized the information is, the better it is remembered.	Kintsch, 2009
For students to become effective metacognitive learners, they must have time during and after a learning experience to evaluate how their learning progressed.	Baker, 2008
Teaching students how to learn needs to be embedded in learning important content rather than taught as discrete skills.	McKeown, Beck, & Blake, 2009
Students learn more effectively when they know content and assessment expectations at the beginning of a learning experience.	Wiggins & McTighe, 2005
Teacher modeling and guided practice lead to pronounced effects in the improvement of reading comprehension.	Duffy, 2002

Text Complexity: Identifying the Author's Craft and Design

2

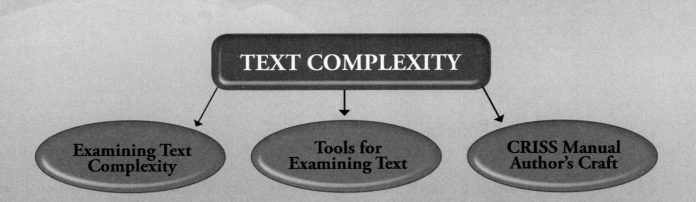

In this dizzying era of constant digital communication, students often take the quick way out and avoid reading complex text. Clicking through websites and doing cursory reading and viewing has become the reading mode for most students and many adults. Given this situation, it is paramount that students know how to use and learn from more complex texts, whether information is available online or in more traditional textbook formats.

An essential element of the CRISS Framework for Learning is an awareness of author's craft. As students progress through school, they face increasingly complex text in multiple content domains. To meet the challenge of this increasing complexity, students must have an insider's understanding about what goes into crafting text and the factors making some text more difficult (or easier) to understand. Attaining an awareness of the author's craft and how to employ this knowledge while both reading and writing is essential to becoming a successful, strategic learner.

While organizing our lessons through the CRISS Framework for Teaching, we, too, need to take the author's craft into consideration. As we design instruction, we must take time to analyze who the author is and how she or he proceeds to guide readers through the text. Once we have a clear understanding of the author's road map, we can plan ways to help students use the author's craft as a comprehension and learning tool.

Chapter 2 is divided into two sections. Section 1 examines text complexity, and Section 2 provides practical tools for evaluating text.

SECTION 1: EXAMINING TEXT COMPLEXITY

In our review of the empirical and practical wisdom about text, it became clear that researchers and practitioners use different approaches to examine text complexity and the author's craft. In this first section of this chapter, we describe these multiple and overlapping approaches:

(1) Quantitative Measures of Text Difficulty

(2) Qualitative Measures Defining Considerate Text

(3) Common Writing Patterns

(4) Student and Text Variables

(5) Content Domain Variables

(6) Student Knowledge and Text Structure

Quantitative Measures of Text Difficulty

Historically, quantitative measures have played a major role in determining the complexity of texts. Numerous quantitative tools exist, such as readability indices, lexiles, and computer software for evaluating the difficulty of text (Armbruster, 2008).

These quantitative tools can be a useful first step in evaluating readability of text. Secondary content area textbooks are typically vocabulary and content dense, putting them at a higher readability level than the grade at which the courses are normally taught. For example, a readability assessment was made of ninth grade biology and geology textbooks from a major U.S. publisher that indicated the complexity of the textbooks landed closer to twelfth grade on the Fry's Readability Graph (Fry, 1977). The teachers using the textbooks had real, quantitative data that explained why many students had legitimate trouble reading the text on their own. It was clear that specific instruction would be necessary to bridge the gaps in student understanding. Readability measures also become a factor in the adoption of textbooks. Knowing that textbook reading is commonly assigned as homework or independent reading, teachers can seek out resources that match the grade level or the reading level of the majority of students. But, there are caveats to the use of quantitative tools.

Although these measures are somewhat helpful in matching student abilities with text, their apparent objectivity can be misleading. Most of these readability determinations use some kind of formula, such as the average length of words and sentences within a text. According to these systems, simple vocabulary and short sentences reduce the reading level of texts. Yet, these measures can be deceiving. For example, the *Grapes of Wrath* received a lexile rating appropriate for grades 2-3 because of its seemingly simple dialogue. In this case, quantitative measures can't capture the deeper meaning and complexity behind what appears to be everyday speech.

Quantitative measures have also led to "watering down content." To meet readability requirements for marketing, authors often reduce the reading levels of their texts by replacing key vocabulary terms with shorter, simpler words and by shortening sentence length, often resulting in short, choppy sentences with less elaboration of content. Such writing can actually be more difficult to comprehend. Moreover, quantitative measures do not take into account qualitative factors about how the author has crafted text to make content coherent and interesting or how texts differ by content domains. A volume of poetry reads quite differently than does a scientific report. As you will see from this review of research, text comprehensibility encompasses many factors that cannot be reduced to a mathematical formula or reading level.

Qualitative Measures Defining Considerate Text

A more productive approach to evaluating text incorporates qualitative features that can only be measured by an attentive reader. Basically, well-structured texts or what Armbruster (1984, 2008) describes as considerate texts, cue readers about how to construct meaning. Researchers consistently find that considerate texts are easier to comprehend than poorly written materials. This topic has been studied extensively, and several conclusions emerge that have important implications for reading materials used in schools.

Typographical Features. Students remember information better from texts that use typographical features such as italics, underlining, bold print, color, and special fonts. In addition, students' abilities to summarize ideas from text improve when they use text that effectively incorporates typographical features (Lorch et. al., 2001).

Internal Features. Written clues within the text that help the reader understand structure and guide the development of main ideas influence recall of information. Readers tend to organize and remember information better when authors use signal words. For example, to indicate main ideas, an author might use, *"The most important point is . . ."* To signal sequencing of ideas, an author might use, *"First . . . second . . . and third . . ."* To show how disparate parts of text relate, an author might use, *"As discussed earlier . . ."* Making the structure of the text more salient improves comprehension and retention (Armbruster, 2008).

Presentation of Main Ideas. Beginning in the 1980s, researchers confirmed the common sense notion that readers more readily comprehend important ideas when authors note them directly in statements and questions (Baumann, 1986; Beck, McKeown, Sinatra, & Loxterman, 1991). In these studies, researchers presented readers with different versions of the same content. For example, Bauman rewrote science passages from four popular textbooks. In these revisions, he presented general topics in the titles and subheadings and made sure the main ideas were explicit in paragraphs. Fifth grade students read either the original passages or the revisions and then were tested on the key ideas in the selection. Students who read the rewritten passages did better than those reading the original.

<u>Clarity and Elaboration of Content</u>. The most critical aspect of text comprehensibility has to do with whether or not authors include sufficient explanation for developing concepts. Authors tend to "cover" content without going into sufficient depth for students to grasp essential information. One idea after another is "mentioned" without sufficient explanation or interconnectivity of ideas. The following excerpt introducing the Russian Revolution is typical:

"The Russian Revolution was the most violent and radical revolution since the French Revolution. In March 1917, the czar abdicated and provisional government took control. Then led by V. I. Lenin, the Bolsheviks seized power in November, 1917. This marked a new era of Soviet rule. Russia had become the world's first socialist state, and Lenin intended for the revolution to spread." (Glencoe, 2010).

While lifting an excerpt from text is not entirely fair to the authors, this example demonstrates how authors pack information—in this case, at least twelve discrete pieces of information into four lines of text. Packing content makes comprehension particularly difficult for students with little background knowledge about the topic. Covering or "mentioning" content, rather than explaining it, is the norm in most content texts.

It is hardly surprising that readers find tersely written explanations of key concepts more difficult to understand than elaborated explanations. When authors explain concepts well, students do better on measures of comprehension (Armbruster, 2008). For example, Holliday (1991) describes Herman's 1984 study examining the effects of inadequate explanations on student learning in a situation where eighth grade students read one of two versions of a description of the heart. The original version, published in a popular middle school text, was tersely written. The revised version was designed to provide students with a clearer explanation of the same topic. It contains more detail, including an explanation of how various parts of the heart function and relate to each other. Text passages below show the original and revised explanations:

Original Version:

A human heart is a cone-shaped muscular organ about the size of a large fist. The heart is located in the center of the chest behind the breastbone and between the lungs.

A human heart contains four chambers—right atrium (AY tree uhm), left atrium, right ventricle (VEN trih kuhl), and left ventricle. Right and left refers to the body's right and left sides. A wall separates the chambers on the right from the chambers on the left.

Revised Version:

The heart is the part of the circulatory system that pumps blood throughout the body. The heart is located in the center of the chest behind the breastbone and between the lungs. The human heart is suited for pumping because it is a hollow, cone-shaped muscular organ about the size of a large fist. Being hollow, the heart can easily fill up with blood. Once filled, the heart muscle provides the power necessary for pumping the blood through the body.

A human heart contains four hollow chambers made for receiving and sending blood. The right atrium (AY tree uhm) and right ventricle (VEN tru kuhl) receive and send blood to the lungs, while the left atrium and left ventricle receive and send blood to the rest of the body. (Note that right and left refer to your body's right-hand and left-hand sides.) The right and left sides of the heart are separated by a wall of muscle. This wall keeps blood going to the lungs separate from the blood going to the body. (Herman, 1984).

As predicted, students learned more about the heart from the revised version. These eighth graders benefitted from an elaborated explanation.

<u>Vocabulary Development</u>. Text complexity is driven by vocabulary complexity (Beck, McKeown, & Kucan, 2002). While we have devoted an entire chapter to this important topic (see Chapter 9), several factors are important to keep in mind about the relationship between text difficulty and vocabulary.

The first factor has to do with the number of potentially unfamiliar words contained in a reading selection. What makes a text easier or more difficult to read is related to the density of new vocabulary. Some content texts are basically studies in new vocabulary. For example, Holliday (1991) noted the number of words presented in most science books far exceeds the number of words taught in most foreign language classes. Therefore, as we examine content texts, a critical feature is the number of new words presented. Word density is important because there are limits to the amount of vocabulary a student can learn. Has the author of your textbook packed text with too many technical and non-technical words that might be unfamiliar to most of your students?

The next factor is whether or not all of the technical vocabulary is necessary for explaining important concepts. Holliday (1991) notes that content materials, particularly science texts, frequently contain too many complicated terms. Authors tend to label concepts and phenomena with unnecessarily technical vocabulary, or jargon. Technical words become jargon when they are (1) difficult for most students to learn, (2) used only by experts, (3) used for academic testing purposes, or (4) introduced too soon in a student's schooling. As you examine the technical vocabulary in your student course materials, consider whether or not it is necessary for the concepts being explained.

Another important consideration is how well the author identifies important concepts. Texts are more readable when authors feature key concepts explicitly in bold print, as main topics in paragraphs, and when appropriate, with visual information. Will the importance of a technical term be obvious to the reader, or will the reader have to guess the author's intention?

Explanations that lack clarity make some texts far more difficult than others. Look carefully at the words and examples used by the author to explain new concepts. Sometimes authors use vocabulary and examples even more obtuse than the word being explained. When evaluating vocabulary in course materials, ask students to help. Have them read and circle concepts they don't understand. They may identify technical terms you felt were clearly explained within the text and non-technical terms you assumed they already knew.

To recap our discussion so far, qualitative features of text influence a reader's ability to comprehend. Clear presentation of main ideas, the presence of typographical and internal features, and clarity and elaboration of information make informational text more readable. Also important to keep in mind are factors involved in the relationship between vocabulary complexity and text complexity, including the sheer number of new words in texts, how well important words are featured, and the clarity of explanations.

Common Writing Patterns

Another aspect of text structure has to do with identifying the writing patterns authors use to craft their ideas. Even though there is little hard data about how different writing patterns may affect students' comprehension, literacy experts recommend teaching students how to recognize and use common writing patterns as a way to transform information (Buehl, 2009).

While patterns vary from source to source and by grade level (K-college), authors of the Common Core Standards loosely divide informational writing into two broad categories: explanatory and argumentative (Common Core, 2010). With explanatory writing, authors begin with a concept or controlling idea and then teach the reader about it through relevant examples, facts, and details. Authors often explain ideas by sequencing information, making comparisons, and explaining issues with problems, solutions, and processes. For example, authors develop explanations by posing and defining a problem along with information about the causes, effects, and possible solutions. Authors frequently emphasize problem-solution relationships describing events where individuals must figure out ways to deal with problems and to generate solutions. Similarly, math texts are primarily structured around problems and solutions. Content texts are also replete with comparative writing where authors examine an idea by comparing or contrasting it with other ideas or concepts. The intention with these various structures is not to persuade or analyze a situation or a new concept, but to explain it.

Argumentative writing has a different goal in that the author not only provides information, but also takes a stance and works to convince the reader by developing arguments and presenting evidence and counter-evidence from varying perspectives. Argumentation patterns are prevalent in most content subjects and are frequently embedded in social studies and current events articles.

Of course, authors may use a variety of organizing patterns in the same selection. For example, a scientist might begin a piece by analyzing issues following a comparative pattern, and then conclude with a proposition followed by supportive evidence.

Even though writing patterns do play a role in text comprehension, the reader's purpose is what ultimately drives the transformational process. For example, if the reader wants to examine the pros and cons of global warming, he or she uses this purpose to sift through information from a variety of reading selections. The reader then transforms information across these varying sources and an assortment of writing patterns based upon his or her purpose.

Being sensitive to the writing patterns within a piece as well as the reader's purpose lays groundwork for selecting CRISS strategies (e.g. Two-Column Notes, Concept Maps, Conclusion-Support Notes, Problem-Solution Notes, etc.) to help students transform information. If the text contains comparisons, and the readers' purpose is to understand and explain information by making comparisons, they may find a Venn Diagram useful for transforming the content. With argumentative writing, students may find Proposition-Support Notes useful. Similarly, a math text explaining the solution of linear equations might be best transformed using Process Notes.

In summary, taking a qualitative approach to examining text makes the most sense for selecting appropriate reading materials. Our students deserve to read well-written text. Becoming aware of qualitative features, such as explicit main idea presentation, the clarity and elaboration of content, and the prevalent writing patterns within a selection, guides us in planning instruction and is integral to both CRISS Frameworks.

Student and Text Variables

Any discussion about text structure and comprehension has limitations. As one would predict, reader variables, such as an individual's background knowledge, personal experiences, goals and, as just noted, the reader's purpose interact with text comprehensibility (Kintsch, 2009). The following paragraphs briefly summarize this research.

Background Knowledge and Text Structure. As we will discuss more fully in the next section of this chapter, comprehension depends on the domain expertise of the reader. Think for a moment about your own comprehension. When you know a lot about a topic, you can pick up practically any material related to your own expertise and comprehend it. Your pre-existing knowledge allows you to bridge the gap in understanding new perspectives, elements, or main ideas. Text structure makes little difference to your comprehension.

However, if you know little about the topic, you need to problem-solve your way through the text, consciously searching for relevant background knowledge and employing explicit strategies to figure out what the author is saying.

Research documents this reader-text interaction (Kintsch, 2009). In most situations, the more domain-specific knowledge readers have about a topic, the less important text structure is to their comprehension because they can readily supply the structure themselves. Yet, there is a caveat. In some situations, expertise can become detrimental. With a high level of expertise, readers tend to slack off when presented with challenging, well-structured materials, thinking they already know the content. They don't put in as much effort building new understandings as they would with more difficult, less obviously structured text. In most cases, our students don't have this level of expertise. In fact, most have little background knowledge about our subject areas. Therefore, it is always better to select considerate reading materials with clearly stated main ideas and with embedded structural cues to help the less knowledgeable reader with comprehension and retention of the material (Goldman & Rakestraw, 2000).

<u>Background Knowledge, Interest, and Purpose</u>. Interest and purpose also play key roles in text comprehensibility. Readers become more engaged in text and comprehend a selection better when they find the material interesting. Background knowledge affects interest. For example, interest in a topic tends to be low when a reader has little or no relevant background knowledge (Armbruster, 2008). This conclusion makes sense. If you don't know anything about a topic, it is difficult to be interested in it. Interest, as well as subsequent comprehension, increases with some knowledge about the topic (Kintsch, 2009). However, Kintsch notes a point of diminishing return—too much knowledge doesn't help. If a reader already knows the content of a selection, his or her interest diminishes. Therefore, a student's interest and background knowledge influence the potential impact of text structure.

Students also need a reason or purpose to be interested in what they are reading. Kintsch (2009) describes a study where middle school students learned how to write summaries as a means to transform content for deep understanding. A crucial variable was whether or not teachers provided students with a purpose or reason for doing the summary writing. In control classes where summary writing was introduced as just another decontextualized activity, students failed to learn anything. Students need reasons for putting forth an active effort.

<u>Writing Style and Reader Interest</u>. An inviting writing style can also enhance interest, making text more readable (Kintsch, 2009). Material may be interesting not because of what is said, but because of how it is said. For example, writers can increase interest by using active rather than passive verbs, by including examples that make the writing less abstract, and by using vivid and unusual words.

Beck, McKeown, and Worthy (1995) noted that voice, the quality that helps a reader view text as communication between an author and reader, had a positive effect on recall. They compared four versions of the same text: the original textbook passage, a voiced version (natural, expressive written language), a coherent version (well-structured main idea development), and a version that was both voiced and coherent. The combined voiced and coherent version produced the highest recall.

The issue of voice is important in analyzing informational text. Too many of the texts used in school are voiceless. Think about the difference between reading an article in *The New Yorker* and reading a chapter in a secondary textbook. Typically, teams of authors create content texts, making them voiceless, flat, and boring. Voiceless texts make engagement more challenging.

Other factors also influence reader interest. Researchers find imagery and concreteness positively relate to interest and comprehensibility (Zoss, 2009; Wade, Schraw, Buxton, & Hayes, 1993). When readers can visualize information, they tend to find the text more engaging and consequently easier to remember and understand.

What's clear from this discussion is the interaction between reader and text. A reader's background knowledge and interest influence comprehension. Students find text more interesting when they have some (but not too much) background knowledge, have a clear purpose for reading, and when they perceive the author as having an inviting style of writing.

Content Domain Variables

Another way to examine text complexity is through the lens of varying content domains. Students face tremendous diversity in the texts they encounter as they move from mathematics to history to science classes. As educators, we not only need to understand and use general factors defining considerate text, but we also need to recognize and use text features unique to our own content areas.

In fact, some researchers suggest moving away from a more generalist notion of content area literacy to approaches more linked to disciplinary texts (Heller & Greenleaf, 2007; Moje, 2007; Moje, Stockdill, Kim, & Kim, 2011; Shanahan & Shanahan, 2008). They recommend that strategic learning approaches be nested in specific content, mirroring the analytical thinking required in the discipline. This means we need to figure out the textual features unique to varying domain texts and become more aware of the kinds of thinking required in different subject areas.

<u>Exploring Text Features and Reading Processes</u>. Shanahan and Shanahan recommend that content teachers take on the responsibility for figuring out what is unique about their subject areas in terms of author's craft as well as the thinking processes required to succeed in understanding their respective subject areas. What thinking processes do experts in science, social studies, and mathematics use when they read texts in their own areas of expertise? How are these processes reflected in the written texts? What features of domain-specific text do expert readers use while reading in their fields of expertise?

Shanahan and Shanahan (2008) describe a study where teams of disciplinary experts in chemistry, history, and mathematics read texts in their own disciplines and did think-alouds about textual features and their own reading processes. Preliminary results indicated that the disciplinary experts approached reading differently when reading in their own fields of expertise. For example, mathematicians talked about the importance of attending to how authors develop vocabulary and how they had to read a passage multiple times before they could apply what they read to a new situation or to solve a problem. One high school math teacher talked about the importance of visualization when reading math texts. He found diagramming and converting problems to sequence designs helped him understand. Science teachers described how they connected the visuals, graphs, charts, and diagrams to the text. They kept looking back and forth from the text to the diagram to make the content understandable.

What's important from this work is that we take time to explore what is unique about the way authors craft text in our own content domains. Take a hard look at the written materials you use and think about what makes them subject-specific. What thinking and reading processes do you use when reading challenging material in your area of expertise? Because we, as content specialists, are so steeped in our fields of expertise, we frequently have trouble figuring out what might be challenging reading for outsiders. To help in this process, you might want input from a colleague in another discipline who does not have your level of expertise. Choose a complex article in your own content domain. Use this brief list of questions as a starting point for analyzing the kinds of thinking and challenges inherent in text from your discipline. Think aloud as you read to give your partner your insider's perspective.

- What are the features of the text that are unique to your content area and how can they be used to help your students learn?
- What reading processes do you use to untangle challenging content?

- What do you have to do to transform the information?
- How do you incorporate different blocks of information (e.g. sidebars, graphs, data tables) into your processing of the text?

As you read, your colleague can help you identify the kinds of thinking you use with the text features commonly found in the written materials of your discipline. Conversely, it might also be helpful to ask that colleague to read and think aloud as s/he reads one of your texts. S/he may find issues of text complexity different from your own.

Recognizing the Author's and Reader's Perspective. Another aspect of text complexity arising from the Shanahan and Shanahan study is the author's perspective. The historians in Shanahan and Shanahan's study described how they read critically based on the context and the perspective of the author. Historians read text as interpretation rather than truth. If the author is a member of a right-wing fundamentalist group, the text will read differently than if he's a left-wing liberal.

So, while analyzing the author's craft, it's important to recognize the writer's purpose. Awareness of an author's perspective is particularly important in examining periodicals, newspapers, and primary sources. Most of these resources are not neutral, but instead represent particular points of view. Readers need to understand the meaning embedded in print and what lurks behind the black and white symbols. To guide your assessment of course materials, see below: Examining an Author's Perspective. To analyze an author's perspective and reliability, see the online reproducibles for Chapter 2, Critical Analysis of the Author's Perspective and Reliability.

Examining an Author's Perspective

Questions to ask about the author or composer:
- Who composed the text? (If more than one author, ask the following questions about each author.)
- What credentials does this author have that make this information credible or not?
- To what groups/organizations does this person belong (political, military, environmental, religious, etc.)? How would membership in these groups/organizations influence the author's message?
- What does the composer of the text want you to know or do? Why?
- Is the author writing to sway your mind, to rouse you to action?
- What do you know about the composer's values and interests?

Questions to ask about the text:
- What is the text about?
- Are main ideas or key points supported with facts or opinions? Evaluate supporting evidence by checking several resources.
- Evaluate the adjectives and/or descriptions used to describe people and events. Are they fair and unbiased or colored by the author's views?
- Are there people, events, or critical information missing from the text? If so, how does that impact the author's message?
- What views of the world are advanced by this text? Should these views be accepted?
- What points of view are excluded from the text?

Questions to ask about the message:
- Who benefits from the text?
- How does the message fit or not fit with your own belief system?
- How do authors craft text to promote a particular point of view?

Coupled with recognizing how authors write from a personal perspective is the need for readers to consider their own purposes and values while reading a selection. Not all of us will get the same meaning from the same text. We interpret differently based on our own points of view. Critical readers keep both their own and the author's perspectives in mind. Therefore, analyzing an author's craft is always "colored" by our own values. As you read and analyze how an author presents content, think about your own background knowledge and how your values may influence your analysis of the author's message.

- How does the author's perspective color your understanding of the message?
- How has your thinking been influenced by the author's perspective?
- How does your perspective impact your understanding of the message?
- How has your thinking been influenced by your point of view?

Student Knowledge of Text Structure

What's important throughout this entire discussion about examining your own text is providing students with insider information about how authors craft text in general and in our own content domains. Researchers confirm that the reader's knowledge of text structure plays an important role in comprehension (Goldman & Rakestraw, 2000; Duke & Pearson, 2002). If students know how authors structure their writing, they can more readily understand and remember what they read. When readers become privy to an author's style of presentation, they can use it to guide their own understanding as well as their representations of content.

What's also clear is students tend to pay little attention to how writers write. They remain oblivious to bold face print and topic headings, introductory paragraphs, the placement of main ideas, and common patterns in text unless they receive explicit instruction. After reviewing the research in this area, Duke and Pearson conclude that almost any approach to teaching the structure of informational text improves comprehension and recall. Students knowledgeable about the craft of their text learn more from expository material than students who are not aware of structure. Being sensitive to the author's perspective and voice as well as the varying writing patterns in a piece lays groundwork for selecting organizing formats (Two-Column Notes, Concept Maps, Conclusion-Support Notes, Problem-Solution Notes, etc.) to best structure the content of the assignment. (Chapter 3 of this manual focuses on teaching strategies to help students recognize and use the author's craft as a comprehension tool.)

▲ ▲ ▲

In the next section of this chapter, we use information gained from the qualitative features defining considerate text as well as other text variables—common writing patterns, content domain variables, the author's and reader's perspectives—as a foundation for the development of rubrics and checklists useful for our own examination of text.

SECTION 2: TOOLS FOR EXAMINING TEXT

We begin this discussion with an overview of a Content Textbook Assessment Rubric (see the online reproducibles for Chapter 2) appropriate for most informational text. This rubric takes a generalist perspective and is probably most useful for examining chapters found in typical content textbooks. For this assessment, we encourage you to create assessment teams of three to five people comprised of colleagues in your content area, in other content areas, and those who work with special needs students. Assessment teams such as these do an excellent job identifying the strong and weak features of content textbooks and analyzing how these materials will work for all types of students. Following this rubric, we include content-specific adaptations for evaluating social studies texts and mathematics problem sets. In addition, we provide a checklist for analyzing an author's perspective.

Content Textbook Assessment Rubric

To select considerate text for our students, we have to move beyond the "splash" of beautiful pictures, bold face print, fancy graphics, and support materials to analyze the author's style of presentation. We encourage you and your textbook assessment team to take an editorial stance and carefully examine the author's strengths and weaknesses.

We divided this rubric into six parts:

1. Overall Content and Correlation with Standards
2. Features for Preparing Students
3. Text Organizational Features
4. Features for Reflection and Assessment
5. Teacher's Guide and Other Teacher Resources
6. Ancillary Materials for Students

The components listed in the rubric indicate features of a well-written, considerate text. To determine if your text has these features, look at several chapters—remember most textbooks are written by teams of authors, so the features of one chapter may not be consistent throughout the book. Use the "Evidence/Comments" section of the rubric to support your point score. (Note: The online reproducible provides more space for comments than the following model.) Before most sections, we have written a few guidelines and referenced page numbers; you will find it helpful to keep this manual handy as you work through your analysis.

Part 1: Overall Content and Correlation with Standards

Part 1 should be completed by content area experts; you are the ones who can best evaluate the content and assess how that content relates to the appropriate standards.

Component	Evidence/ Comments	Points (0-3)
The content of this text reflects the essential concepts of this discipline.		
The content flows in a logical progression appropriate for this topic (e.g., from simple to complex, chronological, topical, etc.).		
The content, including illustrations and examples, appropriately addresses human diversity.		
The content addresses local/state/national standards.		
Other		

Part 2: Features for Preparing Students

The features identified in this section relate to the PREPARE step of the Framework for Learning. If the author provides guidance in these areas, students will need less guidance from you. This type of information usually occurs at the beginning of the book and/or at the beginning of chapters and sections. Frequently this type of information is presented in boxes or in the margins.

Component	Evidence/ Comments	Points (0-3)
Background Knowledge—Review Chapter 1, pages 11-12		
At the beginning of the chapter, the author helps students relate their own life experiences and previously learned information to the topic.		
The author builds on the students' prior knowledge within the chapter subsections.		
Purpose Setting—Review Chapter 1, page 12		
The chapter begins with a list of objectives, statements, or questions indicating what students will learn in this chapter.		
Section headings are specific enough that students can convert them to focus questions which direct their reading.		
Author's Craft—Review Chapter 1, pages 12-13		
The author provides students with an overview of the textbook organization and features.		
Other:		

Part 3: Text Organizational Features

In this section, you will evaluate the following components:

- The author's writing style. Will the author's style engage your students?
- Overall organization of information. The Table of Contents will help you determine the organization of the book. In addition, review several chapters looking for a logical, consistent presentation of content.
- Presentation of main ideas and details. Look for consistency and a thorough explanation of the main ideas. Avoid texts guilty of only "mentioning" or "covering" information.
- Vocabulary development. Make sure the most important, content-based vocabulary is included, highlighted in some way, and defined using more than just a definition. Look for appropriate context clues, examples and counter examples, descriptions, explanations, illustrations, and diagrams.

Component	Evidence/ Comments	Points (0-3)
Author's Writing Style: Review pages 29-30, Writing Style and Reader Interest		
The author's style engages students; sentence structure is varied and not overly complex, and verbs are mostly in the active voice.		
The author uses imagery and concrete examples to help students visualize information.		
Organization of Information: Review page 25-28, Typographical and Internal Features and Common Writing Patterns		
The text is organized logically, concepts build on each other, and students can easily take notes.		
The author uses a writing pattern that is appropriate to the content—explanatory or argumentative.		
Signal words are provided to indicate how ideas in the section are related to one another.		
The presentation of main ideas and details is consistent in each chapter.		
Main ideas: Review pages 25-26, Presentation of Main Ideas		
Titles of sections within the chapter indicate the main idea of each section.		
The main idea is clearly stated and easy to locate.		
Support for Main Ideas: Review pages 25-27, Clarity and Elaboration of Content		
Main idea explanations are thorough and include an adequate number of details and examples.		
Charts, pictures, and other graphics support the main ideas and are appropriately located.		
Interesting details are included to expand on the essential information in the text and to engage students.		
Vocabulary Development: Review pages 27, Vocabulary Development		
Important words/concepts are emphasized in the text (bold, italics, highlighted, color).		
Important words/concepts are clearly defined or explained within the reading.		
Concrete examples or analogies are included to clarify abstract ideas.		
The author provides more than just a definition (e.g., pictures, examples, analogies, counter examples, and other context clues).		
The number of highlighted vocabulary terms is appropriate for the concepts being explained. Author avoids excessive jargon.		
Other:		

Text Complexity: Identifying the Author's Craft and Design

Part 4: Features for Reflection and Assessment

As you read through the textbook, look for features that will help students identify if they are reaching chapter goals.

Component	Evidence/ Comments	Points (0-3)
Metacognition—Review pages 3-6 in Chapter 1		
The author provides questions within each chapter to help students check their understanding. (These might be in the margins, at the end of a section, or within the written text.)		
The author provides questions at the end of each chapter to help students check their understanding. They correlate to the chapter objectives, encourage higher order thinking, and promote class or small group discussion.		
The author provides chapter or section summaries that give students the gist of the content.		
The author provides opportunities for students to test their knowledge through application activities, such as labs, problem solving, creating products, and developing projects.		
The author suggests appropriate instructional strategies for organizing chapter information and provides prompts at the end of the chapter to evaluate the student's application of those strategies.		
Other:		

Part 5: Teacher's Guide and other Teacher Resources

Component	Evidence/ Comments	Points (0-3)
The teacher's guide and resources include suggestions for modeling and applying specific instructional strategies to help students organize and learn content.		
The suggested instructional strategies match the content and help students reach the stated purposes of the lesson (rather than being just fun activities or busy work).		
The teacher's guide and resources include suggestions for helping students lead their own discussions and work in cooperative groups.		
The teacher's guide and resources provide suggestions for modifying content and goals so they are appropriate for all levels of learners.		
The teacher's guide and resources provide reflection questions for both the teacher and students to evaluate learning.		
Other:		

Part 6: Ancillary Materials* for Students

Component	Evidence/ Comments	Points (0-3)
Ancillary materials expand knowledge of content by focusing on essential ideas.		
Author's perspective or bias is explicitly stated or obvious to the reader (see checklist, page 31).		
Ancillary materials are differentiated to meet the varying needs of individual students.		
Other:		

Sample Subject-Specific Rubrics

<u>Social Studies Rubric</u>. Notice how social studies teachers in one high school changed the information from the Content Textbook Assessment Rubric to develop a rubric for evaluating potential textbooks. This streamlined version contains most of the key features found in the original, but was far better suited to their specific needs.

Social Studies Textbook Rubric

Text Title: American Social Studies Publisher: Santa Publishers
Grade Level(s): Eighth Pages/Chapter(s) Reviewed: Early Exploration (pp. 21-55)

3 = Excellent   2 = Fair   1 = Poor   0 = Missing

Component	Evidence / Comments	Points (0-3)
The content aligns with curriculum standards.	Yes. Early Exploration 1000-1600	3
The content is covered in depth.	Yes.	3
Information flows logically (i.e., from simple to complex, chronological, topical, etc.)	Yes. Time line at beginning of chapter to preview events that will be discussed.	3
The chapter begins with objectives, statements, or questions indicating what students will learn.	Yes. Main ideas are stated and the purposes for reading the information are clearly identified at the beginning of the chapter-"Section Theme.	3
The main ideas are clearly presented with adequate supportive details to make the material easy for students to understand.	Main ideas are clearly outlined-Title in large red print, main ideas in blue, supportive details in green. Easy to form a power outline from this text.	3
The charts, pictures, and other graphics are adequate and appropriately placed close to the text they illustrate.	Pictures of historical events w/ thorough explanations/maps with geo. skills/keys for important information presented/direct quotes set off with bold quotation marks/activities for analyzing visuals provided.	3
Key vocabulary words/concepts are identified and clearly explained within the text.	Key terms are identified at the beginning of the chapter. Vocabulary terms are in blue print within the text and defined within the sentences in which they are found.	3
High-order thinking questions correlate to the chapter's objectives, and include writing and reflection for understanding and application.	Definitely! Section assessments include higher order thinking questions: Compare and Contrast, analyzing information, drawing conclusions, applications to the real world.	3
Cooperative group activities have been included for discussion and problem solving.	Think-Pair-Share and cooperative discussion group activities have been included.	3
There are quality multi-level, multi-genre resources and ancillaries to enhance the core text.	Literature Libraries, Primary Source Documents, CD-Rom.	3

Possible Points =   Total Points = 30

Additional Comments:

Textbook Reviewer's Name: _____   School: _____

Number of classes you teach in which this textbook would be used: _____   Date Submitted: _____

Mathematics Textbook Rubric. Project CRISS staff worked with teachers in a high school mathematics department in Illinois to develop the following supplement to our rubric. The teachers were in the final stages of their textbook adoption and wanted to assess the practice problems included with their geometry textbook selections. They needed to make sure the problems fit with mathematics standards and the ACT standards. We created the following rubric based on those standards and other concerns voiced by the geometry teachers.

Standards/Criteria	Evidence/ Comments	Points (0-3)
1. There are a sufficient number of problems.		
2. Students are asked to create problems as well as solve them.		
3. The author allows for more than one way to solve a problem.		
4. There are open-ended problems— those with several correct answers.		
5. The problems are practical and "real world."		
6. The problems involve hands-on applications to real situations.		
7. The problems use information learned in other math classes, e.g., algebra.		
8. The problems use information learned in non-math classes.		
9. The problems provide for the use of appropriate, up-to-date technology.		
10. The problems correlate to the ACT standards and the following state goals: Goal 7 (7.A.3a, 7.A.4a, 7.A.4b, 7.C.3b, 7.C.4a, 7.C.4c, 7.C.5b) and Goal 9 (9.A.5, 9.B.3, 9.B.4, 9.B.5, 9.D.3, 9.D.4, 9.D.5)		
TOTAL POINTS (30 Possible)		

Ask students to help with the evaluation, so they, too, can become experts of text structure. Talk about the results and begin to think about how to use the information. For example, if your choice for materials provides little help in bringing out prior knowledge, work with your students to develop ways they can do it for themselves—perhaps skimming headings and looking at pictures, then writing a journal entry about what they already know.

▲ ▲ ▲

Summary

The various approaches researchers and practitioners use to examine text complexity and the author's craft provide valuable insights for examining classroom materials. These approaches also helped us, as CRISS authors, become more conscious of our writing in this text. In fact, let's step back for a moment and take a brief look at this book.

Organization of this CRISS Manual

In writing this book, we have kept you in mind, and tried to be considerate by making each chapter's design consistent. Here is an overview:

- Before each chapter, we provide a graphic that shows the chapter contents and structure (see page 23 in this chapter).

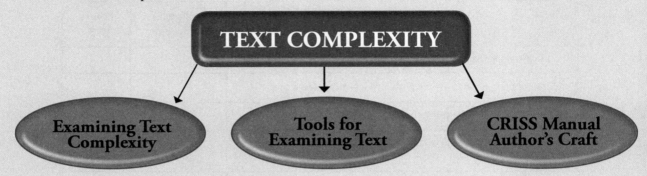

- Each chapter starts with an introduction that presents the key topics.
- Following this introduction, we summarize the relevant research supporting each topic.

Topical headings within the chapter reflect each section's content (see page 24):

SECTION 1: EXAMINING TEXT COMPLEXITY

Strategies are indicated by the following colored bar and triangle (see page 75):

▶ Think-Pair-Share

- We divide the presentation of our research-based instructional strategies into two sections (see page 75):

Introduction, Modeling, and Reflection provides a step-by-step protocol for teaching the strategy. We include relevant examples and templates when needed.

Introduction, Modeling, and Reflection

Support and Extensions shows how the strategy can be applied and adapted for grade- and content-specific implementation. This section frequently includes real teacher and student samples.

Support and Extension

- We tried to eliminate jargon, to use active verbs, and to keep our sentence structure relatively simple.
- Each chapter closes with a summary that reviews the key ideas from the chapter (see page 39 in this chapter).
- To help our research-minded readers, we synthesized the key research components for each chapter (where appropriate) into a chart found after the last page of the chapter (see page 41 in this chapter.)

As fellow teachers, we respect how busy you are and want this manual to be your friend.

CHAPTER 2 RESEARCH BASE

Research Conclusion	Reference
Clear presentation of main ideas, the presence of typographical and internal features, and clarity and elaboration of information make informational text more readable.	Armbruster, 1984, 2008
Students remember information better from texts with typographical features such as italics, underlining, bold print, color, and special fonts. In addition, students' abilities to summarize ideas from text improve when they use text that effectively incorporates typographical features.	Lorch, Lorch, Ritchey, McGovern, & Coleman, 2001
Readers more easily comprehend important ideas when authors note them directly in statements and questions.	Baumann, 1986 Beck, McKeown, Sinatra, & Loxterman, 1991
Text comprehensibility is influenced by vocabulary complexity.	Beck, McKeown, & Kucan, 2002
An inviting writing style enhances interest, making text more readable.	Kintsch, 2009
Reader variables such as an individual's background knowledge, personal experiences, goals, and the reader's purpose interact with text comprehensibility.	Kintsch, 2009
The more background knowledge readers have about a topic, the less important text structure is to their comprehension because they can readily supply the structure themselves.	Kintsch, 2009
The writer's voice, the quality that helps a reader view text as communication between an author and reader, has a positive effect on recall.	Beck, McKeown, & Worthy, 1995
When readers can visualize information, they tend to find the text more engaging and consequently easier to remember and understand.	Zoss, 2009 Wade, Schraw, Buxton, & Hayes, 1993
The reader's knowledge of text structure plays an important role in comprehension.	Goldman & Rakestraw, 2000 Duke & Pearson, 2002
Recognizing the author's and reader's perspectives is critical to text comprehension.	Shanahan & Shanahan, 2008
Researchers suggest moving away from a more generalist notion of content area literacy to approaches more linked to disciplinary texts.	Heller & Greenleaf, 2007 Moje, 2007 Shanahan & Shanahan, 2008

Analyzing & Applying Basic Patterns & Structures

3

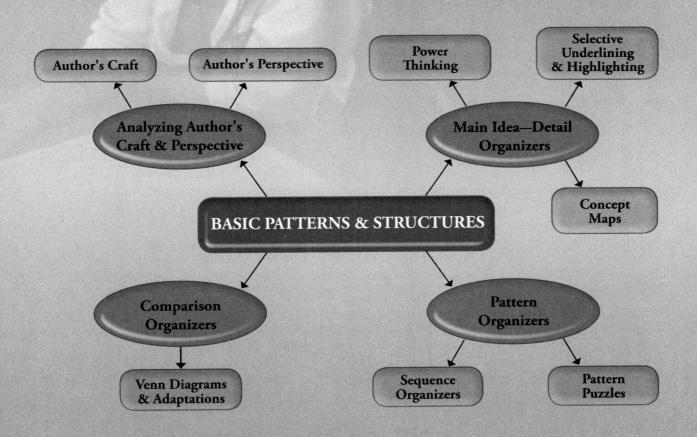

The next several chapters describe the comprehension and learning instruction offered in Project CRISS. To facilitate instructional planning, we have packaged the presentation of these learning strategies into discrete chapters, but the ideas intermingle across chapters.

A couple of points are worth mentioning as a general introduction to these practical approaches to teaching and learning. First, Project CRISS strategies are a means to an end; they are tools for building knowledge. They are not skills learned out of context; they are embedded in the CRISS Frameworks for Teaching and Learning. Our focus is on guiding students to build representations of knowledge by employing discussion, writing, and transformational tools. Our goal is not for students to become adept at using a strategy for the sake of learning a strategy; we want learning champions, not strategy champions.

A comprehensive study conducted by McKeown, Beck, and Blake (2009) directly addresses the issue of strategies for strategies' sake. In a two-year study with fifth graders, they compared two approaches to instruction, a content approach and a strategy approach. In the content approach, the teachers focused student attention on understanding the content of the selections. They did this by engaging students in conversations about content where they talked about important ideas and connections. Reading was stopped at selected points and discussion initiated to examine characters, problems, events, etc. The entire focus was on the meaning students were generating from the text. In the strategy approach, the teachers had students read a portion of text, stop and then do one of several strategies such as making an inference, asking a question, making a prediction, or developing a brief oral summary. The focus was on doing the strategies effectively, not on delving into the meaning of the text. It turned out that the students in the content approach did better on measures of comprehension than did the students participating in the strategies approach. According to McKeown et al., doing the strategies without also focusing on meaning actually distracted readers from building a coherent representation.

The important message from this study is that strategy instruction without a content focus does not lead students to a deep understanding of content. While students need to develop proficiency in using a variety of strategies, instruction should always be nested within the Framework for Teaching. Otherwise, strategies become distracting activities taking students away from what we want them to accomplish in our academic disciplines.

With this said, our second point has to do with how we present strategies in this book—which at first blush might seem a bit confusing given what we just discussed. We have gone back and forth about how to best organize the presentation of these tools. We considered presenting them in sample lessons, similar to what we do in the CRISS workshop, but this approach turned out to be too constraining because many CRISS strategies can be used at various points in a lesson; tying them down to a single lesson created too much specificity. We decided to take a more generalized approach and cluster strategies into broad categories as reflected in our chapter titles. Presenting them in this way makes lesson planning easier. Keep in mind the bigger picture. CRISS strategies are a way of learning academic content. They mix and flow as part of the CRISS Framework for Teaching.

This is the first chapter where we begin presenting learning strategies in a consistent instructional sequence: (1) Introduction, Modeling, and Reflection and (2) Support and Extensions.

(1) Introduction, Modeling, and Reflection

This sequence progresses from teacher modeling to student independence. In numbered steps, we provide instructional guidance for teachers beginning with the teacher explicitly telling students what the strategy is and why it is useful. This is followed by teacher modeling of the process used to implement the strategy, including guidance as to when and how to apply it. The teacher demonstrates the thinking involved and the questions asked throughout the process. Students are given time to practice the strategy in the context of a lesson (using simpler content at first if the strategy is complex!). As students progress in their learning of the content and the new strategy, they need time to reflect on what they are doing as learners. The last step in this section, found in a shaded box, provides sample reflection prompts. This metacognitive reflection, typically written or oral, is vital. Framed by the teacher, this reflective process conference allows students to examine how the strategies assisted them in applying the different elements of the Framework for Learning to new content. Over time, students internalize this reflection process and are able to approach new content as independent, self-directed learners.

(2) Support and Extensions

This section contains suggestions for supporting students as well as adaptations and extensions that go beyond the basic structure of the given strategy. Every teacher, in every content discipline and grade level, will have different instructional needs, depending upon their students and their content materials. Some students will require more scaffolding to reach the state of independent application, while others will need very little guidance before they can use a strategy independently. In some teaching situations, the basic process and structure of a strategy needs to be adjusted to meet the demands of the content—and students need to see that the strategies are not set in stone. When appropriate, we have provided examples of specific extensions created by teachers in the field, as well as student work.

▲ ▲ ▲

It makes sense to begin our discussion of CRISS strategies by describing how to help students effectively read and learn from the various texts they must use in school. Also, in this chapter, we present some fundamental tools for organizing information across varying text patterns. These basic tools—identifying main ideas, making comparisons, and sequencing ideas—are fundamental to understanding essential ideas in practically all content domains. Moreover, most of them partner nicely with the other strategies presented later in this manual.

In the previous chapter, we provided an overview of research describing how the author's craft and design affects comprehension. Now, we examine ways to apply some of these principles to practice.

ANALYZING AUTHOR'S CRAFT AND PERSPECTIVE

Analyzing Author's Craft

As a precursor to any of the basic organizing strategies offered in this chapter, students should analyze how an author presents essential ideas in his or her writing. The style of writing will differ according to content domain. Therefore, it is essential to walk students through the kinds of writing they will meet in our classrooms. When students know the author's style of writing, they gain control over their reading and their own writing. This fits precisely with the research presented in Chapter 2—readers who understand how authors structure their writing more readily understand and remember what they read (Duke & Pearson, 2002; Goldman & Rakestraw, 2000).

Introduction, Modeling, and Reflection

1. Select a typical reading assignment in your content area. Photocopy the selection (or a portion of the selection) so students can practice underlining and making margin notes while you model.

2. Begin with an explanation of Author's Craft (see Chapter 2).

3. Next, project a copy of the text and begin with a quick walk-through of the chapter, thinking aloud as you proceed. Summarize text features that describe the author's style and what the author does to help students learn the information. With each feature you identify, see if students can explain how it will help them learn. Your walk-through should address the following questions or topics:
   - Does the author provide information about the text organization and features in the introductory pages of the text? If so, use this information as part of your walk-through.
   - What one-of-a-kind features do you find in this textbook? Glossary, appendices, answers to problem sets, etc. Share these features and see if students can determine how each feature will help them learn.
   - Look for features repeated within chapters. Here are some features to look for:
     - ✓ Guiding information before or at the beginning of each chapter/section (purposes, learning goals, vocabulary terms, note taking suggestions, etc.)
     - ✓ Chapter/section titles, headings and sub-headings that clearly present the main ideas of the section they represent.
     - ✓ Main idea placement in paragraphs. Look for explicitly stated main ideas in the same location of each paragraph, e.g., the first sentence is the best-case scenario. Implied main ideas or those that are inconsistently placed will be more difficult for students.
     - ✓ Identification and explanation of key vocabulary concepts. How are vocabulary terms typographically identified (e.g. boldface print, highlight, color)? Look for multiple sources of information to define the terms—defined in context; clear explanations with examples and counter examples; illustrations, photos, and other helpful graphics that build understanding; appropriate comparisons to known objects or concepts; etc.
   - Identify features that may be specific to your discipline.

4. Talk about how the author's structure can be used to determine how to organize the information for learning. Are there prevalent writing patterns in the text—comparative analyses, cause and effect, hypothesis testing, or problem-solution relationships—that students can use to dictate their note-taking organization? Should they organize it with a Venn Diagram, Two-Column Notes, Hypothesis-Proof Notes, or Problem-Solution Notes (see Chapters 5 and 6)?

5. Follow the same progression with other materials used in class—especially with the less friendly texts. *What does this author do to hinder your learning? What makes this text more difficult? What can we do to learn from this text?*

Reflection

How do you think being aware of the author's organizational structures will help you learn? How did this strategy help you? How can you use this process on your own?

Support and Extensions

- Divide students into groups. Have each group take a chapter from the text. Ask the recorder from each group to write down what the author does to help or hinder learning.

- Copy several pages of your text or other classroom materials. Pair students and have them read the selection together and write down in the margins or on sticky notes their think-alouds about the author's plan. Students can also record text information using Two-Column Notes:

Text Features	How can you use it to learn?

- Talk about the qualities of well-written text as described in Chapter 2. Give students portions of the Content Textbook Assessment Rubric found in Chapter 2 of this book. Working in small groups, students can evaluate their text to decide if it is considerate.

- If your text is problematic, have students take on the role of an editor. Ask them to write a letter to the publisher of the book, giving the author suggestions for revisions. Send the letter. Students can also take on the role of a textbook adoption committee member and write an evaluation of the book.

- Have students read the introduction, bold print topics, and conclusion, and then using a "map," have them predict the organization of the chapter. (Notice the Concept Map of this chapter on page 43.)

- If students identify problems with a text, have them work in teams to establish a procedure for overcoming the difficulties. (They may decide to use other materials, work with the librarian to discover other sources of information, or ask their teacher for help.)

Analyzing the Author's Perspective

Teaching students to become aware of the author's intention is critical in this era of non-stop communication. The explosion of visual and printed texts, supposedly offering factual information, bombards and shapes our view of the world. This shaping often happens unconsciously. As mature learners, we know texts are representations of reality, and we base our interpretations on our own personal realities. We know our personal beliefs narrow the focus of what we read and hear. Our task is to help students recognize the ideological assumptions that underwrite what they read, view, and hear. To be critical readers, students must understand how their own social and political beliefs influence their interpretations. We need to guide students so they can broaden their knowledge base by recognizing and analyzing multiple perspectives and, hopefully, they will learn to see the potential value of a variety of information sources—even those that challenge their beliefs and ideas.

Introduction, Modeling, and Reflection

1. Provide students with an article on a current issue where the author has presented a biased point of view. Editorials and letters to the editor from your local newspaper are always excellent sources.
2. Model how you preview the article by noting authorship, the type of article, headings, etc. to get a preliminary understanding of what the author is presenting.
3. After previewing the article, ask students to think about what they already know about the topic and generate a discussion about their varying opinions. List different points of view. Then talk about how their own thinking about the topic can influence their interpretations.
4. Read the article together, stopping to note substantiated or unsubstantiated opinions and facts as well as biased language or tone.
5. Talk about why the author might have wanted to write this piece. Who do you think might want to read this article? Who would agree with the author's message? Who would disagree with it?
6. After reading and talking about the article, develop a list of questions critical readers/viewers think about when examining the author's perspective. Your list might be similar to the following:

   What is the topic?
   What are my own opinions about this topic?
   What kind of an article is it (e.g. editorial, advertisement, public service information)?
   Who is the author? What does the author believe?
   Does the author take only one side of an issue, or are other points of view presented?
   Who would agree with this article? Who would disagree?
   Has the author included emotion-arousing words?
   How has the author developed and supported his or her point of view?
   How can I verify or dispute the veracity of an author's data and claims?

Reflection

How do your own opinions and values about a topic influence your understanding of information? How do you filter information based on your world view? Why is it important to understand the author's perspective when viewing or reading information

Support and Extensions

- Ask students to select a controversial topic to research using periodicals, online sources, etc. Use the questions generated above or the Questions for Critical Analysis of Author's Perspective (see the following chart or the online reproducibles for Chapter 3) to direct their examination.

QUESTIONS FOR CRITICAL ANALYSIS OF AUTHOR'S PERSPECTIVE	
Coverage	**Evidence/Support**
What new information or insight does this work contribute to its field?	
Is this a primary or secondary source? How will that impact how you use this information? Primary sources are the raw material of the research process, the originating documents. Secondary sources are based on primary sources.	
Audience	**Evidence/Support**
Who is the intended audience of the piece?	
Is the publication aimed at a general audience or a specialized group?	
Is this source too elementary, technical, advanced, or just right for your needs?	
Reliability	**Evidence/Support**
Is the information fact, opinion, and/or propaganda? *Facts* can be verified; *opinions* (although they can be based on facts) are based on interpretations of facts and involve judgment; *propaganda* is information slanted to promote a specific belief or cause.	
Is the information valid and well-researched, or is it questionable and unsupported by legitimate evidence? How do you know?	
Are ideas and arguments presented in a manner similar to other reputable works in the same field/on the same topic? The more radically an author departs from the views of peers in his/her field, the more carefully the ideas should be scrutinized.	
Assess the author's point of view. Is it objective and impartial? Or is it biased?	
Does the author present arguments in opposition to her/his own?	
Is the language free of emotion-arousing words and bias?	
Perspective	**Evidence/Support**
What is the author's professional affiliation? How might this affect her/his perspective?	
What is the publisher's interest in this issue?	
What evidence does the piece contain about the perspective or bias of the author?	
What conclusions can be drawn about the perspective or bias of the author of the article?	
Other Notes	**Evidence/Support**

- Have students listen to liberal and conservative television newscasts and identify how the presenters show their values and worldviews.
- Ask students to examine political cartoons and other visuals to determine the author's or the composer's motives and intentions.

Once students have an idea about how an author presents information, they can use organizing strategies to transform content based on their learning purposes. For example, organizing information around main ideas and details is a skill fundamental to all content domains whether the text comes from a scientific journal or from a history text. Other fundamental processes are making comparisons and sequencing ideas. The

Analyzing & Applying Basic Patterns and Structures

strategies presented in the rest of this chapter are loosely clustered into three basic patterns of organization: Main Idea—Detail, Comparison, and Sequence.

MAIN IDEA—DETAIL ORGANIZERS

Power Thinking

Power Thinking helps students differentiate between main ideas and details (Buehl, 2009; Sparks, 1982). The process is easy for students to use because main ideas and details are simply assigned numbers. Main ideas are Power 1 ideas, while details are Power 2s, 3s, or 4s. Students can use Power Thinking as an organizational tool for reading, writing, and studying.

Introduction, Modeling, and Reflection

1. Begin instruction by providing students with the following information:

   Power 1: Main idea
      Power 2: Detail or support for a Power 1
         Power 3: Detail or support for a Power 2
   (and so forth)

2. Start working with Power Thinking by using individual words. Later, students can incorporate sentences and phrases. Show your students examples such as the following:

   Power 1: Animals
      Power 2: Dogs
         Power 3: Collie
         Power 3: German Shepherd
      Power 2: Cats
         Power 3: Siamese
         Power 3: Calico

Note: Ideas or words having the same Power numbers must have a similar relationship to the Power above. For example, "bear" could be another Power 2, but "grizzly bear" would be too specific for a Power 2. If "bear" were the Power 2, then "grizzly" and "polar" could be Power 3s.

3. Pick a Power 1 idea on a familiar topic such as sports, food, or TV shows. Have your students give you power 2s, 3s, and 4s. For example:

Teacher:	Power 1 is "sports." What could be a Power 2?
Student:	*Football*
Teacher:	Great, now give me another Power 2 that is "parallel" to football.
Student:	*Basketball*
Teacher:	Right, now give me Power 3s that will fit under basketball. Remember, they must relate to basketball in the same way.
Student:	*Hoop, court, and basketball—they are all things or equipment you need in order to play.*
Teacher:	Good. Now may I add "Lakers" as another Power 3 under basketball?
Student:	*No, because it's a team and not equipment. It wouldn't be parallel.*

As students give you these ideas, write them on the board or overhead

    1. sports
      2. football
      2. basketball
        3. hoop
        3. court
        3. basketball

Note: You can also write this in a nonlinear format. The following example incorporates mapping with Power Thinking.

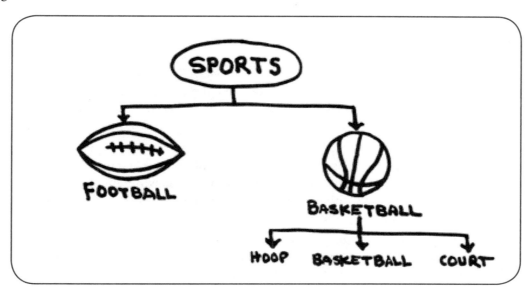

Reflection

How does Power Thinking help you understand the content? How might you use Power structures to organize information? Why is organizing information into main ideas and details so essential to learning? How might you use Power structures in combination with other note-taking strategies?

Analyzing & Applying Basic Patterns and Structures

Support and Extensions

- Write two similar Power structures on the board:

  ```
  1                           1
      2                           2
          3                           3
          3                           3
      2                           2
          3                           3
          3                           3
      2                           2
          3                           3
  ```

  Provide the Power 1s such as "TV shows" and "movies." Divide the class into teams and have them race to fill in the different items in order from top to bottom. Ask students to check the winning team's work to make sure they really won. When students are comfortable with the Power structure, choose Power 1s from your content area. This can be used to bring out background knowledge or as a review.

- Write Power 1, 2, and 3 words on separate 3" x 5" cards for several topics. Mix them up and distribute one card to each student. Have students move themselves into category groups and then into Power structures within each category. The Power 1 person can stand, the 2s kneel and the 3s sit to create a "pyramid."

- Power structures are useful tools for young children as well as high school seniors. In the first example below, a first grader used Powers and drawings to organize information about colors. In the second example, a high school senior took Power Notes about the government.

• 52   Chapter 3

- Power Writing. One way to introduce students to paragraphing is to first have them develop Power Thinking outlines using words and phrases, similar to the Power Thinking example on page 50. Next, ask them to expand their ideas into sentences and then combine these sentences into a paragraph. Begin with simple 1-2-2-2-1 Power Writing structures.

  1. I have several favorite sports.
    2. Skiing in the winter is first on my list.
    2. During the summer you will find me on my roller blades.
    2. I love playing tennis.
  1. My favorite sports keep my body and mind fit.

  In the beginning stages, you may find it helpful for students to include the number of items or reasons in their topic sentence, e.g., "My three favorite sports..." After students have a good understanding of the Power 1 and 2 structures, they can begin adding Power 3 and 4 ideas and conclude with another Power 1 sentence.

  1. My three favorite sports, skiing, roller-blading, and tennis, make me healthy and happy.
    2. Skiing provides a great way to get through the winter.
      3. I love the feel of gliding through the snow.
    2. During the summer, however, you will find me on my roller blades.
      3. Roller-blading builds balance and strong muscles.
      3. I really enjoy skating around town.
    2. Finally, I love playing tennis.
      3. It is so much fun to run around the court and hit the ball.
      3. I always feel so good when I hit a clean shot over the net.
  1. My three favorite sports keep my body fit and my mind sharp.

  Keep in mind that these structured paragraphs are only an intermediate step to freer forms of writing. Many students will not need such tight structures in order to develop coherent paragraphs. Over-structuring writing can hinder creativity and hamper students who have already internalized a sense of structure in their writing. Once students have an awareness of main idea and detail paragraph development, they will no longer need to think about their writing in this structured, numbered form.

- Expand Power structures from paragraphs to multi-paragraph essays using Spool Papers (see page 200).

- Power structures guide students in taking notes and in writing summaries. In the following example, a high school social studies teacher used a news article Power Writing Guide to help her students organize information.

News Article Power Writing Guide

Name _____ Date _____ Period _____

Read the news article. Complete the following outline and then write a summary.

1. After reading the news article, "_____," I found two interesting facts:
  2.
    3.
    3.
  2.
    3.
    3.

1. Summary: _____
_____

Analyzing & Applying Basic Patterns and Structures

Selective Underlining and Highlighting

Underlining and highlighting are probably the most used and the most abused study strategies. For underlining to work, students must be selective and have an idea of their purposes for reading. Otherwise, they will underline too much, hemorrhaging their yellow markers across the page without really transforming the information. In these situations, underlining isn't very effective. It only works when students take time to preview the material; they must skim or read the material first and then highlight.

This entire instructional sequence can be modeled using electronic text. Underlining is most easily accomplished by selecting the chunk of text to be underlined and using the U icon on the formatting toolbar in Microsoft Word. You can also highlight the passage by selecting the text and clicking the highlighting icon and color of choice.

Introduction, Modeling, and Reflection

1. Explain to students that underlining and margin notes are critical tools for analyzing main ideas and details. Talk about the importance of underlining selectively and having purposes in mind before reading. *Don't start marking words before doing some careful previewing and purpose setting. In fact, underlining works best after you have read the selection.*

2. Model how to preview the assignment. Show them how to read the introductory paragraph(s) and bold print headings, to examine the pictures and graphs, and to read the concluding paragraph(s). *Stop and think about what you might learn from the selection and what you already know.* Next, guide students in a discussion about developing purposes for reading. Read the selection silently one paragraph at a time, and then demonstrate how you selectively underline. Think-aloud as you demonstrate.

3. With the students, develop and record procedural steps:
   - Skim or read through the selection first.
   - Reread one paragraph or section at a time and begin underlining.
   - Choose key words or phrases to highlight, never whole sentences.
   - Organize main ideas and details by Powers or other types of notations.
   - Generate topics or categories for ideas and write them in the margins.
   - Discuss and justify underlined information with a partner..

Reflection

How does selective underlining help you transform information? Why is it essential to be selective and to organize information as you underline? How does selective underlining help you become more metacognitive, particularly when given opportunities to talk about why you have underlined certain information?

Support and Extensions

- Provide students with opportunities to underline selectively. Use electronic texts, old textbooks, or photocopy sections of your assignments. Have students work with a partner to make decisions about what to underline.

- Underline main ideas (Power 1s) and details (Power 2s and 3s) with different colored markers. For example, main ideas could be in blue while details are in red and green. When main points are not explicit, generate your own main points and jot them in the margins.

- If you want students to underline, but don't have disposable copies, provide students with clear transparencies they can clip to a page of text and underline with dry erase or overhead pens. Before cleaning the transparency for the next page, students need to transfer the key ideas to their classroom notes. After a while students will not need to underline with a transparency. They will be able to pull out main ideas directly and add them to their notes.
- Have students underline key ideas on tests (see page 54) and in their notes.

Concept Maps

Concept Maps are another tool for helping students organize the essential ideas and supporting details from a selection. Concept Maps show concrete representations of the relationships among ideas in order to help readers organize the subordinate and superordinate components of a concept. Students find Concept Maps useful before, during, and after reading and as a procedure for organizing and remembering information. Concept Maps help students read poorly-structured text and enhance understanding and retention for those who typically have difficulty making meaning from text (Goldman & Rakestraw, 2000). In a comprehensive review of research, Trabasso and Bouchard (2002), found that teaching students to use Concept Maps to structure textual information improved comprehension and retention, particularly in the areas of science and social studies.

The effectiveness of using Concept Mapping as a learning strategy fits well with what we know about learning and memory. When we first take in new information, we store it temporarily before it becomes part of our background knowledge. If processing goes well in our working or short-term memories, information will be retained. As noted by Marzano (2004), certain learning activities are essential to effective processing for long-term retention: the information must be processed multiple times, the learner must add details, and the learner needs to make associations among ideas. Asking students to transform information into Concept Maps involves all of these processes.

In addition to improving general processing of information, using Concept Maps works particularly well with materials lacking cohesive structure (ideas are scattered throughout the piece). It also works as an excellent summarizing procedure in conjunction with other strategies such as K-W-L (page 112) and Two-Column Notes described in Chapter 6.

Introduction, Modeling, and Reflection

1. Model with a familiar word or concept such as "music" (Power 1). Post it where students can see it. Allow space to write additional information.

2. Have students discuss and agree on four or five general subdivisions (Power 2s) for the topic—for music, they might select rap, hip-hop, rock and roll, and country. Let the students know that typically their topics will be chapter titles or headings in their reading materials or topics dictated by their purposes for writing.

3. Next, divide students into groups and assign one category to each group. Have students brainstorm five to ten key pieces of information they know about their category. They should think about how the ideas relate to each other and to their category. Power Thinking might help, because they will be responsible for adding their information to the class Concept Map.

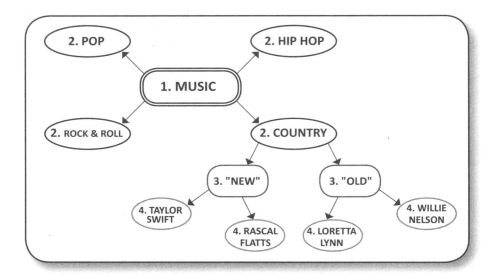

4. Have each group record their details on the class map. Let the other groups critique the quality and organization of the information.

5. Finally, work with the class to develop a Concept Map using course materials. As a class, have them preview a section of text, determine a topic, and pick out several sub-categories of information that match their purpose. Individually, have them read and pick out appropriate details for their maps.

Reflection

While creating the Concept Map, how many different ways did you transform information? How does this strategy fit within the Framework for Learning?

Support and Extensions

- Have students use their Concept Maps to write a summary about what they have learned.

- Mapping provides an effective structure for organizing information for research and for narrowing topics to specific areas. For example, each arm on the map (the Power 2 categories) becomes a topic for research.

  Consider assigning students research projects in cooperative teams. One student from each team researches one or two topics from the map, and then the team comes back together to share information, drafting a group report or class presentation.

- Have students use large sheets of newsprint or chart paper to develop their maps, and then they can add to the map as they learn more about each topic. Encourage students to draw pictures and add graphics to clarify information. Alternatively, students can use an electronic mapping tool to capture their learning. Then students can use their maps for their presentations. Because mapping has helped students to organize their thoughts, these oral reports usually surpass those presented without this tool.

- Concept Maps work well for taking notes on people. While reading a novel or biography, or while studying a famous person in history, students can use Character Map to record the main events of a person's life. They can then use their notes for writing.

In the following example, sixth graders used a Character Map to organize information as they read about Henry VIII.

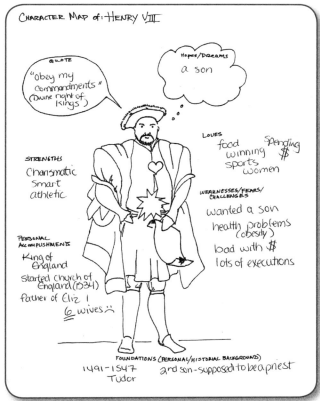

- Use Concept Maps to prepare students for discussion. In this example, Jadie Meyer asked her high school psychology students to read an article about the twelve principles of learning. Students worked in pairs to organize the information into a Content Frame (see page 158) and then transformed it again into a Concept Map. Students kept this map in their learning logs as a reference.

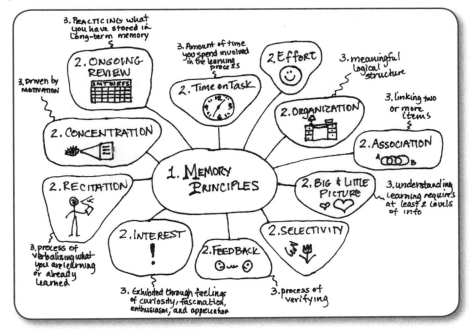

Analyzing & Applying Basic Patterns and Structures 57 •

- Pre- and Post-Reading Concept Maps.
    - ✓ Have students brainstorm all the information they know or think they know about the topic.
    - ✓ List the information and then have students help you categorize it. These categories will become Power 2s in their Pre-Reading Concept Maps.
    - ✓ Next, students read, view, and/or listen to information about the topic.
    - ✓ After learning, students change, delete, and/or add information to their Pre-Reading Concept Maps, making them Post-Reading Concept Maps.
    - ✓ Additional categories (Power 2s) may be added as needed.

In the following nutrition example, the new information about "benefits" is in the thickly-outlined Power 3 boxes. Information that was proven incorrect has been crossed out.

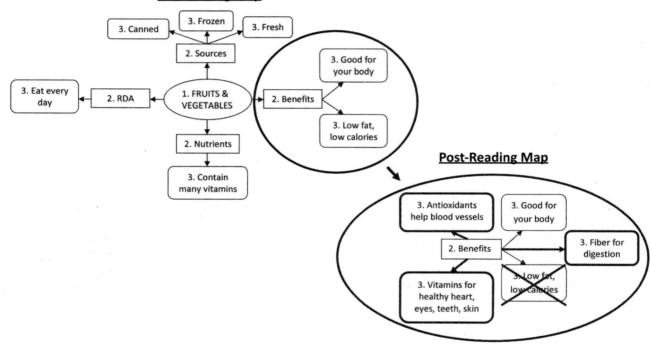

COMPARISON ORGANIZERS

Making comparisons is fundamental to understanding essential ideas across the content domains. Comparing depends on one's ability to analyze similarities and differences between two or more things. The most commonly used comparative structure is the Venn Diagram.

Venn Diagrams

Students label the two circles (or ellipses) with the names of the two items to be compared. The area within the overlapping circles is for recording similarities; the traits that are specific to each item are recorded in the remaining part of the circle. This format helps students untangle similarities and differences among concepts, characters, and events. (See online reproducible for Chapter 3.)

• 58   Chapter 3

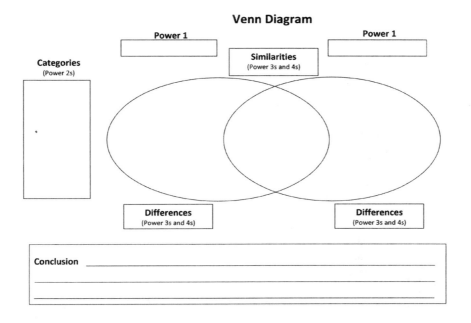

Introduction, Modeling, and Reflection

1. Introduce the Venn by inviting two students to the front of the classroom. Interview them and note similarities and differences on the Venn organizer. The following Venn Diagram was used to introduce students to each other in a Spanish II class. Students were given some general categories to get them started.

2. Model how to use the Venn Diagram to compare specific information, characters, or events in your content area.

Analyzing & Applying Basic Patterns and Structures 59 •

3. Determine several comparisons topics from previous content—concepts, people, things, events, etc. Divide students into small groups and assign each group one pair of items to compare using a Venn. When done, have each group explain similarities and differences using their Venn Diagram.

In the following example, geometry students compared rational and irrational numbers.

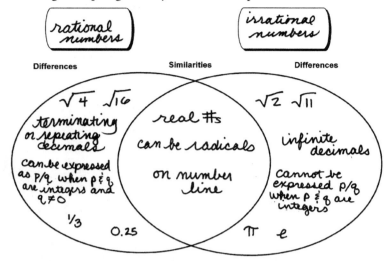

In this example, biology students used a Venn to clarify their understanding of DNA and RNA.

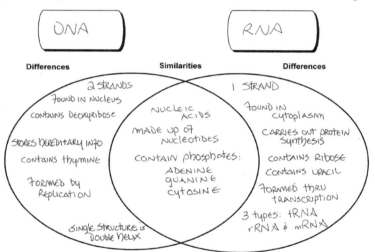

Reflection
How did the Venn Diagram work for you? How did it help you transform ideas and review important concepts? How might you apply the Venn Diagram to other material you are studying? Where does the Venn Diagram fit in the Framework for Learning?

Support and Extensions

- The Venn Diagram is an effective assessment tool when the teacher provides a set of comparison categories to guide students' responses. In addition, having students write a conclusion based on their entries provides additional information for assessment. The following science example shows both of these modifications.

• 60   Chapter 3

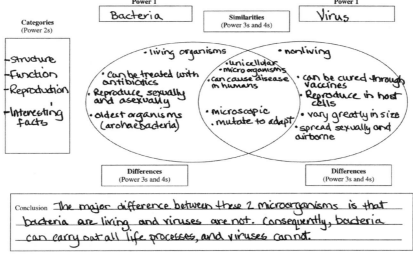

- Have students use visuals. For example, a geography teacher had her students do reports on European countries. When they finished, each student paired with another student who had selected a different country. They compared their two countries using a Venn Diagram with comparison categories of their own choice. Instead of two circles or ellipses, the students overlapped the outlines of their two countries.

- Have students draw visual representations (symbols or icons) rather than writing words in the Venn Diagram. This is especially powerful for second language acquisition students and younger students.

- V-Diagram. Because it's not always easy to write similarities in the overlapping circles, an alternative comparison diagram, the V-Diagram, provides more space. Notice in the following Mitosis/Meiosis example how the teacher provided scaffolding. In heterogeneous classrooms, this kind of differentiated assignment is easy to create. Advanced students receive a blank diagram and complete it independently. Students in need of some support get the partially-completed V-Diagram.

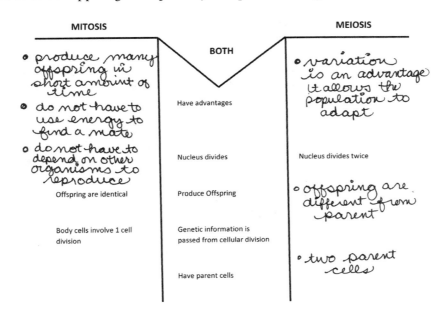

Analyzing & Applying Basic Patterns and Structures 61 •

In the following example of a V-Diagram, the student completed the graphic organizer and then wrote a summary sentence.

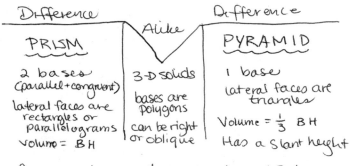

- Contrast and Compare Chart. The Contrast and Compare Chart is helpful for comparing two items or concepts which might be easily confused. Because brain research indicates we remember best what we do at the beginning of an activity, we to ask students to list differences first and then itemize the similarities. In the following example, literature students compared two poems, *The Fawn* by Edna St. Vincent Millay and *The Meadow Mouse* by Theodore Roethke. Before beginning the discussion about differences and similarities, the class decided on the areas of focus and listed them on the "With regard to" sections of the chart. Deciding on these focus areas first helped them analyze the poems.

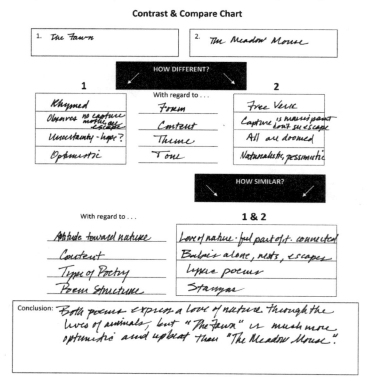

• 62   Chapter 3

- Differences and Similarities Chart. The following comparison format, similar to the Contrast and Compare Chart, has students identify the differences between two items before looking at their similarities. For example, if students are comparing two short stories, they start by listing on a separate sheet of paper things they notice about characters, point of view, or literary devices. Or, if they are comparing two kinds of plants, they list what they observe about each. Next, they categorize the information in the chart—identifying the differences first and then the similarities.

	Topic 1	Topic 2
Differences		
Similarities		

- Triangular Comparison Diagram. This diagram is used to identify the similarities and differences among three concepts. It can be expanded by choosing polygons with more sides (e.g., a square is used to compare four items, a pentagon, five). Several levels of complexity are possible with the Triangular Comparison. The first diagrams provide the simplest versions with the least amount of information required. The second diagram, modified from the original by a high school teacher, Jayson Foster, requires students write the individual traits of each of the three concepts to be compared along the sides of the triangle, the traits shared by all three go in the middle, and the common traits between any two of the concepts go in the corner diamonds between the two items being compared (an art history example follows). If more focus should be placed on the similarities, rather than the concept, switch the location of the information by placing the concepts in the corner diamonds and the similarities along the sides of the triangle.

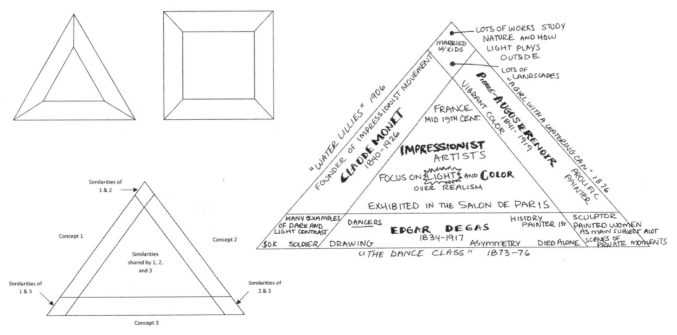

Analyzing & Applying Basic Patterns and Structures

PATTERN ORGANIZERS

In this section, we include two strategies: Sequence Organizers and Pattern Puzzles. Sequence Organizers focus on information presented in a distinct order, e.g., directions, steps in a process, events in a story. You will experience a variety of linear and graphic representations to meet the demands of varying texts and tasks. Pattern Puzzles can be used in a variety of ways to prepare for learning and to help students engage with and practice content information. Through sequencing, grouping, or developing a hierarchy of ideas, this strategy reinforces the patterns learners experience while reading, viewing, and listening.

Sequence Organizers

Sequence Organizers provide a structure for analyzing story events, determining character changes, identifying sequential processes of scientific investigations, and solving mathematics problems. The format changes depending upon the task. The information contained in sequence organizers flows naturally into writing.

Introduction, Modeling, and Reflection

1. Model with a familiar topic.
2. Choose a framework that works for the topic (e.g., comic strip, flow chart, timeline).
3. Develop the sequence together with your students.

   In the following example, an art teacher worked with her students to clarify the steps used to critique a work of art. She emphasized the importance of starting objectively with facts and observations, and then easing into the more subjective evaluations.

Objective	Objective	GUESS (with support)	Subjective
Describe (objectively) what you see—record size of work, medium, processes used; indicate the subject with details; list the elements of art used.	**Analyze** the organization of the work. How are the principles of art used to organize the elements of line, color, shape, form, space, and texture?	**Interpret** the artist's message. Explain the meaning or mood of the piece. Your opinion must be based on visual facts, but be daring and creative!	**Judge** the success of the piece. Determine the degree of artistic merit. Judgment has two parts: personal, (Do you like the piece?) and intellectual, (Does the work successfully communicate its message?).

4. Next, work with your content materials and pick something from a previous unit with which students can create Sequence Maps or other sequence organizers. Talk about different formats for their organizers, but let individuals or small groups select the format they think is best. Have groups share their final products.
5. Finally, have them create Sequence Organizers with new content.

Reflection

How do Sequence Organizers help identify each step of a process? How does discussing each step lead to a clearer understanding of the whole?

Support and Extensions

- Use pictures with text. In this example, a high school student demonstrated his understanding of the rock cycle.

- Working on computers, ninth graders in cooperative groups developed Sequence Maps for solving math word problems (see the following example). Each group paired with another group, printed their maps, and then completed a set of problems to evaluate how well their partners' map worked.

Analyzing & Applying Basic Patterns and Structures 65

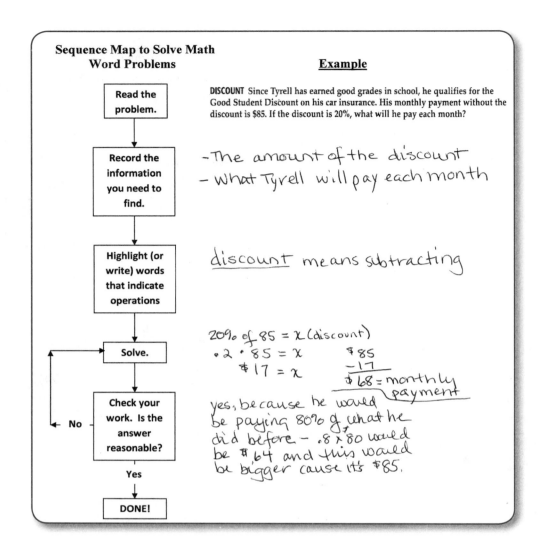

Pattern Puzzles

One way to engage students in exploring various organizational structures is to use Pattern Puzzles, where students physically manipulate words, phrases, sentences, images, or a combination of these into various configurations, depending upon their purpose. Pattern Puzzles are often used to help students identify sequence or procedural steps or chronologies. Students also use them for categorizing concepts into groups and hierarchies, and for matching vocabulary terms with definitions and/or illustrations.

Introduction, Modeling, and Reflection

1. The first time you introduce Pattern Puzzles, use simple concepts with easily recognized potential relationships—you want students to learn the process first so they can move through the content without being distracted by the process.

   For example, a geography teacher might provide students with cards labeled with the names of the following countries: United States, South Africa, Iraq, Brazil, Russia, Canada, Egypt, China, Mexico, India, and Japan.

2. Display the concept cards in a random arrangement and think aloud as you find ways to group the concepts in meaningful ways.

• 66   Chapter 3

The country cards can be configured in a variety of different groupings depending on the learning goal and the grade level of the students: population, continent, geographic features in common, economy, government, etc.

3. After providing a few examples, have students offer alternative groupings.

4. Once students understand the procedure, identify the key concepts related to your content goal and create sets of note cards or paper slips (textboxes if done electronically) with one concept per card for each student. You may want corresponding images or definitions on additional cards, depending upon learning goals.

5. Ask students to manipulate the cards into logical groupings (or sequence or matches) that make sense for these concepts. Instruct students to look for relationships among concepts and to predict how the terms can be organized for learning.

6. Discuss the different configurations students generate, focusing on the meaning (students sometimes start with simple pattern identification, e.g., color, letters in common, etc.). Encourage students to demonstrate their thinking with a partner or in small groups.

Reflection
How did Pattern Puzzles help you organize information logically? Were you actively engaged? Did you have opportunities to talk about your ideas?

Support and Extensions

- After completing a unit of study, have students list topics, sub-topics, and bold print vocabulary on separate cards. Place in envelopes. As a post-reading activity, have students organize these into Power 1, 2, and 3 hierarchies.

- In the following math example, a geometry teacher gave her students strips of paper that included the components of a two-column geometric proof, solvable in several ways. When done, students shared their different correct responses on the board and looked for similarities and differences across the set of proofs. Some students even suggested using different properties to prove the relationship.

Pattern Puzzle	
[Diagram of triangles with points A, B, C, D, E]	**Given:** $\overline{AD}$ bisects $\overline{BE}$ $\overline{AB} \parallel \overline{ED}$
	Prove: $\overline{AB} \cong \overline{ED}$

Statements	Reasons
$\overline{AD}$ bisects $\overline{BE}$ and $\overline{AB} \parallel \overline{ED}$	Given
$\angle E \cong \angle B$	If two parallel lines are cut by a transversal, the alternate interior angles are congruent.
$\overline{BC} \cong \overline{CE}$	Definition of a segment bisector
$\angle ACB \cong \angle DCE$	Vertically opposite angles are congruent.
$\triangle ABC \cong \triangle DEC$	Angle—Side—Angle
$\overline{AB} \cong \overline{DE}$	Corresponding parts of congruent triangles are congruent.

- Have students write sentences, describing the main events of a sequence (scientific experiments, the steps to solve a math problem or a geometric proof, the plot of a short story). Cut the statements apart, and place the slips into envelopes. Have pairs of students

Analyzing & Applying Basic Patterns and Structures

organize them into correct order and then explain their thinking.

- Use Pattern Puzzles as a tool for helping students with basic paragraph structure. With younger children, begin with a single paragraph that contains a well-developed topic sentence and supporting details.

    Write each sentence on a separate strip of paper. Mix up the strips and demonstrate how to organize them into a paragraph. Talk about topic sentences and transition words. Encourage multiple solutions, as there are a variety of ways to organize any paragraph. Try out different sequences before deciding which sentence order seems to work best.

    Take multiple copies of another paragraph and cut them apart, sentence by sentence. Put all the strips from each paragraph into an envelope and give one envelope to each group of two or three students. Instruct them to work together to organize the sentences into a well-written paragraph. Ask students to discuss why they organized the sentences into a specific pattern. Remind them about Power 1, 2, and 3 ideas.

    With multi-paragraph selections, leave the first paragraph intact, but cut the remaining paragraphs into individual sentences. Make sure there is one sentence per slip of paper. Put all of the slips into an envelope and distribute to pairs of students. Then have the students place the paragraphs and the individual sentences in the correct order. Suggest they find sentences containing Power 1 ideas. Then organize the Power 2 and 3 ideas appropriately.

- Pattern Puzzles can be used to help students explore a variety of structures. For example, use poetry to help them identify rhyme patterns, use a classroom text selection to help them identify the author's craft, and have students use their own written pieces to help them discover different and/or better ways to structure sentences and paragraphs.

▲ ▲ ▲

Summary

In this chapter, we have focused on some fundamental ways to help students construct meaning from text. When students know how authors structure their writing and from what perspective writers present their information, they can more readily understand and remember what they read. They can decide if the author's organizing structures will help them attain a deeper understanding of textual information, or if they need to select something more applicable to their purpose for reading. This chapter featured tools for organizing information into main ideas and details, for making comparisons, and for sequencing information. With each strategy, we demonstrate, encourage, and model. Then, we gradually step aside and assist only when necessary. We teach a variety of strategies and then encourage flexibility and reflection so students can begin adapting these strategies to their own unique qualities as learners.

Remember, even though we have presented these basic strategies out of context, they mix and flow as part of the CRISS Frameworks for Teaching and Learning.

CHAPTER 3 RESEARCH BASE

Research Conclusion	Reference
"Doing strategies" without focusing on meaning (content learning) distracted readers from building coherent representations.	McKeown, Beck, & Blake, 2009
When students know the author's style of writing, they gain control over their reading and their own writing. Readers who understand how authors structure their writing more readily understand and remember what they read.	Duke & Pearson, 2002 Goldman & Rakestraw, 2000
Concept Maps help students read poorly structured text and enhance understanding and retention for those students who typically have difficulty making meaning from text.	Goldman & Rakestraw, 2000
Teaching students to use concept maps to structure textual information improved comprehension and retention, particularly in the areas of science and social studies.	Trabasso & Bouchard, 2002
For long-term retention, information must be processed multiple times by adding details and making associations among ideas.	Marazano, 2004

Discussion: The Conversation of Learning

4

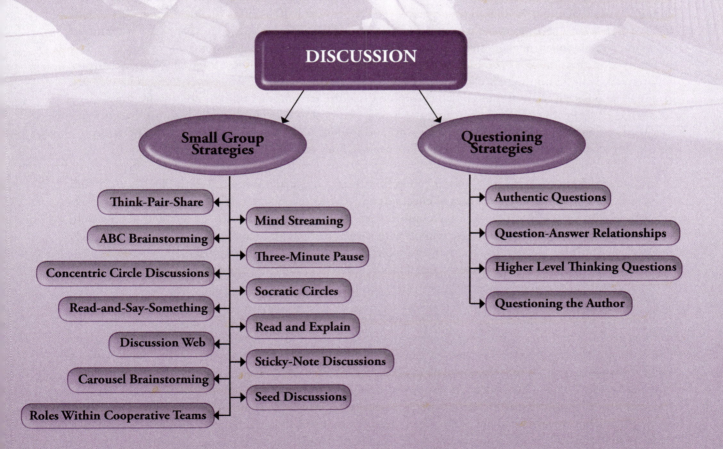

We talk to learn. Learning is a social enterprise. As social beings, we are innately wired for collaborative learning. Learning grows from social interactions where students have real discussions. They enter our classrooms with some information, but no one has the whole picture. Through talk, students make ideas grow. They make connections, ask questions, and pool their understandings. Engaging in meaningful conversations about content leads to deeper and deeper levels of understanding. Through thought-provoking conversations, students emerge with a deeper knowledge and a clearer focus for learning.

Unfortunately, rich classroom discussions where students engage in thought-provoking conversations about course content are rare. The typical scene in classrooms is all too familiar; most of us remember how it feels to be a student in a classroom dominated by teacher talk and interrogation. The teacher asks the questions. One-by-one, students reluctantly reel off answers until someone hits on the correct one. The teacher is the sole evaluator and controller of the discussion. Cazden (1988) calls this model of discourse IRE: the teacher initiates (I) talk by asking a question; a student responds (R), and the teacher evaluates (E) the response. In these situations, teacher-student dialogue is a means of assessment rather than instruction. Students rarely acquire the depth of knowledge that allows them to make their own inferences or draw their own conclusions.

Our own school experiences reflect what has occurred historically in education. In a comprehensive review of research on classroom discourse and reading comprehension, Nystrand (2006) noted that researchers in the early 20th century found recitation with rapid-fire teacher questions the dominant pedagogy. For example, as early as 1912, Stevens claimed that the predominance of recitation in classrooms made them places "for displaying knowledge instead of a laboratory for getting and using it" (as cited in Nystrand, 2006). In the 1950s, Benjamin Bloom found that teachers talked at least half of all instructional time and more than 80% of all teacher questions focused on recitation of textual information. Little has changed. For example, Nystrand and his colleagues conducted a study in 8th and 9th grade English classrooms where they found 85% of observed instruction was a combination of lecture, recitation, and seatwork. Moreover, Nystrand further reports a study in 58 ninth grade classes where he found that open-ended, higher-level discussions averaged about 15 seconds a day. Even though rich classroom discourse remains rare in most classrooms, literacy research is replete with evidence supporting the strong relationship between dialogic discourse (where students talk with one another and the focus is on content) and student achievement. Students achieve better in classrooms where the discussion is dialogic (Wilkinson & Son, 2011).

Some of the most compelling research comes from work on effective schools. Judith Langer (2009) did a five-year study examining the features of effective and less effective high schools. She classified schools as effective and ineffective based on high stakes assessments and course performance. Langer and her research team compared effective and ineffective schools with similar demographics ranging from schools in high poverty areas to those situated in suburban and middle class neighborhoods. They learned that effective schools, regardless of demographics, have significantly different school cultures than their less effective counterparts.

Effective schools in middle class and in high poverty areas are more caring; everyone goes "the extra mile" to show kindness and to create a sense of belonging for staff and students. Among other things, adolescents find these schools are safe places where they can try out new ideas and have a strong support network to keep them from getting lost. Teachers are part of engaging professional communities and share a similar philosophy of education. Langer and her colleagues also noted striking differences in classroom contexts. They observed far more instances of dialogic discussion where students asked questions and took more responsibility for leading their own discussions. Langer described these classrooms as "intellectual playing grounds for the development of whole people who can engage in both critical and creative thinking." This interactive context contrasted sharply with the less effective schools, which were also far less welcoming. Students often worked alone. Teacher talk and questioning dominated. Rather than encouraging student questions, teachers treated student questions "as evidence that a student has not learned well, didn't read the text, or failed to do the homework."

Another line of research supports the positive relationship between discussion and reading comprehension. Saunders and Goldenberg (1999) found that fourth and fifth grade children of varying levels of English proficiency who engaged in instructional conversations (small group discussions) to construct their own meaning did better on measures of factual and interpretative comprehension than did children in the control group assigned to read and study the selection. Similar results occur with high school students; for example, Sweigart (1991) found that exploratory talk in student-led discussion groups helped high school seniors understand difficult content more effectively than conditions where students listened to a lecture or participated in a whole class discussion. Moreover, students participating in the small group discussions produced better opinion essays (scored for clear thesis and elaboration of ideas) than did students in the other two conditions. Sweigert concluded that student-led small group discussions provide a means for "developing understanding of complex topics and can facilitate writing about these ideas."

Considerable research on discussion comes from work on using literature for reading instruction (Morrow & Gambrell, 2000). Researchers find that discussion promotes deeper understanding of text, leads to higher-level thinking and problem-solving, and improves communication skills (Gambrell, 1996). Student-led discussions foster greater student participation than those led by teachers, and they improve communication skills—including the ability to take on different points of view. Such discussions also increase student sensitivity, encouraging recognition and acknowledgment of others in the group (Almasi, 2008). Given these conclusions, the challenge is that students don't do a very good job in student-led discussion groups without teacher guidance, and yet, if the teacher is involved, students tend to make their responses to the teacher rather than to their peers (Adler, Rougle, & Caughlan, 2004).

Promoting rich classroom discussions can be complicated by the instructional histories students bring to the classroom. Connolly and Smith (2002) remind us that "discussion is as much a social activity as it is an intellectual one." In a qualitative study with ninth graders, they investigated student conceptions about discussion. Connolly had his 9th grade honor students participate in discussion and then reflect upon their discussion experiences by writing and talking. The results were rather surprising. Even though Connolly's students were used to participating in small group discussions, they still regarded their teacher as the ultimate authority—even in situations where he was doing his best not to be the authority. Students felt the teacher's opinion outweighed the opinions of fellow students. This comment pretty much sums it up: "If another student says their opinion, we feel free to challenge it, but when the teacher says his opinion, it stands."

Another complicating variable has to do with student relationships. Students in Connolly and Smith's study acknowledged how risky whole class discussion can be. Even these 9th grade honor students feared being ridiculed by other students. Their peers might think they were stupid for asking questions or sharing comments, so they kept their mouths shut. Students worried when their opinions differed from the majority and from the teacher's point of view. One student said, "I think the problem with the large group discussions was that it made you exposed to the special brand of teenage cruelty."

The personal worries were not so prevalent in small group discussions. Most students felt they learned more from small group discussions where they had a chance to get to know other group members. Small groups are "a less threatening forum. . . one has a chance to express their thoughts and opinions without feeling stupid or awkward." This qualitative study speaks to the importance of establishing strong relationships with students and to creating a classroom atmosphere where students feel safe to take risks and be vulnerable without fear of retribution. Connolly and Smith recommend opportunities for students to "talk about talk." Teachers and students need to become more open not only about content, but to recognize their feelings and their own roles within the micro-culture of their classroom.

A challenge for all of us is to help shift the deeply-rooted paradigm of classroom discourse. Students expect the teacher to impose questions, to call on them for answers, to dispel erroneous information, and then provide the answers before transitioning to the next questions. Changing the power and voice in the classroom is essential for engaging students in deep learning. For example, Copeland (2005) describes how he works to build an emotional climate supportive of rich discussion between his high school English students. At the beginning of an academic semester, he allows time for students to get to know one another by doing a series of classroom climate activities. Students learn about one another's interests, histories, and personalities in preparation for understanding another's opinions and ideas.

Most CRISS strategies, particularly those described in this chapter, help shift power to students. Conversations among students about content naturally occur when small groups focus on accomplishing a task, such as developing a Character Map or creating Conclusion-Support Notes. When students take a moment to write about their thoughts before sharing them with a partner or small group, they are more likely to participate in the discussions that follow (as in Think-Pair-Share, Sticky-Note Discussions, and Seed Discussions). In other situations, the focus might be on authentic questions that individual students have recorded in their journals or questions that teams develop for discussion with the entire class (e.g., Question-Answer Relationships and Higher Level Thinking Questions). Students can also assume specific roles in their discussion groups. This chapter contains a variety of discussion options in which student talk, rather than teacher talk, remains central. The key ingredient behind each of these approaches is to establish a classroom atmosphere in which risk taking during discussion is an important goal. For this to occur, we as teachers must model how to listen and respond to our students. Students must know expressing their voices is safe.

Discussion Guidelines

Before using any discussion strategy, establish some ground rules for student-led conversations. Develop these collaboratively with your class. Begin by specifying several which you feel are critical. Here are a few ideas:

- Listen to what your discussion partners have to say.
- Let each person complete his or her thought; do not interrupt.
- Repeat the main points of the previous speaker before making your own comment. Repeating another person's idea will help you listen and will also let the speaker know that you have heard his or her message.
  - *I get what you are saying about . . .*
  - *Another way to think about what you said is . . .*
  - *Let me make sure I understand what you said about . . .*
- Challenge or support ideas, not people.
  - *I hear what you said . . . but I have a different idea . . .*
  - *What do you feel about . . . ?*
- Support your ideas with examples and facts from the materials you are reading.
- Keep an open mind.
- Make sure everyone has a chance to talk.
- Look at the person who is speaking.
- BE RESPECTFUL!

Post these guidelines in your classroom so they can be referred to when necessary during discussion periods. Refine them as needed.

We organized this chapter into two sections, small group discussion strategies and questioning strategies.

SMALL GROUP DISCUSSION STRATEGIES

Think-Pair-Share

Think-Pair-Share is a particularly powerful discussion strategy (Kagan, 1989) that allows every student to become an active participant. It works well before and during reading, as a problem-solving strategy, as a break in a lecture, or as a follow-up activity. In each case, the procedure is similar.

Introduction, Modeling, and Reflection

1. The teacher begins by suggesting a topic or asking a question.
2. Students *think* and write down what they know or have learned about a particular topic.
3. After students have written, have them *pair* with another student or with a small group of students and discuss their ideas.
4. Conclude with a whole-class *share* discussion.

Reflection
How does Think-Pair-Share exemplify the CRISS Framework for Learning? How did this strategy prepare you to read this assignment? How did writing about your own ideas before discussing help you participate? How did talking with a partner help you understand the content?

Support and Extensions

- Students generate their own questions or topics and use them within discussion groups or with the whole class.
- During a reading assignment, ask students to stop after they have read about an important concept in the selection. Pose a question about the topic and have students do Think-Pair-Share in response to the question. After pairs have shared with the whole class what they learned, invite them to read the next section.
- Use Think-Pair-Share in place of brainstorming. In the following example, a middle school math teacher wanted her students to understand that finding a fraction of a number involves multiplication. She began her lesson with a Think-Pair-Share about the following questions:
    a. What does it mean to find 1/3 of 2/3?
    b. Will the number be greater than 2/3?

    After one minute, students discussed their answers with the person next to them, and then shared their answers with the whole class.
- Use to prepare students for a writing assignment.
- During a lecture or video, stop and ask students to respond individually to a few questions focusing on the content presented so far. Use open-ended questions assisting students to think critically about the content: *What is the most important point made so far? What information do you agree or disagree with? What ideas are obscure or difficult to understand?* Then, divide students into small two- or three-person "buzz" groups (Copeland, 2005). Copeland finds that buzz groups help students become more comfortable with one another

by providing them with brief and frequent opportunities to speak persuasively based on content just presented. After a few minutes, share comments with the whole class and then continue with the lecture or video.

- Doug Buehl (2009) suggests a variation of Think-Pair-Share where students assume different roles. Identify one member of the pair as an expert whose role is to explain the topic to someone who knows nothing about it. The expert explains difficult vocabulary and concepts so the novice understands. The novice asks questions to make sure the expert makes sense. Students then switch roles. This adaptation works well as a review for an examination where students work in pairs to explain how they would answer probable test questions.

Mind Streaming

Students work in pairs to bring out their background knowledge about a topic or to review learned information.

Introduction, Modeling, and Reflection

1. Student A talks for one minute about the topic. Student B listens and encourages student A, but does not talk.
2. The roles reverse. Student B talks for one minute about the topic and student A listens and encourages student B.

Reflection

How does Mind Streaming exemplify the CRISS Framework for Learning? How did this strategy prepare you to read this assignment? How does talking and listening in this manner help you as a learner? How might you use this strategy on your own?

Support and Extensions

- Mind Streaming also works effectively as a post-reading/listening strategy in which students do one-minute paired retellings of what they have learned from a reading assignment, video, or lecture.

- Use Mind Streaming as a component of Think-Pair-Share. Students can "mind stream" after they have written down what they *think* they know about a topic.

- Paired Verbal Fluency (Buehl, 2009). Use this adaptation at points in the lesson where you want students to review what has been learned. Partner A talks for one minute about what they have gained from their reading so far. The partners switch and change roles. Partner B adds additional information without repeating anything described by Partner A. By not repeating information, students must listen carefully rather than thinking ahead to what they might say when it is their turn.

ABC Brainstorming

The ABC Brainstorming strategy can be used to elicit information before a lesson or before writing.

Introduction, Modeling, and Reflection

1. Ask students to write the alphabet down the left side of a sheet of notebook paper. Before reading or listening, provide the topic and ask students (alone or with a partner) to brainstorm their background knowledge relating to the topic that begins with each specific letter.

2. Students can be assigned certain letters or can brainstorm ideas for the entire alphabet.

3. After reading or listening, ask students to return to their ABC Brainstorming. What can they now add? What can they verify as correct information?

4. ABC Brainstorming also works well as a pre-writing tool. Once writers have listed what they know, they can begin to organize their ideas for writing.

Reflection

How does this strategy fit into the Framework for Learning? How did ABC Brainstorming prepare you for learning new material? How else can you use this strategy?

Support and Extensions

- Students can also use ABC Brainstorming as a during—and after—reading strategy. Kathy Kerby had her literature students work in dyads to develop ABC charts about Christopher Boone, the main character in the book, *The Curious Incident of the Dog in the Night-time*.

Alibi	Bus	Cow	Driving Mothers Car	Ed Boone his father
Faces	Groans Alot	*The Curious Incident of the Dog in the Night Time*	Hitting People	Intelligence is normal
Judy Boone his mother	Knows something!		Love's Math	Mrs. Alexander tried to help Christopher
Neighborhood	Organized		Patterns	Q ? who killed ? the dog? ?
Refusing to use his toothbrush if anyone had touched it.	Screaming or smashing things when angry	Christopher Boone	Teacher	Understands everything
Victory over autism.	Wellington the dog	X(e)xcellent teacher	Y Hates Yellow + Brown things	Zoo

Discussion: The Conversation of Learning

- ABC Brainstorming can also be adapted to demonstrate students' understanding of content. Donna Duval had her U.S. History students create ABC Stories to show what they learned about the 1920s.

    Al Capone made the 1920s fun and dangerous.
    Being a bootlegger, he brought alcohol to everyone.
    Corrupt presidents even drank in the White House.
    During this time some people were haters.
    Even "good" people joined the KKK.
    For they thought they were being good Americans... Wasn't "100% American."
    Going one step further, the government created quotas.
    Hate-filled quotas on immigrants from countries we did not like.
    Inside, people must have been sad, but they drank and partied the Twenties away.
    Jobs started to become obsolete as technology improved.
    Keeping people rich wasn't a problem. The stock market made plenty of "money."
    Letting people buy on margin, brokers bet the market would be good forever.
    Millionaires were said to have tripled during the Twenties, but were they real?
    National heroes emerged to make us feel good, like Charles Lindbergh and Amelia Earhart.
    Over the oceans they flew—risking life and, for one, giving her life.
    People also rushed to Harlem, where the musicians were black but the audience couldn't be.
    Quiet the Twenties were not.
    Right when we thought they were okay, the
    Stock Market crashed on Black Tuesday.
    To many this was a sign of the end.
    Ugly days lay ahead with bank runs and no cash to be found.
    Very soon people would find that buying on margin is costly.
    Women and children would find they had no money, no home, and sometimes no spouse (suicide).
    X extraordinary people lost it all.
    You have to ask yourself, was it all due to greed?
    Zero money... zero hope.

Three-Minute Pause

In order to learn and remember information, we have to stop and take it in; otherwise information will flow through our minds without sticking! The Three-Minute Pause (Buehl, 2009) provides an effective way to stop the flow to save it in our memories.

Introduction, Modeling, and Reflection

1. Students pause while reading, watching a video, or listening to a lecture and turn to their partner or group for a Three-Minute Pause. They
    a. summarize what they have learned.
    b. identify something they found particularly interesting.
    c. ask any questions about confusing information and/or make a prediction about what they might learn next.

2. Explain to students that pausing about every 10 to 15 minutes helps them "fix" new information in memory. Discuss why stopping and reflecting upon what they are learning is metacognitive and helps them learn and store new information. Why is hearing and viewing information not enough for constructing new meaning?

> **Reflection**
> How did discussion with a partner help you construct meaning? How might this strategy be useful in studying for a test?

Concentric Circle Discussions

Concentric Circle Discussions (Kletzien & Baloche, 1994) work well for reviewing content in whole-class groups or in groups of six or more. With little teacher intervention, the students can review key concepts, offer personal interpretations, and review vocabulary. This turns out to be a great way to review for a test.

Introduction, Modeling, and Reflection

1. Give each student an index card. On their cards, they review or explain a key concept.
2. Place students in two concentric circles facing each other.
3. Students in the inside circle pair with students in the outside circle.
4. Students use the cards to explain their concepts to one another. (Give students a time limit of one to two minutes per person.)
5. The partners ask questions to make sure they understand the information.
6. After completing both explanations, the two students trade cards. The outside circle moves clockwise one person, and each student is now paired with a new partner.
7. Students must now explain the information described on the new card to a new partner. The process is repeated until all students have learned and taught all concepts and have received their original cards back.

> **Reflection**
> How does the strategy assist you in learning/recalling the information? How does the active listening and discussion of Concentric Circle Discussions help you learn?

Support and Extensions

- <u>Fishbowl</u> (Gilmore, 2006) is a modification of Concentric Circle Discussions. Students form two circles with the smaller circle comprised of three to five students inside the larger one. Select a controversial topic or a key concept for discussion. Follow these rules:
    - ✓ Only the students in the inner circle can speak.
    - ✓ No student leaves the inner circle until s/he has contributed to the discussion.
    - ✓ After a student talks once, he or she changes places with a student in the outer circle.
    - ✓ A student cannot re-enter the inner circle for two minutes.

Socratic Circles

Copeland (2005) provides a rich and detailed description of how he has incorporated Socratic discussions into his high school English classrooms. While we have space in this manual only to describe his work briefly, we recommend his book, *Socratic Circles: Fostering critical and creative thinking in middle and high schools* as an excellent resource. He describes Socratic dialogue as a "quest for understanding that has no definite beginning or end . . . Socratic dialogue is about accepting multiple perspectives on a certain topic and re-examining our own experiences and opinions in light of those perspectives."

Introduction, Modeling, and Reflection

1. Hand out a short passage of text. Ask students to read, analyze, and take notes on the text.
2. Randomly divide students into two concentric circles–an inner and outer circle. Students in the inner circle sit on the floor facing each other and participate in the discussion. Those in the outer circle sit in chairs and silently observe the behavior and performance of the inner circle.
3. With difficult text, inner circle students take turns reading the passage aloud.
4. For the next ten minutes, the inner circle discusses the text. The teacher sits on the outside contributing questions and comments to keep the discussion going smoothly.
5. After the discussion, the outer circle students spend ten minutes providing feedback about the inner circle discussion (e.g. strong points, questions, process).
6. Students in the inner and outer circles switch roles and places.
7. The process continues with the inner circle holding a ten minute discussion followed by ten minutes of feedback from members of the outer circle.

Copeland's Guidelines for Ensuring the Success of Socratic Circles

- Select a text worthy of discussion. It needs to be rich in ideas and content and can be taken from literature, history, math, philosophy, current events or even a musical score or a piece of art.
- Be flexible in allowing student's voice in the discussion, yet instill in them a desire to push beyond the simple answers and examine all issues thoroughly and in detail.
- The feedback provided by the outer circle is essential to the success of the discussion. Begin the feedback process by asking each student for some initial impressions.
  - What were some of the strong points about how the discussion went?
  - What were some of the obstacles?
  - Did everyone have a chance to participate?
  - Did students really listen to one another?

Directly witnessing how the discussion went prepares the outer circle to become a more effective inner circle.

> **Reflection**
> How does the process of Socratic Circles help you gain a deeper understanding of the ideas in the text? How does this process improve your conversations about the content?

▶ Read-and-Say-Something

Read-and-Say-Something works effectively for difficult materials; rather than letting students struggle with the meaning alone, have them read and discuss the ideas with a partner or in a small group.

Introduction, Modeling, and Reflection

1. Have students work in partners or small groups. The leader reads the first paragraph or section of the assignment out loud, or all group members read the first section silently.

2. After reading the first section, the student to the right of the leader says something that relates to the information and/or the purpose for reading. S/he may react to ideas, descriptions, images, and/or comment on confusing parts. Others in the group may comment after the first person says something.

3. When discussion about the section ends, or when time is up, the person to the right of the leader (the first say-something person) reads the next section and the process continues.

4. Conversations about the meaning of the article occur naturally. Students conclude the session by writing down questions they want answered by the whole class or other groups.

> **Reflection**
> How did Read-and-Say-Something help you understand the ideas in this selection? Were you actively engaged? How did it help you to be metacognitive?

Support and Extensions

- Use this strategy as a way for students to review class notes. Have them read through their notes with a partner and then say something to one another.

- Incorporate Read-and-Say-Something as part of problem solving in mathematics.

- Focus discussions on specific topics. For example, a language arts teacher might have students talk about descriptive writing; a history teacher might have students pay attention to issues regarding human rights.

▶ Read and Explain

Read and Explain, a modified version of Read-and-Say-Something that is linked directly to the text content, provides a more explicit way for readers to examine their own understanding. Frequently, students don't know when they aren't comprehending. Read and Explain works well to slow readers down so they can carefully process text. In addition, it's a powerful metacognitive strategy. If students can't explain what they read, they know they didn't "get it" and need to apply additional strategies.

Introduction, Modeling, and Reflection

1. Divide a section of text into several paragraphs or chunks.
2. Model Read and Explain by asking a student to be your partner. Read aloud the first section of the assignment. Pause at the end of a paragraph or section and explain what you read to your partner. Talk about any questions that come to mind or comprehension difficulties that occurred.
3. Your partner adds any additional information.
4. Switch roles. Your partner reads the next section aloud, explains the content, and you add additional information if necessary. Continue reading and explaining until the selection is completed.

Reflection
How did Read and Explain help you understand the ideas in this selection? Were you actively engaged? How did it help you to be metacognitive?

Support and Extensions

- This strategy works well as an informal and non-intimidating assessment of a student's comprehension. Many students can read the words, but they aren't comprehending. Sitting beside a student and reading and explaining together is a gentle and effective way to diagnose problems students have with comprehension.

- Read and Explain works well in a one-to-one situation to help struggling readers. By modeling how you read, stop, and explain content, you are demonstrating what it means to comprehend and to monitor your own comprehension as a metacognitive learner. During your modeling, make sure to use fix-up strategies—look up a word in the glossary, reread a sentence or two, ask your partner. Show how you apply strategies to increase your understanding. Eventually, students will become proficient at processing the reading and be able to Read and Explain independently, in their heads.

Discussion Web

As teachers, we know that classroom discussions encourage students to think, but involving everyone is difficult. We don't want the debate monopolized by a few vocal students; everyone needs an opportunity to rethink a topic, to acknowledge or challenge viewpoints. Adapted from Alverman's Discussion Web (Alvermann, 1991; Buehl, 2009), this strategy helps students untangle different points of view by actively involving everyone. It also helps them understand opposing sides of an issue.

Introduction, Modeling, and Reflection

1. Model with a whole class discussion. Make or project a copy of the Discussion Web organizer (pictured on the next page and available in the online reproducibles for Chapter 4). Begin with a controversial and familiar topic, one that you know will generate some "heat."

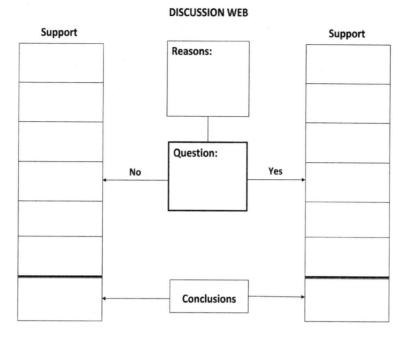

2. Write the question in the middle of the grid (e.g., Should the Alaskan wilderness be opened for oil exploration? Should there be stronger gun control laws?). Discuss and record the reasons for selecting the topic, e.g., *We need more oil so we aren't so dependent on the Middle East.*

3. Next, have the class brainstorm opposing arguments (see example that follows). Challenge students to take sides contrary to their personal views.

4. Develop conclusions on both sides.

5. Then, ask students to work in pairs and decide which conclusion seems more valid.

DISCUSSION WEB

Support (No)	Reasons / Question	Support (Yes)
Handguns not a major cause of death and injuries	**Reasons:** • Recent shootings • School violence • Enforcement of current laws	Direct relationship btwn # of guns and high rates of murder
Guns necessary for self defense, reduce crime		Guns for self defense translate to personal injuries mostly
2nd Amendment guarantees gun rights		2nd Amend. applies to militia, not individuals
Laws don't stop criminals from purchasing guns	**Question:** Would a national gun control policy reduce violence in America?	National laws will keep people from buying guns
20,000 local and state gun control laws exist		State & local laws not strong enough—need consistent fed. policy
Polls favor right to own guns		Polls favor restriction to gun ownership
A national gun control policy would take guns from people, but not stop criminals. We need to enforce current laws.	**Conclusions**	A national gun control policy would restrict gun ownership and make it impossible for criminals to own guns.

Discussion: The Conversation of Learning 83

> **Reflection**
> How did this strategy help you to analyze both sides of an issue? How were you actively involved in the discussion? How did the Discussion Web help you organize your discussion?

Support and Extensions

- Provide student pairs with reading selections containing opposing viewpoints about a topic and a copy of the Discussion Web. Provide a question relating to the topic that will generate opposing points of view, for example, *Should the United States government support subsidies to farmers?* or *Should wolves be protected?* Remind students to put aside their own opinions to ensure fair representation of both points of view.

- After student pairs have completed their Discussion Webs, ask them to join with another student pair. In these groups of four, see if they can develop one conclusion. Then ask each group to present their conclusion to the whole class. They must explain the reasoning that led them to the conclusion.

- Have students write an analytic or persuasive essay using the notes created with their Discussion Web frame.

Sticky-Note Discussions

Sticky-Note Discussions provide an effective way to engage students with text as they read. They can be used with literature groups, while reading mathematics word problems, or when dealing with challenging science and social studies materials. Ask students to use sticky notes as they read or after they have read a selection to mark the places they want to discuss. These might be questions they have, sections they especially enjoy, humorous bits, or vivid descriptions. Students record key words on the sticky-note to help them remember why they marked the text. For electronic texts, ask students to insert notations for discussion.

Introduction, Modeling, and Reflection

1. Establish a purpose for reading and noting specific information. On the next page, we have provided prompts to guide your purpose setting for the reading.

2. Read aloud. When you come to a spot you want to mark, explain why, and record a few key words on the sticky note. As you model, make a list of the kinds of things you noted.

3. Once students have the idea, suggest they mark one or two places per section. Limiting the number of notes focuses students and ensures broader participation. Students with multitudes of items marked tend to dominate the discussion.

4. Begin Sticky-Note Discussions as a whole class. Start by sharing a place you have marked. Select one that will likely inspire a lot of discussion. Talk about why you marked it, and then ask students for any comments or reactions. This may launch a lively discussion, leading to conversation to other ideas in and out of the text. Once the discussion is over, or if no real discussion has transpired, share another one of your noted areas or have a student share.

Guidelines for younger students in preparation for literature study groups

- Questions I have
- Parts that are beautifully written
- Places that make me sad, angry, laugh
- Parts that make me want to keep reading
- Parts where I learn more about the characters
- Places where I learn about where the story takes place

Guidelines for older students in preparation for literature study groups (elements of fiction)

- Tension: excitement, suspense, nervousness; anticipation that keeps us turning pages
- Character: conversations, actions; descriptions that teach us about the characters
- Place and Time: descriptions that paint mind-pictures; sections creating time and place
- Mood: feelings of reader, characters; parts that arouse emotions
- Symbols: symbols contributing to mood, tension or resolution; what they represent
- Point of View: first or third person; how point of view influences thoughts and feelings about characters

Guidelines for Nonfiction

- Questions I have
- Information I don't understand
- Places where I need more examples
- Powerful images to help me remember
- My opinions, feelings, reactions
- Connections I make to ideas and content

Reflection

How did the Sticky-Note Discussion help you gain a deeper understanding of the story or content? How did listening to other students' comments help with your understanding?

Support and Extensions

- Divide students into small groups and select one student to facilitate. After students have read and marked the selection, have the facilitator lead the discussion by going through the assignment page by page. Each student talks about the parts he or she has marked.
- Have students use sticky notes to add to the author's text (e.g. add illustrations, diagrams, examples, etc.).
- Use two or more colors of sticky notes:

    Argument notes: pink for information that supports opinion; blue for information that defeats opinion.

    Vocabulary notes: pink for words they don't understand; blue for key math/science terms.

    Question notes: yellow for questions to ask the author; blue for concepts that would make good test questions.

- React to the Fact. As students read, they use sticky notes to identify at least three facts. On the notes, they "React to the Fact" with questions, opinions, feelings, and connections. Students then meet in small groups to share their facts and "React to the Fact" comments. Group members take notes and discuss each others' facts and reactions. Once everyone has shared, students use their notes and independently record in the four-column notes (below) what they consider to be the most interesting or controversial facts, reactions from the group, and some final observations and comments that expand on their understanding of the information.

Fact	Pg #	Group Reaction/Fact	Personal Reaction

Carousel Brainstorming

Carousel Brainstorming involves students brainstorming in small groups. It can be used to bring out background knowledge and for review.

Introduction, Modeling, and Reflection

1. Select about five related topics or key concepts to determine your students' background knowledge. Write each topic on one piece of chart paper (at the top). Number the topics (1 through 5) and post them in order around your room.

2. Assign each student a number from one to five, and then have all students move to the paper labeled with their assigned number. Give each group a different color marker to record their information.

3. Give the groups about one minute to write on the chart paper everything they know or have learned about the topic. If they are not sure about their information, they can write a "?" by it.

4. After one minute, signal for the groups move to the topic with the next higher number (group 1 goes to topic 2, etc., and group 5 goes to topic 1). At the next topic, they read what the other group has written, make corrections or additions, write a question mark after information they don't understand, and add any new information they know. As they move to each station, you might want to add a little more time for reading the preceding entries. All writing they do should be with their original color marker (e.g., all of the groups 1's entries on the five topics are in red).

5. Continue this process until each group is back to its original number. After students have read what the other groups added to that topic, they move back to their seats, reading what has been added after their entry to each of the other four topics.

6. One at a time, review the information for each topic (or have the original group read the information). If there are any question marks, give the group writing the unclear statement a chance to explain.

Reflection
How did this strategy help you see the connections among the topics? What else would you like to know? How did this strategy help you determine what you knew and didn't know about the topic?

Support and Extensions

- Rather than having students write freely about their understanding of a concept, ask them to write a One-Sentence Summary on what they think is the most important information about each topic. Follow the same carousel procedure until each group has added a summary sentence to all the charts.

- Ask students to plan their own Carousel Brainstorming review. They determine the key topics, write them on the chart paper, and organize the groups.

- Use for reviewing key vocabulary. Write one word per chart. Ask students to elaborate on the meaning with illustrations, student-friendly definitions, etc. (see Chapter 9).

- Use for analyzing characters in a novel. Write the name of a character on each chart. Students can note motives, goals, and relationship issues of the main characters. As students read the novel, they can add additional information to the charts. Use Carousel Brainstorming several times during the novel unit.

- In math classes, write a problem on each chart. As groups progress through the Carousel, they write one of the process steps required to solve each problem. The successive groups check the steps and then add the next, eventually solving the problem.

- For world language students, write a story or dialogue starter related to a topic for review on each chart. Each group adds the next line. Provide a bank of root words from which students can draw.

Seed Discussions

One way to help students lead their own discussions is through Seed Discussions (Villaume et al., 1994), where students write down one important thing (or seed) about what they are reading and then share it with their group. Effective "seeds" grow into discussions. Less effective seeds wither, resulting in little discussion. Seed Discussions are particularly effective with younger readers or with older students having difficulty comprehending and engaging in small group discussions.

Introduction, Modeling, and Reflection

1. Explain to students they will be leading their own Seed Discussions. Begin your introduction something like this: *While reading this book (assignment) you will be leading your own discussions. You aren't just going to answer my questions. Instead, you are to identify and develop topics important to your own thinking. As you read, think of one important thing to discuss. Write your discussion seed in your journal or on a card. We want strong 'seeds' which will grow into lively discussions about a topic. We'll do the first several seed assignments together.*

2. Together, make a list of possibilities for seeds. Post them on a large chart so students can refer to the suggestions:
   - Information or situations I don't understand
   - Comments about what I have learned
   - Things that seem interesting or surprising
   - Vocabulary I want to know about
   - Descriptive writing I particularly enjoyed
   - Things that remind me of other things that I know

3. Read aloud two or three pages and model your own discussion seeds. Model strong seeds and weak seeds. For example, seeds for the novel *Julie of the Wolves* might be:

   Strong seed:
   I am not sure what this quote means: "Patience with the ways of nature had been instilled in her by her father." Discussions could center on what is meant by "ways of nature." How would "patience" relate to the "ways of nature?"

   Weak seed:
   "Miyax is a pretty young girl." There is nothing to discuss here.

4. Begin the discussion by introducing one seed. Then have at least four students say something about the seed before the next one is introduced.

5. If little can be said about the seed, it means the seed is not strong enough. Continue to model some strong and weak seeds.

6. Also model discussion behavior so students can respond to one another's comments:

   I really like what you said about . . .
   Do you have any other ideas about . . .?
   I agree with you... but I also think . . .

Reflection

How might Seed Discussions help you become a better reader? How did you feel about being part of a Seed Discussion group? How does this strategy help you to become more actively engaged in your reading?

Support and Extensions

- After modeling with the whole class, divide students into groups of four. Begin by asking one group to come to the front of the room and do a demonstration for the whole class; assign each member of the group a role as shown in the following list. After they have modeled with one or two sections of text, have groups lead their own discussions.

ROLE	DESCRIPTION
Leader	Responsible for calling on each person to share his or her discussion seeds.
Manager	Makes sure that everyone has all necessary materials for the discussion (books, journals, cards, etc.).
Checker	Makes sure that everyone has a chance to talk about his or her seeds. Everyone in the group comments on the seed before the next person presents a seed for discussion.
Communicator	Summarizes the main points generated in the discussion for the group and for the class. Lets the teacher know when the discussion is complete. The communicator is the only person who may leave the group.

- Incorporate sticky notes along with the seeds. Students put sticky notes on places that would make good discussion seeds.

Roles Within Cooperative Teams

Another way to promote student-led discussions is to assign students specific roles. Students take on various tasks while reading and discussing (Daniels, 1994, Daniels & Steineke, 2004). Roles combine a variety of strategies within a discussion group. Each group member takes on a role (e.g. Discussion Director, Bridge Builder, Vocabulary Expert, etc.) before reading and then comes to the discussion group prepared to fulfill a specific task. While teachers have used discussion roles most frequently in middle grade and secondary literature classes, they have also modified them for content texts (Stein & Beed, 2004; Wilfong, 2009). Wilfong found that having students take on different roles while reading and discussing science text led to improved performance on chapter tests.

Keep in mind, Daniels and Steineke (2004) recommend using the formal roles for a brief time as a training tool. Using them rigidly over a longer period can stifle rather than energize discussion. The roles are designed to help students internalize different ways of thinking about text. Once they have it, the roles won't be needed; they should be considered one of many tools to turn discussion over to students.

Introduction, Modeling, and Reflection

1. With the whole class, teach and model each role you plan to have students use in their small group discussions. The following three roles, descriptions, and guide questions provide just a sample of options (for more roles, see Support and Extensions for this strategy and the online reproducibles for Chapter 4). Students need to feel comfortable with all the roles you plan to use before they try them on their own in their discussion groups.

ROLE	DESCRIPTION	GUIDE QUESTIONS
Discussion Director	Lead the group in discussion of questions assigned by the teacher and/or developed by you. Think about your purpose for reading, potential controversy in the text that can generate thoughtful discussion, and areas that may be challenging for readers to understand.	Do your questions relate to the purpose for the reading? Do they prompt for the big ideas rather than discrete facts? Have you generated some open-ended questions where more than one answer is acceptable? Have all group members responded? Are you keeping the discussion and comments focused on the question at hand? Did your group generate additional questions?
Bridge Builder	Help the group make connections between the reading, their own lives, what they have seen or experienced, and other texts.	What connections can you make between this reading and your own world? How does this remind you of other things you have read/watched? What bridges can you build? How is this text relevant? This reminds me of . . .
Summarizer	Prepare a brief, written summary of the assigned reading (at least one full paragraph). Present the summary to your group.	What is the major idea of this reading selection? What key details make the major idea understandable? What are the most important vocabulary words you need to understand this content?

2. Teach the role of Discussion Director first. Model how to develop questions from the reading. The Discussion Director develops four or five open-ended questions over the reading as a way to get the discussion going. Remind students about QARs and Authentic Questions (see Questioning Strategies in this chapter). In some cases, the Discussion Director might be responsible for engaging his or her group in a discussion of teacher-developed questions.

Discussion: The Conversation of Learning

3. Model how to use questions in small group discussion. Bring four students to the front of the class and have each in turn ask one question to the rest of the group. When the discussion has run its logical course, divide the remainder of the class into groups of four, and have them use their own questions to conduct discussions.

4. Follow a similar procedure for introducing each of the other roles you plan to use. Once students feel comfortable with roles you have selected, they are ready to apply them within their groups during or after reading assignments.

> **Reflection**
> How did your discussion group function? (Did everyone participate? Was everyone prepared? Were you willing to share tentative ideas? Did you ask questions of one another? Did you give reasons for your opinions?) Were you able to make connections with the world, with other texts, and/or with yourself?

Support and Extensions

- Adapt discussion roles by incorporating CRISS strategies. For example, the following charts show a series of discussion roles adapted from Daniels' work, with modification to incorporate CRISS strategies. These roles for fiction and nonfiction text were created by a team of high school teachers from McMinnville, Oregon. For a master copy which includes more role adaptations with guide questions for students (adaptable to a variety of content disciplines), see the online reproducibles for Chapter 4.

DISCUSSION ROLES FOR FICTION & NONFICTION TEXTS	
ROLE	**DESCRIPTION**
Discussion Director	Lead the group in discussion of questions assigned by the teacher or develop several of your own QARs or Authentic Questions.
Bridge Builder	Help the group make connections to their background knowledge—between the reading and their own lives, what they have seen or experienced, and other texts.
Illustrator	After reading, close your eyes and visualize what you read. Create Picture Notes, a Concept Map, or another illustration to tie key ideas in the text to your purpose for learning. Share your illustrations with the others in your group. After everyone has had a chance to talk, tell them what you think.
Summarizer	Use Read-Recall-Check-Organize-Summarize to prepare a brief, written summary of the assigned reading (at least one full paragraph). Present the summary to your group.
Vocabulary Expert	Find and share complicated, unusual, or important words. Include at least five words from the reading. Select two of the words and develop Student-Friendly Definitions and/or a Concept of Definition Map. Share the words and your definitions

- In addition to including CRISS strategies in the role descriptions, the high school teachers in McMinnville, Oregon created several new roles for nonfiction and fiction text (see the following two charts).

ADDITIONAL DISCUSSION ROLES FOR NONFICTION	
ROLE	**DESCRIPTION**
Graphic Engineer	Create a graph (bar, line, pie, etc.) that represents the information presented in the text. Include a written explanation.
Purpose & Bias Detector	Identify the author's purpose and any biased information. Write at least two paragraphs identifying his/her perspective. Then, create a symbol or slogan that represents the main ideas/viewpoints of the text.
Opinionator	Write at least three paragraphs to communicate your opinion about facts, bias, and related information provided in the selection. Share your ideas with your group.
Argument Anticipator	Anticipate opposing arguments to the views presented in the reading selection. Write at least two paragraphs describing opponents, their motivations, and the quality of their arguments. Share the opposing arguments and your evaluation of them with your group.
Information Locator	Refer to the information provided in the charts and tables in this selection. Write at least one paragraph interpreting the data. Generate at least three test questions that can be answered using the graphics. Make a record of the answers. Share your interpretation of the data with your group. See if they can answer your questions.

ADDITIONAL DISCUSSION ROLES FOR FICTION	
ROLE	**DESCRIPTION**
Literary Analyzer	Select a portion of the text that is particularly interesting, powerful, descriptive, important, etc. and write an analysis of the content and structure of the text (rising action, climax, falling action, etc.). Share your selection and analysis with the group.
Voice Analyzer	Select a portion of the text that demonstrates the author's unique voice. Give examples of the literary devices used (metaphor, imagery, foreshadowing, flashback, irony, etc.). Describe how you reacted as the reader to the author's mood and tone. Share your selection and your analysis with your group.
Purpose & Perspective Detector	Write a reflection on what you determine to be the author's purpose. Consider themes, messages, conflicts, and relationships. Share your thoughts with your group.
Predictor	Make a prediction about the consequences of a character's decisions/actions. Identify the specifics in the text that lead you to this prediction. Share your ideas with the group.
Mediator	Choose a character from the text and write an explanation/justification for why they made the decisions they did. Present your explanation to the group.
View Expander	Select a scene/event from the text and rewrite it from the perspective of a different character (use I, me, we). Share your version with the group.
Character Analyzer	Write a letter to the protagonist or antagonist. Tell him/her how you feel about key events and actions, as well as how you feel about other characters. Read your letter to the group.

DISCUSSION ROLES FOR MATHEMATICS	
ROLE	**DESCRIPTION**
Discussion Director	Lead the group in discussion of questions assigned by the teacher or provided by the author, or develop your own questions over confusing concepts and processes.
Bridge Builder	Help the group make connections to math concepts which have been learned earlier in this class or in previous classes. What bridges or applications can you make between this information and the "real" world?
Example Finder & Creator	Find good examples from the text or another resource that help clarify information in this section. Create your own examples for each concept and share them with your group.
Vocabulary Expert	Find and share at least five complicated or important terms and vocabulary concepts in the text. Write down what you think the word means from context, and then add additional examples and/or information about the word from the glossary, your background knowledge, and other resources. When it is your turn to lead the discussion, have everyone find the word in the reading and then talk about what the word might mean. After the discussion, share your explanation and examples.
Process Server	Identify processes and procedures in this section of the text. Identify the steps in each process. Be prepared to demonstrate the process with an example of your own. Check your work to make sure the steps make sense. Walk your group through your example.
Illustrator	Provide graphic or artistic representations of the key ideas and processes in the text. Show your illustrations to the others in your group. Ask them to interpret your diagrams and tell how they relate to the major concepts and processes in the text.

- The teachers in McMinnville also adapted the discussion roles to be used with poetry (see the chart on the following page). After reading and processing a poem using their role descriptions, group members worked together to complete the following Three-Column Notes.

What takes place in the poem?	Your Thoughts, Connections, Predictions, etc.	Class Thoughts, Connections, etc.
Meaningful quotes and examples from the poem.	Your impressions, reflections, visualizations, interpretations, analysis, etc.	Impressions, reflections, visualizations, interpretations, analysis, etc. gathered from class discussion.

\multicolumn{2}{c}{**DISCUSSION ROLES FOR POETRY**}
ROLE	**DESCRIPTION**
Discussion Director	Develop three questions prompted by the poem for your group. One question must be a "what" question (Right There). One question must be a "why" question (Think and Search). One question must be a "how did the author…" question (Author and Me). Write a one paragraph, personal response to each question. Have your group answer the questions.
Dictionator	Identify the type of language used in the poem. Find at least three key words in the poem. For each word, copy the sentence/phrase/stanza that contains the word and the context clues that help determine its meaning. Identify synonyms for each word and write your own definitions of the words based on those context clues. Discuss connotation and denotation as they pertain to these words. Tell why these specific choices of diction are essential to the meaning of the poem. Then write the actual dictionary definitions (top 3) for each word and a phrase or stanza of your own creation that uses each word correctly.
Illustrator	Draw a picture that represents an important image, symbol, or theme in the poem. Write at least one paragraph justifying your representation.
Bridge Builder	Make connections between the poem and your life (personal experience, family life, school life, etc.) or your general experience (the community, world events, films, etc). Write two paragraphs in which you make at least two connections.
Structure Scout	Analyze how the author uses shape, structure, syntax (sentence structure and length), and punctuation to add meaning to the poem. Write a two-paragraph analysis of the poem's structure.
Imagery Investigator	Identify images, figures of speech, or other poetic devices used to create images in the poem. Write at least two paragraphs explaining how they contribute to the overall meaning and effect of the poem.
Sound Sleuth	Read the verse aloud several times and identify what you hear when you read the poem aloud. Write two paragraphs that discuss the poet's use of literary devices (e.g. assonance, caesura, repetition, etc.), meter, rhythm and rhyme/rhyme scheme. Include your thoughts on how each sound contributes to the poem's meaning and effect.

- As students become comfortable with all roles, allow groups to pick the roles they want to use. Over time and over multiple pieces, students are expected to complete all or most of the roles.
- Have students develop their own roles and create their own role sheets. Encourage students to use CRISS strategies as roles: developing Conclusion-Support Notes, Problem-Solution Notes, or Content Frames. In other situations, students might be prepared with sticky notes, discussion seeds, visualizations, authentic questions, or summary statements. Practically all of the strategies described in this chapter would work well to define a role. The roles differ according to what students have experienced and the kind of assignment they are reading. Once students understand the different roles, each student in a group can take on a different role within the group. Ask students to give oral presentations using information from their discussions.

QUESTIONING STRATEGIES

As noted in the introduction to this chapter, the role of questions in teaching has a rich but checkered past. For years, researchers have documented how teachers have dominated classroom talk. Teacher questioning accounts for 80% of discussion with most teachers being unaware of just how much their own questioning dominates classroom interactions. For example, Nash and Shipman (1974), as reported in Marzano et al. (2001), found that elementary school teachers who thought they were asking 12 to 20 questions per hour were actually asking from 45 to 150 questions per hour. Years later, Marzano et al. (2001) and Nystrand (2006), documented the same result.

Another insight comes from studies on the types of questions teachers tend to ask (Almasi, 2008). Researchers conclude that higher-level thinking questions—those that require students to apply knowledge or restructure information—produce deeper learning than questions focusing on lower-level factual information. These results seem logical. Yet, most teachers ask lower-level questions leading to student disengagement by stymieing and diminishing student dialogue (Almasi, 2008). So, the research tells us that teachers flood their classrooms with endless low-level questions, which tend to create passive, insipid learning.

Further insight comes from studies on the relationship between questioning and wait-time, which is the amount of time teachers wait for students to respond after asking a question. Longer is better! Not only is this common sense, but brain researchers have documented that our brains need time to retrieve and organize information. How many times have we caught ourselves quickly answering our own questions without giving students time to think, the students' answers tend to respond? Yet, when teachers pause several seconds after asking a question, allowing students time to think, the students' answers tend to be far richer and much more extensive. Wait-time also increases student-to-student interaction and stimulates more discussion (Marzano et al., 2001). We have to keep reminding ourselves not to jump in so quickly; it is okay to wait, even if the quiet feels a little uncomfortable.

One final issue focuses on who is asking the question: Which questioning approach leads to better comprehension? Should teachers ask the questions or should students generate their own? The best answer is—it depends.

If your goal is for students to know specific information from their reading, ask them a question about it. Teacher questions do help readers focus on particular content and lead to improved comprehension and memory for specifics. However, if you seek more generalized improvement in comprehension—beyond the content of particular questions—and want students to become more independent, then invite them to ask their own questions (Trabasso & Bouchard, 2002). When students generate questions about what they are reading (particularly why and how questions), they actively process text information and monitor their understanding. Some evidence suggests that teaching students how to ask their own questions leads to improvement on standardized test performance (Trabasso & Bouchard, 2002). Two implications arise from this body of research. First, question generation during reading is an important strategy for improving comprehension; second, students need to learn about effective questioning strategies. This instruction should include teacher modeling and guided practice, as well as opportunities for readers to practice developing questions with teacher feedback. With this brief overview, let's turn to some practical ways to implement effective questioning practices in our classrooms.

Authentic Questions

Accomplished readers spontaneously ask questions before, during, and after reading. Self-questioning deepens one's engagement and understanding of text. Proficient readers speculate about meaning and the author's perspective or intent. They know many of their curiosities and questions will not be answered by the author, but will be left to their own interpretation. Being bombarded by your own questions is a good thing. Having questions is not a sign of comprehension failure–it signifies a successful reader, who monitors his or her own comprehension. Our task is to inspire students to unleash their own ideas and questions. As Doug Buehl (2009) says, we want students to "wonder" through texts, to embrace the authentic questions that come to mind. Our task is to guide them in the process of composing their own questions during reading and viewing.

Introduction, Modeling, and Reflection

1. Provide students with an engaging piece of text. Ask them to walk through the text noticing whatever grabs their attention–the title, photographs, captions, and other visuals. Tell students to be aware of their thoughts and questions.

2. Ask them to write down two or three ideas or questions on sticky notes or on a chart similar to the following in the "Before Reading" column:

What Questions Do You Have?	What Have You Learned? (Answer Questions Here)	Additional Thoughts and Questions
Before Reading		
During Reading		
After Reading		

3. Have them share with a partner and then with the whole class.

4. Next, have students record in the middle row additional questions that occur as they read. If they find answers to their "Before Reading" questions, have them record the information in the "What have you learned?" column. Talk about why "wondering as you read" deepens comprehension and makes learning more enjoyable.

5. After reading, have students note additional new things they have learned and record any dangling thoughts and questions that capture unresolved curiosities. Throughout this entire process, encourage students to talk with their partners and share ideas with the whole class.

Reflection

How did creating Authentic Questions help you become more engaged in reading? Why is self-questioning critical for all learning? How does self-questioning help you become more metacognitive?

Support and Extensions

- Ask students to keep a list of questions as they read a novel. Read aloud the first chapter and model a variety of possibilities. These might involve Authentic Questions about (1) vocabulary, (2) predictions, (3) who did what and why, and (4) how a situation evolved.

    In the following example, Rose Peck's high school language arts students were reading the novel, *Factory Girls*. The teacher's goal for the day was to have student-led discussions over the first half of the book. She projected question starters (see the chart on page 100) and gave students time to develop questions individually. Next, she had them decide on categories based on their questions (e.g., character, author, culture/Chinese life, literary, and personal connections). One person in each group was designated as the discussion leader, who selected the questions to ask and called on group members to respond. The student-led discussions moved from one category to another with the time spent on each topic determined by the teacher. Sample questions (categories in parentheses):

    Why do you think the author wrote this book about migrant workers? (Author)

    What is the relationship between the people who spoke Cantonese and those who spoke Mandarin? (Culture)

    What motivated the girls to be content with working in a factory all of their lives? (Character)

    Do you agree with the actions of Min when she left the factory? Why or why not? (Personal)

    Would Factory Workers have been as effective if the author had been more positive? Why or why not? (Literary)

- Demonstrate the importance of student-generated questions by using them for discussions or essay questions. Once students realize their questions are taken seriously and that it's safe to ask questions, Authentic Questions will become a bigger part of their response to reading. As a result, discussions will become richer and more student-centered.

- Use Authentic Questions with various media (e.g. video, diagrams, demonstrations, etc.).

Question-Answer Relationships

Taffy Raphael and her colleagues (Raphael, 1986; Raphael & McKinney, 1983; Raphael & Au, 2005, 2010; Raphael & Wonnocott, 1985) developed an important technique to help students identify sources of information for writing and answering questions that is applicable across grade levels and subject areas. They considered this question: If students know how questions are written, in other words, if they understand the "craft of question-writing," will they become more proficient at answering and asking questions? To test this, she ingeniously simplified the world of questioning into two broad categories: **In the Book** (text-explicit questions) and **In My Head** (text-implicit questions). She then distinguished between *Right There* and *Think and Search* text-explicit questions. Similarly, she classified text-implicit questions as either *Author and Me* or *On My Own*. See online reproducibles for Chapter 4 for the following chart.

Question-Answer Relationships - 4 Types of Questions

In the Book QARs	In My Head QARs
Right There The answer is in the text, usually easy to find. The words used to make up the question and words used to answer the question are in the same sentence.  Sample *Right There* Questions 1. In what year was the Declaration of Independence signed? 2. In *The Wizard of Oz*, what is the name of Dorothy's dog?	**Author and Me** The answer is <u>not</u> in the story. You need to think about what the author tells you in the text (author), what you already know (me), and then put the two together. Sample *Author and Me* Questions 1. Which right in the Bill of Rights is most important to you and why? 2. Why do you think _____ (character in story) behaved the way she did?
Think and Search *(Putting It Together)* The answer is in the selection, but you need to put together different pieces of information to find it. Words for the question and words for the answer are not found in the same sentence. They come from different places in the selection.  Sample *Think and Search* Questions 1. Give several reasons why people should exercise. 2. Explain two ways to find a percentage of a number.	**On My Own** The answer is not in the selection. You can even answer the question without reading the selection. You need to use your own experience and prior knowledge.  Sample *On My Own* Questions 1. What do you know about good nutrition? 2. Name a person you admire and explain why.

Raphael taught this system, which she termed **Question-Answer Relationships (QARs)**, to her students. Once students became proficient in using QARs for writing and analyzing questions, they answered questions significantly better than students who lacked this understanding. Raphael's four question types guide students in developing their own questions. Several national reports and articles on research-based practices (Roe, Smith, & Burns, 2005; The National Reading Panel Report, 2000; Rand Reading Study Group, 2002; Vacca et al., 2010) recommend QARs as an effective process for improving comprehension, for assisting student with metacognitive processing, and for improving the teaching of metacognition as part of content learning (Wilson, Grisham, & Smetana, 2009).

Sample Text with QAR Examples

Popcorn

Have you ever wondered why popcorn pops? Popping corn has more moisture inside each kernel than regular corn. As the kernel is heated, the water inside turns into steam. Pressure begins to build inside until the hard coat on the outside of the kernel explodes, turning inside-out.

If you are careful about how you prepare it, popcorn turns out to be a very healthy snack—higher in protein than ice cream or potato chips, without the fat and sugar. Air-popping is the best way to prepare popcorn because it doesn't require oil; this keeps the popcorn low in calories. To add a little zest to your snack, forget the butter or caramel flavors. Instead, try melting a few tablespoons of peanut butter and stirring that into your popped corn. Or add sunflower, pumpkin, or sesame seeds.

Right There: What is the best way to prepare popcorn? (Air popping.)
Think and Search: What are some ways that you can make plain popcorn taste better?
(Add sunflower, pumpkin, or sesame seeds or peanut butter.)
Author and Me: Why do you think the author wrote this article about popcorn?
(To teach the reader how to prepare healthy popcorn, to convince us to eat healthy snacks, to sell us on the idea of popcorn as a snack.)
On My Own: What is your favorite snack?

Introduction, Modeling, and Reflection

1. Introduce QARs with a reading selection. Use the "popcorn" example or a selection of your choice. Explain to students that you are going to teach them about questions: *There are four general types of questions. If you know these four general types, you will not only be able to ask better questions, but you will also be able to answer questions more easily.*

2. Demonstrate how to develop questions based on the QAR framework. Project a copy of the framework or provide them with their own copy (see online reproducibles for Chapter 4).

3. Go over the framework. Your explanation might sound something like this: *You can divide questions into two types—***In the Book** *and* **In My Head**. *The answers to* **In the Book** *questions are found in the book.*

Continue modeling:

Notice that there are two kinds of **In the Book** *questions— Right There and Think and Search. The answers to Right There questions are found in one sentence in the selection. Right There questions are easy and require very little thought. You just have to find the relevant sentence in the book. For example: How is popping corn different from regular corn?*

Another type of **In the Book** *question is Think and Search. This is a little bit harder because to find the total answer you have to incorporate information from more than one place in the selection. You won't find it all in the same sentence. Find all of the information relevant to the question and then pull it together. For example: How can popcorn be a healthy snack? Or, why does popcorn pop?*

In My Head *questions force you to work harder than* **In the Book** *questions. There are two types of* **In My Head** *questions, Author and Me and On My Own. To answer Author and Me questions, you have to take what you know from the text and think about it. You can't find the answer in the book, but you have to read the selection in order to answer the question. For example: Why do you think popcorn has become such a popular snack in our country? Has the author convinced you to eat popcorn as a snack? Why?*

The answers to On My Own questions come directly from your own head. It helps to read the text because it helps you think about what you already know, but you don't have to read it to answer this sort of question. For example: Why is it important to eat healthy snacks? Explain that On My Own questions are useful for bringing out background knowledge before reading.

4. After modeling several questions of each type, explain that you are not going to lead the discussion over the selection. They are. It is better for them to ask their own questions than to answer your questions. They will understand more and become better readers by developing their own questions. Ask them to take turns leading the discussions over the selection.

5. Select a few pages of content text. Divide students into cooperative teams. Have each team produce examples of the four types of questions. Then have each team present their questions to the class. Use the following steps:

    a. Have one team read the question without telling what type it is.

    b. Don't ask for the answer; ask the class to tell you the type of question it is.

    c. Make sure students tell you why it is a certain type of question. Ask them to justify their answer by explaining why the question fits into one of the four categories.

    Justifying the answer always produces lively debate, particularly if the question happens to be a Think and Search or Author and Me type. Often students have valid arguments supporting a question as both types. In the end, it does not really matter if a particular question fits within a specific category. It is the thinking that occurs in justifying answers that is important. The process is far more important than the end result. If students are upset with the ambiguity, have them rewrite the question so it can be interpreted only one way.

    d. Finally, have students answer the question.

    A discussion of the type of question is more important than the answer, so make sure that students explain why a question fits a certain category before they answer it. Remember—the type of question determines the type of answer.

Reflection

How have QARs helped you become more proficient at analyzing and asking questions? How do QARs relate to the Framework for Learning? How might an awareness about question design help you respond to questions on state assessments and college entrance exams?

Support and Extensions

- The following chart provides a way for students to see how the amount of information from the text and/or from their heads varies when they answer each type of QAR question.

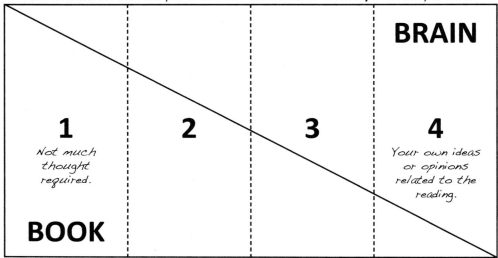

- After students understand how to develop questions and have practice holding discussions as a whole class, small groups are ready to begin leading their own discussions.

- For younger children and struggling readers, Raphael and Au (2005) recommend teaching In the Book QARs and its subcategories first. Once students feel confident with these questions, introduce In My Head QARs. Introducing all at once can be overwhelming.

- Have students prepare questions individually as they read. They should bring their questions to group discussions.

- If students are writing questions in their journals as they read, they can go back and classify the questions they have written. The QARs provide students with a system for evaluating their own questions. If students find most of their questions are *Right There* and *Think and Search*, challenge them to come up with other higher-level questions as they read. Most students will realize that Authentic Questions are usually *Author and Me*.

- <u>Question Starters</u>. To help students develop their own questions, provide them with Question Starters. Make sure students realize that categorizing question starters by type does not limit them to one type of question. Some, particularly those in the *Think and Search* and *Author and Me* categories, can overlap.

Right There	When is . . . Who is . . . What is . . . Define . . . Name . . . Identify . . . Who did . . . What happened . . .
Think and Search	List the . . . What are the parts of . . . Compare . . . What is the problem . . . What is the effect of . . . What are the solutions for . . . Summarize . . . Compare . . .
Author and Me	Predict . . . Anticipate . . . Explain . . . Summarize . . . What if . . . Form a hypothesis about . . .
On My Own	Judge . . . Solve . . . Defend . . . Develop . . . Apply . . .

- QARs work well for content materials. In the following example, students formulated QARs based on a graph from *Global Warming : A Personal Guide to Causes and Solutions* by Sneed Collard (the nonfiction companion book for *CRISS for Sutdents II: Learning To Succeed*).

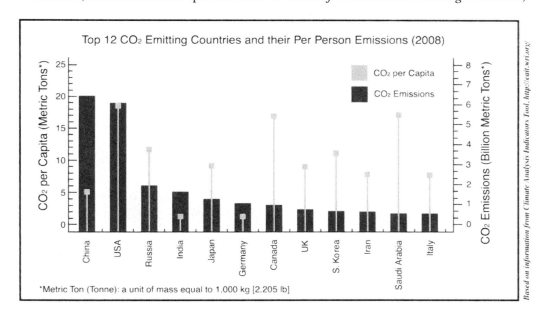

Right There: In 2008, how many metric tons of CO_2 did each person in the United States produce per capita? (The answer is found in one place on the graph. You just have to read it.)

Think and Search: Which two countries emitted the most CO_2 and which two countries emitted the least? (The answer is directly in the graph, but from different locations on the graph.)

Author and Me: On average, how many more pounds of CO_2 per capita did individuals in the U.S. create than individuals in China? (The author doesn't give you this answer. You have to use the data provided by the author plus your own personal knowledge and skills of subtraction and unit conversion.)

On My Own: In ten years, what country do you think will emit the most CO_2 into the atmosphere and why? (The answer is not on the graph. You have to use your own background knowledge to answer this question. Answers will vary.)

QARs also work for the humanities as shown in the following examples in art and music:

	ART	MUSIC
Right There	What is the subject of the painting?	What kind of music is this—band, orchestra, piano?
Think and Search	What colors did the artist use?	What instruments do you hear throughout this piece?
Author and Me	How did the painter show perspective in this piece? What feelings do you think the artist was trying to convey?	What feelings do you think the composer was trying to convey? How did the composer create feeling?
On My Own	How do artists express feelings in their work?	How do specific instruments in music create certain moods and feelings?

Discussion: The Conversation of Learning

- The definitions of QARs can be altered for specific needs. For example, McIntosh and Draper (1995) modified the four types of questions to make them more applicable for mathematics students.

    Right There: The answer is right there in the text in the same sentence. *Example:* State the slide model for addition. Answer: The slide model for addition is . . . (right from the text).

    Think and Search: The question is just like an example in the text, only the numbers are different. *Example:* The text shows an example of how to simplify $-3 + -x + 7$. The Think and Search QAR would be, simplify $-2 + y + -9$.

    Author and Me: The author has given you information in the text that you have to put together with what you already know (perhaps from previous sections or chapters) to get an answer. *Example:* After learning how to simplify (as in *Think and Search* example above), the author shows you how to solve simple equations such as $x + 6 = 10$ and $17 - y = 12$. An *Author and Me* question might be, solve $-3 + t - 4 = 0$.

    On My Own: The answers to these questions are not in the book at all. These questions ask you to think about and use your own experience. *Example:* Negative numbers appear on television in many situations. What real situation might each negative number represent? (a) -1.32 in stock market averages, (b) -9 in rocket launches, (c) -3 in golf.

- QARs can help students prepare for standardized tests (Raphael & Au, 2005, 2010). Rather than typical test preparation practice, spend time teaching students QARs and how to unpack questions. Have students practice categorizing questions on sample tests. Knowing the type of questions used on standardized tests helps students perform better and reduces test-taking anxiety.

Higher Level Thinking Questions

Consider using the revised version of Bloom's taxonomy (Anderson & Krathwohl, 2001; Bloom et al., 1956) as a system for teaching students different levels of questions. Students can also use the taxonomy for analyzing end-of-chapter tests and sample questions on standardized tests. As presented in the table on the next page, the revision contains active verbs delineating cognitive processes rather than nouns. The revision also repositions the top two categories. In the revised version Creating defines the highest level of thinking compared with Bloom's original version which placed Evaluation on top as the most challenging mental function. Anderson and Krathwohl defend this change by explaining that Creating involves evaluating and evolving a new way to conceive an idea or a product. Creating requires one to use all of the other thinking processes in the taxonomy. The revised model seems easier to use than the original. Specifying thinking as verbs and placing Creating at the top makes this revised version more useful for planning instruction and for guiding students to develop their own questions.

Bloom's Taxonomy 1956	Anderson & Krathwohl's Taxonomy 2001	
Evaluation	**Creating**	Reorganizing elements to form a coherent whole—restructuring, putting parts together in a new way, synthesizing, deriving, recombining, assembling.
Synthesis	**Evaluating**	Making judgments—judging, deducing, criticizing, measuring, rating, appraising, estimating.
Analysis	**Analyzing**	Breaking material or concepts into parts—determining interrelationships, dissecting, discriminating, investigating, categorizing, deducing.
Application	**Applying**	Carrying out or using a procedure—operating, simulating, interpreting calculating, translating, illustrating, dramatizing demonstrating, implementing.
Comprehension	**Understanding**	Constructing meaning—interpreting, classifying, summarizing, inferring, comparing, explaining, concluding.
Knowledge	**Knowing**	Remembering, retrieving, recalling, or recognizing facts, repeating, rules, lists. Knowing requires one to retell or repeat information.

Introduction, Modeling, and Reflection

1. Introduce students to the taxonomy. Give students the descriptions of the levels of thinking or post an abbreviated version of the definitions on a chart.

2. Explain that you are introducing a system for asking questions that taps into higher levels of thinking. With a content reading selection, model several questions representing each level.

Reflection

How do the higher-level questions help you to focus on the essential understanding rather than superficial information?

Support and Extensions

- Share a copy of the table (below) with students.

QUESTION STARTERS & FRAMES FOR HIGHER-LEVEL QUESTIONS

Bloom's Taxonomy	Key Words	Question Starters
Creating	Reorganizing, producing, adapting	How can you adapt this information to _____? How can you apply _____ to your own life? Reinterpret _____ to fit with a different point of view. The author has changed my understanding of _____ by _____.
Evaluating	Judging, defending, proving, assessing, criticizing	What is your opinion of _____? What is the best solution to the problem of _____? Defend your opinion about _____. Evaluate the writing of _____?
Analyzing	Examining, categorizing, classifying, comparing, separating, connecting	Compare __X__ to __Y__. In what ways are they the same? How are they different? Categorize the important ideas in _____? What connections can you make to _____?
Applying	Illustrating, interpreting, calculating, applying, relating	What is one way to illustrate _____? How can you apply _____ to _____? How can you relate _____ to _____?
Understanding	Explaining, summarizing, inferring, anticipating, comparing	What will happen next in _____? What is the main idea about _____? Predict what _____? How is this similar to or different from _____? Explain what is meant by _____?
Knowing	Who, what, list, retell, identify, name, when, define	What is _____? Define _____. Identify the _____. Retell _____. Who did _____?

- Invite students to develop questions for reviewing a unit of study—one question for each level of thinking—and present to the class for discussion.

- Guide students to use the frames for developing and analyzing questions specific to different content areas. Provide them with examples like those provided in the table that follows (authors, 2012; Buehl, 2008, 2009).

CONTENT DOMAIN QUESTIONS FOR BLOOM'S TAXONOMY			
Level of Bloom's	Biology	History	English
Creating	Plan an experiment to determine whether the rate of transpiration is affected by the wind. Propose a hypothesis to explain why sap rises in the spring rather than in the autumn.	How has the author changed what I understand about the colonization and development of Africa?	In what ways will this novel change the way I feel about people with disabilities?
Evaluating	Evaluate whether or not it is possible to solve the problem of world hunger by increasing agricultural production?	Who is the author and how has author perspective influenced the telling of this history?	How does this journalist indicate an attitude or bias about the political parties?
Analyzing	Compare annuals, biennials, and perennials. What are the relative advantages of tap roots and fibrous roots?	What were the causes of the American Civil War?	What literary devices does Tim O'Brien use to communicate his feelings? Why does he use these devices?
Applying	How can I apply what I have learned about respiration to aquatic animals?	How can I connect my experience/knowledge to what this author is telling me about Vietnam?	How can I connect this story to my life experiences?
Understanding	What am I supposed to understand about angiosperms and gymnosperms? Where do new cells and tissues develop in plants? Describe the structure and function of fruit.	What does this author want me to understand about the fall of the Roman Empire? How did people in this time period view their lives and world?	How do the characters in *The Cherry Orchard* feel about each other?
Knowledge	Describe two patterns of plant growth.	What do I need to remember to make sense of the past?	What are the major events in Hemmingway's life?

Questioning the Author (QtA)

What can we do to challenge students to build understanding of text ideas and not shut down when confronted by challenging, inconsiderate text? Questioning the Author (Beck, McKeown, & Kucan, 2002; Beck, McKeown, Hamilton, & Kucan, 1997) takes into account that authors are people like us; they might not always be adept at communicating clearly. It places the onus on the author, not the student. Sometimes problems with comprehension may not be the reader's fault, but the author's inability to explain his or her ideas well. Questioning the Author (QtA) assists readers in taking an active, constructivist approach to comprehension.

Queries are the key ingredient of Questioning the Author (QtA). Queries differ from typical questions in that they occur during rather than after reading, and they are designed to assist students in constructing meaning. Queries change the role of the teacher from an interrogator to a facilitator of discussion. Student-to-student interactions increase as learners grapple with an author's text, as they work together during reading to make sense of it. Queries always deal with what the author says or means.

Isabelle Beck (Beck et al., 1997) loosely divides queries into three types: Initiating Queries, Follow-up Queries, and Narrative Queries. The following queries are also available in the online reproducibles for Chapter 4.

SAMPLE QUERIES

Initiating Queries

What is the author trying to say here?
What is making the author's message difficult to understand?
How is the author presenting various types of information?
What does the author expect us to know?

Follow-up Queries

What does the author mean here?
Did the author explain this clearly?
Does this make sense with what the author told us before?
Does the author tell us why?
Why do you think the author tells us this now?

Narrative Queries

How do things look for the character now?
How has the author let us know that something has changed?
How has the author settled this for us?
Given what the author has already told us about this character, what is the character up to now?

In the example below students worked in pairs to question the author of the Preamble to the U.S. Constitution:

> *We the People of the United States, in Order to form a more perfect Union, establish Justice, insure Domestic Tranquility, provide for the common defence, promote the general Welfare, and secure the Blessings of Liberty to ourselves and our Posterity, do ordain and establish this Constitution for the United States of America.*

What does the author expect me to know about a more perfect Union?

What is the author trying to say about We the People? Does the author mean everybody or just white males? How do women and slaves fit in?

Why does the author capitalize the word Order and not the word "defence"? What message is the author trying to convey by capitalizing only certain words?

What does the author mean when he says "insure Domestic Tranquility"? What does the author expect me to know about Domestic Tranquility? How could the author have said this more clearly?

Why does the author choose the word Posterity?

What does the author mean by Blessings of Liberty?

Introduction, Modeling, and Reflection

1. Before introducing students to QtA, take a segment of text and determine the major understandings that students are to construct and then identify the stumbling blocks students might encounter, such as lack of elaboration or density of information that can impede comprehension. Identify places to stop and initiate discussion through QtA to clarify ideas.

2. As you begin modeling, talk about authorship. Identify names and read any biographical information available in the text. *Who are these authors? Are they university professors? Do you*

think they are familiar with what students your age might know about this topic?

3. Start reading and then stop at the first place you think might cause students problems. Ask questions similar to these: *Has the author presented his or her ideas clearly? Where in the text is the author having difficulty communicating? What has the author done to help us understand his or her message?*

4. Continue through the text. Pause. *What is the author trying to say? What does the author expect you to know already? Why do you think the author tells us this now? What additional information could the author have given to help you understand this? How does this relate to what the author has already explained?*

5. Throughout, talk about how QtA helps one really get inside the author's head to figure out the information the writer wants us to take away from the assignment. Discuss how good readers internalize these self-questioning procedures as a way to monitor their own comprehension. Include in your conversations encouraging remarks about not being helpless or frustrated when reading. Explain that in most situations it is not our fault when we have difficulty understanding. Authors often have trouble communicating their message. *Don't feel defeated by an author. Instead figure out what the author is trying to do. He or she may not be very good at getting information across, but don't give up. Rise up to the challenge. It can be very satisfying to tackle difficult text, to grapple with meaning. This struggle defines what good readers do.*

Reflection

How did the QtA help you understand the selections? What kinds of new queries did you create to help you understand the text?

Support and Extensions

- Post a chart of queries in the classroom and/or give students copies. Ask students to take sections of text and put asterisks by difficult and confusing content. Decide on queries that work for each section and use them to facilitate a class discussion.

- Pair students, and ask them to pose queries to one another.

- QtAs are readily adaptable to different content domains. For example some QtAs for mathematics texts might be:

    What does the author do to introduce new math terms?

    What does the author assume I already know in order to understand this concept or process?

    What does the author expect me to know about the steps in solving this problem?

    Is the author explaining this concept clearly?

    What could the author have done to clarify these sample problems?

▲ ▲ ▲

Summary

Dialogic discussion enriches comprehension and creates a classroom atmosphere that honors student voices. Classrooms become safe houses where students feel accepted and respected not only for their ideas but for whom they are as people. Students learn to hear and respect one another when classrooms focus on participatory rather than teacher-centered models. When readers have an opportunity to discuss their interpretations, meaning is made for all. True discussion is an open exchange of ideas and questions with no easy answers. Everyone is involved; everyone is engaged. Dialogic conversations contrast sharply with teacher-directed recitation wherein instructors ask the questions, do most of the talking, and limit student-to-student conversation. What's worse–it's boring!

The strategies described in this chapter not only assist students in leading their own discussions but are instrumental in creating positive classroom cultures. In classrooms embracing dialogic conversations, students have more opportunities to feel connected with their peers and to build genuine relationships with their teachers.

Think-Pair-Share, Sticky-Note Discussions, Read-and-Say-Something, Seed Discussions, and the Discussion Web inspire students to take the lead in instructional conversations. Other strategies focus more directly on helping students develop their own questions for discussion. With Authentic Questions students go beyond what they presently understand. QARs, Higher Level Thinking Questions, and Questioning the Author assist students with their own critical inquiries. Students have opportunities to untangle meaning from text and to talk about their insights and questions. All of the strategies in this chapter embrace student-centered conversations. We talk to learn!

CHAPTER 4 RESEARCH BASE

Research Conclusion	Reference
Little student-to-student discussion occurs in classrooms. Open-ended, higher-level discussions averaged about 15 seconds a day.	Nystrand, 2006
In more effective schools, discussion was far more prevalent than recitation. In effective schools students asked more questions and took far more responsibility for leading their own discussions.	Langer, 2009
Fourth and fifth grade children of varying levels of English proficiency, who engaged in small group discussions to construct their own meaning did better on measures of factual and interpretative comprehension than did children assigned to read and study the selection. Similar results occur with high school students.	Saunders & Goldberg, 1999 Sweigart, 1991
Discussion promotes deeper understanding of text, leads to higher-level thinking and problem-solving, and improves communication skills. Student-led discussions foster greater student participation than those led by teachers, and they improve communication skills—including the ability to take on different points of view. Such discussions also increase student sensitivity, encouraging recognition and acknowledgment of others in the group.	Morrow & Gambrell, 2000 Almasi, 2008
Effective discussions are more likely to occur in situations where students have guidance in how to lead their own discussions.	Adler, Rougle, & Caughlan, 2004
Students tend to feel more comfortable leading their own discussion in small groups and within social contexts where they feel safe to express their own points of view.	Connolly & Smith, 2002
Teacher questioning accounts for 80% of discussion.	Marzano, Pickering, & Pollock, 2001
Higher level thinking questions produce deeper learning than questions focusing on lower-level factual information. Yet, most teachers ask lower level questions diminishing student dialogue.	Almasi, 2008
When teachers pause several seconds after asking a question, allowing students to think, their answers tend to be far richer and more extensive. Wait-time also increases student-to-student interaction and stimulates more discussion.	Marzano, Pickering, & Pollock, 2001
When students generate questions about what they are reading, they more actively process text information and monitor their understanding. Question generation during reading is an important strategy for improving comprehension but students need to learn about effective questioning strategies. This instruction should include teacher modeling and guided practice, as well as opportunities for readers to practice developing questions with teacher feedback.	Trabasso & Bouchard, 2002
Question-Answer Relationships is an effective process for improving comprehension, for assisting students with metacognitive processing and for improving the teaching of metacognition as part of content learning.	Raphael & Au, 2005 Wilson, Grisham, & Smetana, 2009

Active Strategies for Learning

5

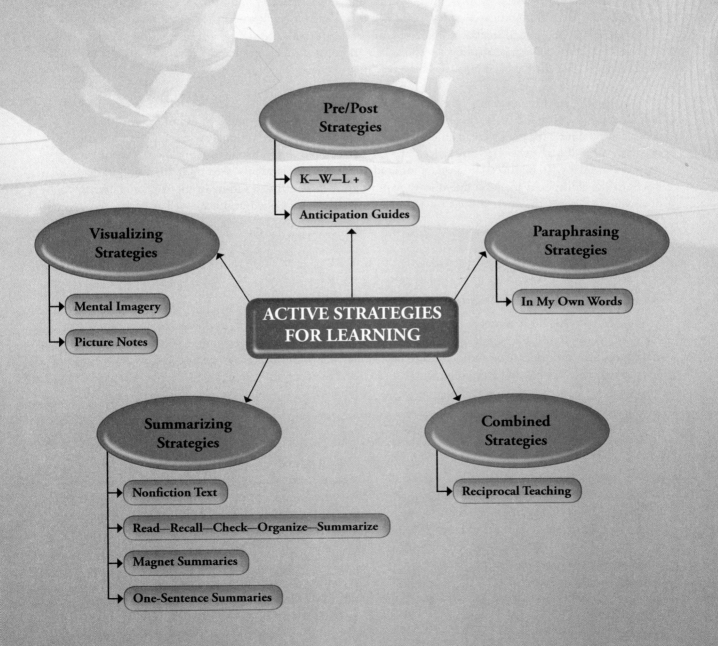

Before continuing our discussion of comprehension and learning strategies, let's step back to Dolores Durkin's classic article on reading comprehension published in the *Reading Research Quarterly* in the late 1970s. Her research uncovered how little comprehension instruction actually occurred in classrooms. Teachers assigned, questioned, and lectured students about the content, but did little to show them how to understand and learn new information. They assessed but did not teach comprehension. Durkin's study helped initiate a revolution in research and instructional efforts that continued through the 1980s and early 1990s–a revolution which focused on instructional strategies for helping students comprehend and retain information from their reading. The effects were particularly striking with poor readers. When students had opportunities to learn how to comprehend and learn, they did far better on all kinds of reading and learning tasks.

Two decades of research provide overwhelming evidence that students can be taught how to use comprehension strategies (Conley, 2008). The case is clear–teaching elementary, middle, and high school students to use a repertoire of comprehension strategies increases comprehension of text (Wilkinson & Son, 2011). Has this research led to changes in classroom instruction? One would assume so, given this convincing evidence and the current pressure of high-stakes assessments which focus primarily on reading comprehension. Yet, the data tell us otherwise. Almost thirty years later, Michael Pressley and his colleagues noted few changes since the time of Durkin's study (Pressley, 2002). In extending Durkin's work, they noted many effective literacy practices being used in classrooms, but witnessed little real comprehension instruction. Instead they observed teachers posing post-reading questions and asking students to read and answer the chapter questions. Even teachers identified as exemplary did little teaching of comprehension.

This lack of teaching may in part explain why so many middle and high school students are in need of literacy support. As noted by Brozo (2010), the statistics remain troublesome. For example, two-thirds of American 8th and 12th graders read at less than proficient level on the National Assessment of Educational Progress, 40% of high school graduates lack literacy skills employers seek, and about 1.2 million students drop-out annually. To be successful readers for academic purposes, students need more than skill in reading words or the ability to read aloud fluently. They must know how to use a variety of sophisticated literacy practices. This is exactly where Project CRISS and the practices described in this, as well as in the next several chapters, come into play.

PRE/POST STRATEGIES

While many of the approaches presented in this manual work well as pre and post strategies, K-W-L + and Anticipation Guides are designed explicitly for preparing students for learning experiences and for helping them recognize and process new understandings. Both of these approaches can be integrated readily into the Framework for Teaching and combined with other CRISS learning strategies.

Know—Want to Learn—Learned Plus: K-W-L +

Donna Ogle's K-W-L + is a classic strategy (Ogle, 1986; Ogle & Blachowicz, 2002; Carr & Ogle, 1987). Teachers from all content areas successfully incorporate and modify K-W-L + in their elementary and secondary school classrooms. This lesson sequence embeds every aspect of the CRISS Framework for Learning as part of three reading phases: Students (1) brainstorm what they **know** (K) about the topic, (2) generate questions about what they **want** to know (W), and then (3) record what they **learned** (L). Students then do the plus (+) part of the sequence by transforming the learned information into a new organizer such as a Concept Map and writing a summary.

After completing all of the K-W-L + steps, the teacher leads students in a process conference, helping them to analyze the strategy's effectiveness. Students can readily see that the strategy exemplifies the major tenets of the CRISS Framework for Learning: The **K** and **W** processes are part of our PREPARE step. Listing learned information (**L**), organizing it, and writing about it (**+**) fall into our ENGAGE step. Process conferences, where students examine why and how the strategy worked (or didn't), make up the REFLECT step of the Framework for Learning and are a key element in transferring ownership from the teacher to the student. This time for reflection is essential!

Introduction, Modeling, and Reflection

1. Choose a reading selection from your class materials.
2. List or project the topic (Power 1) and/or key vocabulary on a K-W-L chart (see online reproducibles for Chapter 5).

What I **K**now	What I **W**ant to Know	What I **L**earned

Categories of Information:

3. Have students brainstorm what they know (or think they know) about the topic and/or key vocabulary before reading, listening, or viewing and place the information in the **K** column. These items represent Power 3s for your Power 1 topic.
4. Have students determine categories for their background knowledge and list them at the bottom of the K-W-L chart. The categories represent Power 2s for the topic.
5. Ask the class to try to record more **K** information for each category, if possible.
6. As a class, have students generate questions they would like to answer or have them *predict* what they think they will learn about each subtopic or category and place in the **W** column. The example on the following page is from a 9th grade health class covering stress.

What I Know	What I Want to Know	What I Learned
• Stress can cause health problems. Kids and adults can have it. Caffeine might increase it. Too much homework can cause stress. • Meditation or yoga might help. • Prozac helps lessen stress. • It makes you jumpy and nervous. • Stress isn't good. • It can give you a headache.	**Definition:** What exactly is stress? Is all stress bad? **Causes:** Can stress be caused by things we eat or drink? Is stress genetic? **Symptoms or Effects** Are there different effects for different levels of stress? Can stress kill you? Are there good effects of stress? **Coping or Cures:** Can medications eliminate or lesson stress? If so, what medications are most successful? How can I get over test anxiety?	

Categories of Information:
  Definition of stress
  Causes of stress
  Symptoms/effects of stress
  Coping with stress or cures

 Have students read or listen to the selection. Afterwards, have them record in the third column what they have learned. Encourage them to develop new categories of information if needed.

What I Learned

Definition:
  Physical or mental tension caused by one's reaction to a situation.
  May be good (able to react quickly) or bad (cause health problems)
  "stressors" = things that cause stress
Causes:
  Physical danger, emotional events, timelines, deadlines, difficult tasks, people
  Caffeine and other stimulants
Symptoms or Effects
  Nervous system activated & specific hormones (adrenaline & cortisol) released
  Hormones increase heart rate, breathing rate, blood pressure, and metabolism
  Blood vessels open—more blood to muscles
  Liver releases stored glucose—increases the body's energy
  Sweat produced—cools body
  Stress response (SR) improves body's functioning, may cause problems when long term, e.g., fatigue, panic attacks, irritability, stomach problems, headaches, skin reactions, sleeping problems, depression and loss of appetite, and weaken the immune system
Coping or Cures
  Good nutrition, avoid caffeinated beverages
  Talk about problems with friends
  Keep physically fit—exercise works off tension
  Get a good night's sleep
  Use breathing exercises, build downtime into schedule, read, spend time with pet, take a bath
  Develop a positive attitude

• 114 Chapter 5

8. Discuss as a whole class what the students learned and recorded in the third column. Ask them to revise their charts by making notations to their pre-reading record. Often students will have misconceptions about a topic. Ask, *Do we need to change any information from our K list?* Together mark (✓) information verified in the selection. Use minus signs (-) to indicate incorrect information or cross it out. In the preceding example, students changed the **K** entry "Stress isn't good" to "Stress can have both positive and negative effects on people."

9. After completing the chart, extend the learning process by adding the "Plus." Ask students to transform the information on the K-W-L chart by developing a Concept Map or other organizer. Talk about how transformation helps them generate additional information and discover new interrelationships.

10. Finally, have students use their Concept Map to orally summarize the information or to write a summary (the final step in **+**).

Reflection

How did this strategy help you understand and remember information from the reading assignment? How well did K-W-L + fit within what we know about how we learn? What CRISS Framework for Learning principles does it incorporate?

Support and Extensions

- After completing their **K** entries, have students preview their assignment and make an outline of topic headings. From these headings have them develop two or three questions they think will be answered in the selection and place them in the **W** column.

- Before students read a selection, have them read the introduction, bold-print headings, and summary and then list key concepts. Have students brainstorm what they already know and what they expect to find out from reading the selection. In the following example, high school reading resource teachers Shirley Jensen and Kathy Theis changed the K-W-L to K-E-L (What we **K**now, What we **E**xpect to find out, What we **L**earned). They found that this subtle change helped students focus more on the major topics presented in their Western Civilization text.

Category	What We KNOW	What We EXPECT To Find Out	What We LEARNED
Religion			
Politics/Government			
Geography			
Social Issues			
Economy			
Culture			
Technology			

- When multiple resources are used, add a fourth column which lists the references from which the information in the **L** column was obtained.

Active Strategies for Learning

- Convert the chart into a Scientific Inquiry Grid by including a fourth section for more questions (Schmidt, Gillen, Zolo, & Stone, 2002).

What I know	What I Want to Know
What I Learned	More Questions
Resources:	

- Laverick (2002) used elements similar to K-W-L in a modified version for high school students which she called B-D-A (Before, During, and After steps). Students begin by brainstorming and recording what they know about the topic before reading. During reading, they write brief notes on new information, and then after reading they write a summary and three questions. They conclude by writing a One-Sentence Summary statement. In the following example, students in Rick Stern's high school social studies class used the B-D-A format as a tool for organizing information from a current events article.

Before	During	After
List everything you know about this topic before reading.	Briefly note new information you find during reading.	Write a summary and three questions.
One-sentence main idea statement:		

- Jenny Stone, a high school art teacher, used a simplified version of a K-W-L to prepare her students for a video about Leonardo da Vinci. Before viewing, they brainstormed what they thought they knew about Leonardo da Vinci. Afterwards they added new information they learned from the video and checked their pre-viewing knowledge for misconceptions.

LEONARDO DA VINCI (1452-1519)
66 yrs old

WHAT DO I KNOW ABOUT LEO?	WHAT I KNOW NOW
1. PAINTED MONA LISA	1. Took pleasure drawing gross + ugly people
2. PAINTED LAST SUPPER	2. Obsessive interest in End of the World + Destruction
3. INVENTOR (WACKY!)	3. Considered "GREATEST" Italian Draftsman
4. ARCHITECT	4. Interested in Anatomy of bones + muscle structure
5. FROM SPAIN	5. Did not complete much of his work
6. LEFT HANDED	6. Wrote a lot, never organized his writings
7. COULD DRAW A PERFECT CIRCLE FREE HANDED	7. engineering or hydraulic project either failed or not started

Anticipation Guides

Anticipation Guides (Herber, 1978; Buehl, 2009) provide an effective way to activate background knowledge before reading a selection. Based on their personal thoughts and experiences, students respond to several statements relating to the content. They agree or disagree with each statement and then explain or defend their positions to a partner or the whole class. This strategy provokes students' curiosity to find out if they are right or wrong and to investigate the topic further. Anticipation Guides are not designed to teach content but to "hook" students into wanting to read and learn more and to discover their own misconceptions. These guides can be used in all content areas and with a variety of learning materials, including videos.

This procedure creates interest, guides students in setting purposes, and inspires learners to higher levels of thinking. After reading or listening, they return to the statements to decide whether or not they still agree with their original choices. Did they have any misconceptions about the content? Do they still agree or disagree with each of the statements or do they need to change their opinion? Why or why not? Having students pull specific quotes from the text (video, etc.) to support their stance further develops their rhetorical skills.

Introduction, Modeling, and Reflection

1. Identify five or six major concepts to be learned in the material (film, lecture, text, science experiment, etc.). Keep the following guidelines in mind when writing the Anticipation Guide statements:
   - Think about what students might already know about the concepts, paying particular attention to common misconceptions.
   - Write statements which reflect large segments of texts rather than specific details. That will force students to read and synthesize the information rather than simply skim to find the answers.
   - Make sure you create both true and false statements.
   - Word statements to provoke critical thinking.

2. Display or hand out the Anticipation Guide and have students complete it prior to reading (viewing, listening).

3. Have students read the selection and then revisit the Anticipation Guide to see if they have changed their minds.

4. Ask students to return to their small groups and develop a consensus about the answers. Remind them to provide evidence to convince others.

5. Discuss the reading as a whole class using the Anticipation Guide, and then have students write in their journals about how their beliefs have changed.

Sample Anticipation Guide for The Restless Decade

Before reading the article, *The Restless Decade*, write Agree or Disagree in the "Before" column to indicate your reaction to the statements. Then, talk to your partner about your choices. After completing the reading, reread the statements and record whether you agree or disagree. Compare these answers with your pre-reading choices. Did anything change? Be prepared to defend your ideas as part of a whole class discussion with evidence from the text.

Before		After
	1. The 1920s was a period of rapid economic growth in all areas of the U.S. economy.	
	2. The people of the 1920s reflected a general breakdown in moral standards.	
	3. During the 1920s the stock market climbed to higher and higher levels.	
	4. The 1920s was similar to every other decade in American history.	
	5. Most people detested prohibition, danced the Charleston, and did well economically.	

Reflection

What did the Anticipation Guide do for you as a learner? How did it focus your reading? How did it help you realize what you knew and didn't know about the topic before you read? How did you deal with misconceptions identified by the Anticipation Guide?

Support and Extensions

- Assign groups to prepare their own Anticipation Guides. Then, ask them to trade with another group and complete their partner group's guide. The very act of developing a guide motivates students to process and to define the essential ideas in a selection.
- Ask students to underline or place sticky notes by evidence in the selection that supports or refutes a statement.
- Develop Anticipation Guides to be completed from different perspectives. For example, give students a role such as an environmentalist or a logger. How would they respond to the following Anticipation Guide before reading an article on clear cutting? How would they defend their point of view?

Environmentalist	Logger	
		Clear cutting is the most economical way to log.
		It is essential that logging companies have unlimited access to our national forests.
		It costs our government more to build roads into roadless areas than the companies take out in profits.
		Logging is essential for preventing forest fires.
		Logging has devastated America's forests.

- Guy Todnem, CRISS National Trainer, adapted the Anticipation Guide for mathematics. Before reading, students read each statement and noted whether or not they agreed with it. After reading, they marked the statements again according to whether or not the text supported or refuted the statement. Students then noted disagreements and had to find evidence from the text which showed that their preliminary thinking about the statement was incorrect. This adaptation provided students with a clear way to examine their own misconceptions and also helped them read the text more critically.

Anticipation Guide for Slope

Directions: In the column labeled "Me," place an "A" next to any statement with which you agree or a "D" next to statements with which you disagree. After reading the text, place an "A" or a "D" in the "Text" column to reflect the information you read. Compare your responses to those of the text. In the last column, for all those statements where you and the text differed, write the words or phrases from the text that support the correct response.

Me	Text	Statement	Text Evidence
		1. Slope refers to the steepness of the line.	
		2. A straight line has several different slopes.	
		3. A slope can be written as a ratio.	
		4. A vertical line has a slope of 0.	
		5. Slope is the ratio of the change in the Y values over the change in X values.	
		6. This line ⟷ has a positive slope.	

VISUALIZING STRATEGIES

"A picture is worth a thousand words"—so goes the old saying which may explain why students' comprehension is enhanced by mental imagery and by depicting thoughts in sketches, symbols, or diagrams. Although little research has been done on transformation through actual drawing, there is a great deal of experimental support for mental imagery (i.e., the reader making mental pictures while reading and listening). When students are given instructions to read text and form vivid images, they can answer more questions about the text and recall more information than students instructed only to read carefully. Asking students to create pictures in their heads while reading also led to higher inferential thinking and recall than students in the control groups.

Indeed, researchers provide ample evidence that creating mental images while reading or listening enhances comprehension and retention for both children and adults (Gambrell & Koskinen, 2002). Imagery seems to help students integrate information across text and encourages more active engagement while assisting readers in monitoring their own understanding.

Imagery turns out to be particularly effective with less proficient readers. Many reluctant and low-ability readers are unable to describe images and pictures as they read. While many students automatically convert printed text into mind movies, struggling readers need explicit instruction (Seglem & Witte, 2009). Through emphasizing and modeling visualization with students, teachers can help students improve comprehension by transforming print into mental images.

Much less data exist on the relationship between comprehension and student-generated pictures. However, while developing Project CRISS, we conducted action research in classrooms which showed a consistent and positive relationship between image production and comprehension. Students who read a selection and then worked in small groups to transform the information into pictures learned the information better than students who just read and discussed it. The effects on long-term retention were most impressive. After a week's delay, students who explained key concepts in physics by drawing pictures remembered them significantly better than students who did not transform the information through art. Therefore, when we want students to process and learn difficult information, Picture Notes becomes our strategy of choice. Keeping in mind this brief overview of research, let's examine how to work with mental imagery and Picture Notes in the classroom.

Mental Imagery

Mental Imagery, visualizing information as one reads or listens, can be a powerful comprehension strategy, but it's not necessarily easy for all students to master. To help students trigger visualizations, Doug Buehl (2009) suggests using "guided imagery" as a first step. In this process, teachers share the images that come into their minds when they think or read about a topic. For example, when eighth grade health students were ready to study the human heart, their teacher shared his Mental Imagery of the heart and its function in the following way.

> *Close your eyes, relax, use your imagination. Imagine that you are an arthroscopic scope—a medical instrument for seeing beneath the skin. You are peering inside your chest, reaching in just to the left and underneath your sternum. You see your heart, a pulsing, writhing mass of muscle. Its color is shades of red, its size—about the size of your fist. Once every second, watch the wall of your heart contract. Move inside one of its four chambers or rooms. The chamber opens; blood rushes in. Now it closes and squeezes the blood out. Watch it open, fill, close, and empty. Open, fill, close, and empty. Feel its rhythm. With each pump, blood spurts from the heart into a tube-like vessel . . .*

Introduction, Modeling, and Reflection

1. Pick a topic or concept from your content that elicits images, and then talk through the images that come into your mind. Your Mental Imagery modeling can happen before reading, similar to the preceding example; during reading, where your modeling would include reading a section of text and then stopping periodically to share images that come to mind; or after reading, where you combine text ideas into one or two images to encompass the key ideas from the entire selection. If appropriate, your "visualizing" may also include sounds, smells, tastes, and textures.

2. After modeling your images, pick another topic (or read an additional section of text) and ask students to talk about their Mental Imagery. What questions come to mind? What else do they want to know?

3. Once students feel comfortable creating and talking about their images, have them read and create Mental Images in pairs or small groups. The process can be similar to Read-and-Say-Something (see page 81), only in this case it would be Read-and-Visualize-Something.

4. Creating and sharing mental images during and after reading is an effective way for students to be metacognitive. They can follow-up their discussions by creating Picture Notes (see page 121).

> **Reflection**
> How does making pictures in your mind help you understand and remember? How does imagery help to clarify meaning and monitor comprehension? How does imagery help you become more engaged with the material?

Support and Extensions

- Have students develop their own guided imagery scripts and lessons in groups of three or four. Have one person in the group read the selection while the others listen and visualize what the passage describes. Groups then discuss their images. As a class, talk about why mental images differ among readers and what aspects of the writer's message lead to vivid mental pictures.

- To improve descriptive writing, have students write, share with peers, and have peers discuss images (or lack thereof) that came to mind as they listened.

▶ Picture Notes

Creating an image can be a visual summarization and/or a depiction of complex information. This transformation of challenging information into visual representations involves deep processing of content and will help students uncover meaning as well as retain information.

Picture Notes, which involve students reading, talking, and then drawing their own representations of content, work well as a small-group activity. In the following example, small groups worked together to explain key concepts in a biology unit (photosynthesis). After developing their representations, they gave oral presentations of their drawings to the class, and then they wrote explanations. Reading, talking, drawing, presenting, and then writing helped these students do multiple transformations to reinforce their understanding.

Active Strategies for Learning   121 •

Introduction, Modeling, and Reflection

1. After students have read an assignment, organize them into small groups. Give each group a large sheet of paper and a set of colored markers. Tell them to determine the important ideas relating to the purpose for reading and to come up with a way of representing their ideas on paper through pictures, diagrams, and words.

2. It's rarely necessary to do any modeling, but if needed, model with previously learned information, not the current topic, and use symbols, icons, and simplistic illustrations. The reason for this is that once students see your representations, it is difficult for them to create something different and, if they see quality artwork from you, they may get discouraged and give up.

3. Explain that the quality of the artwork is secondary to the thinking processes involved in discussing content and deciding how to organize it. The only criterion is to represent central ideas and their interrelationships. Encourage students to use line drawings, symbols, pictures, circles, squiggles, or whatever creative endeavor they feel best portrays their analysis. Changing words into pictures encourages active synthesis of ideas. No two productions will be the same. Several student examples are usually sufficient to launch the rest into creating their own unique representations.

4. Have the teams share their productions with the class. Emphasize that their presentations need to pull together the discrete images into a clear and complete explanation.

Reflection

How did your Picture Notes help you understand and remember the material? What did you have to do to transform what you were learning into pictures? How might you use this strategy on your own?

Support and Extensions

- Decorate your classroom, attaching team projects to walls and bulletin boards. After several days, ask students to recall the content of their Picture Notes or give a more formal test over the information—leaving the posters visible

- Use Picture Notes to review content for tests. Assign different topics to groups who then become responsible for presenting and explaining their topic illustrations to the whole class.

- Ask students to transform written notes into images. Use software and/or clip art for students who are uncomfortable drawing their own images.

- Use Picture Notes as a pre-reading activity to bring out prior knowledge.

- Have students create images to help them remember key vocabulary terms or concepts. See the example below.

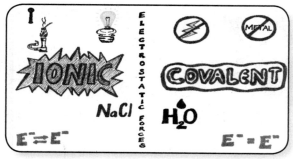

- Review a Book in an Hour. Place students in groups. Each group creates a pictorial representation of one chapter. Images are shared in sequence so that each group can relate their segment to previous chapters.
- Provide examples of political cartoons. Talk about how cartoonists portray emotions in ways printed news stories cannot. Invite students to create political cartoons about controversial issues. In the following example, students captured the essence of the 2000 presidential election between George Bush and Al Gore.

PARAPHRASING STRATEGIES

Paraphrasing, or putting the content into your own words, is a process students can use to monitor and improve their comprehension. Paraphrasing is different from summarizing where one needs to reduce the length of the passage, create a topic sentence, and delete unimportant information. To paraphrase, one doesn't have to focus on reducing text to its bare essentials by ferreting out the important ideas from the less important details. Instead, paraphrasing is less formal and may even be considered a pre-cursor to summarizing. With paraphrasing, students read or listen to information and are encouraged to translate the material into their own words. They are discouraged from simply retelling the message using the language of the author or speaker. When students retell the author's message, they don't have to process it as deeply as they do when converting content into their own words. Teaching students how to paraphrase has been shown to be particularly effective with struggling readers (Kletzien, 2009). Paraphrasing helps learners know whether or not they understand, by tapping into their metacognitive processing. It also inspires students to connect with prior knowledge as they construct their own meaning.

In My Own Words

In My Own Words helps students paraphrase an author's ideas into their own words.

Introduction, Modeling, and Reflection

1. Begin by explaining that paraphrasing is a superb way to check one's understanding. If you can convert a written or oral message into your own words, you know you understand it. Explain that effective learners stop when they are reading, look away from the text and, in their own words, describe what they have just read.

Active Strategies for Learning   123

2. To model for students, read a paragraph or section of text and think aloud as you paraphrase the ideas. Use your own words rather than the author's. As suggested by Kletzien (2009), when modeling, don't remember all of the information. Ask students to participate by paraphrasing the information you missed. Demonstrate how you need to return to the text, check for understanding, and then in your own words, talk about what you read. Incorporate how you make connections with your prior knowledge.

3. After modeling three or four paragraphs or a section of text, invite students to paraphrase the next several paragraphs. Continue modeling as needed until students are able to paraphrase on their own.

> ### Reflection
> How does paraphrasing help you understand text? In what ways does paraphrasing help you be metacognitive?

Support and Extensions

- Divide a reading assignment into segments. Have students work in groups of three or four. One student reads the first segment, stops, and uses his or her own words to talk about the content. Then the reader asks the other group members to paraphrase any additional information from the segment. When students feel they have adequately paraphrased this first section of text, another student takes a turn to read and paraphrase the next piece of the assignment. The process continues until all segments of the assignment are read and paraphrased.

- Use with videos. Have students watch a short segment of video, stop after one or two ideas have been completely developed, and allow time for students to paraphrase the information either as part of a discussion or in writing.

- After students have paraphrased a chunk of written text, a segment of video, or part of a lecture, ask them to convert their paraphrased ideas into a succinct written summary.

- Paraphrasing is a great process to move students from mindless copying and can be used as an element of note taking.

SUMMARIZING STRATEGIES

Reducing information to essential ideas is critical to comprehension. Masses of information bombard us every day. In order to remember and understand this volume of information, we have to filter through the details and arrive at essential meanings. Teaching students this skill is a challenging task, but research confirms its importance to student learning.

A review of research indicates that when students learn how to summarize and can use the strategy effectively, a positive effect occurs on comprehension and recall of textual information (Marzano, 2010; Trabasso & Bouchard, 2002). This positive effect holds only if students have explicit instruction about how to summarize. Just *telling* students to do so is not enough. When students learned how to write brief summaries or annotations in the margins of their texts, their comprehension and retention improved (Simpson & Nist, 2002).

Familiarizing students with varying text structures and teaching students how to organize information based on varying structures is an important part of effective summarizing (Marzano, 2010). For example, understanding the elements of a story (setting, characters, problem, resolution, rising and falling action, theme) is a precursor to summarizing narratives. When students first analyze narratives according to story elements, they do a better job of summarizing than if they go directly from the narrative text to writing a summary. The intermediate step of transforming the information is a critical step in the process. For more information on approaches to summarizing narrative text, see the section on Story Plans in Chapter 6.

Text structure and transforming strategies also play a similar role in summarizing expository text (Marzano, 2010). For example, the processes used to summarize argumentative, explanatory, cause-effect, or comparison text will vary. The organizing strategies described in Chapter 3 (Concept Maps and Comparison Organizers) and in Chapter 6 (Main Idea—Detail Notes, Conclusion-Support Notes, and Problem-Solution Notes) help students extract essential ideas from varying text structures and provide the scaffolding necessary for developing summaries. As noted in our descriptions of these various organizing strategies, developing written or oral summaries is usually the final step in the process.

Before describing strategies for teaching summarization, let's go back to an early study conducted by Taylor (1982), who observed differences between those who can and cannot summarize. Taylor found that those who wrote poor summaries spent little time rereading and taking notes about the selection before they wrote. They did nothing observable in the way of note taking or underlining to organize their thoughts. They went straight from the text to writing their summaries without any intermediary processing. In contrast, the expert summarizers took notes and organized the information, continually monitored their writing progress, and checked back to the original selection to ensure that their efforts preserved its gist. This behavior differed markedly from that of the poor summarizers, who rarely referred to the original.

Share this information about successful and unsuccessful summarizers with your students. Then model the steps for developing summaries

Summarizing Nonfiction Text

Summarizing is a successful learning process because it is difficult and requires students to think, evaluate, and purposefully transform information by recording the most important ideas in a meaningful way. Many students, even at the high school level, arrive at our classrooms having very little experience summarizing text, especially nonfiction. From the research summary in the preceding section, we know summarization is an important comprehension strategy, but only when students receive explicit instruction in the process of summarizing. The following process provides a guide to students for how to summarize the information in their content materials. It's critical that you model multiple times and with different types of text—textbook selections, newspaper or magazine articles, reference books, online resources, etc.

Introduction, Modeling, and Reflection

1. Pick several selections from the same content materials with which to do your modeling and student guidance. Model with the first selection, then gradually have students do more of the work, until they can summarize independently. Both you and the students should follow the next seven steps (numbers 2-8).

2. Review structural aids found in the first selection, such as titles, bold-faced headings, highlighted vocabulary, discusssion questions, and illustrations. Remind students to notice transition words (e.g., first, second) that indicate main points. Note the presence of key vocabulary, repeated ideas, and clue phrases (e.g., the main point is. . . , the most important idea is. . .).

3. Make predictions about what topics or ideas you think will be in the selection.

4. Determine the text structure(s) used by the author. Discuss with students the organizing formats you think might work with this selection. Your final determination will happen as you carefully read and reread the selection.

5. Read for important ideas and describe your thinking processes (teacher "think-alouds") for sorting through main ideas and details. Reread the selection as needed and record key information on the board. Include key words from topic sentences that express the main points of each paragraph. In addtion, model how to annotate the text with brief margin notes as you read.

6. Organize the ideas from your notes into an appropriate structure. You might cluster ideas into a Concept Map, record key ideas in Problem—Solution Notes, or match key ideas and brief details in Main Idea—Detail Notes. Reread if necessary to verify you have the correct relationships between ideas.

7. Write your summary using the information in your organized notes. As you write, cross out any information that does not seem important. Verbalize your thoughts; choices about what to exclude are as important as decisions about what to retain.

8. Reread and edit your summary. Make sure ideas flow together smoothly and that it represents the most important ideas of the selection. Edit if necessary.

9. Next, using the other selections, work with the whole class to create a summary or two. When you feel students understand the process, have them work in small groups to create summaries using the preceding seven steps. As students get more comfortable with the process, let them create their summaries independently. The ease of summarizing depends on the material to be summarized. If it contains unfamiliar content or is poorly written, students will need more support. With well-written and familiar text, students may reach independence fairly quickly.

Reflection

What are the processes involved in effective summarizing? How does the type of text influence how you summarize? How do your background knowledge and the difficulty of the text influence your approach to summarizing?

Support and Extensions

- As students read and reread the selection, have them make Powers Notes (see page 50) in the margins reflecting the main ideas and details. Then, as they write, students should incorporate the Powers into their summaries. To check, students can swap summaries with a partner and try to identify the Powers in each other's writing.

- Once students have written summaries within small groups or independently, have them meet in groups to present their summaries and support their choices for inclusion in a debate format.

- Provide students with Pattern Puzzles (see page 66) of the key information from the text. Have them read the selection and organize the Pattern Puzzle pieces into an order that accurately summarizes the selection.

- Provide students with the key vocabulary terms you expect to see in an effective summary of the selection.

- Provide students with several summaries of the same selection, each of varying quality and completion. Have students evaluate the effectiveness of each and write the missing elements to complete the ineffective summaries.

Read-Recall-Check-Organize-Summarize

With this strategy students read the selection and then recall important information. Their recall becomes the basis of their summaries.

Introduction, Modeling, and Reflection

1. *Read* a selection together. As a whole class, *recall* the information you've read. List the information students brainstorm.
2. Reread the piece to *check* for accuracy of recalled information—add and delete information at this stage.
3. *Organize* the recalled material into a logical format using Powers, a Concept Map, or another organizing strategy.
4. *Summarize* the information together using the organized notes.

Reflection

How does this approach to summarizing influence your understanding and retention of the material?

Support and Extensions

- Pair students and have them read and recall the information, check for accuracy, and organize their final list of ideas. Each pair writes a summary. Students present their summaries to the whole class.

Magnet Summaries

Doug Buehl's (2009) Magnet Summaries help students "rise above the details to construct meaningful summaries in their own words." Students identify magnet words (the key concepts and terms from their reading), select key supporting details, and then combine the magnets and related information into a written summary.

Introduction, Modeling, and Reflection

1. Buehl suggests introducing the idea of *magnet* words with an analogy: "Just as magnets attract iron, magnet words attract information." Read a short, familiar passage to your students and pick out one or two magnet words.
2. Next, write or project the magnet words so students can see your modeling. For example, in Donna Duval's U.S. History class, students read a selection on Progressivism. One of the magnet words was *Muckrakers*.

3. Ask students to recall details from the selection to expand the concept. As you record information around your "magnet" have students write the magnet word and details on an index card (or in their notes). For the magnet word, *Muckrakers*, responses were *writers, exposed horrible working conditions, argued for reform,* and *The Jungle*.

```
  journalists                                    horrible
                                                 working conditions
                       Muckrakers

  argued for reform                              The Jungle
```

4. Model how to combine these words into a summary sentence, e.g., *Trying to improve working conditions in the United States, Muckrakers wrote pieces such as* The Jungle *to expose horrible conditions and argue for reform.*

5. Continue by distributing three or four cards to each student. Read, stop, and talk about possible magnet words and details. Help the students create a One-Sentence Summary (see below) for each card.

```
  working class                                  Debs & DeLeon
                       Wobblies
  union members                                  until WWI
```

One-Sentence Summary: *Debs and DeLeon led the Wobblies, a group of working class union members, until WWI.*

```
  religious organizations                        Salvation Army
                       Social Gospel
  whole person                                   classes, counseling, and
                                                 recreation
```

One-Sentence Summary: *The Social Gospel of the Progressive Era stated that religious groups like the Salvation Army should treat the whole person—providing classes, counseling, and recreational opportunities.*

6. Arrange the sentences into a logical order to create an initial draft of the summary.

7. Model for students how to edit the draft into a finished summary.

Progressivism in the United States grew out of the work of journalists, called Muckrakers, who argued for reform of the horrible working conditions in pieces like The Jungle. *Union members, in groups such as the Wobblies—led by DeLeon and Debs—also fought to improve lives of workers. The rise of the Social Gospel, which stated that religious groups, such as the Salvation Army, should treat the whole person with classes, counseling, and recreational opportunities, also changed people's attitudes in the U.S.*

Reflection

How does this strategy exemplify the CRISS Framework for Learning? How do Magnet Summaries help you transform and own the key information?

Support and Extensions

- Have students use Magnet Summaries to transform and review unit notes.
- Divide students into groups. Have each group take a section of a chapter and develop a Magnet Summary to teach their text section to the class.

One-Sentence Summaries

One-Sentence Summaries guarantee active student participation and provide excellent feedback for the teacher. These brief writings clearly indicate the level of understanding of concepts. They work best after students have had some experience with summarizing and Magnet Summaries. One-Sentence Summaries are typically used to encapsulate essential ideas or the big understandings from a reading selection, lecture, or video. To encourage brevity, ask students to write their summaries on 3" x 5" cards. Four procedures for writing One-Sentence Summaries are covered below; select the procedure that best matches the purpose of the information presented.

Introduction, Modeling, and Reflection

Procedure A: Read, Set Aside, and List

1. *Read* a section of text aloud.
2. *Set aside* the selection and *list* four or five key ideas or words from it.
3. Model how to combine these ideas/words into a One-Sentence Summary.
4. Delete any extraneous words from the summary.

Procedure B: Selective Underlining and Main Idea—Detail Notes

1. After modeling Selective Underlining (Chapter 3), go through the selection and circle key ideas (Power 1 ideas).
2. Show students how to combine these ideas into a One-Sentence Summary.
3. Alternatively, after developing Main Idea—Detail Notes (Chapter 6), have students take the ideas on the left and use them to write a summary sentence.
4. Delete any extraneous words.

Procedure C: Content Frame Summary Chart for Sequencing

1. Present students with the following content frame (Chapter 6) to organize information for a One-Sentence Summary. The example below is from a class studying MacBeth, but the content frame may also be used for a summary with more than one sentence:

Identify the topic being summarized	Tell what it begins with.	Tell what's in the middle. Use words such as: covers, discusses, presents, continues with	Tell what it ends with.
The Shakespearean play MacBeth	witches setting an ominous tone	MacBeth's character begins to change due to his ambition	MacBeth's downfall
The Shakespearean play MacBeth begins with witches setting an ominous tone, continues with MacBeth's character changing due to his ambition, and ends with MacBeth's downfall.			

Identify the topic being summarized	Tell what it begins with.	Tell what's in the middle. Use words such as covers, discusses, presents, continues with	Tell what it ends with.
Multiply two fractions	Changing mixed numbers to improper fractions	Multiplying the two numerators to get the numerator of the answer and multiplying the two denominators to get the denominator of the answer	Simplifying the answer, first by reducing it to lowest terms and then by changing it to a mixed number if it is an improper fraction

To multiply two fractions, you first change any mixed numbers to improper fractions, then continue by multiplying the two numerators to get the numerator of the answer and multiplying the two denominators to get the denominator of the answer, and finally you simplify the answer, first by reducing it to lowest terms and then by changing it to a mixed number if it is an improper fraction.

2. Model with familiar content that is appropriate for this sequence frame. Begin by writing the topic in the first column.

3. Ask students to complete the "begins with" and "ends with" columns first; students often find those columns easier because less information is required.

4. To help students keep the middle concise, ask them to provide just the information that is critical to get from the beginning events to the final events. Record this information in the third column.

5. Write a One-Sentence Summary together based on information from the chart. Delete extraneous words and information.

Procedure D: One-Sentence Summary Frames.

1. Display a copy of the following One-Sentence Summary Frames (Cope, 1991).

One-Sentence Summary Frames for Common Text Structures	
Description	1. A _____ is a kind of ___ that. . .
Compare/Contrast	2. __X__ and __Y__ are similar in that they are both. . . , but __X__ . . . while __Y__ . . .
Sequence	3. _____ begins with. . . , continues with. . . , and ends with. . .
Conclusion/Support	4. _____ is _____ because. . . .
Problem/Solution	5. _____ wanted. . . , but. . . , so. . . . _____ because. . . , but. . . , so. . . .
Cause/Effect	6. _____ causes. . . . _____ is a result of . . .

2. Model how to develop a summary sentence using several of these frames.

> **Reflection**
> How did putting the material aside and writing down key words help you transform the information? How do combining Selective Highlighting and Main Idea-Detail Notes work for you? Why was summarizing easier once you had underlined or taken notes on the material? Under what circumstances might you use the chart to help you summarize information? How were the frames helpful? Which of the One-Sentence Summary procedures works the best for you? Why?

Support and Extensions

- Sometimes students struggle to incorporate all of the content information into a single sentence. As a means of differentiating, it's acceptable for students to expand the summary into a paragraph. For example, this Problem-Solution summary came from Kathleen Hocker, a CRISS Trainer. In response to *An Inconvenient Truth*, a student wrote:

    <u>The climate crisis</u> that Mr. Gore talked about included global warming and how it's affecting our earth. <u>Because</u> of the climate crisis, animals are dying and becoming endangered. The ice caps are melting faster, creating the possibility of low-lying cities and towns flooding. <u>However</u>, there are ways to prevent this in the long run: drive less, recycle more, and plant trees. This won't show immediate effects on the planet, <u>but</u> in the long run, it will help. <u>So</u> just do it!

- Ask students to reduce paragraph summaries to a One-Sentence Summary by deleting less important information and by combining similar ideas.

- After listening to a lecture or watching a video, have students combine key ideas from their notes into a One-Sentence Summary.

- Include summaries in examinations. List three or four key concepts which students combine into a paragraph or a One-Sentence Summary.

- At the end of a class period, ask students to write a One-Sentence Summary explaining what they learned during the period.

COMBINED STRATEGIES

Rarely do teachers design a complete lesson using a single strategy. In most cases, they include a variety of strategies to lead students to deep understandings of content. In other words, teachers bundle strategies to meet the needs of students. One approach, Reciprocal Teaching, stands out by combining several reading processes within a single model of instruction. Because of its widespread recognition by researchers and educators as a "premier" reading and learning methodology, it is no accident we feature our discussion of Reciprocal Teaching as the final strategy of this chapter.

Reciprocal Teaching

Reciprocal Teaching includes a transactional model of teaching (teacher modeling → guided practice → student ownership) in combination with four powerful comprehension strategies:

- Summarizing
- Questioning
- Noting Difficult Parts
- Predicting

Reciprocal Teaching is one of the most extensively investigated and most promising instructional procedures to emerge in the last thirty years. Ann Marie Palinscar and Ann Brown (1984, 1986) evaluated this procedure in a variety of content settings. In all instances, they found students who participated in Reciprocal Teaching made far greater gains in reading comprehension than did students using more traditional approaches. A decade later, Rosenshine and Meister (1994) conducted an extensive review of work on Reciprocal Teaching and found its effectiveness increased as students progressed. In fact, multiple strategy instruction becomes increasingly important as students face escalating academic demands. Trabasso and Bouchard (2002) found that weaker readers benefit most from Reciprocal Teaching.

The positive effects of Reciprocal Teaching also transfer to peer teaching. Teachers trained seventh-grade tutors to carry out these four activities with their tutees. Tutors and tutees both made substantial gains in comprehension. Moreover, tutors became very effective in modeling and in providing specific feedback to their tutees.

Introduction, Modeling, and Reflection

1. Begin with a section of your content text which contains a series of well-written paragraphs.
2. Explain you are going to demonstrate four different strategies: *summarizing, questioning, noting difficulties,* and *predicting.*
3. Read through the first paragraph. In one or two sentences, summarize the gist of the material. Talk about how you developed your summary.
4. Ask a question about the paragraph's content. Discuss what you did to come up with your question.
5. Note any difficult vocabulary or unclear statements in the paragraph and comment about what you think they mean. Ask students if they notice any other difficult parts that need clearing up.
6. Predict what you think you might learn in the next several paragraphs.
7. Continue modeling over a period of several days until students are comfortable with the strategies. In the beginning, you will be doing most of the work, but instruction shifts as students take on more responsibility.
8. After you have modeled multiple times, ask a student to be the facilitator and do the four-strategy sequence with a paragraph. Provide feedback about the summaries, questions, and predictions.
9. Other students and the facilitator answer the questions and provide alternative questions, summaries, and predictions. Provide support as needed through praising, prompting, modeling, and coaching.
10. Have students take turns being facilitator until the reading assignment is complete.

> **Reflection**
> How did Reciprocal Teaching help you read and understand better? How did Reciprocal Teaching help you become more metacognitive? How does discussion and collaboration help you understand more? How can you apply Reciprocal Teaching when reading on your own?

Support and Extensions

- While reading challenging content, have students work in pairs and take turns using the four strategies.

- Include Question-Answer Relationships (page 97) in the Reciprocal Teaching process. Students take turns asking one another questions following the QAR model.

- Use Reciprocal Teaching with a whole class, with small groups, and in one-on-one tutorials with students who need extra help with reading. Reciprocal Teaching works well as a component of Special Education and Title 1 programs.

- Use Reciprocal Teaching on sample tests in preparation for state reading assessments and standardized exams such as the SAT and PSAT. After students have processed a reading selection using Reciprocal Teaching, have them answer the test questions.

▲ ▲ ▲

Summary

The strategies described in this chapter deepen our own and our students' understanding of the CRISS Framework for Learning—particularly the principles of background knowledge, purpose setting, and transformation. Pre/post strategies such as K-W-L + and Anticipation Guides build a deeper awareness about background knowledge and purpose setting. Our students don't arrive as blank slates. When we take time to learn about what they know before asking them to read, the momentum of our lesson changes. Students become more curious about reading. By brainstorming what they think they know, talking with peers about their ideas, and then coming up with questions about the topic, students begin to have a stake in their own learning. They become engaged and want to learn more.

Imagery, paraphrasing, and summarizing are some of the tools that facilitate knowledge acquisition through transformation. Students don't learn much by just listening to our lectures or by simply reading our assignments. They must transform information in order for it to become their own Reciprocal Teaching incorporates an instructional model that exemplifies CRISS philosophy as teachers guide students in taking more and more responsibility for their own strategic comprehension.

Finally, the strategy presentations are all nested in a Framework for Teaching with teacher modeling and guided practice. CRISS teachers don't just test comprehension, they teach it.

CHAPTER 5 RESEARCH BASE

Research Conclusion	Reference
Teachers tend to assign, question, and lecture students about content, but do little to teach students how to understand and learn new information.	Durkin, 1979 Pressley, 2002
Teaching elementary, middle, and high school students to use a repertoire of comprehension strategies increases comprehension of text.	Conley, 2008
Creating mental images while reading or listening improves comprehension and retention for both children and adults.	Gambrell & Koskinen, 2002
Teaching students how to paraphrase is particularly effective with struggling readers.	Kletzien, 2009
When students learn how to summarize and use the strategy effectively, they do better in comprehending and recalling textual information.	Marzano, 2010 Trabasso & Bouchard, 2002
Students who participate in Reciprocal Teaching make significantly greater gains in reading comprehension than students participating in more traditional instructional procedures. These results are consistent within a variety of content domains and grade levels.	Palinscar & Brown, 1984 Rosenshine & Meister, 1994
Weaker readers benefit most from reciprocal teaching.	Trabasso and Bouchard, 2002

Organizing for Learning:
Two-Column Notes, Frames, and Story Plans

6

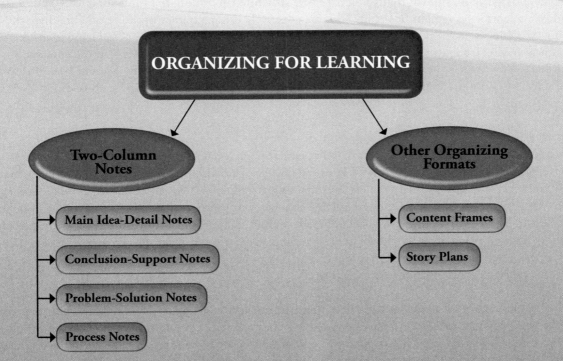

In this chapter, we present a number of approaches which help students organize and remember information. Too many students think they can magically read a text and remember the information without imposing structure on the incoming information. They don't realize our memory has limitations for disorganized, discrete bits of information and how organizing information provides coherence to otherwise incoherent texts. By imposing structure on information, we bring order to the chaos of discrete facts and have an opportunity to achieve cognitive clarity. Organizing strategies also encourage learners to process text more deeply and to become more highly engaged with text.

While teaching students organizing strategies receives strong support from experts in memory and learning (Bransford, Brown & Cocking, 2000), these approaches are also supported by the concept of generative learning (Wittrock, 1992). Generative learning, or meaningful learning, occurs when readers themselves generate meaningful relationships among the ideas in the text and with the ideas they already know. Rather than just recalling facts, generative learning is about building relationships among ideas. In order for this to occur, teachers create situations that lead students to use their generative processes. Wittrock tested his model in a variety of situations, documenting that learning through constructing relationships (e.g. constructing graphs and charts, composing titles, writing summaries) results in better comprehension than in situations where students did not use these processes.

Our job is to show students how to use their generative processes to construct meaning. This means they need competence in a variety of ways to organize information in order to develop their own personal systems. To gain this expertise, they must experience different ways of structuring content that take into consideration the author's purpose, style of writing, and most importantly, the author's content domain.

Different content domains have different organizing properties. The organizing strategies useful in mathematics will not necessarily work for organizing information from a Shakespearean play. While a world geography passage about human rights might be best structured according to problems, effects, causes, and solutions, a scientific text might be organized more effectively using a framework for evaluating hypotheses by using data and scientific evidence. If the goal in a civics lesson is to analyze proposed legislation on issues such as health care, students may need to organize content from varying perspectives. In the end, savvy readers know how writers present information and how those presentations vary by content area. Authors may organize ideas around problem-solution relationships, cause and effect relationships, a chronology of events, a series of comparisons, descriptions, or they may present an argument using propositions and supportive information.

In addition to figuring out the best way to impose structure on texts from varying content domains, students must also adapt organizing strategies to the quality of an author's presentation. If expository materials happen to be fairly well structured with obvious main ideas and details, Power Notes might be the strategy of choice. When materials have less obvious structure or where authors have scattered information throughout a piece, Picture Notes may work better for obtaining key points and details. Unfortunately, students too often face poorly written materials which make the task of imposing structure more challenging. The organizing strategies described in this chapter help students structure information from various content domains as well as impose order on confusing, poorly written text.

Finally, the organizing strategies work best after students have actively read and processed the content information. Once they understand the essential ideas, they can select the appropriate organizing structure to connect these ideas and the relevant supporting information. If students use organizing strategies while reading, it's important for them to brainstorm background knowledge, to preview the assignment, and to develop purposes for reading. Otherwise, they will have difficulty sorting the wheat from the chaff.

TWO-COLUMN NOTES

Two-Column Notes work best as a post-reading strategy or in situations where students have sufficient familiarity with the topic to be able to organize information as they read. The format of Two-Column Notes will vary depending upon the subject area, instructional goals, and the structure of the text. These notes can be used in situations demanding higher levels of thinking, including supporting conclusions and organizing for persuasive papers, analyzing problems, and improving process skills in science and mathematics. We include four different formats (plus a variety of adaptations) in this chapter: (1) Main Idea—Detail Notes, (2) Conclusion-Support Notes, (3) Problem-Solution Notes, and (4) Process Notes.

Main Idea—Detail Notes

Main Idea—Detail Notes help students organize main ideas and details from subject area reading assignments. This format works particularly well with text structured around concepts and definitions. Students divide their papers into two columns and record main ideas in the left column and details on the right. Main points can take the form of questions or key words. Students can then use their notes as a study guide. Covering the information on the right, they test themselves by using the key words or main idea questions on the left as prompts.

Introduction, Modeling, and Reflection

1. Project a selection of text for modeling with students. Provide students with their own copy so they can underline and make margin notes as you model the process.

2. Preview the assignment. Read the introduction and bold print headings; examine visuals, and read the summary and end-of-chapter questions. Brainstorm background knowledge and develop a purpose for reading. *Why do you think the author wrote this selection? What do you think some of his/her big ideas might be?* Consider using Questioning the Author (see page 105) as a during-reading strategy.

3. After reading, return to the selection and demonstrate how to use the author's clues to identify main ideas. For example, if the author happened to develop main ideas through bold print and rhetorical questions, your instruction might be similar to the following: *We can use the author's clues to develop notes on the important information in the selection. In the left-hand column of our notes, we want to include the main ideas asked through rhetorical questions. In addition, we want to include bold print vocabulary and main points from pictures and diagrams.*

4. Model how to convert these clues to notes. Model while students write down their own notes at their desks. Talk about how to abbreviate the questions and other key points. *Do not use complete sentences in your notes. Use brief phrases to summarize ideas. It takes too much time to write sentences.* Model how to include main ideas and vocabulary essential to content in the left column. In the right column, record information that elaborates on main points. *Write the author's information in your own words. Making the author's message your own ensures better comprehension and retention.*

Organizing Learning: Two-Column Notes, Frames, and Story Plans

5. Demonstrate how to use the notes for self-testing and for reviewing information. Show students how to cover the right-hand column with a sheet of paper. Model how you self-test by using the questions and key words on the left.

   Now watch me as I use my notes to study. I cover all of my notes to the right and use the ideas on the left as triggers to test myself. I first ask myself how much information is needed (i.e., two causes for . . ., three steps in . . . , etc.). Next, I ask myself what the information is. After reciting what I know, I uncover my notes and check. Finally, I see what else I know—I draw some conclusions, list additional examples, use the information in some way, or make applications to other situations.

   Point out that this last piece is your metacognitive check: *If you can't add anything to the information, you probably don't know it. It has only been memorized. Go back to the original and reread.*

   After the demonstration, ask students to work alone or in pairs and use their "triggers" in the left-hand column to test themselves.

6. Continue to model the note-taking process with input from students. Once students start to understand the process, have them work in pairs and/or small groups to complete notes, and then have them model the process for each other. When students start to feel comfortable taking notes, have them try it independently—continue to scaffold the process for students needing more help.

Nature's Clean-Up Organisms: Scavengers & Decomposers

Scavengers	
What are they?	large & small animals
Examples:	big animals - coyotes, lions, vultures
	smaller - slugs, beetles, tadpoles, grubs
Habitat	litter: dark, moist food-note: one rotting apple can have 100,000 roundworms, also found in cow manure
What do they do?	begin cleanup - eat dead matter
Decomposers	
What are they?	microscopic, fungi, bacteria, microscopic animals 1000's of different kinds
Examples:	mushrooms
Habitat	different decomposers in each ecosystem
What do they do?	change litter & waste back to basic materials
	[diagram: Decomposers → Enzymes → Litter and waste → CO₂, water, minerals, other nutrients → Soil, other organisms]
Decomposition	Breakdown of dead material into basic materials by decomposers

---

Reflection

How did the process of developing Main Idea—Detail Notes help you focus on and record the most important information from your learning? How did reviewing your notes help you learn and remember the information? Which elements of the Framework for Learning did you use when developing and studying with these notes?

Support and Extensions

- <u>The 12 Minute Study</u>. This process encourages brief, but frequent, studying in preparation for a test.

    Within 24 hours of learning new content, students return to their notes for a 12 minute review using the process outlined in step 5. Then, they should study and self-test themselves for 12 minutes at least twice each day before a test (class time, study hall, after school, evening). No more than 12 minutes! Explain that frequent, brief study sessions tend to lock information in memory better than longer, less intense sessions. It is hard for your mind to wander if you only have 12 minutes!

    After students practice using their Main Idea—Detail Notes for studying, lead a discussion about what a test over the material might look like. Plan the test together.

    Next, give the students a test. Use questions developed previously in your discussion. On the test, ask the students at what times they studied and for how long.

    When the tests are returned, talk to the students about how the studying process related to their grades. Ask students to comment about the 12 Minute Study as a process for learning.

- Continue modeling how to take and use Main Idea—Detail Notes throughout the year. Each selection students read will probably be structured differently, and they will need help in understanding how their text is written.

- Have students incorporate QARs (see page 97) in the left column of their two-column notes. Encourage them to use mostly *Think and Search* and *Author and Me* questions. *Think and Search* questions encourage students to put details together. *Author and Me* questions can be added to tap higher levels of thinking. You will need to model the use of these questions.

- In content area subjects, students may need help distinguishing important from unimportant information. As part of every pre-reading activity, provide students with clear purposes for reading. *As you read your social studies text, make sure to take notes on these topics . . . .* List essential ideas on the board so students know to include that type of information in their notes.

- Have students work together on their notes. Assign small groups the same or different parts of a reading assignment and ask each team to present their notes to the class for discussion.

- Use Main Idea—Detail Notes as part of discussions and lectures. As you present, develop and project your notes. Initially develop a complete set of notes with the main points of your lecture on the left and details on the right. Then begin to write down less information, allowing students to fill in more of the details as you talk.

- Consider incorporating Powers (see page 50) into Main Idea—Detail Notes. In the following example, the chapter subheadings have been turned into Power 1 topics. Each Power 2 reflects the main idea of one paragraph in the section.

Chapter 4: The New England Colonies	
Main Ideas	**Details**
1. Puritans in Massachusetts 2. Who were the Puritans?	3. Wanted to reform Church of England 4. Wanted simpler service, do away with customs taken from the Catholics 3. Different from Pilgrims who wanted to separate from the Church

2. Reasons for leaving England	3. They felt uncomfortable and unsafe in England.
	     4. England's King Charles did not like Puritan ideas. Took away their business charters, had them kicked out of schools, and even had some jailed.
	 3. In 1629, royal officials gave Massachusetts Bay Co. (formed by Puritans) a charter so they could form a colony in New England.
	     4. Colony based on laws of God
	     4. Not watched by England, so had some freedom
	     4. Many non-Puritans joined to get land and a new start.

- <u>Fact-Reason</u>. Teachers have found Fact-Reason notes to be an effective two-column organizing approach in science (based on Tovani, 2000). In the following example, Bruce Marshall's earth science class read about volcanic eruptions.

Fact-Reason	
Write key facts from your reading	**Explain why you think these facts are important**
Volcanic eruptions and climate change: Mount Tambora (1815) blanketed Indonesia in darkness for three days.	The global effects were not felt until the next year.
As volcanic ash and gas spread through the atmosphere, they blocked out sunlight and caused global temperatures to drop.	During large-scale eruptions, enormous amounts of volcanic ash and gases are ejected into the upper atmosphere.

Different types of volcanoes:
     Shield
     Cinder Cone
     Composite
	Knowing the different types helps to identify differences and activity levels. The Hawaiian islands are examples of shield volcanoes while Crater Lake and Mt. St. Helens are examples of composite volcanoes. Parícutin Volcano in Mexico is a cinder cone.

- <u>Fact-Opinion</u>. Billie Jean Fogle wanted her middle school students to understand the importance of reading multiple sources on a topic and to become aware that writers have biases. Students read two short biographies about Christopher Columbus—one depicted him as a hero, the other as a villain. After students read both biographies, she modeled how to go back into the texts and determine if information was either a fact or opinion. They talked about how emotionally charged words can lead to an opinion and misconceptions even when they are coupled with facts. After students analyzed information using their Fact-Opinion

Notes, they wrote paragraph summaries on the life of Christopher Columbus using only factual information:

Fact-Opinion

Fact	Opinion
Explorer	Greatest explorer
Born in Genoa	No Fear
Had no real schooling	Hero
Read ancient Greek philosophy and medieval astrology	Columbus' spirit lives on in the new world
	May have spent many evening gazing at the sea

- <u>Main Events—Significance</u>. Language arts teachers have found Main Events—Significance Notes effective for helping students prepare for a discussion about literary themes in short stories and novels. Students use the information in their notes to develop a summary of the story's theme:

Main Events—Significance

Main Events	Significance

- <u>Three-Column Notes</u>. Add a third column for studying, pictures, notes from films, and class discussions/comments which relate to key ideas in the left-hand columns.

Three-Column Notes

	BOOK NOTES	CLASS DISCUSSION
Advantages of the North	More people More factories and mills Better infrastructure	People were also clustered in more urban areas—easier to pull together (more soldiers) More people to produce goods South had to get goods from Europe
Advantages of the South	Defensive war Better generals, Robert E. Lee was far better, many surprise moves	Defensive war—people very protective of their homes, makes them fight harder

Organizing Learning: Two-Column Notes, Frames, and Story Plans

Conclusion-Support Notes

Students' academic achievement depends upon their ability to analyze and organize information from varying viewpoints. They also need to be able to articulate arguments both orally and in written form. As noted by Mason, Benedek-Wood, and Valasa (2010), about one-third of the fourth and eighth grade students taking the 2007 NAEP assessment wrote unacceptable responses to selections where they had to analyze argumentative information. They had difficulty teasing out arguments and consequently were unable to develop a coherent and convincing response. Too often students can specify a conclusion, but do not know how to go about explaining why it makes sense. Conclusion-Support Notes can help.

Conclusion-Support is a two-column format in which students develop and support arguments with evidence (Santa, Dailey, & Nelson, 1985). This approach stresses critical thinking skills with both expository and narrative text. Students write their thesis or conclusion in the left-hand column and use the space in the right-hand column to record evidence from their reading. They may then use their notes to develop persuasive written arguments. This format also works well to identify and record authors' opinions (left-hand column) and the support for their opinions or conclusions (right-hand column).

Introduction, Modeling, and Reflection

1. Find a selection that will inspire strong reactions from the students. Conclusion-Support is particularly effective with controversial characters or issues. Pick an issue that might be controversial at your school, such as whether or not students can leave campus for lunch.

2. Divide the class and assign pro and con positions. In these roles, students discuss the issue for two to five minutes.

3. Have a whole class discussion and together develop pro and con Conclusion-Support Notes:

	Conclusion	**Support**
Pro	Students should be allowed to eat off campus.	1. Support local lunch businesses 2. Gives students a break from school—come back feeling recharged 3. Teaches students more responsibility
Con	Students should not be allowed to eat lunch off campus	1. School cafeteria would lose money 2. Causes problems for neighbors near school 3. Creates tardies to afternoon classes

4. Conclusion-Support Notes evolve naturally into persuasive writing. Demonstrate how the thesis or the conclusion statement becomes a topic sentence which students support with sentences developed from their notes. Conclusion-Support Notes can also be used for longer papers. The notes in the above example can readily be woven into an argumentative paper following the Spool format (see page 200). In this case, the introduction presents two points of view. The subsequent paragraphs present each conclusion along with support, and the paper concludes with a comment about which of the two opinions seems to make the most sense.

Reflection

How did Conclusion-Support work for you as a strategy? How did it help you think through an issue? How might Conclusion-Support Notes help with questions or writing prompts on assessments? How did it help you write a better persuasive essay?

Support and Extensions

- Conclusion-Support works well as part of cooperative group discussions and debates. Ask students to form opinions about a character or issue and develop Conclusion-Support Notes. Ask them to bring their notes to small group discussions. Each student presents his or her conclusions and support to the group. Team members ask questions leading to clarifications of opinions. After students discuss their ideas, they write persuasive papers.

- Ask students to find exact quotes in a selection and mark them with sticky notes. Record these quotes and clarifying statements to help support each conclusion.

- Students can also create character Conclusion-Support Notes through pictures. This is especially helpful for second language learners. They write their conclusion (e.g. the character is brave, weak, misunderstood, etc.) and then illustrate the qualities or actions of the character which support their conclusion.

- <u>Conclusion-Support-Interpretation Notes</u>. Another way to help students elaborate on arguments is to use three-column Conclusion-Support-Interpretation Notes. Students use the support column for textual evidence and the how/why column for explaining why the evidence lends support to the conclusion.

Conclusion	Support	How / Why

- Another version of Conclusion-Support Notes helps students organize their thinking around questions that guide their responses to counterarguments (adapted from Felton & Herko, 2004).

What is the issue?			
What is your position on the issue?	What are your reasons for this position?	What are the counterarguments?	How are you going to respond to the counterarguments?
What is your conclusion?			

- Combine Power Thinking with Conclusion-Support Notes. Frequently, students record random facts to support their conclusions and the reasoning behind their choices is not always evident. When students must record in the right-hand column the Power 2 information (the facts) and the Power 3 information (why the facts support their conclusion), a higher level of thinking is employed. Note the use of Power Thinking employed in the next example.

- Use Conclusion-Support to explore and expand upon issues in content subjects. In the following example, students in Kimin Mitchel's class examined whether or not animal experimentation for scientific purposes is ever justified. Students began with Carousel Brainstorming (see page 86), focusing on aspects of animal rights. She then divided students into expert groups responsible for reading and responding to questions about their topic. Next, students took either pro or con notes which they presented to one another. Finally, students used their notes to develop argumentative papers.

Conclusion	Support

1. Animal Experimentation is always justified.	2. Huge advances controlling diseases
	   3. Polio-crippling disease, irong lung
	      4. Vaccine-experimentation with monkeys
	      4. Albert Sabine-no oral polio vaccine without animal experimentation
	   3. AIDS—all experimental treatment done on animals—when a cure is found it will be because of research on animals
	2. Sacrificing an animal to save many human lives is justified
	2. Hands-on research using animals better for scientists
	2. Only safe and effective way to develop therapeutic drugs—everyone benefits from research involving animals

1. Animal Experimentation is never justified.	2. Animals suffer
	   3. Improperly anaesthetized animals facing surgery
	   3. Does superior power of human give us this right
	   3. Mistreating animals for our gain
	2. Doesn't always lead to better medical knowledge
	   3. Animals not similar enough to humans for combating disease
	   3. Effects of drugs different with humans
	      4. Drugs testing safe for animals not always safe with humans
	2. Animals used for testing cosmetics

Student example:

A debate continues about whether or not animals should be used for medical research. Some feel the cruelty done to animals for the sake of medical advances is wrong because animals suffer. Others feel the ends justify the means. Animal research has led to incredible advancements in improving the health of people.

Those against using animals in medical research studies have strong opinions. Humans shouldn't use their power to mistreat animals. Animals have the same right to live as we do. Some say that animal research does not always lead to better medical knowledge because animals are not similar enough to humans. Testing drugs on animals can give us false information. Some drugs work differently on animals than on humans which means that drugs are not always safe for humans. Animals should not be used for non-medical purposes like testing for cosmetics. There is no need to practice surgeries on animals now that we have the technology to do simulations. Those against using animals in research think it is immoral to make animals suffer.

Others feel that using animals for medical research is the right thing to do. Animal-based research is an effective way to develop therapeutic drugs and save lives. An example is polio. In the 1940s and 1950s lots of children and young adults died or were crippled by polio. In 1961 the polio vaccine was given to every child in America, and the disease pretty much disappeared because of the research conducted on monkeys. Even though the monkeys died, thousands of lives have been saved. Hopefully, the same will happen with AIDS. Some believe that sacrificing animals to save human lives is the right thing to do.

Even though I hate the thought of animals suffering, I think experimentation on animals for medical purposes should continue. Look at polio. If it weren't for animal testing, there would still be people walking around in iron lungs. If animals are the most effective way to get an accurate result, then it is justified. Care must be taken so that the animals don't suffer, and research should only be done for medical reasons. Animals should not be used for testing cosmetic products. Scientists should continue using animals when necessary but do it in a way that animals don't suffer.

- Use Conclusion-Support Notes to help students analyze issues from varying perspectives and to help students build tolerance for varying opinions. For example, Rick Stern, a social studies teacher, asked students to identify their political preferences. Next, he instructed his students to shift their political perspectives and take on those initially in conflict with their own biases. *If you identified yourself as a Republican, shift your perspective and become a Democratic senator. Likewise, if your political preference is Democrat, take on the role of a Republican senator.* Students then gathered evidence supportive of their perspective on healthcare reform using Conclusion-Support Notes. They used a variety of resources: news magazines, Internet sites, YouTube videos, and information from television news. Students then used their notes as a basis for developing a mock congressional debate.

- <u>Advantages—Disadvantages</u>. An alternative format for helping students analyze issues is to examine a topic according to advantages and disadvantages before arriving at a conclusion. In the following example, students read an article about parents monitoring their teenager's driving with a GPS, "GPS Helps Parents Track Teens: Lifesaver or a 'Big Brother?'"

Use of GPS to Track Teens	
Advantages	**Disadvantages**
Keeps kids honest	Invasion of kid's privacy
Improves safety	Doesn't work in all areas
Tracks car speed	Creates trust issues
Easy to download	Replaces more personal communication

Conclusion:

- Janet Luberda, a chemistry teacher, used Conclusion-Support Notes as a means for students to take notes on a laboratory experiment identifying mixtures.

Conclusion	**Support**
Mixture 1 is a solution	no settling no particles on filter paper blue in color - Tyndall effect transparent
Mixture 2 is a colloid	cloudy no particles no settling white in color + Tyndall effect
Mixture 3 is a suspension	opague settling has particles - Tyndall effect looks like chocolate milk

- Use Conclusion-Support to prepare students to write persuasive essays–a prevalent feature in most state assessments.

- Proposition-Support (Buehl, 2009). Proposition-Support is a more advanced form of Conclusion-Support. As students progress through school, they need to become increasingly adept at analyzing an author's point of view. The Proposition-Support framework helps older students critically analyze an author's conclusions or propositions by identifying different ways to build a case using facts, statistics, examples, expert authority, and logical reasoning. By untangling the various dimensions of argumentation, students can more readily analyze oral and written text containing differing viewpoints, opinions, hypotheses, and theories. This framework guides students in writing persuasive papers, in preparing speeches and debates, and in conducting research. Completed notes also prepare students for more focused classroom discussions. In addition, Proposition-Support Notes provide a superb way to analyze political and environmental issues.

When introducing Proposition-Support to students, begin by defining the term proposition as a statement expressing a judgment or opinion. Choose a text containing a clear proposition and various forms of argumentation.

Next, read the selection together using the Questioning the Author strategy (see page 105) to arrive at the author's intended point of view or proposition.

Continue by analyzing and categorizing the varying arguments.
- ✓ Does the author make a convincing case? How? What makes it convincing?
- ✓ Do you reject or accept the proposition?
- ✓ Has the author used one form of argumentation more than another?

Scrutinize how the author might do a better job of supporting the proposition.
- ✓ Are the arguments logical?
- ✓ Are they based on research and examples?
- ✓ Are one or more expert authorities cited?

In the process of analyzing these questions, students become far more astute thinkers, writers, and debaters.

In the following example, high school health students read an article about the safety of the food we eat and organized their notes into the Proposition-Support format.

Proposition Much of the food we eat is unsafe	Support
Facts	1. Salmonella from contaminated pork 2. Fish, cattle, broiler and laying chickens now raised in food factories—conditions favor contamination 3. E-coli wide-spread in cattle herds 4. Families eat out more often; more chance of contaminated food
Statistics	1. The Center for Disease Control and Prevention (CDC) reports 76 million people each year suffer from food born diseases 2. CDC reports 5,000 people die per year 3. FDA took samples of food in Washingon DC, 20% samples had Salmonella bacteria 4. Study by consumers' union: 2/3 of chickens in U.S. grocery stores contain campylobacter that causes extreme abdominal pain and vomiting
Examples	1. Uncooked eggs and egg products (Caesar salad, eggnog) 2. Rare cooked meats 3. Blue cheese, camembert 4. Poorly washed fresh vegetables
Expert Authority	1. Patricia Griffin (CDC)—Increasing risk of eating contaminated food 2. Frederick Angulo (CDC)—animals eat contaminated food that they carry in their bodies 3. Carmela Velazquex—hand washing essential
Logic and Reasoning	1. Change eating habits—fewer fast foods 2. Need better disposal of animal wastes 3. Food cannot be made risk-free 4. Insist on cleaner meat, poultry, eggs, and vegetables 5. Raise own food, community gardens

- <u>Hypothesis-Evidence</u>. Hypothesis-Evidence Notes help students think like researchers. The analysis of written materials according to theoretical assumptions and evidence is integral to the research process.

  Start with sharing a research article with students. Talk about how researchers present their hypotheses or theories in the opening paragraph and then dedicate the rest of their paper to presenting evidence supporting their theories.

  Read through the article, underlining the theory and supporting evidence. After reading, develop Hypothesis-Evidence Notes together.

  Finally, have students evaluate the researcher's evidence to determine if it is convincing and write their conclusion at the bottom of their notes.

  Once students understand how to take Hypothesis-Evidence Notes, find articles which have different theories on the same topic. Divide students into teams and have each team take notes supporting one hypothesis. Then have each team present its Hypothesis-Evidence Notes.

  In this example, students were asked to read articles about the disappearance of dinosaurs.

Question: Why did dinosaurs disappear?	
Hypothesis	**Evidence**

1. Hypothesis:
An asteroid, six miles in diameter, hit the earth.
	2. Tremendous amount of dust in atmosphere
	   3. Drop in temperature changed weather
	   3. Dust blocked off light
	     4. Plants died (destroyed food supply)
	2. Extinction went quickly
	   3. Fossil record
	   3. Iridium layer around the world
	2. Physical Evidence
	   3. Yucatan crater

Agree or disagree with hypothesis: Yes. Strong Evidence	

  Model how to use Hypothesis-Evidence Notes for writing a summary paragraph. Sometimes a Writing Template (see page 195) will help students develop summaries from their notes:

      The author/s conclude . . .

      First, the author/s say . . .

      Next . . .

      Finally . . .

      I think . . .

Student example:

*__The authors of the articles conclude__ that dinosaurs disappeared because of a giant asteroid that hit the earth. **First, they say** the asteroid probably caused a drop in the temperature of the earth. The drop in temperature may have caused the dinosaurs to die because the weather changed quite drastically. **Next,** when the asteroid hit, it created a lot of dust and particles. The dust probably kept sunlight from reaching the ground, so plants couldn't live or grow. Without plants to eat, the dinosaurs and other animals that were herbivores would have starved, and the meat-eating dinosaurs wouldn't have had any animals left to eat. **Finally,** the geologic record reflects the fact that dinosaurs died quickly. The dust from a huge asteroid probably caused them to die fast. There is a layer of iridium dust that separates a time when many dinosaurs were living and then none were. There is also a crater in the sea floor of the Yucatan that is from an asteroid hitting the earth.*

__I think__ the theory might be true. Animals would die if they didn't have any food and that would have happened pretty fast. The iridium layer is all over the world, and it marks a change in what animals were living before and after it. There is also a gigantic hole where the asteroid hit the earth.

Problem-Solution Notes

The Problem-Solution two-column format lists four questions in the left-hand column: (1) What is the problem or issue? (2) What are the effects of the problem? (3) What are the causes of the problem? (4) What are the solutions to the problem? Answers to the questions are recorded in the right-hand column of the page. This format provides students with a guide for thinking and writing about issues in novels and in content subjects. The format works well as a discussion guide and for taking notes from reading assignments. It is particularly effective for analyzing social issues, ecological issues, current events, and conflict in short stories.

Introduction, Modeling, and Reflection

1. Model Problem-Solution Notes using a current school, community, or national issue about which the students have some knowledge.

2. Develop a problem statement and write it in the right-hand column, opposite the "Problem" question.

3. Brainstorm possible effects, causes, and solutions to the problem, and record them in the right-hand column opposite the appropriate questions.

4. Next, model with a short, simple content article. First, skim the article to determine the problem being addressed and record it in the Problem-Solution guide. Then, read through the article more carefully and underline the effects, causes, and solutions. You can label them in the margins of the article with an "e," "c," or "s" to keep the underlined information straight. Finally, transfer the underlined information to your Problem-Solution guide. The following Problem-Solution Notes are based on an article about erosion.

What is the Problem or Issue?	America's topsoil is eroding away at an alarming rate.
What are the Effects?	ugly ditches cut through the hillsides creek beds choked with topsoil soil can't produce as many crops more land will have to be put into production
What are the Causes	over-tilling the soil not rotating crops burning fields after harvest
What are the Solutions?	no-till farming new fertilizers strip farming

5. Model how to use the Problem-Solution Notes to write a paper. The first paragraph identifies and explains the problem. The subsequent paragraphs cover the effects, causes, and solutions.

Example:

A huge problem for American farmers is erosion. Topsoil is eroding away at an alarming rate. This problem must be stopped.

You can see the effects of erosion any time you drive into the countryside. After a rain, deep, ugly ditches cut through the hillsides where the rains have washed the top soil away. Creek beds become choked with soil as the water sweeps the soil away. Too much soil in a stream will destroy animals and plants that live in and around the stream. In addition, the remaining topsoil in the fields becomes thin and can't produce abundant crops. This means that more land will have to be put into production, which leaves little left for supporting native plants and animals.

There are several factors which lead to the problem of soil erosion. Farmers like to plant one crop on their land so there is nothing to stop whole hillsides from eroding away. After a crop is harvested, farmers plow the soil until it is too fine, which makes it easy for the rain to wash the soil away or for winds to blow it away. Other farms burn their fields so all of the organic matter is destroyed, and there is nothing to hold the soil during heavy rains.

How can the problem be solved? Farmers need to do strip farming where different crops are planted next to one another in strips. There might be a strip of winter wheat next to a strip of green peas. If the water starts to flow through the land planted in peas, it will stop when it comes to the wheat crop. Another idea is to use no-till farming where farmers just plant into the stubble rather than cultivating it first. Also, farmers should not burn their fields after harvest. There are many things farmers can do to keep their land productive and, at the same time, protect against soil erosion.

Reflection

Why is this strategy helpful for analyzing problems and solutions? How did identifying the ingredients (problem, effects, causes, and solution) of a problem or issue help you analyze it? How did this framework help you with discussion? With writing? What other elements of the Framework for Learning did you use?

Support and Extensions

- Problem-Solution Notes can serve as a basis for small group discussions. Students work together identifying problems and solutions and then present their ideas to the whole group.

- Some school counselors and administrators use Problem-Solution Notes with students who receive disciplinary referrals. Students must complete the Problem-Solution guide before meeting with an adult. Administrators report this is a good way to prevent incidents from recurring since the students have to determine their own solutions. Also, administrators and counselors use the Problem-Solution Notes before dealing with groups of students who are in trouble. Students must work together to complete one form before talking to an adult. This helps the students to see both sides of the problem and to resolve their issues more effectively.

- These notes can help students think about problems confronting characters in novels and short stories. Students can take brief notes from each chapter using Problem-Solution Notes. This note-taking strategy works well for literature because chapters usually build around one or two problems which the main character or characters need to resolve. Asking students to take Problem-Solution Notes individually and then bring their notes to cooperative team discussions works well as a discussion strategy.

- Mickey Conway, a language arts teacher, used the following modified framework to assist her sophomores in reading and discussing *The Scarlet Letter*. Students brought their completed reading guides to their literature discussion groups.

What characters have we met so far?	What seems to be the main conflict/problem at this point?	Questions I had while reading	My predictions about what will happen next.

Organizing Learning: Two-Column Notes, Frames, and Story Plans

- <u>Problem-Solution Graphic Structure</u>. Another format teachers find useful for generating discussion and writing is the Problem-Solution Graphic Structure. In the following example middle school students read an article about eating disorders and used the organizer to guide their reading and discussion:

PROBLEM: EATING DISORDERS

Problem
- Who: American women
- What: Want to be thinner, unhappy with their bodies
- Why: Daily images of thin models and actresses

Steps to Solution

Attempted Solutions:	Consequences:
1. Don't eat junk food, and eat only when you are hungry	1. Will be able to eat healthier food
2. Don't hang out with others who diet or have eating disorders	2. May end up just like these people
3. Don't judge yourself against the "beautiful" people on TV or movies	3. Most people look better in print or film than in person–i.e., images are touched up
4. Don't keep a scale in your room or bathroom	4. You won't be thinking about your weight all the time

End Result
- Healthier attitudes
- Better self-esteem
- Self-confidence goes up

- Problem-Analysis Notes. George Rusnak, social studies teacher, created the following Problem-Analysis template for students to take notes, discuss, and write about specific problems in history and current events. It will also work for conflicts in literature and for problems in science.

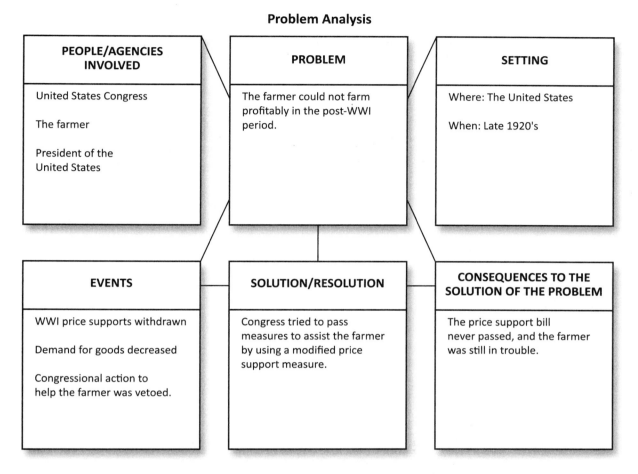

- Cause-Effect (or Because-Effect). These notes are particularly useful in the social sciences. In this example, history students analyzed issues leading to the American Revolution:

Cause (Because)	Effect
Colonist paid taxes on sugar, tea, and stamps in 1765 and saw no benefits	Colonists were frustrated and very tired of paying taxes. They even had to pay taxes to buy stamps. Colonists rebelled against taxes in Boston Tea Party. Problem is still the same today; people are anti-tax.

- History-Change Frame (Buehl, 2009). History texts appear to be an endless flood of names, dates, and events with authors mentioning one fact after another. Buehl's History-Change Frame helps students begin to make more sense of history, in that it is a story of change and people's reactions to change. Change forces us to rethink old ways and creates new problems for us to resolve. This framework helps students begin to think about how changes affect groups of people, and it guides students to go beyond the facts and think about bigger ideas or essential issues.

Organizing Learning: Two-Column Notes, Frames, and Story Plans

Group: Nez Perce Indians	Group: U.S. Military
What problems did they face? • Homesteaders and prospectors claimed their land.	**What problems did they face?** • The Nez Perce Indians would not move from their land and abide by the government established treaties.
What changes led to these problems? • White settlers moved west. • Gold was discovered on Nez Perce land.	**What changes led to these problems?** • White settlers moved west. • Gold was discovered on Nez Perce land.
What did they do to resolve the problems? • Agreed to treaties with U.S. government • Peacefully resisted moving • Had some skirmishes with army troops • Retreated to Montana • Chief Joseph surrendered.	**What did they do to resolve the problems?** • Negotiated treaties to reduce Nez Perce land • In 1877, planned to force NP into Idaho reservation • Troops pursued NP 1,500 miles through ID, WY & MT. • Caught Chief Joseph, moved him and people to reservations in Kansas and Oklahoma

Process Notes

Students seldom realize that they use processes daily to achieve results in all aspects of their lives. They seem to think they get from one point to another by random acts or by luck. Whenever students need help learning how to do a step-by-step process, consider Process Notes as a tool. Process Notes help students work through the steps and procedures for negotiating a multitude of tasks such as conducting scientific experiments, building furniture in a woodworking class, and solving those dreaded word problems in mathematics.

Introduction, Modeling, and Reflection

1. Give students a blank copy of the Word Problem Process Notes (see online reproducibles for Chapter 6).

WORD PROBLEM PROCESS NOTES

Write the question.	
List clue words and facts.	
Identify the variable(s).	
Make a drawing.	
Choose a strategy.	
Solve the problem.	
Write your answer in a complete sentence that answers the question.	
Checks: *Credibility* (Does your answer make sense?) *Mathematical*	

2. Model using the Word Problem Process Notes tool while students follow along and complete the Process Notes in their notebooks.s

3. Have students practice using this tool in pairs or small groups to complete assignments.

4. Model each type of problem students need to solve using this tool and allow students to practice.

5. Model other types of problem-solving formats (see pages 149-153) so students can record them in their notebooks and refer to these models when doing their assignments.

Sally Hunt shared with us that even her best math students struggled with word problems. "They'd freeze and lose confidence because they had difficulty breaking down the information from word problems–they wanted to do everything in one step." Therefore, she and her algebra students developed mathematical Process Notes that made problem solving less intimidating and assisted them in becoming better problem-solvers. An example from algebra is below:

Sample Problem

When rating movies, movie critic Ms. Thorson gives four thumbs up to every five thumbs up given by movie critic Mr. Lang. If Ms. Thorson gives thumbs up to 68 movies, how many movies does Mr. Lang rate favorably?

Write the question.	How many movies does Mr. Lang rate favorably?
List clue words & facts.	clues: 4 thumbs up to every 5 = ratio Fact: Ms. T gives 68 thumbs up.

Identify the variables.	T = Thorson's # favorable
	L = Lang's # favorable

Make a drawing.	movies (drawing of thumbs up pairs labeled T and L, numbered 1-5)
Choose a strategy.	Set up a ratio of favorable picks T to L. Then solve a proportion by using product of means = prod. of extremes.
Solve the problem.	$\frac{T}{L} = \frac{4}{5} = \frac{68}{L}$ $4L = 5 \times 68 = 340$ $L = \frac{340}{4} = 85$
Write your answer.	Mr. Lang rates 85 movies favorably.
Check math & reasonableness.	math $\frac{68}{85} = .8 = \frac{8}{10} = \frac{4}{5}$ which is the ratio of T to L reasonable? Yes, since Mr. L would rate ¼ more than Ms T.

Reflection

How did process notes help you tackle word problems? How did the notes help you internalize the steps needed to solve the problems?

Support and Extensions

- The following example is an elementary version of Process Notes. The students used the two-column format to answer the following word problem: *A boat sailed 750 miles from Vancouver to San Francisco, another 412 miles to Los Angeles, and on to Panama 3,000 miles away. What was the total length of its journey?*

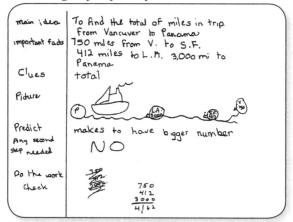

- Modify the process notes as needed to make it relevant for your content materials. The following is an example from a geometry class:

MAIN IDEA	IMPORTANT FACTS	PICTURE	DETERMINE ANSWER	WRITE ABOUT THE PROCESS
What is being asked for?	What facts are necessary to solve the problem?	Draw a picture of the situation.	Solve and show your work!	Tell what you did and why you did it.
to find the measure of the 4th angle	lot shaped like trapezoid has 2 right angles (90° + 90°) 3rd angle = 80° sum of all angles should be 360°	[sketch of trapezoid with 80°]	$\angle x + 90 + 90 + 80 = 360$ $x + 260 = 360$ $x = 360 - 260$ $x = 100$ 4th angle is 100°	I know the sum of all angles of a quadrilateral is 360°. In this trapezoid, I know three of the angles, so I just need to subtract the sum of those three angles from 360° to get the measure of the fourth angle.

GEOMETRY: A lot for a new house is shaped like a trapezoid, with two right angle corners. If the third corner is an 80 degree angle, what is the measurement of the fourth angle?

- You can also adapt Process Notes for students to record information from scientific explorations. Afterwards, students use their notes to write a scientific report (see example below).

TOPIC/RESEARCH ?	PROCEDURE/MATERIALS	RESULTS	CONCLUSIONS	FURTHER QUESTIONS
What is the topic of the experiment? What is the research question?	What are the steps in the process? What materials are necessary?	Describe the results of the experiment.	What's the answer to the research question?	What questions remain in the light of this research experiment?
MOLD — HOW DOES MOLD GROW? POSSIBLE CONDITIONS: LIGHT < WET < COLD/WARM, DRY < COLD/WARM; DARK < WET < COLD/WARM, DRY < COLD/WARM	8 PIECES OF BREAD 1 FOR EACH CONDITION 1. DAMPEN BREAD STORE IN PLASTIC BAGS 2. DARK - USE ALUMINUM FOIL 3. COLD OR WARM AREA OF ROOM	AFTER 1 WEEK, THE BREAD IN THE DARK, WARM AREA HAD THE MOST MOLD.	MOLD GROWS BEST IN DARK, WARM PLACES. MOLD DOES NOT GROW AS WELL IN SUNNY, COLD PLACES.	WHAT INFLUENCE DO FOOD PRESERVATIVES HAVE ON MOLD?

Student example:

In this experiment, we studied mold. We wanted to know what makes mold grow. We used eight slices of bread. We put water on half of the bread and then stored all pieces in plastic bags. Some bags were in light places. We put tin foil around some of the bread to keep out the light. After one week, we decided which pieces of bread had the most mold. The wet bread kept in tin foil had the most.

- As part of the reflection process, have students use Process Notes to reflect on how they dealt with a challenging task encountered during a lesson.
- <u>Problem-Solving Organizer</u>. Jim Devine developed the Problem-Solving Organizer as a way to help fifth, eighth, and tenth graders prepare for the Florida Comprehensive Achievement Test (FCAT) in mathematics. Students were not only being asked to solve a problem, but also had to explain the process. The explanation part of the assessment presented, especially for the middle school teachers, a unique challenge. Jim developed this Problem-Solving Organizer in response to teachers' pleas for help (available in the online reproducibles for Chapter 6). He notes that the organizer also helps teachers better understand students' thinking processes. Consequently, they can provide precise feedback about how students might approach problems more effectively.

To use the organizer, first select problems which have multiple steps, as in this sample problem:

Anna's allowance is $5 a week. She can earn more by doing extra chores. She can earn $1 per day for feeding and walking the dog, and $1 per day for helping with meals and doing dishes. How much can Anna make in four weeks if she does every chore? Show how you figured it out and write a brief explanation of your process.

Model how to paraphrase the question by asking, *What does the problem ask you to do?* This information goes in the box at the top of the page.

In the boxes, numbered "1" and "2", write your mathematical plan using numbers and symbols. Come up with several different plans demonstrating that there is more than one way to solve the problem.

Below each step in the mathematical plan, develop a written explanation for what you did

In the last box, model how to synthesize the information into a concluding statement that includes the answer to your original question. This organizer prompted students to begin by paraphrasing the question, and then asks them to refer to the same question as a writing prompt for their concluding statement.

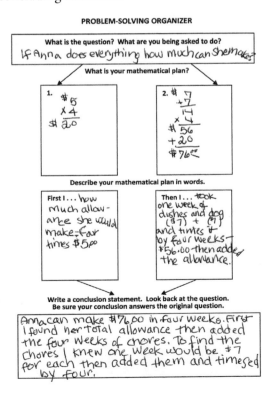

Organizing Learning: Two-Column Notes, Frames, and Story Plans

Jim created a more advanced form of the Problem-Solving Organizer shown below.

THINK: What is the question? What are you being asked to do? Rewrite the question.		
SOLVE: What is your mathematical process? Show your work.		
Step 1	Step 2	Step 3
EXPLAIN: What is your thought process? How did you solve the problem?		
First, I . . .	Then, I . . .	Finally, I . . .
WRITE: Make sure your conclusion answers the original question.		

OTHER ORGANIZING FORMATS

Content Frames

Frames provide another way to organize and compare information. Content Frames work well in situations where you want students to analyze the interrelationship of ideas. Consider using frames when authors structure the material so that main topics are compared with similar subtopics. Content Frames serve to pull information together from a variety of sources. It's important to remember with Content Frames, that students create the guiding information in the top row and first column and then they fill in the remainder of the information from reading and from additional research if necessary.

Introduction, Modeling, and Reflection

1. Preread (or brainstorm) content materials that have elements you want to compare. Using a think-aloud as you scan the materials, model how you use headings and subheadings as clues to frame categories. Ask these two questions:
   - What are the important categories of information?
   - How might these categories be subdivided?

2. Read through the material together. Continue modeling how text features can cue your identification of key information. Note Power 1 ideas or topics with a star (*) and underline Power 2 ideas or subtopics. When necessary, write topics and subtopics in the margins.

3. Together, build a Content Frame for the information. Then read through the material again to complete the frame. Talk about whether or not your chart works for each topic. Make changes or additions in the Content Frame as necessary.

4. After the Content Frame is complete (you may need more than one resource), model how to use it for self-testing.

The following examples represent some sample Content Frames from a variety of contents:

Science

Julie Johnson's biology students organized information about genetic disorders into a Content Frame. First, as a class, they examined the organization of their textbook chapter and determined the categories of information presented and the subdivisions into which the categories were divided. Then, as they read, they recorded the information to complete their frames.

CONTENT FRAME ON GENETIC DISORDERS

Genetic Disorder	Chromosome Error	Dominant or Recessive	Symptoms (How it affects a person)
Albinism	#11	Recessive	no melanin, pigment in hair or skin, sensitive to light
Cystic Fibrosis	#7	Recessive	Respiratory + digestive problems, delayed growth, thick mucus builds up b/c of sodium channels of cells, males = infertile, pale stools, coughing, weight loss, most fatal inherited disorder affecting Caucasions in USA
Tay-Sachs Disease	#15	Recessive	usually in Jewish people, start to appear @ 3-6 mos. progress rapidly + death = 4-5 yrs, deafness, dimentia, seizures, paralysis, loss of muscle function, delayed mental growth
Sickle-Cell Anemia	#6 blood disorder	Recessive	joint pain, fatigue, breathlessness, rapid ⌒=RBC heart rate, delayed growth, ulcers on lower ⌒=S.C. norm legs, jaundice, bone pain, attacks of abdominal African pain, fever, excessive thirst + urination, chest pain Am.
Phenylketonuria (PKU)	#12 bad PAH Enzyme	Recessive	Severe mental retardation, can be tested for + prevented w/ sp. diet by low protein diet, "diet for life"
Huntington Disease	#4 muted gene	Dominant	onset = middle age (late 30's-40's), kills brain cells, loose control of muscles, lyn.g breakdown, European descent, death w/in 15 yrs. of onset, mood swings, depression, loss of movement + memory

In this sixth grade example, the students used a Content Frame before and after reading about Polar Bears.

	food sources	appearance physical characteristics	behaviors	environment + habitat	Other
BEFORE READING	fish, seals, eggs, ~~penguins~~, snow ferets	fur white/clear black skin	swim, hibernate	Arctic	coke ads
AFTER READING	baby ring seals, fish, seaweed, eggs, rodents, berries	fur is clear sun reflects off it + makes it look white, black skin helps keep them warm, nostrils close under water	super swimmers, hunt a lot, females have cubs in winter, build dens in fall, snatch seals when come for air	global warming threatens habitat, Alaska, Russia, Norway, Canada, Greenland	for long time killed for fur like winter

Organizing Learning: Two-Column Notes, Frames, and Story Plans

Mathematics:

In this example, students created and completed their frames using a computer.

Name	Symbol	Label	Key Word	Definition (own words)
Plane	▱	▱	2-D or flat	A plane is a flat surface like the top of my desk.
Point	•	•M	dot	A point has no dimension, just a location. Group together to make lines.
Line	←——→	K↔L	Straight	A line is a set of points, determined by any 2 points. It is horizontal, vertical, or oblique (angle).
Line Segment	•——•	R•—•S	Endpoints (R&S)	A part of a line with points on the ends to show where it ends.

Social Studies:

In this example, students completed Content Frames about the Democratic and Republican parties.

Political Party	Environment	Education	Social Programs	Local vs Central
Democrats	Stewardship enjoy but leave no trace preserve	public unions tend to support fed leadership national stand.	take care of citizens welfare, health care, keep social security	Fed gvmt knows best
Republicans	for humans to use for resources & recreation	private vouchers no fed dept of ed	no handouts cut programs	Local control

Reflection

How did the Content Frame help you organize the author's information? How can you use a Content Frame to organize information from a variety of resources? How might you use a Content Frame to study for tests?

Support and Extensions

- As part of pre-reading activities, have students make some decisions about the best ways to organize information. Ask students to think about these questions:

    What does the author want us to learn?

    How does the author structure his/her writing for presenting main points?

    How is the material organized?

How should I transform the information?

Are there categories of information that reflect the major concepts in the materials? If so, perhaps a frame might work better than other transformation strategies.

- Have students work in small groups or pairs. Ask them to design a frame they feel works for the materials. Teams present their frames and explain how they represent the content and structure of the material.
- To differentiate instruction, provide Content Frames with varying levels of completion for students with reading and learning difficulties.

Story Plans

Story Plans (also called Story Grammars) are organizers used for understanding narrative structure. Teaching students about the plan or structure of a story leads to improved comprehension. Trabasso and Bouchard (2002), in his review of research on story structure instruction, found that teaching students to analyze stories improved comprehension as measured by performance in answering questions and in recalling information. In addition, knowledge of story structure led to higher standardized test performance, particularly for less able readers in grades 3-6.

Story Plans characterize the general structure of stories by defining what most have in common. They are, in effect, a summary of the plot and setting of a narrative. When students understand the architecture of fiction, they can use these generic frameworks in comprehending literature and in drafting their own stories. In addition, they are effective props for story retellings.

Story Plans usually contain the following key elements: major characters, setting (time and place), problem (character's attempt to solve problems), goal (character's plan to solve the problem), main events of the story, and resolution (see the online reproducibles for Chapter 6).

Story Plans provide a concise way of summarizing stories because readers choose only the events leading directly to the resolution of the problem. If students first define the problem and resolution, they will have a way to sort through the story details. They can narrow down details to those that directly lead to the solution of the problem.

Introduction, Modeling, and Reflection

1. Explain to students that most stories have certain elements in common and understanding these components leads to improved comprehension.
2. Model how to develop a Story Plan with a simple story such as *The True Story of the Three Little Pigs* by A. Wolf as told to Jon Scieszka. Guide the discussion with questions:

Setting questions	Where did the story occur? When did the story occur?
Character questions	Who is the main character? Who is this story most about?
Problem and Goal questions	What major problem does the main character face? What does the character hope to achieve?
Problem and Goal questions	Does the character solve the problem? Is the character defeated by the problem? Does the character learn to live with the problem?

Organizing Learning: Two-Column Notes, Frames, and Story Plans

A completed Story Plan for *The True Story of the Three Little Pigs* might look something like this:

Setting	Wolf's neighborhood, way back in "once upon a time"
Characters	Wolf, three pigs, reporters, police
Problem	Wolf doesn't have any sugar for his Granny's cake
Goal	Make a birthday cake for Granny
Events	Wolf visits first neighbor pig in straw house to get sugar—no answer; wolf sneezes, house falls down and accidently kills pig. He eats it.
	Visits next neighbor to get sugar; house built out of sticks; pig tells him to go away, he sneezes, house falls down, accidentally kills second pig. He eats it.
	Visits third neighbor pig; house built with bricks, pig is obnoxious, tells him to go away, makes fun of his granny, wolf tries to destroy house, goes to jail.
Resolution	Wolf goes to jail; doesn't get to make cake.

3. Together use the Story Plan to write a summary.

Reflection

How does the Story Plan help you analyze narratives? How might you use Story Plans in your book discussion group? Why are Story Plans an excellent way to summarize narratives? How might they be used to help in the writing of original stories?

Support and Extensions

- Have students do several different Story Plans for a selection. Each plan should have a different problem statement. For example with *The True Story of the 3 Little Pigs* the problem statements might be:
    - The wolf is misrepresented in the original story of the *Three Little Pigs*.
    - The wolf has a bad cold.
    - The wolf is a murderer.

    After students have brainstormed different problem statements, divide them into groups. Have each group develop a Story Plan for one problem statement. Then have groups present their plans and convince other class members that the story events and the resolution provide evidence that their problem is developed in the story.

- Story Plans can be adapted for more challenging texts. The following example summarizes, *New Directions* by Maya Angelou.

Story Plan/Title: "New Directions" by Maya Angelou		
Setting	What is the time and place?	1903, rural Arkansas
Main Characters	What is the major difficulty the main character is facing?	Annie Johnson, illiterate and poor, was abandoned by her husband and left to care for their children without financial support. Annie is facing survival for herself and her children.
Goal	What does the character hope to achieve?	Annie hopes to make a living without neglecting her children. She hopes to have the skills and the ambition to "cut a path" to survive.
Events	What are the key steps the main character takes to achieve the goal?	Decided not to work at the town's cotton gin or lumber mill, but to "cut a new path." Walked to both factories carrying stones to see how much food she could carry. Made and carried meat pastries to sell at the factories each day. Built a stall between the two factories so the workers would come to her for hot lunchtime provisions. The stall eventually became a successful store where customers bought many commodities.
Resolution	Does the main character solve the problem? How does the story end?	Yes, Annie was a survivor. She became a successful storeowner and was able to care for her children. The story ends by telling us that "we have the ability to assess the roads which lie ahead, and those which we have traveled, and if the future looms ominous or unpromising, and the roads back uninviting, then we need to gather our resolve and carrying only the necessary baggage, step off that road in to another direction." In other words, no matter what the obstacles, you must persevere.

- Once students have a basic understanding of a Story Plan, extend their understanding by explaining that problems in stories are resolved in one of three ways: the character can solve the problem, the problem defeats the character, or the character simply learns to live with the situation. Students can use this format for thinking through problem-resolution in class novels and in their independent reading. Use the Story Plan Map that follows as a tool for analyzing the three possible resolutions.

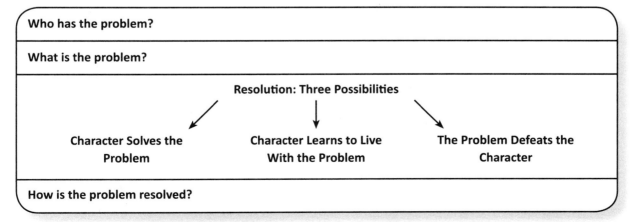

Organizing Learning: Two-Column Notes, Frames, and Story Plans

- Have students develop Story Plans for media presentations (e.g. television, movies).
- Have students use Story Plans for drafting their own stories. Before students write, encourage them to think about the characters, setting, problem, and solution. After students have drafted their stories, use Story Plans for revision conferences. They can use a checklist similar to the following for making decisions about revision:

    Will the reader be able to describe the setting?

    Who is the main character?

    What is the main character like?

    What problem does the main character need to resolve?

    How is the problem resolved? Do we know?

    If students find out they do not have these components in their stories, they will have some specific ideas for revision.
- Modified Story Frames can be used for non-fiction situations. Following are some examples.

History

After reading about an event in history or a current event article, have students in pairs or cooperative groups fill out a Story Plan from the perspective of one of the parties involved. In the Teapot Dome scandal example that follows, students filled out the frame from the perspective of Secretary of the Interior Albert Fall.

Event	Teapot Dome Scandal
Setting	Washington, DC & Teapot Dome, WY - 1923
Characters	Pres. Warren G. Harding, Interior Secretary Albert B. Fall
Problem	Oil rich land in Wyoming is to be used by the Navy.
Goal	Secretary Fall wanted to get rich.
Events	Harding, overwhelmed by presidency, gives Cabinet positions to friends.
	Profitable oil reserves found in Wyoming are earmarked for Navy Fall, one of the "friends."
	He sells off drilling leases to private companies (illegally & secretly).
	Fall gets cash, stocks, and cattle as bribes from the companies.
	Congress discovers the fraud.
	Harding becomes ill and dies before all is resolved.
	Fall is convicted and sent to jail.
Resolution	Fall loses everything and goes to jail.

Mathematics

Use the modified Story Frame to help students solve open-ended math problems or as an organizer for developing their own written problems.

Example:

Your mother sends you to the store with $5.00 and asks you to buy fruit for a fruit salad she plans to make. She doesn't care what you get as long as you get at least three types of fruit, and so long as it makes enough for exactly 10 people— she wants to have enough, but no leftovers. She gives you the information in Chart 1 to help with your selections. You discover the information in Chart 2 when you get to the store.

Single Serving Size for Various Fruits	
Fruit	**Serving Size**
Orange	1
Apple	1
Kiwi	3
Banana	1
Strawberries	½ pint
Raspberries	½ pint

Grocery Store Prices for Fruit	
Fruit	**Cost**
Orange	3 for $1.00
Apple	4 for $1.00
Kiwi	4 for $1.00
Banana	6 for $1.00
Strawberries	1 pint for $1.50
Raspberries	1 pint for $3.00

The store allows you to buy oranges, bananas, apples, kiwis, and bananas one at a time, but the smallest amount of either strawberries or raspberries is one pint. How much money do you return to your mother and what is your fruit salad recipe?

Setting	Kitchen and grocery store
People/things involved	Mother and me
Goal	Make a fruit salad which costs $5.00 or less, serves exactly 10 people, and contains at least three kinds of fruit.
Important information or "givens"	How much fruit provides enough for one serving (see Chart 1). Cost of the individual types of fruit (see Chart 2).

Steps to Solution	1. Since the raspberries are so expensive, I don't think I will use them.
	2. I will try to use the remaining fruits and a similar amount for each.
	3. Since I can't divide the strawberries, I will buy 1 pt which serves 2 people and costs $1.50.
	4. I have four fruits left and need eight more servings so I will try two servings of each and see how the money comes out
	    2 oranges @ .33 = $0.66
	    2 apples @ .25 = 0.50
	    2 x 3 kiwis @ .25 = 1.50
	    2 bananas @ .17 = 0.34
	5. $3.00 plus the $1.50 for strawberries makes a total of $4.50.

Solution	Return $.50 to mother, salad contains 2 each of oranges, apples, and bananas, 6 kiwis, and a pint of strawberries.
Check Solution	I went back and rechecked my calculations. The answer seems reasonable to me since I have lots of fruit, and I did not go over the $5.00 which Mom gave me.

Science

This modified Story Plan guides student explanations of a process; in this case, photosynthesis.

Process	Photosynthesis
Setting	Daylight, time of year when plants are not dormant (some photosynthesis actually happens in dark, too).
Components	Any green plant (having chlorophyll), light, carbon dioxide, water
Goal	Changing light energy into chemical energy
Steps	Carbon dioxide and water are taken in by the chlorophyll-bearing cells in a plant. When light energy is added, oxygen and glucose are formed. $$6\ CO_2\ \text{(carbon dioxide)} + 6\ H_2O\ \text{(water)} \xrightarrow{\text{Light Energy}} C_6H_{12}O_6\ \text{(glucose)} + 6\ O_2\ \text{(oxygen)}$$
Results	The glucose that the plant forms is used as a source of stored energy for the plant. The chemical energy is used also by animals that eat the plant. The oxygen that is a byproduct is used by animals for breathing.

▲ ▲ ▲

Summary

In this chapter, we explored a variety of ways to organize and structure text information. We know successful readers glean main points from their reading assignments and have specific strategies such as Main Idea—Detail Notes and Content Frames for organizing information they've read. In order to succeed, students must organize and apply information from their reading.

In addition to helping our students understand the main ideas from their reading, we encourage higher levels of thinking. The instructional strategies for evaluating opinions, problems, and issues help students think critically about their reading. Students develop support for opinions, define propositions, analyze problems, identify processes, and analyze the literary elements in narratives. As teachers, we must model options and teach for competence in these strategies so students have the confidence to develop their own individual study plans.

CHAPTER 6 RESEARCH BASE

Research Conclusion	Reference
Organizing information is essential for learning from text.	Bransford, Brown, & Cocking, 2000
Generative learning or meaningful learning occurs when readers themselves generate meaningful relationships among ideas. In a variety of situations, learning through constructing relationships (constructing graphs and charts, composing titles, writing summaries) results in better comprehension than in situations where students did not use these processes.	Wittrock, 1992
Teaching students to analyze stories improves comprehension as measured by performance in answering questions and in recalling information. Knowledge of story structure led to higher standardized test performance, particularly for less able readers in grades 3-6.	Trabasso and Bouchard, 2002

The positive relationship between writing and reading has strong research support. Graham and Hebert (2010) conducted a meta-analysis of empirical research investigating the effectiveness of using writing to improve reading comprehension. The results are clear: writing about text leads to improved understanding. When students respond to text by writing personal reactions and by analyzing and interpreting the text, they have a better understanding of text material. Writing about what is read produces more gains in comprehension than just reading, reading and rereading, and/or reading and studying the material. These effects hold for a variety of content domains and grade levels.

These results make sense when considering what it takes to comprehend and write about text. To comprehend, we must actively engage in building relationships among ideas and in integrating ideas into our background knowledge. Writing engenders active participation and helps us know if we know (metacognition). If we can write about content and explain what we are learning, we can claim knowledge as our own.

During the first weeks of school, we ask students to keep their writing in learning logs. These logs become a regular part of our classroom routines. Learning logs can deepen student ownership by providing a safe place to speculate, seek, discover, and figure things out. Through writing, learning logs are more about *thinking* than polished writing. Nonetheless, the more students record their thoughts in writing, the better writers, readers, and more active learners they become.

We recommend introducing learning logs by explaining why writing is essential for learning. Let students know that entries may include lab results, process steps, observations, and questions about vocabulary or difficult concepts. These entries are often messy, with thoughts scratched out and arrows indicating added information.

While listening to a speaker (invited guest or teacher) or while viewing a video, students might write in their logs two or three times during a class period. Speakers should pause frequently to allow students time for writing down ideas and questions and to let them share their responses before moving on to the next part of the presentation. Mixing writing with listening and discussion helps energize students. It is harder to stare blankly into space when you know you are expected to write about and discuss information from a lecture or visual presentation.

Writing also prepares students for discussion. When they write about their thinking before they talk in their groups or with the whole class community, discussions become richer and more interactive.

Sometimes entries have focus; in other situations, they are completely open-ended. Free-Writes, Dialogue Journals, and Perspective Entries generate more open-ended responses than those where students write explanations, develop pre/post entries, or write about their observations. The response depends upon the content and goals of a lesson. This chapter offers a variety of learning log options.

Free-Write Entries

Whenever students read, view, or listen and then write without a teacher's specific direction about what and how to do it, they are making a Free-Write Entry. By design, Free-Writes help students to connect with the material and to think more deeply about their reading. Readers learn to trust their own instincts while they speculate, question, and find meaning as they write. Free-Writes help students connect with the piece and untangle challenging ideas.

Introduction, Modeling, and Reflection

1. Project a prompt or series of prompts based on your content materials: a novel, an article, a non-fiction book, section of the textbook, or a poem. Prompts may include:
   - quotations pulled directly from the content
   - a key idea from the content/questions based on the content video or audio clips
   - photographs, other images, or special objects that relate to the content

   Display the first prompt. Explain, *Write freely about anything that comes to mind. Express your own opinions, ideas, and questions. No one is going to grade your responses.*

2. Model your own response with items crossed off and words tumbling across the page. Your model will help everyone feel safe about taking risks.

3. After a few minutes, ask students to finish their responses to the first prompt. Display the remaining prompts one at a time, allowing them two or three minutes to write about each one.

4. When students have responded to all the prompts, invite them to reread their responses. *Mark any phrases, questions, words, or ideas you find promising. Note ideas that could be developed further. Talk about some of these possibilities with your partner. Are there any excerpts or ideas you want to share with the whole group?*

Reflection

How do Free-Writes help you become more engaged in reading? How did this strategy work for you? How did it help with your discussions, with your understanding of the selection? How did it help you become more metacognitive?

Support and Extensions

- <u>Stop-and-Think</u>. This adaptation works well for students reading a novel as a class or as part of a literature study group. At the end of a reading period, ask students to *Stop and Think* about what they have read. Ask them to write non-stop. For less able writers and younger students, begin with three-minute writings and gradually work up to ten minutes. Use a timer. Next, ask students to share their entries with the class. Accept their ideas. Listen intensely. Repeat what the writer says. If it seems right, delve more deeply: *I am interested in what you said about . . . What made you say this?* Your modeling and interest show you really care about their ideas. Gradually, students will begin to trust their own ideas and thinking.

Informal Writing to Learn

In the following example, an eleventh grade reader responds to a selection from the novel *The Things They Carried* by Tim O'Brien.

> This isn't a book where you'd expect to find rhythm, but as he explained what each soldier carried — military equipment relevant to their role in the platoon, their responsibility to the other men, their personal baggage, their photographs... all these burdens they carry — physical and mental as they trudge through the landscape. Are these things listed because they will play a part later in the book — or are they included to illustrate each of the characters' particular idiosyncrasies?

- Encourage Free-Write responses in the form of questions. Begin by explaining how good readers constantly question the text before, during, and after reading. Model questions that come to mind as you read a literary excerpt, a current events article, or a math problem. Stop and let students do the same thing.

Here, an Algebra teacher had students develop questions based on the chapter about functions:

I am having a hard time understanding what a function is. The explanation with x's and y's is hard to follow. It has to do with ordered pairs and graphs, but I don't know why the graphs on page 138 are different from the one at the top of page 139. Next question: Can the x value of a pair ever be the value of the function? Next question: Are all linear equations functions?

In this example, high school students wrote freely about a political cartoon. Questions naturally emerged in the writing.

- 172   Chapter 7

- As a pre-reading activity, have students examine pictures relevant to the upcoming topic and write about their feelings, ideas, and predictions. In this example, Florida middle school students observed a photograph of a hurricane before reading a scientific article explaining how hurricanes develop.

> When I see this picture I get scared. I think of Hurricane Wilma 2 years ago. The house was shaking the front door almost busted. We were hiding in my parents closet. We had no power so we had to listen to a portable radio. After it was done we went outside. Trees were down lites were broken in the whole neighborhood. All the neighbors came out. We all helped each other. We missed school for 3 weeks.

- As in the above example, teachers and counselors have students process their emotions in writing. These can be shared or not as appropriate. Students may choose to format them as letters, poems, etc.
- Use Free-Writes as exit slips. During the last few minutes of class, have students write about something they learned, something they have questions about, or something that struck them as being significant or important. The 3-2-1 process is popular; students write 3 things they learned (very brief summary), 2 questions they have, and 1 connection or reaction. Collect these slips as students leave the class. Use their ideas and questions as feedback for planning.
- Ask students to draw a picture of their reaction to what they read or watched.
- If students are having trouble getting started, encourage them with Writing Templates or guide questions. See page 195 for more information on Writing Templates.

WRITING TEMPLATES
Making Connections to the Text
This chapter/section was . . . (Use a descriptive word here - exciting, scary, sad, confusing, etc.) when . . . (Tell what in the selection made it that way)
This chapter/selection made me feel. . . .
_____ from the book/selection reminded me of . . . in my life (in another book, etc.)
I can really relate to . . . because. . . .
I like the way the author . . . because. . . .
I didn't like . . . because. . . .
Explaining Ideas in Your Own Words
Explain this so that a fifth grader would understand. Draw pictures or diagrams if you think it will help clarify your meaning.
In plain English, this equation/selection says. . . .
I could use the information I learned to. . . .
Addressing the Confusion
I was confused when. . . It was confusing because. . . .
I don't understand why the author. . . because. . . .
I don't understand . . . (What is the problem?) because . . . (What makes the problem or selection difficult?) I can figure it out if . . . (How can you get the information your need?)

Informal Writing to Learn

> **GUIDE TEMPLATES**
>
> **Guide Questions**
> - What are you thinking?
> - What does . . . stand for/mean?
> - Why did you write that equation/response?
> - Why does that last step make sense? Explain.
> - What were you thinking about when you did . . .?
> - Could you have done this in a different way?

Double-Entry Reflective Journals

Double-Entry Reflective Journals help students become more aware of their thinking while reading (Tovani, 2000 & 2004). Students divide their papers lengthwise or create a digital table, as if they are going to take Two-Column Notes. On the left side of the paper, readers record quotes, comments, or summary statements from the materials they are reading and then use the space on the right to note their thoughts.

Picture, Direct Quote, or Summary	Thinking Prompts:
(Give source and page number.)	I wonder . . . This reminds me of . . . I predict . . . I am confused because . . . I will help myself by . . . I think this means . . .

Tovani recommends modeling one prompt at a time. After students are comfortable using that prompt, add others.

Introduction, Modeling, and Reflection

1. Select one prompt such as *This reminds me of...* and write it on the top of the right-hand column.

2. Read a selection aloud. As you read, write down a quotation, a single word, or a summary statement on the left side. Think-aloud, demonstrating how the quote ignited connections with your own background or with other things you have read or experienced. Briefly summarize these connections in the right-hand column. Continue modeling.

3. Once students feel comfortable with one thinking option, introduce another following a similar instructional procedure. Take time for reflection.

You might choose an option that illustrates challenges students might meet in a particular piece of writing. Asking students to note their confusion (*I am confused because . . .*) helps prevent them from becoming overwhelmed by difficult materials. In fact, the struggle to wade through obtuse writing can actually be invigorating. In the following example, the teacher asked her advanced chemistry students to read a challenging assignment and complete Double-Entry Reflective Journals. Before students read, she projected a brief list of quotations from the text for students to write about in their journals. Asking students to read and speculate about the ideas turned out to be good preparation for class discussion. She found that students actually read their assignments and came to class prepared with questions about the key scientific concepts. She began her lecture by listing students' questions and then she addressed these questions as part of her presentation.

"Protons, neutrons, and electrons are the most stable subatomic particles."	**I am confused because...** *I don't know what the author means by stable. The author seems to think I should already know this.* **I will help myself by...** *rereading the previous sections in this chapter and by reading further to see if the author explains it. He seems to think I should already know this and I don't. Maybe I can ask my lab partner about it. She always seems to know everything.*
"Atoms contain protons, neutrons, and electrons, all arranged in a definite manner."	**I am confused because...** *I don't know what is meant by definite. Does it mean unchanging? I think this might be the point of this section, but I am not getting it.* **I will help myself by...** *trying to figure out the table. It could have something to do with atomic number, but I don't really understand that either. I am going to ask about this in class.*

Encouraging students to struggle with their confusions helps them to comprehend and guides them to become more active, metacognitive readers, less easily defeated by difficult material. Good readers always have questions.

Reflection

How did identifying meaningful sections of text and responding to them before and after reading help you make meaning? How do the writing prompts fit within the CRISS Framework for Learning?

Support and Extensions

- Make a chart of the thinking prompts as you introduce them.
- In the following example, students were preparing to read an article about the Gilded Age, a period after World War I when there was rapid economic growth and corresponding materialism in the United States. They responded to quotations before and after reading the selection.

Informal Writing to Learn

Quote	Before Reading	After Reading
"Get rich; dishonestly if we can, honestly if we must."	**I think this means...** that some people are so desperate and used to stealing that they have come to think stealing is easier than working. Therefore, it is better.	**This means...** that we are cheap and will do anything to get money for what we want.
"He rewards the loyal, punishes the mutinous, and negotiates treaties. He generally avoids publicity... and is all the more dangerous because he sits, like a spider, hidden in the midst of his web."	**This reminds me...** of a president doing things to help the country, yet not letting anyone know his plan before he strikes.	**This means...** that a typical boss treats his employees like dirt and does favors for nasty people to get money and win elections.

Dialogue Journals

Reading naturally inspires talk. We want our classrooms to mirror real life, in which informal talk about reading and learning occurs everywhere. We also want to encourage students to listen purposefully to one another. One way to achieve this goal is through writing. After students write, ask them to trade logs, read their partner's entries and, without talking to one another, write comments in response. Peer response becomes very motivating. It makes learning more social, and writers get feedback right away. It is also a legitimate way to pass notes in school and creates a context for social engagement.

Dialogue journals work well as online discussions, too. In fact, all of the suggestions offered here for encouraging written conversation can be done digitally. Students can read paper or e-books and respond to the information using electronic journals, blogs, and e-mail exchanges. Introduce students to online discussions by demonstrating login procedures and the features of electronic message boards. Consider using a message board to deliver prompts. For more information on electronic journals see Larson (2009).

Introduction, Modeling, and Reflection

1. Ask students to select partners. Partners will write entries related to the same selection. Provide a purpose or have them do Free-Writes.

2. Model how to respond to a partner. *Write about the ideas presented. Do NOT evaluate your partner's response.* Talk about the language of response. Some starters might be:

    I agree...
    I disagree...
    In my opinion...
    I think...
    I understand what you mean when...

3. Have students pass their logs back and forth or send responses to each other electronically as they read. Challenge them to avoid talking about their entries. *Writing is your conversation.* In this example, the students communicated using a blog. Brandon started the dialogue with a brief blog entry, and then the two boys posted comments in response to each other.

> **A Wrinkle in Time**
>
> *I think the kids are going to the town and get split up. Then one of them will find their father. The other two will probably have to fight the dark thing. And then they will almost get killed and Mrs. Whatsit will save them. – Brandon*

Comments

Jose: *I disagree with you when you say Mrs. Whatsit will save them. I don't think she can. I think Mrs. Whatsit believes these kids will have to solve the problem themselves. She believes in them. Who do you think will find Father?*

Brandon: *I think the Black Thing took over the father and disguised him as the guy with red eyes. Then I think Charles will get into the mind of the guy with red eyes and find out it's Father. Then I think the three kids will release Father from the Black Thing.*

Jose: *I understand what you mean. But I don't agree with you. I think Father is held prisoner somewhere, but not in the guy with red eyes. I think the kids will have to break him out. I am worried that Charles might be a goner. Something seems to be taking him over. What do you think is going on?*

Reflection

How does writing about what you read help you gain more from your reading? How did writing to a partner affect the quality of your entries?

Support and Extensions

- Dialogue entries can be based on field trips, speakers, videos, lab activities, or books students are reading for pleasure. Students can use e-mail at home as well as classroom or laboratory computers to complete their correspondence. Consider connecting your students with email partners from other school districts, states, or countries.

- Include yourself in the conversations. Student-teacher dialogue journals provide a way to "talk" with your students about books they are reading or concerns and ideas they have about content. You also learn more about individual students in your classroom. Frequently, writing brings forth more personal ideas than does talking. Keep it manageable by writing to three or four students in your class each day and by responding digitally. By the end of several weeks, you will have written at least once to each student. Use your responses to focus students on important content and on analytic ideas. Notice how Donna Duval does this in her response to one of her student's entries.

> Article: From Sea to Supermarkets
>
> Source: New York Times
>
> Topics: dolphin hunts
>
> After Reading this Article, I felt sick to my stomach. How could people kill and eat dolphins. I remember swimming with them during a vacation in Hawaii. They are so smart & gentle. They are so cute!
>
> I totally agree. I remember watching Flipper on TV when I grew up. It breaks my heart thinking that people could eat him. Then I thought about how India holds the cow sacred, how Ecuadorians eat guinea pigs or how Asian cultures don't give a second thought about eating dogs. Is it wrong or just culturally different? What do we eat or do that others would find wrong?
>
> Ms. Duvall I haven't thought about it this way, but now that you mention it, it reminds me of NACIREMA! Our culture is odd to others so maybe what they are doing is OK. Maybe it wouldn't be OK if the animals were on the endangered species list. I think I want to investigate this for my final project.
>   Alii'a

- Create "Must Read" wall posters. Feature a book or article. Have groups of students write their dialogue entries on chart paper or as a blog. The entries can focus on texts students are reading as a whole class, in small groups, or individually; other students record brief comments or ask questions about the book on the chart paper. Making these discussions public provides a way to champion books that students are reading or may want to read.

Pre- and Post-Reading Entries

Pre- and Post-Reading Entries provide a natural way for students to link their own background knowledge to content, to set purposes for reading, to note pre-reading misconceptions, and to become more metacognitive.

Introduction, Modeling, and Reflection

1. List key concepts from a reading selection. Ask students to create Pre-Reading Entries in their logs about what they think the concepts mean, and then have them talk with a partner.
2. As a whole class, discuss the ideas and questions generated in the pre-reading discussions.
3. After reading, have students write again, this time adding new information and correcting any misconceptions they might have had about the content before reading. See the Social Studies and Science examples that follow.

Social Studies

Topic: Creation of a federal law

Pre-reading: *I think laws are created by either the president of the U.S. or senators or representatives. They write up what they want and then they all vote on it. If a representative starts the law, then I think just the House of Representatives has to vote on it, plus the president has to agree. I think it is the same in the Senate. If most of the senators vote for a law and the president likes it, then it becomes a real law. I think the Supreme Court might have something to do with it because of the "balance of power" thing, but I'm not sure what they do.*

Post-reading: *I kind of had the right idea, except that what the senators and representatives write up is called a "bill." The bill has to be passed in both houses, and a lot of the time what they pass is different in each house, so they have to get together in a committee. The committee has both House and Senate members and they try to agree on one bill that is between the two different ones. If they can agree and pass the same bill in both houses, and the president signs it, then it becomes a law. The president can veto it if he doesn't like it, but then the houses can override the veto with a 2/3s vote in each house. The Supreme Court gets in there if someone thinks the new law is unconstitutional. If the Court thinks it is too, then the Court can kill it.*

Science

Topic: Glaciers

Pre-reading: *Glaciers form where it is very cold, usually on mountaintops. They are really just lots of snow that does not melt during the summer time. They can be found in Alaska, Glacier National Park, and probably the Alps. They are dirty on the top with cracks where some explorers have fallen into them and died. I think someone died on Mt. Everest by falling into one of the cracks. I think some are really old like a million years ago during the ice age.*

Post-reading: *Some of my ideas were a little off. Glaciers are more than just snow, but they start as snow. When the snow gets really deep—100s of feet—it is so heavy that it packs down the bottom part and turns it into ice. Because of the weight above, the ice flows forward—like when you step on a rubber ball and it squishes out beneath your shoe. This movement is really slow, about one foot a year, but still the glaciers changed the shape of the earth. Like they made mountain valleys and lakes. They also made hills and put a lot of gravel in the soil. The Great Lakes were made by glaciers. There are still glaciers today like I said, and they do have cracks called crevices. The last ice age was actually 11,000 years ago, not a million years ago.*

As an additional post-reading entry, ask students to write a process entry. For example, *What did writing about your ideas before and after reading do for you as a learner?"*

Process: *I felt more interested in reading about glaciers because I thought about it before I read. I was surprised I knew as much about them before reading the assignment. Writing helped me put down what I already knew. It made me more interested in reading because I wanted to know if I was right. Knowing that I was going to have to write when I finished reading made me read more carefully. I learned more.*

Reflection

In what ways did Pre- and Post-Reading Entries incorporate the elements of the Framework for Learning? How did Pre- and Post-Reading Entries help you become more metacognitive? In what ways were you more actively engaged in reading the selection? How was your reading more purposeful? Did the reading either support or contradict anything in your pre-reading entry?

Support and Extensions

- Pre- and Post-Reading Entries can also be used before and after viewing a video, listening to a speaker, doing a lab, or going on a field trip.
- Use Pre- and Post-Reading Entries with online selections. Students first preview for key ideas by viewing pictures, page titles, headings, and subheadings, and then they write an electronic pre-reading entry. After reading, they write again, adding information and correcting misinformation.

Observation Entries

Learning logs are vehicles for seeing more clearly and for developing and recording ideas. Learning logs inspire precise observations which naturally lead to questions. As students write their observations, they discover meaning in what they see.

Introduction, Modeling, and Reflection

1. Ask students to look at an object in your classroom. Model writing your observations. Carefully note each detail; talk aloud as you write about what you see. In this example, a science teacher distributed a fresh cut flower to each cooperative team. The teacher modeled the following entry:

   Observation Entry: *Right below the outside of the flower, the stem thickens into a little case or holder for supporting the flower. It looks almost like a crown. I see a ring of petals. The petals are in two layers. The lower petals are greener and look more stem-like than the upper petals. I wonder what use all of these petals have? Maybe they attract bees. Maybe they protect the flower in some way. Next, I see a ring of petal-like parts in the middle of the flower. There are four of these, and each tiny petal has two sharp parts. Are these the stamens or pistils?*

2. Talk about how writing helps you to think about what you have seen. Notice how observations automatically lead to questions for further exploration.

3. Have students pick an item to observe, and then have them write an observation entry and share with partners and the class.

Reflection
How did writing about the object help you notice more than you realized? How did writing help you better understand what you observed?

Support and Extensions

- Use observation journals as pre- and post-learning activities. In the following example, a biology teacher asked her students to observe an unfamiliar specimen through a dissection microscope. After students wrote their observations, she provided additional information about what they had seen and then asked them to observe the specimen again and do a second journal entry describing the specimen using new information they had just learned.

   Pre-entry: *The size of the creature is about 3 centimeters long and 1.5 centimeters at its peak. It has a flat bottom with a rounded back. It is not circular but more oval. It has a hard shell that is rounded but has a flat fleshy underside. Its shell is blue, brown, and green and appears to have a calcium deposit on it. It has an orifice on the underside and the space between where the flesh begins and the shell ends. This could be used to create a suction to stick to something.*

Post-entry: *The limpet is unusually large at 3 cm long and 1.5 cm at the top of its shell; most limpets are slightly smaller. Limpets often live in tidal areas and the shape of their shells provide protection against the waves. Limpets aren't normally very colorful—I think that the blues and greens on this shell are from algae, the primary food of a limpet. The underside of the limpet is mostly taken up by its foot (the limpet is a gastropod). I thought the gap between the shell and the flesh helped the limpet hold onto rocks but it turns out the foot holds it in place and helps it move. The gap actually helps water flow over the gills. Once I looked more closely, I was able to see the limpet's head which had eyes on tentacles and a tiny mouth.*

- A high school football coach asked his players to view a video from their last game. They wrote about their observations. *What advice would you give to our team? How could we make this play more effective?* Writing helped his players begin to see how they might win the next game.

You Ought to Be in Pictures

When looking at paintings, old photographs in family albums, or photos of historic events, we often imagine what life was like for the people captured in those images. What life events were reflected in Mona Lisa's face? What stories lie behind photos of farm families abandoning their homes during the Great Depression?

Pictures call forth emotions, feelings, and responses that can communicate far beyond the written word. Frequently, photographs and other visuals embedded in text are ignored, or at best receive cursory attention as readers rush to complete assignments. Yet a few minutes spent walking through the visuals can bring readers into the text before they start to read. You Ought to Be in Pictures (Buehl, 2009) invites students to step inside an image and become a quiet observer, connecting conceptually and emotionally with people and events in the scene.

Introduction, Modeling, and Reflection

1. Identify a photograph or series of photographs that connect to your enduring understandings and will evoke emotions and/or pique the interest of your students. Images should capture ideas and themes.

2. Display the image for students and direct them to examine the details. The first few times, guide students by modeling your thought processes as you analyze the picture contents and then imagine yourself as a participant.

Riis, J.A. (ca. 1890). *In the home of an Italian rag-picker, Jersey Street* [photograph]. From How the Other Half Lives (1901).

Your think aloud might go something like this:

The title of the photo is "In the home of an Italian rag-picker, Jersey Street". It was taken around 1890 in New York City. I'm going to spend some time thinking and writing about this picture, using a strategy called You Ought to Be in Pictures.

As I look at this photo, the first thing I notice is the expression on the woman's face. She looks resigned, but almost hopeful. Notice the slight upturn of her lip – is she smiling? What could that mean? In her arms is a baby. It's wrapped up in a lot of cloth – it makes me think it's a cooler season. Look at her hands! Those are not dainty hands – she obviously works hard. They look banged up. But they are holding the child, protecting it.

Now, I let my eyes travel around the space. There's a ladder, but I can't see what it leads to. Maybe a loft where they sleep? I don't see any bedding anywhere.

She's got piles of what looks like burlap bags around her. I read somewhere that ragpickers dig through trash and collect rags to sell – I wonder if that's what those bags are. What else is there? A barrel, some metal basins… on the right in the foreground there's a cast iron stove, but no wood or coal. Everything is barren; there's nothing personal – like she's just borrowing the space. It looks cold. Dirty. A harsh place to have to be.

Now that I've looked at the photo from an outside perspective, it's time to step into the picture and do some writing from the perspective of one of the people in the photo. I can choose the mother or her baby. Let me show you.

The teacher models the act of writing for students in real time. She writes:

When we left Italy, we were promised good jobs and a good living. We gave up everything we had to pay our way. It was a difficult trip, but we made it to New York. We were so excited to see the Statue of Liberty – the proud lady welcoming us. But the fates and the crooked men who made false promises, had something else in store for us.

We live in a slum. It's dark and dirty. There are no good jobs, so we sift through trash and ashes at the dump heaps every day, searching for scraps to sell. I want more for my bambino – a better life; not this.

Or from the baby's perspective:

I was just a little bambino when my mother lived in New York. She tells me it was a dark time. They spoke no English. They survived by renting space in the slums. They had nothing of their own but the clothes on their backs. She worked long, hard hours, and it was years before they could save enough pennies to get out of the slum. As difficult as it was, she was proud. She did her best to keep things clean and keep me fed.

Students in Donna Duval's high school history class completed You Ought to Be in Pictures journal entries after learning about the Gilded Age in America. This example, using the same Ragpicker photograph, demonstrates how students start to get a feel for life in another time.

> I work all day and clean and watch the child. I try my best to keep things clean, but I never seem to get it clean enough. I pray that my child doesn't have to live like this forever. I work so hard with my husband — we can barely pay the rent for this dingy place. We have nothing. Was it worth leaving our family in Italy for this?

3. Using another image, ask students to take on the persona of one of the characters in the image and write a diary entry, a letter to someone from the time, a letter to the grandchild of someone in the picture (from the perspective of the grandparent), or the thoughts of the person as s/he lives in that moment. Some guide questions for students include:
    - What are you thinking?
    - How do you feel?
    - Why are you where you are? What got you here?
    - What do you predict will happen tomorrow?
    - What are your memories of this day and the events that took place?

4. Provide time for students to share their writing. Guided trips into visual history like this humanize events in ways text rarely can, and making these kinds of connections opens students to deeper learning about the content.

Reflection
How did viewing and writing about an image help to engage you in learning? How did "getting into" the visual improve your understanding of the content? How does this strategy fit into your Framework for Learning?

Support and Extensions

- Using photographs or diagrams from other content areas (e.g. science, math, literature), ask students to become witnesses to details which may or may not include people. For example, they can step inside photographs of deforested areas to explain what they see and how it makes them feel, or join a character on an epic journey and record his/her observations and feelings as a member of the team, or even step inside a diagram or figure and discuss the relationship of one element to another – such as a point on a graph or a variable in an equation.

- Walking Through a Painting (Granat, 2004). Share pictures from art calendars, museums, and other sources. Ask students to look carefully at one of the pictures. After about three minutes, have them jot down answers to the following (or similar) questions:

    What is the first thing you notice in the picture?

    Describe one of the images in detail.

    What are the predominant colors?

    How do the colors make you feel?

    What is the mood–peaceful, melancholy, cheerful?

    Look at any lines in the work. Are they narrow, wide, curved? Do the lines control the way you look at the picture?

    How effective is the composition of this work? Does it add to or detract from its impact?

    After students have recorded their answers to these questions, ask them to "step inside" the picture and write about what is going on around them. *Do you feel comfortable? What do you see, smell, and hear? What happened right before this painting was frozen in time? Does the picture remind you of a place you have been?*

Perspective Entries

In Perspective Entries students can take on the roles of characters, animals, famous people, even inanimate objects. Students might choose a literary character and write what that person is thinking and feeling. They can write from the perspective of a water droplet moving through the water cycle. Or, they can choose to be a point in a normal statistical distribution.

Introduction, Modeling, and Reflection

1. Select a character from a story or a person in history or from a current event. Talk briefly about the person's situation, and then brainstorm how that person might feel or act, what decisions the person might make, or what actions that person might take.

2. Next, have students select a person, animal, or thing from a previous unit of study (e.g., students in a history class might choose a famous explorer or leader). *Develop entries giving clues about the person's life. Think aloud about the person's circumstances. Put yourself into the mind of the character. Find your voice. What are you feeling? What are your goals? Challenges? Worries? Write what you imagine s/he/it would write in a diary, letter, or blog.*

This example shows a progression of journal entries throughout the life of Meriwether Lewis:

> **July 27, 1779** — Today Daddy died. Why I don't know, but he did!!! Mummy will be so sad.
>
> **April 4, 1788** — Mother has remarried to a different man. He will be my new father, but I will always remember my real dad.
>
> **Oct 9, 1792** — The President has asked me to be his private secretary. He is a good fellow with a kind heart. I will live with him at Monticello when he goes there to escape the torrid summer in Washington.
>
> **Oct 13, 1793** — After being with the president one year, he has been very kind to me. He has been the father I have never had. He even asked me to head the Voyage of Discovery that will take my travels through the Louisiana Purchase territory. This should be very interesting! I will leave soon to start this wonderful journey

Reflection

How did writing a Perspective Entry help you transform and change information? How do perspective journals compare with writing a traditional report on a famous person? How did taking on the persona help you understand?

Support and Extensions

- Use Perspective Entries for novel studies. Taking on the role of a character helps students empathize with a character's feelings and problems.
- Students can take on historical and scientific perspectives. In the following example, students took on the role of a kapok tree in Ecuador. The oil barons are coming to convert the rainforest to an oil field. The tree "keeps" a journal of observations and changes.

Informal Writing to Learn 185

Entry 1

I am so tall that I see for miles, stretching over the tops of all the trees. My relatives live in Africa. I grow beside the Napo River in Ecuador. The Huaorani villagers tell me I may be close to 200 years old. My limbs reach over 100 feet high and my trunk is so wide–at least 15 feet across.

Entry 2

Humans have been my friend for over 200 years. Right now Amo and Enqueri are in their tree fort which I shelter for them. None of the other children in their nearby Huaorani village know our secret. I always nestle my leaves close around them so they can't be seen in their hideout.

Entry 3

I see a group of Huaorani elders meeting with members of the Shell Oil Company. The company wants to build a road into the rainforest so they can cut down trees and take the oil. I have seen trees fall all around me as they build this road. I think I will be next. There is no way the Huaorani can fight with an oil company.

Explanation Entries

When students write explanations of ideas and concepts, they discover whether or not they truly understand. These entries are powerful ways to learn vocabulary concepts or to understand the steps of a process in science (photosynthesis), mathematics (solving a problem), art (throwing a pot), and technology (adding a video to a PowerPoint presentation).

Introduction, Modeling, and Reflection

1. Talk about the importance of writing complete explanations so someone who doesn't know the concept or process can clearly understand it and/or follow the steps.

2. Model by asking students to write the steps involved in a simple process with which they are familiar, such as tying shoelaces. After they have created their written explanations, have them read their steps out loud while someone tries to follow the directions. Make sure listeners don't do anything not included in the written directions. In most cases, the author will leave out critical parts of the explanation, e.g., the person tying laces is never told to *pick up* one lace with one hand and the other lace with the other hand. Have students rewrite the directions until their explanations are complete.

3. Next, select a familiar process or concept within your content. Together write an explanation. Have students check the explanation by carrying out the task. In this mathematics example, a teacher models the thinking behind multiplying decimals.

When you are multiplying two decimal numbers, the procedure is really quite simple. For example, remember when you multiplied two numbers such as 32 x 105? It looked like this:

$$\begin{array}{r} 105 \\ \times\ 32 \\ \hline 210 \\ 315 \\ \hline 3360 \end{array}$$

Well, let's say the numbers you wanted to multiply were 1.05 and 3.2. You would do the multiplying exactly the same way, but there has to be a decimal in the answer. You can figure out where it goes in two ways. First, just look at the numbers. The first one is about 1 and the second one is around 3. If you multiply 1 x 3 you get 3, so in the decimal problem your answer would be just a little more than three, or 3.360. Another way to do it is to count the numbers to the right of the decimal in the two numbers to be multiplied. There are two in the first number (1.05) and one in the second (3.2). If you add them you get three, so that tells you there should be three numbers to the right of the decimal point in your answer, 3.360 again!

4. Once students are writing explanations on their own, pair them or have them form small groups to test out each other's explanations.

Reflection

How did writing explanations help you be metacognitive? How does writing help you learn and remember the steps in a process?

Support and Extensions

- Explanation Entries are a natural fit for the visual arts. In the following example from Emily Thiessen's art class, a high school student created a linoleum block print entitled *I Miss You* and then wrote an explanation of her thinking behind the creation.

"I Miss You" explains one of the few memories I have with my mom. In short, my mom gave me a red balloon when I was younger, and I ended up in trouble, and she let my balloon go. In this print, my hand is reaching for the balloon as it's floating away. I feel that this print is very symbolic of the relationship between my mother and me. —Chelsie

Informal Writing to Learn   187

- Writing for younger audiences provides older students with an incentive to write clearly. In this case, high school general mathematics students paired with fifth grade pen pals. As the high school students reviewed key mathematical processes, they wrote to fifth graders explaining the processes. Then, the fifth graders responded with comments about whether or not the explanations were clear.

Dear Dawn,

You are wondering how to solve this problem, $3x + x = 12.04$. Well, there are three steps you have to take before you can get the answer. The first step is to add the like terms, which are three x and just x. Don't forget there is a one in front of the plain x. If you add them right, you get 4x. Then you put an equals sign on the right side of the 4x and put the twelve point zero four (12.04) on the right side of the equals sign. Then divide both the 4x and the 12.04 by a plain 4. Do not put the x by the dividing 4. When you are all done, you should have gotten the answer 3.01. Here are the steps you should have taken:

$$3x + x = 12.04$$
$$3x + 1x$$
$$4x = 12.04$$
$$4x/4 = 12.04/4$$
$$1x = 3.01$$
$$x = 3.01$$

I hope you can figure it out.

Your friend,
Brandy

- Add some creativity to students' explanations by combining Explanation and Perspective Entries. The following example is from a high school earth science student explaining the water cycle from the perspective of a water droplet.

> I'm a raindrop named Rose. I was floating around in a lake one day when Kip The Cloud, my boyfriend, came floating by. He invited me for a ride. So, with the help of the sun, I turned into water vapor and drifted on up. We headed up the hill to the new pub by the river where Kip proceeded to get cold. He dropped me for a new drip and headed back out to the lake. I had to hitch a ride with the river to finally make it back to the lake. "Look, here comes Thad, the Thunder Cloud!"

- Writing helps students think through steps in problem solving. In this example, a seventh grade math teacher asked her students to write as they did mathematical computations. Students wrote their own word problems and then explained how to solve them.

    Problem: *Last summer we went camping in Yosemite, and the first night we did a dumb thing—we left our food on the ground. A bear came along and ripped up 1/3 of our total number of dried meals. The next day we ate four of the meals and tied the food up in a tree. It didn't seem to help because 1/3 of the meals we had left were ripped open by another bear. During our third day, we ate four more meals and that night, despite everything we did, 1/2 of the remaining dried meals were ripped apart. We gave up, ate the four remaining dried meals, and headed home. Can you tell how many dried meals we started with?*

    Student's written and computation response:

    To get your answer you have to start at the bottom. It says that half of the remaining meals were eaten to give the 4. So you have to multiply by 2 to undo the half.

    $4 \times 2 = 8$

    This gives you 8. Plus the 4 more meals they ate gives you 12.

    $8 + 4 = 12$

    Now if 1/3 of the number before this was ripped apart, that means that they have 2/3 of that number left. So, 2/3s is 12. So, 6 is half of the 2/3 that is left or 1/3.

    $12/2 = 6$

    Then you have to add 6 to 12 to get 18.

    $6 + 12 = 18$

    Let's double check. If you minus 1/3 (6) from 18 it gives you 12.

    $18 - 6 = 12$

    So that's right. Then, they ate 4 more meals to give them 22 meals.

    $18 + 4 = 22$

    The next step you do is the same as the last. 1/3 of the number before this was ripped apart. You have to find out what half of 22 is, because 22 is equal to 2/3.

    $22/2 = 11$

    And that's how much is left. The number is 11. So add 11 to 22 and it gives you 33.

    $22 + 11 = 33$

    That's your answer: They must have started with 33 dried meals.

Managing and Evaluating Journals and Learning Logs

During the first weeks of school, we ask our students to purchase spiral notebooks or create files on their laptops to use as learning logs. These logs become a regular part of our classroom routines. As you have seen in the preceding pages, students can use logs for free writing, for explanations, for comments about their reading, for scientific observations, and for simply collecting personal thoughts.

We recommend reading student logs (not necessarily every entry, nor every student's log every day) to gain rich knowledge about our students and about their understanding of content. Their written questions and confusions can guide your planning and instruction. Whenever appropriate, try to respond to students. Ask students to leave you a space to write back or respond to them electronically. Your responses will encourage them to take their logs more seriously. Nudge students on with your written questions and encourage them to write back to you. This personal dialogue provides the individual attention so often missing for middle level and high school students.

We don't grade the individual entries, but often give points for completion. Some students need "point" motivation to take their informal writing seriously. In most situations, writing supports learning and is worthy of a grade, but we do not recommend weighing journals such that they make or break a grade. Learning logs are not a place for grading conventions or handwriting. If you can understand the ideas, the student should earn credit for the assignment. Another way to address grading is to ask students to work on improving one conventions error per entry (e.g., there/their, capitalization, end punctuation). This lightens the teacher's load, informs future instruction, and provides students with conventions and grammar practice in context.

▲ ▲ ▲

Summary

Our students have many opportunities to write informally during class. Learning log responses take a variety of forms depending upon the purposes of a particular lesson. Free-Writes encourage students to become emotionally engaged in their reading, to generate their own questions, and to make predictions. Double-Entry Reflective Journals guide students to become more aware of their thinking while reading and to revisit those ideas after completion. Dialogue Journals inspire instructional conversations about content and literature, while Perspective Entries encourage readers to examine characters and issues from multiple points of view. Pre- and Post-Reading Entries assist readers with difficult content. Students record what they already know about the topic, develop their own purposes for reading, and afterwards discover how much they have learned. When students write Explanation Entries, they internalize concepts and self-evaluate their own understanding. You can't write about something you don't understand.

Whenever we want our students to process content deeply, we have them write about what they are learning whether the format is electronic or paper and pencil. Class and small-group discussions are far richer if students begin "classroom" talk with learning log responses to help focus ideas, and these quick writings insure that everyone becomes an active participant.

CHAPTER 7 RESEARCH BASE

Research Conclusion	Reference
When students respond to text by writing personal reactions and by analyzing and interpreting the text, they have a better understanding of text material. Writing about what one reads produces more gains in comprehension than just reading, reading and rereading, and/or reading and studying the material. These effects hold for a variety of content domains and grade levels.	Graham & Hebert, 2010

Formal Writing to Learn: Writing Reports and Essays

8

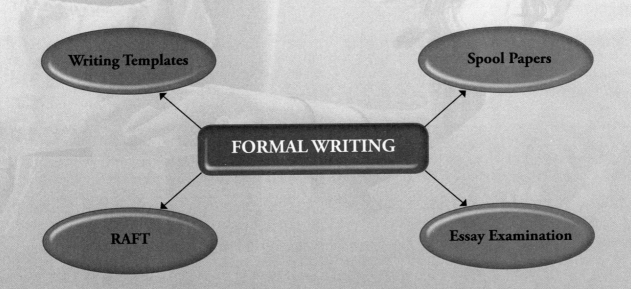

We have high expectations for our students. We not only want them to become adept learners of content, but also be capable of producing new knowledge, which means they must attain expertise in subject matter by questioning and critiquing text as well as creating their own new text. This writing leads to deep learning of content; students become insiders, not only becoming better writers, but also attaining an insiders' perspective. Taking on authorship in specific disciplines helps students internalize the habits of thinking valued and used by a discipline, which in turn leads to improved reading comprehension and learning. Reading comprehension and writing are reciprocal processes.

Research on expository writing strongly supports writing as a tool for learning subject matter (Graham & Perin, 2007; Graham & Hebert, 2010). When adolescents engage in writing text, their reading comprehension improves (Graham & Hebert, 2010).

Becoming producers of content is no small feat when considering the differences among content areas. We must teach students the writing skills and processes necessary for creating text in different content domains. For example, writing like a historian means having an understanding of cause and effect, complex hierarchies, and sequences of interrelated events. Scientific writing requires a command of specific report formats, detailed observation, and research design and implementation. Mathematical thinking and writing requires a deep understanding of vocabulary concepts, knowledge of a variety of process formats, and the ability to create and solve math word problems.

This chapter focuses on tools for helping students become producers of content. This differs from informal writing or learning logs (see Chapter 7) which may or may not lead to completed pieces. While these two chapters focus strictly on writing, we recognize that writing is inherent to most of the strategies presented in this book. Recall how writing emerges from student notes derived from reading. For example, the organizational formats described in Chapters 3, 5, and 6 (Concept Maps, Content Frames, and a variety of Two-Column Notes) evolve naturally into writing. Once students have organized information from their reading, they can readily use it for writing. For example, Conclusion-Support Notes become a tool for persuasive writing, Problem-Solution Notes can easily become analytical papers, and Main Idea—Detail Notes contain the essential ingredients of a summary.

We begin the present discussion of formal writing with structured approaches (Writing Templates and Spool Papers) that assist fledgling writers in writing reports and expository papers. We also describe RAFT assignments and multi-genre research papers before concluding this chapter with a section about negotiating essay examinations. Throughout this chapter, we explore ways to adapt these general tools within specific content domains. Before beginning this discussion, we first offer some general wisdom about the teaching of writing.

All writers, irrespective of content domains, go through various overlapping and recurrent processes in producing a piece: pre-writing, drafting, revising, proofreading, and publishing. While we discuss strategies that can be applied at different points in the process, it is not within the scope of our work to delve deeply into the writing process. We also intentionally left out information about Analytic or 6 + 1 Trait Writing (Spandel & Stiggins, 1997; Culham, 2003, 2010), which involves idea development, organization, voice, word choice, sentence fluency, conventions, and presentation. For rich descriptions about teaching writing, refer to the work of Nancy Atwell (1998, 2007), Lucy Calkins (1994), Ralph Fletcher (2010), Kelly Gallagher (2006), Donald Graves (1994), Linda Rief (2007), Laura Robb (2010), and Tom Romano (1987, 1995, and 2004). We selected strategies for this chapter that are designed more specifically for content disciplines with the implicit understanding that students have opportunities to take their pieces through the writing process and they are aware of analytic traits.

We also focused on what it means to be a considerate writer. Considerate writers (regardless of subject area) assist their readers by leading them through their thinking and explaining their ideas fully. As writers, we don't want to mirror unfriendly textbook authors afflicted with the mentioning problem—the simple listing of concepts without any explanation. We always assume that our readers know less than we do about the topic, and our job is to teach by explaining with clear examples and details. We strive to make our verbs active, to vary sentence lengths, and to write simply without jargon and clutter. We also want our work to have a clear beginning, middle, and end, with transitional features guiding the reader smoothly from one idea to the next.

With this said, let's begin with an overview of some general tools for helping students become better writers of content.

Writing Templates

Strong writers consciously or unconsciously use a set of internal structures or templates in their writing, but many students have no real grasp of the mental structures more advanced writers use intuitively. Making these mental structures explicit through the use of Writing Templates helps students cope with a variety of writing tasks. Some templates exist for writing memos, business letters, and thank-you notes, as well as formats for writing persuasive pieces, laboratory research, and that ambitious doctoral dissertation, but as with any strategy or tool, explicit modeling and explanation are key to effective use.

Writing Templates provide skeleton formats for organizing key ideas and supportive details. Within these templates, transition words guide the structure of student writing. Template design varies from simple main idea-detail constructions to more complex structures such as comparative, problem-solution, and persuasive formats. Writing Templates are particularly effective for assisting students with essay examinations. Once students understand how to compose a well-organized paper, scaffolding the structure with a template won't be necessary. And, as with any strategy, if using a template hinders the advancement of a strong writer, the teacher should not limit the student's creativity to a set format; Writing Templates are scaffolds, not straightjackets.

Writing Templates work particularly well for assisting struggling writers and younger students with more coherent writing. They also provide support as students learn.

Let's begin this discussion at the most basic level–simple paragraph writing—and then progress to Writing Templates used as tools for helping students write in the academic disciplines.

Introduction, Modeling, and Reflection

1. Explain how to structure a paragraph Writing Template.
    - Begin with a topic sentence specifying a general statement or opinion.
    - Conduct a think-aloud in which you compose three to five sentences which provide examples that develop the topic or opinion.
    - Use transitions when needed to connect sentences together (see chart that follows).
    - Encourage the use of a variety of sentences—long and short, simple and complex.
    - End with a concluding sentence containing a restatement of the topic or opinion.

TRANSITION SIGNAL WORDS
Continuation Signals: Warning, there are more ideas to come!
a final reason, again, also, and, and finally, another, first of all, furthermore, in addition, last of all, likewise, more, moreover, next, one reason, other, secondly, similarly, too, with
Change-of-Direction Signals: Watch out, we're doubling back!
although, but, conversely, despite, different from, even though, however, in contrast, in spite of, instead of, nevertheless, on the contrary, on the other hand, otherwise, rather, still, the opposite, though, while, yet
Sequence Signals: There is an order to these ideas.
after, always, before, during, earlier, first (second, third), for one thing, into (far into the night), in the first place, last, later, next, now, since, then, until, while
Illustration Signals: Here's what the principle means in reality.
for example, for instance, in the same way as, much like, similar to, specifically, such as, to illustrate
Emphasis Signals: This is important!
above all, central issue, distinctive quality, especially important, especially relevant, important to note, it all boils down to, key feature, major development, major event, more than anything else, most of all, most noteworthy, pay particular attention to, primary concern, remember that, should be noted, significant factor, the basic concern, the chief outcome, the crux of the matter, the main value, the principle item
Conclusion Signals: This ends the discussion and may have special importance.
as a result, consequently, finally, from this we see, hence, in conclusion, in summary, last of all, therefore
Cause, Condition, or Result Signals: Condition or modification coming.
as, because, but, consequently, due to, for, from, if, in order that, of, resulting from, since, so, so that, that, then, therefore, thus, unless, until, whether, while, yet
Comparison-Contrast Signals: We will now compare idea A with idea B.
also, although, analogous to, and, best, better, but, different from, either, even, however, less, less than, like, more than, most, much as, opposite, or, rather, same, still, then, though, too, while, yet

2. Give students an example of a Writing Template similar to the following science one and work together to write a response using it as a guide.

Prompt: Discuss how you think our city's solid waste management problem can be solved and support your argument with three pieces of evidence.

Essay Template	Topic Sentence	I think _____ would be the best solution to our city's solid waste management problem.
	Prompts for support	First . . . Second . . . Third . . .
	Prompts for conclusion	So . . .

<u>I think</u> recycling <u>would be the best solution to our city's solid waste management problem</u>. <u>First</u>, surveys have shown that paper takes up the most space in our landfill, and I think it would be

fairly easy for families, schools, and businesses to collect their paper for recycling instead of just throwing it away. <u>Second</u>, I called the paper mill in Jonestown, and they said they are already using some recycled paper. They could use more. <u>Third</u>, I called two grocery stores, and they said that recycled paper products sell quite well. <u>So</u>, it seems to me that if it is easy to recycle paper, if the mill can use the recycled products to make new products, and if people buy those products, the best solution to our landfill problem must be recycling!

3. Provide writing prompts that are appropriate to your course content and/or have students develop their own topics.

4. Organize response information into some kind of notes (e.g., for the prompt in #2 above, students first took Conclusion-Support Notes [see page 142]).

5. Work together to develop a topic sentence.

6. Decide on appropriate transitions or prompts that will guide the amount of support and the conclusion.

7. Ask students to complete the paragraph and then edit their drafts. As they write, they may want to change the transitions—encourage this ownership since it shows they are starting to internalize the structure (and expand beyond it!).

Reflection

How did this Writing Template help or hinder your writing? How did the template teach you to structure your own writing?

Support and Extensions

- Continue using paragraph Writing Templates as a guide until students begin to develop their own plans for structuring their ideas. For less able students, templates work well to differentiate instruction—allow them to use templates after other students have discarded them.
- Relate Powers (see page 50) to Writing Templates. The first sentence is the Power 1 statement. It indicates the number of items to follow. For example:

    1. *Democrats differ from Republicans in two ways.*
        2. *First . . .*
            3. *For example . . .*
        2. *Next . . .*
            3. *Because . . .*
            3. *Finally . . .*
            3. *Such as . . .*
    1. *In conclusion . . .*

- Challenge students to develop different paragraph Writing Templates for the different formats of note taking they use. The templates for Conclusion-Support Notes, Concept Maps, and Problem-Solution Notes will NOT be the same.

- Invite students to develop their own Writing Templates (may be longer than one paragraph) to structure different types of texts, such as analytic papers, laboratory research reports, or math word problems.

Formal Writing to Learn: Writing Reports and Essays

- Include a Writing Template essay question on a test. Convert the question to an opening statement and guide content with sentence beginnings and/or Power numbers. The following example comes from a twelfth grade government class.

    The United States government is based on a system of checks and balances. This system maintains a balance of power among . . . Some of the checks and balances are . . . and . . . In summary, our forefathers' idea of checks and balances was developed to . . . because . . .

- Writing Templates can be used across the curriculum to guide thinking or as an assessment. Consider the examples that follow.

Mathematics: Process Sequence

Dividing fractions requires several steps. First . . . Next . . . Then . . . Finally, remember . . .

<u>Dividing fractions requires several steps.</u> <u>First</u>, you need to change any mixed numbers into improper fractions. <u>Next</u>, change the division sign to multiplication and change the second fraction (the one you are dividing by) to its reciprocal (flip it upside-down). <u>Then</u>, multiply the two top numbers—that will be the top number of your answer. Multiply the two bottom numbers—that will be the new bottom number. <u>Finally, remember</u> to reduce the fraction to its lowest terms and change it to a mixed number if the top number is bigger than the bottom one.

Language Arts: Writing about Literature (Grade 6 Example)

In the story _____, I think . . . In the text it says . . . I think . . . According to the story . . . It seems to me . . . The author also tells us . . . In the end . . .

<u>In the story</u> "Maggie and Mitch," <u>I think</u> Maggie and her family were responsible pet owners. <u>In the text it says</u> she let him drink out of the faucet. She gave him tuna water and shrimp crunch with cantaloupe seeds. She really knew what her cat liked. <u>I think</u> Maggie observed her cat and tried to give him what he liked. My dog, Pickle, will only eat certain kinds of dog food. I want him to be healthy so I buy it. He is just like Mitch.

<u>According to the story</u> Maggie tried to convince her mom to give Mitch some medicine when he was sick. She also let him go outside when he needed to go out. <u>It seems to me</u> that Maggie took good care of Mitch. Pets can't feed themselves or go outside. So, she did it. <u>The author also tells us</u> that Maggie was worried about Mitch when she let him go outside. Maggie definitely cared for Mitch. When Mitch was sick, she tried to make him comfortable. <u>In the end</u>, Maggie went above and beyond to try to take care of Mitch. Unfortunately, he died and they buried him in the back yard.

Language Arts: Character Analysis (High School Example)

_____, a character from the classic novel _____ by _____, seems to have been a (an) _____ (adjective) person. An example of this was when . . . Another example was . . . Finally . . . This character, always . . .

> Huck Finn, a character from the classic novel The Adventures of Huckleberry Finn, by Mark Twain seems to have been an adventurous boy. An example of this was when he decided to run away from the widow's house where he was staying. Another example was when he and his friend Jim rode a homemade raft down the Mississippi River by themselves. Finally, Huck decided to adventure back to the widow's by himself. This character, Huck Finn, always dared to do exciting things.

Social Studies: Author's Perspective

The author of this article believes . . . His/her point of view seems biased/fair because . . . An example of this is . . . because . . . In another place he/she says . . . which leads me to think . . . The language contains emotionally charged words such as . . . Another example of questionable evidence is . . . Based on . . . I think . . .

Social Studies: Problem-Cause-Effect-Solution (4 paragraphs)

A critical problem for _____ is . . . This is a problem because . . . In addition . . .

This problem resulted from several causes. First . . . Next . . . Finally . . .

Several important effects have been attributed to the problem of _____ . On the positive side, one sees . . . Some of the negative consequences are . . .

_____ (the problem) could be solved/resolved in a number of ways. For example . . . This would help solve the problem because . . . Another way to solve the problem is . . . This solution seems plausible because . . . A final solution is . . .

Science: Scientific Paper

Introduction: Topic and Question	I conducted a research study on _____. This topic was important to investigate because . . . The hypothesis for my study was . . .
Methods and Procedures	In order to investigate this question, I followed these procedures. First, I . . . Second . . . Third . . . Finally . . .
Results and Discussion	My main result was . . . In addition, I found . . . These results proved/disproved my hypotheses because . . . Some other questions I have about my research are . . . Therefore, I plan to . . .

Formal Writing to Learn: Writing Reports and Essays

- Patricia Tylka (2010) uses Writing Templates to help her students prepare for the ACT writing test. The test requires students take a position on an issue, provide evidence for and against their position, and organize ideas logically. Students must specify reasons and examples to support their point of view and to refute opposing arguments. She has students practice using the following templates:

	Ten Concession/Refutation Templates
1.	Of course, some may disagree with the assertion that . . . They may believe . . . However, it's important to remember that . . .
2.	Some people might argue that . . . However, there are several reasons to oppose this view.
3.	While it is true that . . ., the benefits of . . . outweigh the drawbacks because . . .
4.	At first glance, it appears that . . . But on closer inspection . . . It is better in the long run because . . .
5.	Those who believe . . . may have overlooked . . .
6.	By focusing on . . . overlooks the deeper problem of . . .
7.	I admit that . . . Nevertheless, it does not follow that . . . It is also vital to consider . . .
8.	_____ is only partly the case. The other side of the story is . . .
9.	Even though both sides have merits, the greater good will come from . . .
10.	The statistics are misleading, however, because they do not show . . .

Spool Papers

While some students seem to develop ways to structure writing on their own, most will acquire report writing skills more rapidly when they learn organizing structures. These structures are similar to learning how to ride a bike with training wheels. They help the fledgling writer hold an essay together. Once students have a sense of structure, they can get rid of the training wheels. They begin to move away from the rigid form and apply principles of effective non-fiction writing in more innovative ways.

A Spool Paper is a basic format for writing reports in any content area. It provides an organizational system in the shape of an old-fashioned spool of thread. It starts broad, with an introductory paragraph containing a definite thesis, narrows to detailed supporting paragraphs, and broadens again in a concluding paragraph. The Spool Paper may vary in structure depending upon its purpose. Some Spool Papers are short and concise; others are long and involved.

You can structure students' Spool Papers as tightly as necessary. Ask them to start their papers with an *introductory paragraph* beginning with a lead to draw the reader into the piece, followed by some additional introductory comments and concluding with a thesis statement that previews the topics developed in the subsequent paragraphs or *body* of the piece. The number of paragraphs and the presentation of ideas in the body paragraphs are directed by the thesis statement. Students then conclude their paper with a *summary paragraph* which includes a restatement of main points.

In this example, high school students had just completed *House on Mango Street* by Sandra Cisneros. The teacher introduced students to the Spool Paper format by using a sample essay she wrote about why she chose this book for her class. The students then analyzed the piece to identify the features of a Spool Paper.

Lead

Introduction

As a teacher, sometimes I wonder if I've made the right choice. It's not easy to stick to your guns when faced with antagonistic comments and repeated complaints from students. Why hadn't the students connected with *House on Mango Street*? I didn't expect their negative responses. After all, I love this book. They hadn't appreciated the author's spare, luminous prose. They hadn't walked in the character's footprints or even empathized with Esperanza's rageful and poignant journey into womanhood. Had I made a mistake in selecting this book? For a moment, their complaints made me wonder. As I thought harder, though, I realized I had made a good choice. I had my reasons. Sandra Cisneros writes magnificently and I wanted my students to begin to read like a writer. I wanted them to use her work as their teacher. **I wanted them to see**

Thesis **how a writer crafts sentences, uses powerful verbs, and creates images.**

Body

Sandra Cisneros writes eloquently and sparingly. She slices each sentence to the essence of meaning. She reminds me of Ernest Hemingway, who revised and revised each sentence to the bones. For example, notice the mother's words in the vignette, "A Smart Cookie": "Shame is a bad thing, you know. It keeps you down. You want to know why I quit school. Because I didn't have nice clothes. No clothes, but I had brains." Her writing is clean. No clutter. Every word works. Notice how effectively she uses phrases and, in this example, simple sentences? "She met him at a dance. Pretty too, and young…. And how was she to know she'd be the last one to see him alive. An accident, don't you know. Hit-and-run." Some of her sentences are long; others short. Some are one-word utterances. She clips every line to its core and uses a variety of sentences.

Sandra Cisneros surprises us with her choice of verbs. Note her verbs in these sentences: "Some days after dinner, guests and I will sit in front of a fire. Floorboards will squeak upstairs. The attic grumbles. Rats? they'll ask. Bums, I'll say, and I'll be happy." The verbs *squeak* and *grumble* add color and voice to her writing. Verbs capture the terror of Angel Vargas "...nobody looked up not once the day Angel Vargas learned to fly and dropped from the sky like a sugar donut, just like a falling star, and exploded down to earth without even an 'Oh'." The reader can't escape from the horror painted by these words. An angel exploding and nobody cared! Her clean, precise language, particularly her use of verbs, creates haunting images.

Body

Personification and similes permeate her writing. Attics grumble and squeak. Observe how she uses personification in describing her house on Mango Street. "It's small and red with tight steps in front and windows so small you'd think they were holding their breath. Bricks are crumbling in places, and the front door is so swollen you have to push hard to get in." The inanimate becomes animate. The house takes on human qualities. She uses similes like an artist's thin brush stroke. Notice how she paints the three sisters. "They came with the wind that blows in August, thin as a spider web and barely noticed. Three who did not seem to be related to anything but the moon. One with laughter like tin and one with eyes of a cat and one with hands like porcelain." I also like the way she uses unusual similes in her closing sentences in the vignette, "Linoleum Roses": "She looks at all the things they own: the towels and the toaster, the alarm clock and the drapes. She likes looking at the walls, at how neatly their corners meet, the linoleum roses on the floor, the ceiling smooth as wedding cake." She animates her writing with personification and unusual images.

Conclusion

Susan Cisneros paints pictures with sparse, clean sentences. She teaches us about writing with her distinctive style. **She chooses her verbs carefully so they aren't bland or boring, but precise, clean and filled with voice. Finally, she teaches us about figures of speech.** We learn from phrases like, "Only a house quiet as snow, a space for myself to go, clean as paper before the poem." Thank you Sandra–you teach us well.

Perhaps, my dear students, you now understand why I chose this book. Have I convinced you?

As the class analyzed the paper, they noted how the writer drew the audience into this piece with a lead—in this case, the worries of a teacher facing students who don't yet understand her choices. As part of this modeling, the teacher talked about some different possibilities for leads (see online reproducibles for Chapter 8). Following the lead, she included a few introductory remarks and concluded with a thesis statement or Power 1 sentence (bold). In the example, the three Power 2 ideas developed into paragraphs are in the thesis: how a writer (1) crafts sentences, (2) uses powerful verbs, and (3) creates images. Notice how the paragraphs are in the same order as specified in the thesis. Each paragraph is also highly structured, with a clearly stated main idea (in italics) followed by sentences that explain the main point (Power 2 and 3 ideas). The concluding paragraph repeats the thesis (bold) with a few summary comments.

While the Spool format is not particularly conducive to creative writing or personal responses to literature, it is an excellent tool for reports, business letters, persuasive letters to the editor, and other content writing. As a basic expository writing format, it helps students begin to internalize a sense of structure.

Writers learn how to explore different leads, to set up the thesis for their readers, to develop their ideas, and then to present a strong conclusion. The Spool format helps writers understand how to guide their audience through their writing. Once students have internalized this basic format, they should be encouraged to structure their writing less rigidly.

By writing Spool Papers, struggling readers also learn about main ideas and supporting details. The Spool Paper structure provides an excellent tool for teaching and assessing a student's understanding of concepts. Moreover, it prepares students for the reading and writing tasks found on many state language arts and reading assessments. If students can write a Spool Paper, they will not only be able to write a coherent response, they will also be able to understand how authors use main ideas and supporting details in materials they read.

To help students plan a Spool Paper, encourage them to draft their ideas in a Power outline. Encourage the use of transition words and phrases to connect their Power ideas.

Use the following instructional sequence to introduce your students to Spool Papers.

Introduction, Modeling, and Reflection

1. Your explanation and modeling might go something like this:

   What comes to mind when you hear the word "spool"? Are you thinking of a spool of thread or perhaps the big phone cable spools which some people use for picnic tables? Although spools come in lots of sizes and shapes, they all organize and transport stuff—from threads to cables. The size and shape of a spool depends on its purpose. In a similar way, the Spool Paper is a Writing Template used to organize and communicate ideas. The size and design of the Spool Paper depend on the purpose of the writing.

   The Spool Paper generally consists of at least four paragraphs, but has no upper limit. The first paragraph is the introductory paragraph. It explains what the paper will be about. The rest of the paragraphs, except for the last one, provide all the details and support. We call this part of the Spool Paper the body. The last paragraph of the Spool is the concluding paragraph. It summarizes the main ideas presented in the paper.

2. Project the Spool Paper planning sheet (also in the online reproducibles for Chapter 8). Explain that the outline is a format for planning a paper that clearly develops several main points. Some students may find the Power structure helpful.

   Introductory Paragraph
   0. Lead/Hook
      1. Thesis statement
         List the power 2 ideas:
         2a.
         2b.
         2c.
   Body
      2a. Topic sentence
         3. Detail sentence
         3. Detail sentence
         3. Detail sentence
      2b. Topic sentence
         3. Detail sentence
         3. Detail sentence
         3. Detail sentence
      2c. Topic sentence
         3. Detail sentence
         3. Detail sentence
         3. Detail sentence
   Concluding Paragraph
      1. Restate thesis using different words
   0. Wind-down, conclusion

3. Select a familiar topic and discuss the audience and purpose of the piece. Brainstorm ideas related to the topic. Narrow the ideas to two or three key issues. Based on those issues, create a thesis sentence. (If you have two points in your thesis, this will be a four-paragraph paper. A three-point thesis will result in a paper at least five paragraphs long.)

4. Collectively, develop a lead or introductory statement (Power 0). A lead might be a question, an interesting fact, a quotation, or a dialogue that will catch the reader's attention. Include the thesis statement as the last sentence in the introduction. You can mark the ideas in the thesis statement as Power 2 ideas. Explain that a thesis is a controlling idea that contains the main ideas developed in the paper. Then brainstorm details that develop the main points in each of the paragraphs, and write the paragraphs together with your students.

5. Finally, draft a conclusion and restate the main points of the thesis.

6. Through class discussion, develop an editing checklist or rubric and demonstrate how to use it with the class paper. Here's an example of an editing checklist.

	Editing Checklist: Check the box if the paper meets the requirements described.
✓	Does the lead make you want to read the rest of the paper?
	Does the first paragraph contain a thesis statement? (Put 2s by the supporting points in the thesis.)
	Does the second paragraph explain the first point in the thesis statement?
	Does the third paragraph explain the second point in the thesis?
	Does each paragraph contain a main idea statement? (Underline the main idea sentences.)
	Does each paragraph contain Power 3 and 4 ideas to develop the main idea? (Selectively underline these ideas.)
	Does the last paragraph pull together the ideas in the body paragraphs in a smooth and complete way?
	Does the last paragraph restate the thesis?

Reflection

How did the Spool Paper format help you organize your writing? If it was too constraining, how might you modify the Spool Paper format to make it less rigid? How did the checklist help you analyze and/or revise your paper?

Support and Extensions

- Divide the class into small groups or pairs. Provide a topic related to the content being studied or ask each group to come up with a topic. Have teams draft a Spool Paper. Then have teams trade drafts and edit each other's papers using a checklist.

- Have students write a "how-to" paper on how to write a Spool Paper (see the example on following page). Ask students to evaluate their work using the Spool Paper checklist.

Example:

"Oh, I can't believe it. I just got another D on a report I wrote."

"Do you know what you did wrong?"

"No, I'm not really sure. The teacher said it was pretty poorly organized. I am not really sure how to write reports. All we did the last two years is write creative stories and poetry. I am pretty good at that."

"Well, I think I have just the thing to help you out. It is called a Spool Paper. It will help you write reports, and it is actually quite simple. **The Spool Paper consists of just three parts, an introduction, a body, and a conclusion.**"

We call the first paragraph of the Spool Paper the "introduction." This paragraph begins with several sentences designed to grab your attention. They might be questions or a quote. We label this part a "lead." After the lead, you will need a thesis sentence. This sentence tells what the paper will be about. Usually several subtopics will be listed or suggested in the thesis.

Following the introduction is the "body." The body consists of two or more paragraphs which support the thesis. Each body paragraph will contain information about one of the sub-topics mentioned in the thesis. Usually that sub-topic is written in the first sentence of the paragraph. The other sentences provide details and examples.

The last paragraph of the Spool Paper is called the "conclusion." The first sentence of this paragraph restates the thesis, but in different words. Several more sentences follow. They are called the "wind down" and should be similar to the lead in the introductory paragraph. These sentences tie the paper together, so the reader isn't left hanging.

Once you understand the three components of the Spool Paper—introduction, body, and conclusion—writing a report becomes easy. Now, wouldn't it be nice if the next conversation you had with your parents went like this:

"Boy, I can't believe it! I just got an 'A' on this paper I wrote for Biology."

"That's wonderful. How did you do it?"

"I wrote the paper in a Spool format."

- Modify the Spool format to fit your content area.

Analyzing an Author's Perspective in Social Studies	
Introduction	State the issue and the author's point of view
Body	Arguments: two or three paragraphs, depending on the number of different arguments the author presents
Conclusion	Restate the author's point of view and then react to his/her position. Are the author's arguments valid?

Analyzing Assertions in Social Studies	
Introduction	Make sure your thesis identifies two or three points you plan to develop in your body paragraphs. Thesis Statement: Do you agree or disagree with _____'s claim that... What is the author asserting to be true? Do you agree with his/her assertion?
Body 1	Assertion Evidence Commentary Evidence Commentary
Body 2	Assertion Evidence Commentary Evidence Commentary
Conclusion	Restate the author's central assertion followed by your opinion.

Lab Reports in Science	
Introduction	State the issue or problem and your hypothesis with the anticipated outcomes that would support your hypothesis.
Body 1	The set up for the lab—lab equipment, materials, and procedure.
Body 2	Results depend on the lab; this may involve several paragraphs.
Conclusion	Restate the hypothesis and indicate if it is correct, partially correct, or incorrect. Provide substantiating evidence from results.

RAFT

We want our students to write about content, but often we find their writing carelessly constructed, brief, and boring. Another issue, exacerbated by this digital age, is plagiarism. Students find it easy to claim knowledge as their "own" by simply cutting and pasting. Our assignments may contribute to both of these problems.

The most common assignment (a student writing an essay for a teacher to explain something), particularly in the content areas, typically produces a bland essay. Why should students feel compelled to teach an all-knowing, critical audience? There's little motivation to compose with vivid voice, imagination, and detail when writing for the teacher. In addition, many of our content assignments lack focus and are too broad in scope for students to wrap their pens around. RAFT assignments shift students out of their familiar roles and inspire them to write for different audiences using formats other than the essay. RAFT invites them to infuse their work with more voice and imagination. RAFT assignments also make it difficult to plagiarize.

RAFT, originally conceived by Nancy Vandevanter as part of the Montana Writing Project in 1982, clarifies the design of assignments. RAFT, an acronym for Role, Audience, Format, and Topic, defines the decisions students must make before they start writing. It helps them consider who they are as writers, for whom they are writing, the most appropriate format for the piece, and the topic they want to address. RAFT also incorporates strong verbs into the topic statement to focus and energize the piece. A RAFT assignment doesn't ask students to write, but rather to plead, convince, or complain. Untangling and labeling these components help students build a better metacognitive awareness of what writers do before they write. Writers don't just pick up a pen and go at it. They do a bit of planning first. Students also begin to understand that writing has possibilities beyond the classroom. RAFT, like other CRISS strategies, serves to demystify what might be an amorphous, complex process by clarifying its components.

R	ROLE	Who are you? A soldier, Abraham Lincoln, an igneous rock, a mathematical operation
A	AUDIENCE	To/for whom is this written/created? A mother, Congress, an integer
F	FORMAT	What form will it take? A letter, speech, obituary, conversation, multimedia presentation, cartoon, memo, journal, etc.
T	TOPIC + *Strong Verb*	**Persuade** a soldier to spare your life. **Demand** equal pay for equal work. **Plead** for a halt to mining in our valley.

RAFT gives students more control over their writing assignments. Allowing students to define their own role, format, and audience when explaining a specific topic preserves some freedom of choice. The results make lively reading and inspire students to do their own work.

Introduction, Modeling, and Reflection

1. Explain that all writers must consider the four components of every written piece: the role of the writer, audience, format, and topic. RAFT assignments are written from a viewpoint other than that of a student, to an audience other than the teacher, and in a form other than the standard essay. Model for students with something simple such as this RAFT for the song *I'm a Little Teapot*.

   I'm a little teapot,
   Short and stout
   Here is my handle (one hand on hip),
   Here is my spout (other arm out straight)
   When I get all steamed up,
   Hear me shout
   Just tip me over and pour me out!

   See if students can come up with the RAFT components:

Role	Audience	Format	T + *Strong Verb*
Teapot	Young children	Song with movements	*Entertain* children while describing what a teapot looks like and does.

   Talk about the importance of using strong verbs to guide your writing. Seldom do we use the word *write* in our assignments, but instead incorporate strong verbs such as *warn*, *urge*, and *clarify*, which focus the assignment by setting the tone of the response.

2. Brainstorm writing topics from a current unit of study. Select several topics from those presented.

3. Write RAFT on the board and list possible roles, audiences, formats and strong verbs appropriate for each topic. Roles and audience are dependent upon the unit of study, but can be silly, professionally-oriented, traditional, or very creative (e.g. a point on a line, the y-coordinate, a scientist, a congressional committee, a story character, a radio announcer, a historical figure, an atom, etc.). See the chart below for ideas about formats and strong verbs. Make sure students are familiar with the formats. They may need to research or collect samples of obituaries, resumes, etc.

RAFT Formats

advertisement	epitaph	obituary	review
apology	eulogy	pamphlet	riddle
application	graffiti	petition	sermon
art exhibit	interview	photo essay	ship's log
cartoon	joke	poem	script/screenplay
bumper sticker	journal/diary	poster	slogan
commercial	keynote	public service announcement	telegram
complaint	legal brief		travelogue
confession	letter to the editor	radio play	wanted poster
conversations	marriage proposal	recommendation	warning
dramatic monologue	news story	resume	will

Strong Verbs

admonish	confide	encourage	guide	pester	tattle
accuse	congratulate	entertain	harass	plead	taunt
advise	convince	excite	honor	prod	teach
apologize	dazzle	excuse	identify	protest	tease
attack	defend	explain	inquire	question	testify
beg	demand	flatter	interpret	resign	urge
blame	deny	flaunt	justify	reward	warn
boast	disagree	forbid	laud	satirize	welcome
clarify	discourage	foretell	notify	scare	woo
complain	emphasize	formulate	pacify	sell	yield
condemn	evaluate	grumble	proclaim	shock	

4. Provide students with examples of RAFT assignments similar to those on the following pages.

5. Have students write one of the generated assignments.

In the following example, Joyce Clark, an assistant principal of Curriculum and Instruction, co-taught a RAFT lesson in a twelfth grade ESOL classroom. After completing the book, *Animal Farm*, the class developed a chart with possible RAFT assignments. They used characters as the roles.

Role	Audience	Format	Topic + *Strong Verb*
Snowball	Napoleon	Letter	*Complain* about your eviction from the farm and *convince* Napoleon that you should be allowed back in.
Mr. Jones	People of the town	Petition	*Convince* the other humans that they should help you in your assault on the farm to regain power.
Clover	Animals of the farm	Speech	*Confess* to the animals of the farm telling them about all of the bad things you have done.
Napoleon, Squealer, the pigs	Animals and townspeople	Wanted poster	*Design* a wanted poster to be placed around town for the capture of Snowball. List your reasons for wanting him captured.

Science:

A biology student uses a goodbye letter to explain the process of cell division.

Role	Audience	Format	Topic + *Strong Verb*
Chromatid	Fellow chromatid	Letter	*Bid* farewell as you enter mitosis

My dear Twin, even as I write, plans are being made for mitosis of our little cell. With the end of interphase, our entry into prophase is imminent. We will coil into short and thicker chromatids while the already duplicated centrioles move to the opposite ends of our cell. Our protective nuclear envelope will break down and dissolve. Spindle fibers will stretch from the centrioles to our centomeres to ensure our safe traveling. Soon we will enter metaphase. We align ourselves on pre-appointed spindles to prepare for the tedious anaphase.

Formal Writing to Learn: Writing Reports and Essays

During Anaphase we will separate into individual chromosomes as we are pulled to opposite ends of our cell by spindles.

In telophase, we approach the centrioles and group together. We get a brand new nuclear envelope. Our cytoplasm will begin division as we grow a new plasma membrane. After we're done with the cytokinesis, we'll once again lapse into interphase. So it is with a great sadness that I say farewell as we go our separate ways and until we meet again in that great organism in the sky.

With love,

Your Twin Chromatid

Language Arts:
Provided by CRISS Trainer Theresa Sobota, this example makes grammar more interesting for students.

Role	Audience	Format	Topic + *Strong Verb*
Subordinate clause	Human Resource manager	Job interview at local sentence factory	*Convince* human resource manager that you would be a better candidate than an indepedent clause and a prepositional phase for the sentence construction job.

I am a subordinate clause and want the job as sentence constructor in the sentence factory.

I would work well with any independent clauses that might already be employed by you. Independent clauses do not work with others as a team as much as clauses like me do. They like to hurry up and get the job done without details that could be found in other clauses. I like to do a thorough job, so I always work with other clauses in a cooperative way. When the independent clause tells you what happened, I can tell you the cause and effect. Instead of knowing only what the subject did, you will know why the subject acted that way.

Prepositional phrases help provide some of the details, but they don't have the qualifications for this job. A prepositional phrase always contains a preposition and an object, but I always contain a subject and a predicate. While a prepositional phase may tell you where the action is, I can tell you what the action is and who completes it. If a prepositional phrase works alone, it will never make sense. Prepositional phrases are nice to have around, but they are not essential to any sentence structure.

You can clearly see why I am the best choice for this job. I am a cooperative worker, and I communicate more information than phrases.

Mathematics:
In this example, students in Jim Ferwerda's geometry class wrote newspaper ads from an angle in need of companionship.

Role	Audience	Format	Topic + *Strong Verb*
Acute Angle	News readers	Personal ad	Using key vocabulary, describe yourself and what your are looking for in a mate.

I am acute angle named ABC. I am two sided, and I have a brother who is obtuse and never complements me. I am never right, and I am never a three-dimensional figure. My mother was a straight angle and my father was a bisector. I am part of the two-member club known as the linear pair, and we are nicknamed the "Adjacent Angles." I am looking for an acute angle to complement me. If you are an obtuse angle then I would want you to supplement me so I am able to think straight. If we do not get married, I hope we could still correspond with each other.

Social Studies:

As the culmination to a unit on Feudalism, Marc Sonderegger asked students to work in small groups and develop a chart of possible RAFT assignments for the topic—the problem of land ownership during the feudal period. After brainstorming possibilities, students circled the role, audience, format and strong verb they would use to draft their piece. An example follows:

Role	Audience	Format	Topic + *Strong Verb*	
(Monarch)	Mother	Letter	Blame	Persuade
Lord	Friend	Diary	Demand	Plead
Knight	Superior	Conversation	Explain	(Proclaim)
Serf	(Subjects)	(Decree)	Forbid	
	Church	Poster	Inquire	

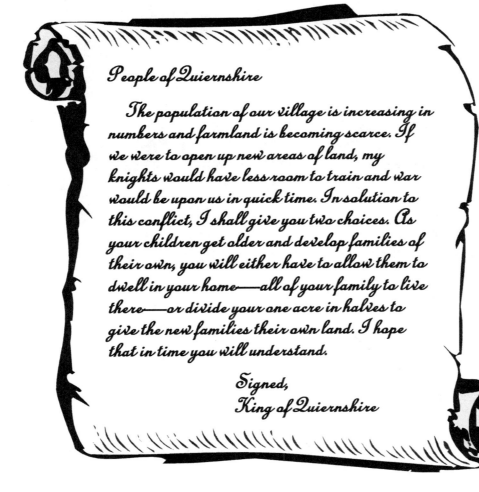

People of Quiernshire

The population of our village is increasing in numbers and farmland is becoming scarce. If we were to open up new areas of land, my knights would have less room to train and war would be upon us in quick time. In solution to this conflict, I shall give you two choices. As your children get older and develop families of their own, you will either have to allow them to dwell in your home—all of your family to live there—or divide your one acre in halves to give the new families their own land. I hope that in time you will understand.

Signed,
King of Quiernshire

Formal Writing to Learn: Writing Reports and Essays

> **Reflection**
> How did your writing change when composing for audiences other than the teacher? How might RAFT help you plan your own assignments? How does RAFT make writing more fun? How can you put yourself into the piece more (living your character's life or place yourself into the scene)?

Support and Extensions

- As part of a unit study, ask students to develop topics for writing and create their own RAFT assignments. Have students take their pieces through the steps in the writing process. Post their completed works on bulletin boards, on web pages or publish in a class magazine. Have a Writer's Celebration where everyone reads their piece aloud.

- RAFTs do not always have to be written demonstrations of understanding. Formal and complex presentations and projects work well, too. Dr. David Long, a high school science teacher, collaborated with Emily Thiessen, a high school art teacher, in an integrated unit. As a culminating project, the students created ceramic plates depicting the phases of cell division.

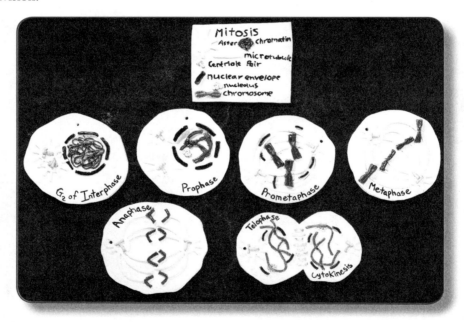

- <u>Multi-Genre Report</u>. Challenge your students to write a multi-genre research paper (Romano, 1987). Rather than the rigid Spool Paper, ask them to come up with other formats. One cooperative team of four students chose to do their research paper on the Civil War using a newspaper format. They wrote reports from the battlefield, songs, obituaries, and "Dear Lizzie" columns. In effect, they combined a series of RAFT assignments into one publication.

- Multi-genre reports also work well as individual assignments. After reading *To Kill a Mockingbird*, a sophomore wrote a factual piece about some of the main historical events occurring during the time of the book, a poem about prejudice, and a journal from Jem's perspective (one of the characters). She also included some of her own illustrations.

The Essay Examination

Think back to those dreaded essay questions in your high school English class or college history course—cold sweat, butterflies in your stomach, rushing against time, not remembering the stuff well enough to actually explain it, being the last one to turn in the test. Or were you one of those irritating kids who always finished on time and scored high, while the rest of us struggled? Unfortunately, some of the authors of this book don't fit in this second category. Yet, we might have, if just one teacher had taught us how to take essay tests. Instead, our teachers assumed too much, and no one ever taught us what to do. Taking essay tests was part of the underground curriculum no one talked about. Imagine how our testing lives might have been different.

Some students negotiate essay tests confidently; most do not. Most begin writing without reading the question carefully, without planning the response, and without having any clear plan about how to organize their ideas quickly. They stop, start, and begin again only to find that they have spent far too much time and have to rush through the rest of the test. Or they simply admit defeat and leave the question blank. To compound the torture, essay examinations have become more important, as written responses are included on state and national assessments.

Teaching students how to read a question and set up an answer will make a dramatic difference in how well they perform on essay examinations. For example, if the question or prompt requires analysis or evaluation of an issue, brainstorm known information into a Conclusion-Support framework. If the question requires the analysis of a problem, use a Problem-Solution organizer. In other situations, the question might require an explanation with a listing of several different ideas, a Power outline to organize, and then the answer can follow a Spool format. Many of the CRISS strategies we've discussed work in concert with improving test performance.

In order to succeed on written assessments, have students follow these steps:

	Preparing for an Essay Exam
Step 1	Read the question with particular attention to the verb and key words.
Step 2	Focus the answer by recasting the question as the topic sentence in the response.
Step 3	Determine the type of organizational format required to answer the question and brainstorm information into that format.
Step 4	Write the response using information from the notes.
Step 5	Reread the question and the answer to make sure all parts have been addressed.

Introduction, Modeling, and Reflection

1. Introduce the five steps to students.
2. Model with a prompt from one of your tests or a sample state assessment.
3. Read through the question or prompt. Underline the verb and key words, particularly those noting the number or order of ideas. Talk about how verbs give important clues about the answer (e.g. evaluate, compare, contrast, describe, explain, criticize).

Formal Writing to Learn: Writing Reports and Essays

4. Rewrite the question as the topic sentence of the essay.

5. Transfer key information into an appropriate note format. For sample note taking formats, see the examples that follow.

6. Write a response based on the information in your notes. If a short response (paragraph) is appropriate, create a brief Writing Template to guide your writing. If a longer, more formal response is required, use the Spool format. Using these formats is a great way to keep students focused on the critical information that needs to be included in their essays.

7. Reread the test question and your response to make sure all parts of the question have been addressed.

8. With students working in Paris, have them practice this process by working through a different test question.

The following examples will help students walk-through the process.

Science

Step 1: Read the question. Note each part of the question that needs to be answered. Underline the verb and key words, particularly those that note number or the order of ideas.

Question: Should the U.S. government grant access to logging wilderness areas in the Rocky Mountains? Present both points of view followed by your own conclusion.

Step 2: Develop a topic sentence.

People have different points of view about whether or not the U.S. government should grant access to logging wilderness areas in the Rocky Mountains.

Step 3: Select an organizing framework and brainstorm key information. Conclusion-Support Notes

Conclusion	Support
Government should grant access to logging wilderness areas.	1. Logging industry needs support. 2. Trees are renewable. 3. Wilderness areas have the best timber. 4. Logging helps in forest fire suppression. 5. Timber damaged by fire and disease isn't wasted.
Government should not grant access to logging wilderness areas.	1. Only a few virgin forests are left. 2. Logging will destroy these forests forever. 3. The forests are habitat for endangered species that need protection, such as the spotted owl and grizzly. 4. They are great for recreation: hiking, fishing and camping.

My conclusion:
I think the goverment should allow logging only in areas of designated wilderness in our part of the country when the majority of trees are dead due to the pine beetle, disease, and forest fire.

Step 4: Write your answer. If a short response is required, a template similar to the following would focus the response appropriately.

People have different points of view about whether or not the U.S. government should grant access to logging wilderness areas in the Rocky Mountains.

Those for logging say . . .
While those against logging say . . .
I feel the best solution is . . .

If a longer response is required, a four-paragraph Spool Paper (see page 200) would work well—the first paragraph states the thesis sentence and the other three paragraphs expand on the prompts listed above for the Writing Template.

Step 5: <u>Reread the question and your answer.</u> Make sure your response addresses all parts.

Social Studies

Step 1: <u>Read the question.</u> Underline the verb and key words, particularly those noting number or the order of ideas.

Question: During the 1920s what were three <u>major factors</u> that led to the economic collapse of the Great Depression?

Step 2: <u>Develop a topic sentence.</u>

In the 1920s, three major factors led to the economic collapse of the Great Depression.

Step 3: <u>Select an organizing framework and brainstorm key information.</u> Power Notes

> 1. Three factors leading to economic collapse
>   2. Farmers had a difficult time
>   3. Over-production
>   3. High costs of materials and machinery
>   3. Land costs high
>   3. Low prices for farm goods
>   2. Banks unstable
>   3. Couldn't get enough farm loans
>   3. Banks closed
>   2. Mass production
>   3. Workers replaced by machines
>   3. Wages
>   3. Corporations didn't pass profits on to workers

Step 4: <u>Write your answer.</u> If a short response is required, a template similar to the following would focus the response appropriately.

In the 1920s, three major factors led to the economic collapse of the Great Depression.

    First . . .
        Because . . .
    The second factor was . . .
        This was the result of . . .
    Finally . . .
        This was a major reason for the Great Depression because . . .

If a longer response is required, a five paragraph Spool Paper would work well; the first paragraph relates the thesis sentence, three paragraphs expand on the three factors leading to the Great Depression, and a concluding fifth paragraph ties the essay together.

Step 5: <u>Reread the question and your answer</u> Make sure your response addresses all parts.

> **Reflection**
> What makes essay questions difficult? How does the five-step plan help overcome these difficulties? How does changing the question into your thesis statement help focus your answer? Why does taking time to figure out an organizing pattern for brainstorming help you recall what you know about the topic and help you structure your answer? How might the procedure for responding to essay prompts help you feel more confident about taking tests?

Support and Extensions

- Teach the format for essay questions used on state and national assessments. In some states, students read a selection and can refer to it as they write a short or extended answer to an essay question. They need to use information from the selection to answer the question. Show students how to use key words from the question to develop their first sentence and how to go back into the reading selection to find supporting evidence. Model how to do Selective Underlining and margin note taking. Students can then use this information directly in their response or convert it to an appropriate organizing format such as Power Notes or Conclusion-Support Notes.

- Have students develop essay questions as an on-going component of studying. After taking Main Idea—Detail Notes or developing a Concept Map, have them design an essay test question tapping higher order thinking. Ask them to practice answering their question orally and in written form. As part of reflective conferences, talk about essay questions that make sense for a particular content topic and then practice answering them. If they can answer their own questions, they will be prepared for questions the teacher might ask.

- Have students practice writing and answering questions in small groups.

▲ ▲ ▲

Summary

Our students deserve to write constantly in our classes. Writing is what we do to learn, to understand, and to explore ideas. We want students to become expert learners capable of creating new knowledge for others to read. The strategies described in this chapter provide scaffolding to help fledgling writers move ahead on their own. Given the scope of this book, we had to limit our discussion to a handful of strategies—strategies we have found to be particularly useful in content classrooms. We invite you to learn more. If you haven't read the work of Nancy Atwell, Lucy Calkins, Ralph Fletcher, Kelly Gallagher, Donald Graves, Linda Rief, Laura Robb, Tom Romano, and Ruth Culham, indulge yourself. You are in for a treat.

Writing Templates and Spool Papers are designed to help students begin to internalize structure in their writing, to carry their audiences forward, moving from one idea to another in a logical progression. Warning: These approaches are transitory, used only as long as students need them. Spool Papers and Writing Templates can be overdone! Once students have internalized a sense of structure and know how to communicate to their readers about what they know, the rigidity of these formats becomes too confining. Know when to remove the training wheels.

With RAFT and multi-genre reports, writers discover more flexible dimensions of writing. These innovative assignments encourage students to discover their own voices using unconventional formats to present their ideas. Writing experts tell us that students need opportunities to choose their own topics. School writing, they say, should mirror the work of real writers; it should be on topics of personal value for real audiences. As we think of ourselves as writers, we understand the validity of this argument. Yet content teachers want their students to write about the material. Allowing students to choose their own role, format, and audience when explaining a topic preserves some freedom of choice even when the content is necessarily limited. As a result, content writing also becomes livelier and more fun to read.

Take the mystery out of the dreaded essay test by teaching students how to approach it. Don't leave this important skill to chance, particularly in these days of high stakes assessments. Show students how to analyze questions, plan their responses, and write logically.

We invite you to try some of the ideas described in this chapter. Writing touches the heart of learning by penetrating the external shell of memorized facts and superficial understanding. When we can explain things to ourselves and to others, we can claim new knowledge as our own.

CHAPTER 8 RESEARCH BASE

Research Conclusion	Reference
When adolescents engage in writing text, their reading comprehension improves.	Graham & Perin, 2007 Graham & Hebert, 2010
Writing facilitates the learning of content.	Graham & Hebert, 2010

Vocabulary

9

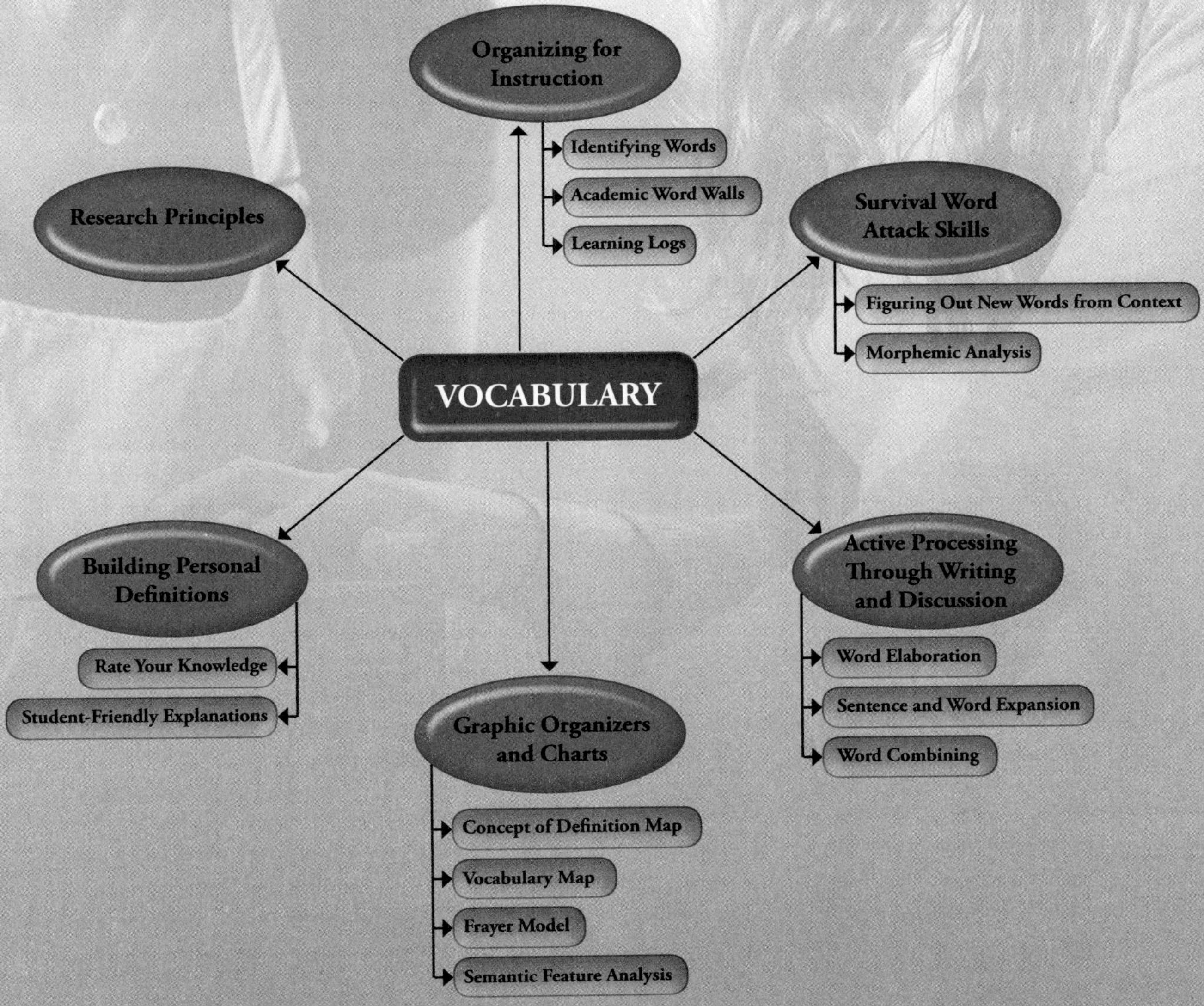

- **VOCABULARY**
  - Organizing for Instruction
    - Identifying Words
    - Academic Word Walls
    - Learning Logs
  - Research Principles
  - Survival Word Attack Skills
    - Figuring Out New Words from Context
    - Morphemic Analysis
  - Building Personal Definitions
    - Rate Your Knowledge
    - Student-Friendly Explanations
  - Graphic Organizers and Charts
    - Concept of Definition Map
    - Vocabulary Map
    - Frayer Model
    - Semantic Feature Analysis
  - Active Processing Through Writing and Discussion
    - Word Elaboration
    - Sentence and Word Expansion
    - Word Combining

One of the most investigated areas of literacy research is vocabulary acquisition. During the last twenty years, review chapters, research articles, and books summarizing the scientific evidence pertaining to vocabulary teaching and learning have enriched our theoretical and practical understanding of the field. The National Reading Panel (2000) also generated a flurry of interest when they identified vocabulary as one of the five areas crucial to literacy. Rather than providing a detailed review of vocabulary research, we have consolidated this work into seven principles that seem most important for guiding our practice. For some excellent research summaries see McKeown and Curtis (1987) and Pressley, Disney, and Anderson (2007).

RESEARCH PRINCIPLES

(1) <u>Vocabulary and academic success</u>. Our first and most fundamental conclusion coming from research on vocabulary acquisition is that a rich vocabulary is the hallmark of an educated person. Over the years, researchers have documented that high school seniors achieving at the top of their class know about four times as many words as underachieving students. Vocabulary knowledge is also related to social class. Children in middle and upper class families come to school with far richer vocabularies than do students from poor families. Consequently, longitudinal studies document that children who grow up in language rich households end up doing better in later reading achievement than do students from language poor families (Beck, McKeown, & Kucan, 2002). In fact, the relationship between vocabulary and reading proficiency is so powerful that there is some evidence that vocabulary size in kindergarten is an effective predictor of reading comprehension and achievement in later school years (Beck, McKeown, & Kucan, 2002).

(2) <u>Vocabulary development and wide reading</u>. Vocabulary development intertwines with the literacy experiences of the reader. As expected, the more one reads, the richer one's vocabulary. Given that we learn vocabulary incidentally through wide reading, some researchers contend that increasing the reading time is the most powerful thing we can do to increase vocabulary learning (Gambrel & Headley, 2006). Learning an unfamiliar word requires repeated encounters in multiple contexts. Struggling readers typically do not read widely enough to have sufficient encounters with unfamiliar words. Individuals who read extensively have far more opportunities to construct meanings of words compared to students who read infrequently. Learning the nuances of words takes multiple exposures within rich contexts.

Even though wide reading is essential to vocabulary development, researchers point out that wide reading coupled with explicit vocabulary instruction provides the best combination. Students learn even more words when wide reading is augmented by lessons and activities connected with subject matter being studied (Baumann, Ware, & Edwards, 2007).

(3) <u>Vocabulary knowledge and reading comprehension</u>. A central premise is the reciprocal relationship between vocabulary and comprehension–a larger vocabulary leads to greater comprehension and better comprehension leads to learning more vocabulary words (Stanovich, 1986). Beginning with the early work of Thorndike (as cited in Pressley, Disney, & Anderson, 2007) researchers documented a significant relationship between reading comprehension and vocabulary knowledge. Students with a larger vocabulary do better in reading comprehension tasks than do students with poor vocabularies. Over the years, this relationship remains consistent across a variety of methodologies including factor analysis, correlation, and readability research (Stahl & Fairbanks, 2006).

The positive relationship between vocabulary knowledge and reading comprehension can be best explained by the reader's background knowledge (Nagy & Scott, 2006). Vocabulary knowledge provides a general measure of background knowledge—students with extensive vocabularies undoubtedly have a richer background knowledge than do students with poor vocabularies.

(4) <u>Pre-teaching vocabulary and comprehension</u>. Students do better comprehending a selection when pre-taught important vocabulary in the assignment. When students study unfamiliar vocabulary in an upcoming reading selection, they do better than their control counterparts in comprehending the selection containing these words. There is one important caveat–learning key vocabulary in a reading selection helps one comprehend the selection containing this vocabulary, but one's comprehension does not necessarily improve with reading selections not containing these words (Nagy & Scott, 2006).

(5) <u>Selecting words to teach</u>. We can't teach all of the words students meet in their reading, especially in the content areas. In fact, many content classes, such as science and mathematics, are in effect, studies in vocabulary. Bill Holliday (1991) notes some high school chemistry texts contain 3,000 technical words unfamiliar to high school students. This staggering number exceeds the vocabulary taught in most foreign language classes. It is impossible for students to learn them all. We must think critically about the words our students really need to understand. Beck, McKeown, and Kucan (2002) suggest the in-depth teaching of about ten words per week.

Related to the issue of selectivity is recognizing vocabulary knowledge rests on a continuum from shallow to an ever-deepening level of understanding (Beck et al., 2002). The first time we meet a word, we attain a surface, superficial knowledge which might suffice for comprehending a selection. In other situations, the reader might need a deeper understanding of a concept in order to grasp essential ideas in the content. To attain this understanding and to have a word become part of our working vocabulary, we have to use it multiple times and in different ways (e.g., vocabulary mapping, adding contextual information, writing, and speaking). Therefore, as educators we not only make decisions about what words to teach, but also about those words worthy of the most instructional attention. For less essential words, we might note them briefly before a lesson, but for those warranting deep understanding, we should use a more multifaceted, rich approach.

(6) <u>Rich vocabulary instruction</u>. In a meta-analysis of research on vocabulary instruction, Stahl and Fairbanks (2006) concluded that effective vocabulary instruction requires multiple exposures in varying contexts along with activities requiring deep processing. Repetition and elaboration are key. Most studies with positive effects involve methodologies where students do multiple "things" with vocabulary. Just looking up words in a dictionary, defining word parts, or analyzing contextual clues in themselves are insufficient. Singular approaches don't fill the bill. However, if these methods are part of a broader approach to learning vocabulary where students also use the words in a variety of written and oral activities, these methods become effective components of the whole. Owning a concept involves creating as many connections as possible between a new word and prior knowledge. In other words, ownership calls for rich instruction (Beck, McKeown, & Kucan, 2002).

(7) <u>Metacognition</u>. Given our CRISS Framework for Learning, it is no accident that we have saved the over-arching concept of **metacognition** as the final principle critical to vocabulary development. To be successful, students must know how to learn new vocabulary (Stahl & Fairbanks, 2006). What does being metacognitive about vocabulary learning involve? Three things emerge from the literature. First, most students have misconceptions about what it takes to know a word. From years of past schooling, they think copying down synonyms or recording definitions from a glossary is sufficient. We must help students change these misconceptions. Second, they need to recognize word learning as a continuum. In what situations is it OK to know a word superficially and when is it essential to have a deep understanding of a concept? Part of being metacognitive involves gauging one's own continuum of understanding in light of learning needs. Third, students need strategies for learning words. Again this involves ridding students of old habits such as glossing over unknown words met in print or memorizing simple definitions. As you have heard time and time again in this manual—we have to make the "how" of learning totally clear to our students. What does one do when encountering a new concept? Model. Be explicit about your own cognitive struggle. Talk aloud. Identify what you do so students gain an understanding of a variety of strategies.

These research principles provide a rich underpinning for the practical strategies described in the next portion of this chapter. We must think hard about the vocabulary our students need to know in our content areas. We need to help students understand what it takes for deep learning of concepts: a rich multifaceted approach going far beyond rote memorization. It also requires showing students how to learn important vocabulary through teacher modeling of systematic but varied instruction.

Probably the most astute advice transcending the nuts and bolts of the vast literature on vocabulary acquisition is to facilitate ENGAGEMENT. Learning vocabulary can actually be fun. After all, we are innately wired as linguistic wizards. Showcase your own enthusiasm. It's catching. The practical ideas offered in the next part of this chapter should make vocabulary learning more inviting for both you and your students. Use sophisticated words in your own speech. Challenge students to do the same. One way to share your enthusiasm is to invite students to explore online word-a-day applications, which introduce a word a day along with the definition, pronunciation, etymology, usage, and a quotation. Enjoy learning new words along with your students.

We have parceled the rest of this chapter into four major parts. The first section, Organizing for Vocabulary Instruction, covers word identification, academic word walls, and vocabulary learning logs. We chose these topics as starting points since they are integral to practically every strategy we describe in this chapter. What are the words worthy of rich instruction; once words are selected, how can they be featured on an academic word wall; and how might students keep track of words they are learning? The second section focuses on survival word attack skills—context and morphemes. Students need to have a basic understanding of contextual relationships within text as well as know the building blocks for learning new words. The next section includes building personal definitions with two general strategies—knowledge rating and Student-Friendly Explanations. The final section contains instructional strategies designed for deep learning of essential academic vocabulary. To provide some cohesiveness to these diverse approaches, we organized this section into two subsections: (1) graphic organizers and charts, and (2) active processing through writing and discussion.

ORGANIZING FOR VOCABULARY INSTRUCTION

Identifying Words Worthy of Rich Instruction

The first step in effective vocabulary instruction is word selection. What words are worthy of rich, multifaceted instruction? What words will students probably get on their own and which words need only superficial attention? How do we choose?

One way to help in the selection process is to think about choosing words based on their utility. Some teachers have found it useful to select words according to a classification system. Probably the best known system is the tier approach developed by Beck, McKeown and Kucan (2002) who recommend classifying words according to tiers ranging from common everyday words (Tier 1), to words occurring less frequently but considered important for literate language users (Tier 2), to content specific words (Tier 3). They suggest expending the most instructional effort teaching Tier 2 words since these tend to be generally more useful for one's literate life.

Flanagan and Greenwood (2009) offer a selection procedure potentially more practical for content teachers. Their procedure focuses on content specific words and also considers word selection as part of an overall lesson plan. They offer a "four-level-framework" as an adaptation to Beck et al.'s three-tier system (Tier 3 domain-specific words can fit into all four of the levels outlined below, depending on text and the instructional goals.).

Level 1 words (*critical before words*): These core content words require deep and thorough exploration for students to succeed in reading the selection. These are the big concepts which need explicit pre-teaching in order for students to learn further information about them during and after reading. Is the word found in curriculum guides and state standards? Important vocabulary words are usually mentioned in these documents. Don't be swayed by all of the highlighted words in text. Many highlighted words as well as those listed in the teacher manuals may not serve your instructional goals and therefore don't deserve attention. Examples of Level 1 words from CRISS Level I training include *nonrenewable, misinterpreted,* and *endangered species.*

Level 2 words (*important before words*): These "foot in the door" words are important for students to know at a surface level before reading an assignment. Students need some familiarity with them for comprehending the "gist" of the selection, but they don't warrant the same amount of before reading instructional time as the Level 1 words. Examples of Level 2 words from the CRISS Level I training include *speakeasy, scandal, megawatt,* and *bounty.*

Level 3 words (*critical after words*): Level 3 words represent concepts defined clearly in the text that can be dealt with during and after reading once students have a better idea of the content. Examples of Level 3 words from the CRISS Level I training include *hydroelectric, mass production,* and *alpha male.*

Level 4 words (*words not to teach*): Words classified as Level 4 words may or may not be familiar to students, but they aren't essential to the lesson objectives. These may also be words which the authors explain clearly within their text. If students read their assignment, they should be able to understand them. *NIMBY* is an example of a Level 4 word from the CRISS Level I training.

Flanagan and Greenwood recommend reading the assignment and determining the essential understandings students are to take away from the lesson. A word's importance depends on the goals of the lesson. Determine a vocabulary list. Then narrow it down to a manageable number and organize the words into levels. Select words needing thorough or superficial attention before students read and identify those that can wait for post-reading discussions. Discard those not linked to the goals of your lesson. Remember, less is more!

Teachers may find some published resources helpful for selecting words in their academic content areas. For example, Marzano (2004) has compiled lists of academic vocabulary for 11 different subject areas: mathematics, science, English, history, geography, civics, economics, health, physical education, the arts, and technology.

Academic Word Walls

Once you have made your list, consider writing words on note cards for placement on an Academic Word Wall. Include essential words from a unit or lesson. Keeping them in full view reminds students about their importance and makes them readily accessible for use in oral and written work. Placing important words on the wall also provides students opportunities for multiple exposures to the words they need to master and having them in full view helps in reviewing for tests. Display words currently in play. Keep them up for the duration of the unit but don't leave words up indefinitely. The point is to use them in a variety of contexts. Keep them active.

Don't make word walls complicated. Reserve a place in your room—a magnetic board, the space above the windows, a bulletin board—for creating the wall. Consider laminating the cards and attaching them using something that facilitates moving them around. Organize them using any arrangement that makes sense—alphabetically, conceptually, thematically, etc. Throughout the term, add new vocabulary to the wall as needed for understanding essential ideas.

Invite students to create ways to make the words on the wall memorable. They can write the words on large index cards and embellish them with pictures, symbols, and definitions as a way to create deeper levels of meaning. For example, Harmon et al. (2009) asked students in a seventh grade English class to develop a word wall. With guidance on how to select important words for study, teams of students chose words for display on the wall. Once the class agreed on the words to study, students then worked in pairs, wrote their selected words on index cards, and elaborated definitions through words, pictures, and symbols. When compared with a control group using a more traditional vocabulary notebook, students in the word wall experimental group demonstrated a higher level of understanding of word meanings on a delayed test of sentence completion. When interviewed about the effectiveness of the word wall for learning new words, students unanimously agreed that the word wall helped them remember word meanings.

Consider developing an electronic Academic Word Wall. Create a background or border with the words using a smart board or a screen saver which students keep on their laptops. Students can also create their own individual word walls using power points slides.

Actively engage students in the use of the Academic Word Wall in conjunction with many of the vocabulary strategies described later in this chapter.

The picture below is an example of a Academic Word Wall from a high school art class.

Vocabulary Learning Logs

Even though we have an entire chapter on informal writing and learning logs in this book, we have included a brief reminder here about how important it is for students to keep track of words they are learning. We recommend students have sections of their notebooks reserved just for vocabulary. This learning log might be a separate spiral notebook or included as a section of a course binder or in an online journal as part of a digital portfolio.

Vocabulary selection can be as simple as asking students to choose words from their reading that they find new, interesting, or unusual, or more teacher directed where they keep track of the academic vocabulary essential to learning the content. Entries may involve graphic organizers, writing explanations, visual images, examples, applications, or a combination of approaches.

Students can use vocabulary journals to expand definitions as in this middle school math example:

Math Vocabulary

Word	Meaning	Description or picture	How will I remember it
Area	The measure inside of a figure	[grid rectangle]	The space inside a shape
Perimeter	The measure outside of a figure	[rectangle with 7, 5, 7, 5]	outside a shape
Volume	L x W x H	[cube with 3, 2, 7]	it's 3D
Prism	[prism drawing]	[prism drawing]	[prism drawing]
Estimate	rounded	7 → 10	educated guess
Cube	6 faced figure	[cube] 6 faces	[die] Like dice
Face	[square] one side of a 3-D figure	[cube] 1 face	one of the sides
Edge	[cube] where 2 faces intersect	[shape] 3 edges	where 2 sides meet — a line
Vertex / Vertices	[square with dots] Points on a square	[shapes with arrows to vertices]	[square with dots] corners

SURVIVAL WORD ATTACK SKILLS

We call learning words through contextual and morphemic analysis survival skills because they lay the foundation for students to progress toward learning vocabulary independently. Since these skills are basic to acquiring new vocabulary, they are components of most vocabulary strategies. Effective word learners approach unknown words by reading the surrounding context, by breaking the word into meaningful parts, or morphemes, by hypothesizing the meaning of the larger word, and then by checking their meaning with the context and their own background knowledge.

Vocabulary 225

Figuring Out New Words from Context

New words should be introduced in context as the starting point for instruction; however, it is not so easy to learn words from context since natural contexts are not always all that informative. Even so, written context is clearly an important source of information for any reader.

Keep in mind, readers don't learn much about a word from any single encounter. Meeting an unknown word in context gives readers a vague familiarity with the word, but it requires more to make it part of a working vocabulary. Students may misread contextual information or the author's clues may be interpreted in multiple ways. What's clear from the research on contextual analysis is students don't know how to use contextual information effectively.

Our task is to teach students how to hone their abilities to figure out new words in running text. This means we must model our own thinking about what we do when meeting an unfamiliar word. We use the surrounding text—contextual clues, pictures, interrelationships among sentences—to come up with a tentative idea of what a word might mean. Once we have a vague idea, we can confirm definitions by using a glossary or dictionary. Finally, we can demonstrate ways to consolidate word meaning by using a variety of rich vocabulary strategies.

Start by helping students understand the contributions, as well as the limitations of context to word meaning. Sometimes authors are explicit with synonyms, bold print, clear examples, and direct definitions. In other instances, where authors suggest some vague relationships or attributes, the context is not helpful.

Introduction, Modeling, and Reflection

1. Model what you do when confronted with an unfamiliar word in text. After noting the unfamiliar word, talk aloud while you search for clues before and after the word.

2. Talk about the strength of various clues. Are the clues close to the word or are they several sentences away? Some context clues might be strong, clarifying the meaning. In other situations, the clues might be confusing and even misleading. Reread the sentences around the word to see if the meaning you've determined fits.

3. Notice any consistencies in the types of clues. Determine if the author uses specific types of context clues in the text. Authors of science and math texts tend to use context differently than do narrative writers. Develop a chart illustrating the different types of context clues used prevalently in your text. Contextual clues typically fall within these three categories:

    <u>Definition or synonym</u>: Definition and synonym clues are the easiest. The author explicitly embeds the information in the text.

    The patient suffered from **amnesia** or *loss of memory*.

    A **dilemma** is a situation that requires *a choice between two equally unfavorable options*.

    The water ran quickly through the **gully**, *a deep ditch*, then slowed as the land became level.

    <u>Properties or characteristics</u>: This type of clue is a little more difficult. You are given only the properties or characteristics of the word and must infer the meaning.

    A **friend** is someone you *like and trust*—someone who understands and helps you.

    The **cypress** has *scale-like leaves* and *round, woody cones*.

    The **pike** lives in *fresh water* in the Northern hemisphere. It has a *long snout* and can grow to over *four feet* in length.

<u>Examples and/or non-examples</u>: This type of clue is even more challenging. The reader has to figure out what critical characteristics the examples have in common or what critical characteristics the non-examples are missing in order to have some idea of what the word means.

Domestic animals, such as *cats, dogs, and cows*, can live comfortably on a farm.

Several kinds of **marsupials** live in Australia, for example *kangaroos, koalas,* and *wombats*

Squares, rectangles, and rhombuses are **quadrilaterals**, but *triangles* and *circles are not.*

4. Once students have a basic understanding of the different ways authors go about clarifying words through context, guide them with the following questions:
   - Is the word in bold print, italics, or highlighted?
   - What contextual clues does the author provide?
   - Are there other aids, such as pictures, illustrations, graphics, or marginal notes?

Reflection

Why is it important to determine whether or not the author has provided sufficient context for initially understanding a new word? How might you apply some of these same authoring techniques to your own written explanations?

Support and Extensions

- Photocopy selections with key vocabulary concepts circled. Instruct students to underline contextual information that explains the concepts. Ask them to note whether or not the contextual information was helpful. If so, have students create their own definitions derived from the contextual information and then check their definitions using a dictionary or glossary. Using note cards, expand definitions using pictures, synonyms, examples, and non-examples.

- Using the following chart, ask students to skim through their reading assignment and record unfamiliar words. Or, you can be more directive and provide a list of academic vocabulary. During or after reading, students examine whether or not the author provided context clues for each word. Remind students to attend to headings, italics, bold print, and visual information. Next, record the page number and predict the meaning from context. Afterwards use a dictionary to check the definition. Then write the word in an original sentence illustrating its meaning or, as an alternative, have students develop a Student-Friendly Explanation (see page 233). Finally, ask them to use the word in oral and written conversations.

Word in Context	Page	Definition in Context	Dictionary Definition	Original Sentence
For some people, however, stress can cause (alienation) feeling isolated and separated from everyone else.	122	Alienation can be caused by stress. It makes people feel alone with no support. They are unable to get help from others.	A withdrawing or separation of a person or a person's affections from an object or position of former attachment.	I had feelings of alienation because I was the last person to be chosen for a team.

Morphemic Analysis

A morpheme is the smallest linguistic unit of a language that has meaning—affixes (prefixes and suffixes) and roots. Fisher and Frey (2009) talk about "learning words inside and out." We learn words from the outside through contextual information embedded in a sentence, a paragraph, a picture, or the whole text. We also look inside the words for clues to meaning. In other words, expert readers become skilled at generating possible meanings based on their knowledge of roots, prefixes, and suffixes. This seems logical, particularly since a majority of English words are built from a few hundred common roots. When learning one word, you actually learn far more. For example, when you learn the word *courage*, you will probably also know: *courageous, courageously, encourage,* and *discourage*.

Analysis of word structure is a resource for learning new words, but research about the effects of morphemic instruction on increasing vocabulary knowledge is both sparse and inconclusive (Beck et al., 2008; Pressley, Disney, & Anderson, 2007). What we do know is students who know how words are formed by combining prefixes, suffixes, and roots tend to have larger vocabularies and better reading comprehension (Kieffer & Lesaux, 2007). While students can learn the meanings of prefixes, suffixes and roots, this knowledge doesn't always result in improved vocabulary learning. Even though supportive research is sketchy, most experts agree that teaching word parts should not be ignored. Many students—even high school students—are unaware that breaking a word into parts can be a way to determine meaning.

The question that remains is what to teach. While lists are available containing hundreds of prefixes, suffixes, and Greek and Latin roots, it is not reasonable to teach them all. Experts agree that less is more. Teach the most commonly used or important elements. For example, only twenty prefixes account for 97 percent of the prefixed words. The same recommendation holds for restricting instruction to the most commonly occurring Greek and Latin roots. Don't ask students to memorize these lists. Instead, teach those relevant to your content. We have included the most common prefixes and suffixes as well as the most commonly occurring Greek and Latin roots on the following page (Bromley, 2007). You can also access these lists in the online reproducibles for Chapter 9. For content areas it makes sense to develop relevant lists. For example a biology teacher's list might include *phototrophs, chemotrophs, autotrophs* derived from the Greek morpheme, *trophs* meaning, "nourishing."

Some caution is warranted. Just as contextual clues don't always illuminate the meaning of a word in text, the same problem occurs with word roots. They can be misleading. For example, knowing that the root *sist* means "stand" doesn't really help in figuring our many of the words containing the root: *assistance, irresistible, consistency* or *persistence*, while learning that the Greek root *hypo* meaning "below" or "beneath" might be helpful in learning the words *hypodermic* and *hypothermia*.

The best advice is to first select the words essential for students to know in a unit and then explore how word parts might help students learn these words. Whenever possible, cluster words into "root" families so that students begin to see how the prefixes, suffixes, and roots function together to affect word meaning.

THE MOST FREQUENTLY APPEARING AND MOST COMMONLY TAUGHT PREFIXES, ROOTS AND SUFFIXES

Most Common Prefixes

Prefix	Definition	Example
re-	again	review, revoke
un-	not	unable, untrue
in-	into or not	insight, inert
en-	in, put into	enliven, ensnare
ex-	out	exit, extinguish
de-	away, from	deflect, denounce
com-	together, with	commune, communicate
dis-	apart	dishonest, disagree
pre-	before	prevent, predict
sub-	under	submerge, submarine

Most Common Roots

Root	Definition	Example
tract	drag, pull	tractor, distract
spect	look	inspect, spectacle
port	carry	portable, important
dict	say	diction, dictionary, prediction
rupt	break	interrupt, rupture
scrib	write	inscribe, describe, scripture
cred	believe	credit, discredit
vid	see	video, evidence
aud	hear	audience, auditorium, audible

Most Common Suffixes

Suffix	Definition	Example
-ly	having the quality of	lightly, sweetly, weekly
-er	more	higher, stronger, smoother
-able/-ible	able to	believable, deliverable, incredible
-tion/-sion	a thing, a noun	invention, suspension, tension
-cle	small	particle
-less	without	treeless, motionless
-est	most	biggest, hardest, brightest
-ment	quality or act	contentment, excitement, basement
-ness	quality or act	kindness, wildness, softness
-arium	a place for	aquarium, terrarium
-ling	small	duckling, gosling, hatchling

Introduction, Modeling, and Reflection

1. Make a list of academic words having common roots and or prefixes.
2. Model how to analyze a word for morphemes. Based on the word parts, make a hypothesis about the meaning. Check the hypothesis for viability within the context.

3. Teach students an overall word learning strategy combining contextual and morphemic analysis. For example, when coming to an unknown word in text, have students complete the following chart:

Word	Morphemic Clues	Before Reading Prediction	After Reading Meaning	Contextual Clues

Guide the students through the process:

See if you can divide the word into parts—separate the prefixes and suffixes from the root. Hypothesize a meaning based on what you know about the meaning of individual word parts.

Use the surrounding context—read the sentences around the word to gather additional information about the word's meaning.

Check in the dictionary or glossary for added information.

Reflection

How might you use Morphemic Analysis to extend your vocabulary? In what situations is it useful? What do we mean by learning words "from the inside out"? Why is this a metacognitive strategy?

Support and Extensions

- Label sections of your Academic Word Wall for prefixes, roots, and suffixes. Consider using different color-coded index cards differentiating prefixes, roots, and suffixes so students can more readily build and deconstruct words. Categorize the words by roots or prefixes and build words by combining morphemic structures.

- Have students or buddies make derivational trees or charts. They can access a dictionary of Greek and Latin roots online or have them bookmark it on their computers. This kind of dictionary is particularly helpful for figuring out science terms. They can also use this resource for building word maps similar to the following example.

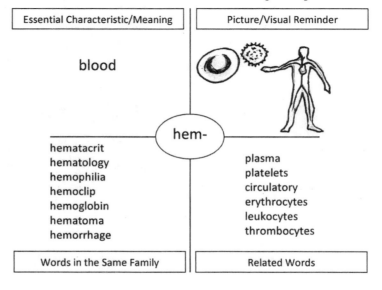

- Project a list of Greek and Latin roots. Challenge students to use their text or dictionary to develop word lists based on these roots.

    Malum, mali (Latin for evil or harm): malaria, malady, malcontent, malevolent, malicious, malignant, malnourished, malodorous, malpractice

    Omnis (Latin for all): omnipotent, omnipresent, omniscient, omnivore, omnivorous

- Students can make their own "possible" vocabulary using word parts appropriate to the text. For example a science teacher might ask students to create three vocabulary terms that might be in the text on photosynthesis with the word parts: *auto, chemo, photo, hetero.*

- Many words in English and Spanish are cognates (have a similar derivation). Knowing a word meaning in one language will help you understand its cognate in the other. For example, if students know the word *identification* in English, they will have no trouble learning the Spanish word, *identificacion*. Some excellent resources on cognates are available online.

BUILDING PERSONAL DEFINITIONS

Our goal is for students to own academic vocabulary. We want them to use a word comfortably in both written and oral contexts. They need to personalize new words to make them their own. Begin vocabulary instruction by having students acknowledge their starting point with a new word. Do they have any idea what the word means? Have they had any experience with it? Inviting students to examine their own background knowledge begins the personalization process and builds curiosity. The conclusion of vocabulary lessons should provide students opportunities for developing their own Student-Friendly Explanations. Therefore, we can think about vocabulary instruction as having two end points–a beginning where students determine their personal status with a word, and an ending where they have explored a word sufficiently to develop their own definitions based on what they have learned about the word. Rich vocabulary instruction is what occurs between these two end points. Rate Your Knowledge and Student-Friendly Explanations provide good ways to begin and end most instructional sequences. These approaches are based on the work of Beck et al. (2002), Dale (1965), and Buehl (2009).

Rate Your Knowledge

Because we learn vocabulary incrementally, Rate Your Knowledge is a great first step as students begin the process of learning key vocabulary terms. Students assess their level of understanding and identify their current background knowledge related to the terms.

Introduction, Modeling, and Reflection

1. Select words from materials students will read in class. Choose words worth your instructional time that are important for understanding the central ideas of the piece.
2. Pronounce the words. If students can't pronounce the word they will shy away from using it in their discussions. Read the words chorally. Consider writing the word on the board with a simplified phonetic guide.
3. Prompt students to rate their own knowledge of the word using the criteria below:

    K – I **k**now it. I can define it and use it in my speaking and writing.
    H – I have a **h**unch about what it means. I have some idea about the word.
    S – It is **s**omewhat familiar; I have seen it, but I don't know it.
    N – It is **n**ot familiar. I have never seen it before.

4. Invite them to work in pairs discussing the words and the rationale behind their ratings.

5. Assign students to read the selection containing the words, and then lead a discussion where they analyze the contextual presentation for each word. If appropriate, remind them to use morphemic cues: prefixes, root, and suffixes.

6. Finally, pairs discuss the word and develop Student-Friendly Explanations (next strategy). If necessary, check definitions using a dictionary.

7. Return to the rating scale. Revise. How would they rate their knowledge now? Talk about how their ratings have changed.

> ### Reflection
> How does examining your own knowledge about a word help prepare you for a more in depth understanding of the word? How might misconceptions about a word influence your learning? Why is it a good idea to be aware of potential misunderstandings about a word?

Support and Extensions

- Vocabulary Knowledge Chart. Before students read, ask them to divide their vocabulary journals into six columns and create a Vocabulary Knowledge Chart. Select important words from the passage. Note key vocabulary on the Academic Word Wall or on the board. Read and pronounce the words. Ask students to discuss the possible meanings with a partner, then record the words in the first column and check (✓) the column that best describes their knowledge. Conclude by asking students to write Student-Friendly Explanations for each word (see page 233).

Word	Know it (K)	Have a Hunch (H)	Somewhat Familiar (S)	Not Familiar (N)	Student-Friendly Definition

Note: Consider using sticky notes instead of check marks so that students can shift the columns as they become more familiar with them. (Adapted from Blachowicz & Fisher, 2006).

- Encourage students to use their Vocabulary Knowledge Charts for test preparation. These charts help student assess their progress learning key vocabulary. They can use the chart as a review to see if they can now mark all the words with a K and talk or write about the words using Student-Friendly Explanations (see next strategy).

Student-Friendly Explanations

Invite students to glance through a dictionary, read aloud a few definitions, and talk about potential problems using a dictionary as the primary tool for learning new words. Note that most definitions are terse statements comprised of vague language and with vocabulary often more difficult than the word being defined. Talk about why just looking up words in the dictionary and copying definitions is considered by experts a dubious vocabulary practice especially when used alone without expanding upon the definition through writing and conversation. Yet not all is lost—definitions can be extremely effective when students know how to create their own.

Introduction, Modeling, and Reflection

1. Model an explanation of a word using multiple contexts. Help students bring a word to life. Explain what it means by using everyday language within a variety of situations. Anchor your explanations with familiar events using the words <u>you</u>, <u>someone</u>, or <u>something</u>.

    *If <u>someone</u> is **obstreperous**, they are being cranky and unpleasant. When <u>you</u> are **obstreperous**, <u>you</u> aren't going along with someone else's plan. <u>You</u> are acting stubborn, not wanting to be controlled. <u>Someone</u> being **obstreperous** with you is not doing what you asked and tends to be rather loud and obnoxious. <u>Something</u> I have learned about **obstreperous** people is that they are difficult to be around.*

2. Talk about who might use the word in their conversations and in written work. Then, compare your explanation with how it is defined in a dictionary or glossary. Evaluate which was more helpful—explaining the word or reading the definition out of a dictionary.

3. Invite students to offer additional explanations of the word using <u>you</u>, <u>someone</u>, <u>something</u>, or using a new context. For example, an *obstreperous* speeder pulled over by a policeman is more likely to receive a ticket. In a hospital, an *obstreperous* person might be strapped to his bed.

Reflection
Why are Student-Friendly Explanations more helpful than the typical dictionary definitions?

Support and Extensions

- Ask students to select three or four words from an assignment or have them select a word from a list identified as essential to understanding the content. Have them work together in pairs or groups to develop Student-Friendly Explanations to teach the class. Prompt students to keep records using a guide similar to the following:

Word in Context	Explanation Using Everyday Language	Example Sentences Using Words: *You*, *Something*, and *Someone*

- Provide Sentence Frames for students to complete that guide them to Student-Friendly Explanations of a word.

    The _____ was *obstreperous* because…

    When _____ is *insolent*, s/he…

Frames are particularly helpful to students whose "explanations" look like this: *The boy was obstreperous*. After providing some model fames, students can start creating their own. Make sure they understand they must include prompting words such as *because* or *when*.

- Ask students to elaborate with more extended writing. For example, think of a time when you were *insolent* and write a paragraph about it.

- Reinforce Student-Friendly Explanations by playing vocabulary games (Townsend, 2009):
    - *Academic Taboo* Divide students into teams. Give each team a target word which they explain using descriptive words. However, they can't use synonyms or definitions in their descriptions. Instead, they talk around the word by describing people and events where the word might be used.
    - *Pictonades* (Pictionary + Charades) One person is given a word card and asked to silently draw the word meaning within a limited amount of time or by acting out the word meaning. Other participants guess what the word might be.

- Assign students the job of becoming a Word Expert for three or four words (Richek, 2005). Give each student a large note card. Ask them to write the word on the front and use the back to expand the definition. *Find the word in context and record the sentence; write the dictionary definition; note roots and affixes; draw a picture; write an original sentence including the words you, someone or something*. Students then use their note cards for peer teaching. Add the expert cards to the word wall.

- Ask students to compare Student-Friendly Explanations with definitions in the glossary or dictionary. For example, they might compare the following:

Science (*homeostasis*)

Glossary definition: The maintenance of a stable equilibrium, especially through psychological processes.

Student-Friendly Explanation: You want your body to be in *homeostasis*, or in a state of balance. Someone who gets too hot because they have the heat set too high will start sweating to bring his or her body temperature to *homeostasis*. Something that upsets *homeostasis* is a high fever.

Mathematics (*equation*)

Glossary Definition: Equation: A mathematical sentence that contains an equal sign, "=" (Glencoe, Algebra 1).

Student-Friendly Explanation: Someone can create an *equation* by determining two mathematical expressions that are equal in value and then placing an equal sign between them.

An *equation* is like a balance scale because you can add the same thing to both sides or subtract the same thing from both sides and the *equation* or scale stays in balance.

You can usually solve a linear *equation* by simplifying both sides of the equals sign. Usually this involves adding or subtracting the same thing (number or variable) to/from both sides and then by multiplying or dividing both sides by the same number.

GRAPHIC ORGANIZERS AND CHARTS

Word maps and charts help students expand word meanings and discover relationships. They also help students develop elaborated friendly definitions rather than simple one- or two-word explanations. In addition, they provide students with a way to learn vocabulary independently.

Concept of Definition Map

Too many students have a narrow conception of what a word's meaning includes. Most conceive definitions as simplistic, imprecise statements lacking elaboration and personal comment. Schwartz (1988) and Schwartz and Raphael (1985) designed an instructional approach for teaching students a broader concept of a definition, one that encourages them to integrate their own knowledge into the components of a definition. Once students understand the qualities of a definition, they apply this general knowledge in order to expand their own vocabularies and master unfamiliar concepts.

Introduction, Modeling, and Reflection

1. To help students visualize the components of a definition, show a Concept of Definition Map (picture below and available online in the reproducibles for Chapter 9). The map includes three relationships essential to a rich definition:
   - What is it? (Category)
   - What is like? (Properties)
   - What are some examples? (Illustrations)

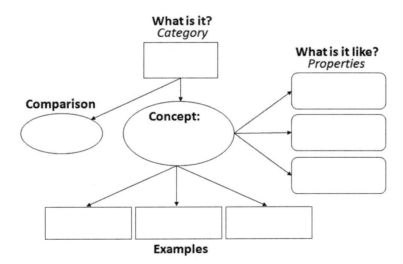

2. Model the process using a familiar concept. For example, ask students about a favorite pet, such as a type of dog—a *terrier*. Write the word *terrier* in the center box. Above terrier (in the top box) write a word that describes the category of animal under which *terrier* fits—*dog*. On the right side, list the properties of the terrier, answering, "What is it like?" In these boxes, you might write *wiry hair, vary in size, bred to hunt small animals*. The bottom boxes are for examples of terriers. In these boxes, you could put *Cairn Terrier, West Highland Terrier*, and *Jack Russell Terrier*.

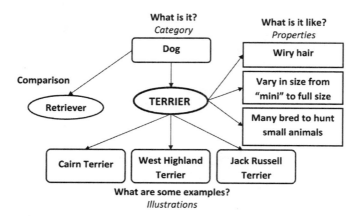

3. Sometimes, when thinking about properties, it is helpful to have a comparison item. In this case, a comparison could be *retrievers*, another type of dog. Write this to the left of the "Terrier" box and connect it as shown to the top box—Dog.

4. Once students have completed the Concept of Definition Map, ask them to write a Student-Friendly Explanation using the information on the map.

   One of my favorite types of dogs is the terrier. The terrier breed is different from the popular retriever breed in several ways. First, terriers have coarse, wiry hair quite different from the smooth or silky retriever coat. Unlike the larger retriever breed, terriers come in all sizes, from a five-pound Yorkshire terrier to an eighty-pound Pit Bull Terrier. They were bred to be tireless while chasing small animals such as rats, rabbits, and badgers. Three of the smaller types of terriers are the Cairn Terrier, the West Highland Terrier and the Jack Russell Terrier.

5. Display vocabulary words on the Word Wall using Concept of Definition Maps. Use for developing Student-Friendly Explanations.

Reflection

Why are expanded definitions so much better than those typically found in a dictionary? Do you have a better understanding of the word? How does expanding a definition help you really know it?

Support and Extensions

- As part of the pre-reading discussion, ask students to brainstorm what they already know using the Concept of Definition Map. Next, have them skim the selection and add information or illustrations to their brainstormed map. After students read, have them work in pairs to fill in additional information and make corrections as necessary. Students then present their maps for discussion.

- Students can use their maps as a guide for note taking from discussions and content texts. For example, a sixth grade class defined concepts from a social studies unit on state government. One of the terms was *lobbyist*. The students read and took notes on several articles. They organized their notes on a Concept of Definition map and then wove their ideas into a friendly definition.

- Assign students to develop Concept of Definition Maps for concepts and key terms as a strategy for studying and reviewing for tests as in the following math example:

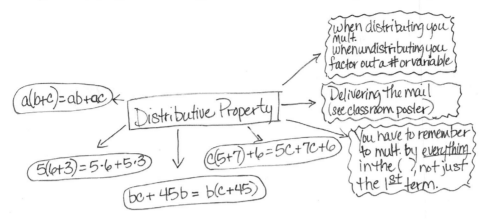

- Encourage students to modify or create their own Concept of Definition Maps. In the following example, sixth graders were studying the Commonwealth of Nations. They decided that these were the important things to know about the concept: *a definition, the facts, reasons for its existence,* and *examples of countries comprising the commonwealth.* Students took notes from their social studies text and then used their notes to write an explanation or a Student-Friendly Explanation.

- Modify maps for taking notes on biographies. In one class, fifth graders reading biographies of American heroes developed maps defining the unique qualities of these historical figures. Their maps served as pre-writing material for brief reports.

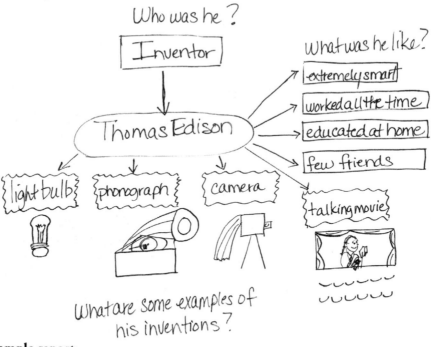

Sample report:

Thomas Edison was a famous inventor. He thought of all sorts of things. He invented the light bulb and made a talking movie. He also invented a phonograph and camera. He must have been very smart. He was such a hard worker that he didn't have many friends. He also didn't make friends at school. He must have been kind of lonely.

Vocabulary Maps

Students can use Vocabulary Maps to elaborate on concepts by recording definitions, sentences, synonyms, and pictures.

Introduction, Modeling, and Reflection

1. Explain to students that developing Vocabulary Maps provides another way to elaborate on important concepts.

2. Model with a familiar word. List the word in the center of the page and surround it with the following information: the definition (in their own words), a synonym or explanation, a picture illustrating the word or statement, and an original sentence containing the word. Remind students to include the words *someone, you,* or *something* in their original sentence (or words that could replace it, like "Nicole" in the following paragraph).

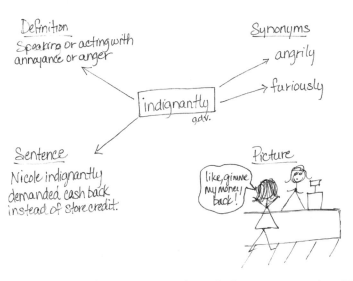

Pair students, and have them develop several vocabulary maps together. Then, ask them to present their maps to the class.

Reflection
How does expanding definitions help you attain a better metacognitive awareness about how well you know a concept? If you can't map a word, what does that tell you about how well you understand it? Why does mapping a word lead to long-term retention of the concept?

Support and Extensions

- The Vocabulary Map works extremely well for learning vocabulary in a second language, as in this Norwegian example.

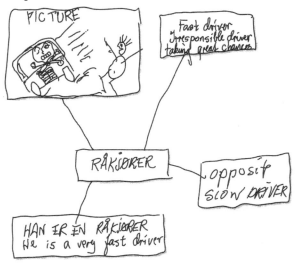

Vocabulary 239

- Students studying mythology in a ninth grade class also expanded words with pictures, definitions, and sentences. In addition, they linked the words to their roots in mythology.
- <u>Vocabulary Flash Cards</u>. Encourage students to expand definitions using Vocabulary Flash Cards. Challenge them to include pictures, explanations, examples, and original sentences as in the following example.

- For another variation, have students create a flipbook to hold important vocabulary words from a unit of study along with appropriate word maps and charts.
- Include Vocabulary Maps and Concept of Definition Maps on the Academic Word Wall.

Frayer Model

Think about how we learn a new concept. Initially we have a superficial understanding, perhaps a one- or two-word definition. As we meet the concept over a period of time, we start to understand it more deeply. We begin to know its essential and non-essential characteristics and to understand examples that illustrate it. We follow the process of deepening understanding described in the Frayer Model of concept development (Frayer, Fredrick, & Klausmeier as cited in Fisher & Frey, 2008).

The Frayer Model is a visual organizer containing four sections: essential and non-essential characteristics and examples and non-examples.

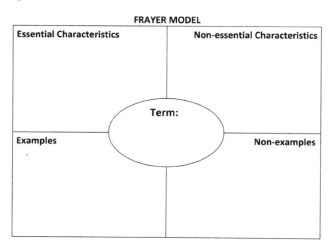

This model helps us differentiate characteristics that define the concept and those only marginally associated with it. Let's try it with the concept "metacognition." What does it mean to be metacognitive? What are the essential characteristics? Non-essential characteristics? What are some examples of being metacognitive? Non-examples?

Essential Characteristics	Non-Essential Characteristics
active learning	answering chapter questions
self-monitoring	listening
self-reflection	reading

METACOGNITION

Examples	Non-Examples
self testing	rote learning
process conferences	reading and rereading text
understanding author's craft	always using the same note-taking system

Introduction, Modeling, and Reflection

1. Review the Frayer Model format. Model digitally using an interactive whiteboard or have students divide a paper into four sections and label it with the four categories (or see the online reproducibles for Chapter 9).

2. Model the Frayer by using a familiar concept—a type of music, sports equipment, something related to a hobby or school activity. Although entries may seem obvious to students, have them imagine they will use the Frayer to explain the concept to someone older, younger, or from another country who doesn't understand the term. Essential and non-essential characteristics are the most difficult. Here are some points to help your students understand these concepts:

   Essential Characteristics: These are things that must be a part of your concept. Without the essential characteristics it wouldn't exist. These traits are critical.

   Non-essential Characteristics: These are characteristics that may be attributed to the concept, but they aren't required. They may be options or traits that aren't always present.

   > *Models of essential and non-essential:* It's *essential* that a coffee cup can hold liquid, that it has a handle or other device that allows a person to use the cup without burning his or her hands, and its size and shape are appropriate for drinking coffee. The composition of the cup—pottery, glass, or plastic—is a *non-essential* characteristic. Insulation and a lid to maintain temperature are non-essential characteristics.

   Examples: These should have all of the essential characteristics. For "coffee cup," students might say, "Mom's china coffee cup" or "a Starbuck's insulated mug." These examples have all of the essential characteristics.

   Non-examples: The best *non-examples* have some of the essential characteristics, but not all. A plastic water bottle is a non-example. The plastic water bottle cannot protect you from burning your fingers, but it can hold coffee and the size and shape are appropriate for drinking. A pencil is also a non-example, but not a good one since it lacks all of the essential characteristics.

3. As you model with students, record one or two items in an area of the Frayer Model, and then ask for input. For some concepts, it might be best to start with examples, and then talk about the essential or shared characteristics of the examples. Discuss the types of information you know about the concept and where this information should be placed in the Frayer Model. Is this item truly essential? Does this non-example have some of the essential characteristics?

In the following example, American history students used a Frayer Model to extend their knowledge of *progressivism*. Students discussed what they already knew about it before reading, and then revised their maps after completing the reading. Using the Frayer Model as a pre-reading activity guided students in setting goals for their reading and provided them with a way to organize their notes and check their understanding of a key concept.

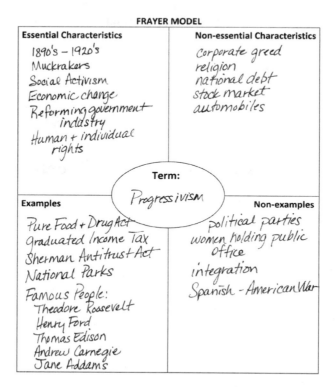

Reflection

Why does analyzing a concept using examples and non-examples help in clarifying concepts? How did the Frayer Model help to organize your thinking?

Support and Extensions

- Create a Frayer Model for words posted on the Academic Word Wall. Ask students to use the Frayer model to expand definitions in their learning logs. Using the Frayer Model, have students create Student-Friendly Explanations using at least one word from each quadrant, as in this example based on the Frayer above:

    *In the late 19th and early 20th centuries, if you supported **progressivism**, you most likely were a social activist and would spend your time trying to get the government to do something about the injustices that you saw around you. In addition, you would want a goverment that wasn't corrupt. You could be a member of either political party—Republican President Theodore Roosevelt and Democrat industrialist Henry Ford were both associated with **progressivism**. Journalists linked to **progressivism** were called muckrakers. They exposed corporate greed that resulted in poor working conditions, child labor, and unsafe food and medicine. Some good things came out of this era of **progressivism** such as the Pure Food and Drug Act, enforcement of Sherman's Antitrust Act, and the establishment of national parks.*

- Ask students to list the major concepts in a unit and then work in pairs to complete a Frayer Model over one or two concepts. Make sure all concepts are covered by at least one group. They can present their models to the class, and then you can post their work around the room as a class review.

- Use the Frayer Model to assess understanding of important concepts. List three or four key concepts from a unit. Students use an adapted Frayer Model to elaborate on the concepts. In this example, chemistry students completed a Frayer Model as an assessment in chemistry.

DEFINITION	CHARACTERISTICS
a substance made up of 2 or more different elements — combined chemically	chemically combined — not just mixed. In formula H_2O "2" tells # of parts of each element. 2-H's to 1-O
EXAMPLES	NON-EXAMPLES
H_2O (water) $C_{12}H_{22}O_{11}$ (sugar) $NaCl$ (salt)	H (one element) an atom of same thing

Concept: Compound

- Use the Frayer Model as a tool for character analysis.

- Students can create a Frayer Model for use as a study guide or a writing tool.

- Some teachers find it unnecessary to use the non-essential characteristics of the Frayer Model. They have simplified it to include essential characteristics, examples, and non-examples.

- Geometry teacher John Skoog modified the Frayer to help his students learn about theorems and their converses. He started by having students read and discuss a theorem in their book, and then he handed out the modified Frayer and asked students to develop a conjecture about the converse of the theorem. In the following example, students predicted the converse of the Same-Side Interior Angles Theorem.

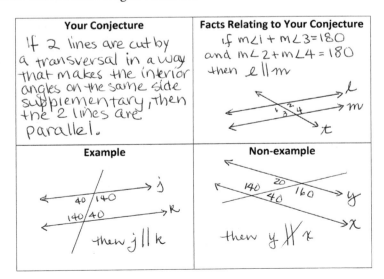

Vocabulary 243

Semantic Feature Analysis

Semantic Feature Analysis (Johnson & Pearson, 1984; Fisher & Frey, 2008) helps students link key vocabulary to major ideas from a content selection. It is a graphic display that focuses on the features that distinguish words in a particular category. Using a matrix grid, students analyze the distinguishing features of concepts according to key characteristics.

Semantic Feature Analysis (SFA) is well grounded in research (Anders & Bos, 1986). Students use background knowledge, become actively involved in relating ideas, and with practice can learn to use the procedure independently. More importantly, the strategy leads to improved learning, particularly for students who have reading difficulties.

Introduction, Modeling, and Reflection

1. Project a blank SFA grid (available in the online reproducibles for Chapter 9) and model using a familiar category such energy sources.

2. Solicit examples (e.g. petroleum, wind, etc.) and write them in the spaces on the vertical column. For the horizontal column ask students to think about characteristics or attributes of the different sources of energy and write these in the horizontal spaces (see the following example).

3. Model how to code the examples and the attributes. Discuss relationships between the features and the terms. A plus (+) represents a positive relationship and a minus (-) represents a negative relationship. In cases where there is no relationship, a zero (0) is appropriate.

4. Have students substantiate their decisions for the various codes (+, -, 0).

Energy Type/Source	Renewable	Greenhouse Gases	Toxic Waste	Clean	Explanation
Petroleum	-	+	+	-	
Coal	-	+	+	-	"Clean coal" technology under development
Nuclear	-	-	+	-/+	
Wind	+	-	-	+	
Solar	+	-	-	+	
Waves	+	-	-	+	
Hydroelectric	-/+	-	-	-/+	Flowing water is renewable, but the construction of dams creates other problems.

Reflection

How might you organize other concepts using SFA? How does analyzing concepts by attributes help deepen your understanding?"

Support and Extensions

- Use SFA as a pre-reading activity. After students read, have them revise the codes and modify existing features. Encourage them to include additional features and terms on the matrix.

- After students have read a novel, list the main characters in the first column and personality features (sensitive, evil, manipulative) across the top row. As part of discussion teams, use the matrix to analyze characters. Teams can then present their matrices as part of a whole-class discussion.

- Students can readily use the information organized in the matrix to write about the topic.

- Use the matrix as a review for a test or as an alternative way to assess as in the following chemistry example:

Directions: For each word listed below, put a "+" in the box if the characteristic is true for the word. Put a "-" in the box if the characteristic is not true.

	Solid, liquid, or gas	Has mass	On Periodic Table	Seen with Naked Eye	Has Chemical Formula	What it's Made of Cannot Change	Heterogeneous or Homogeneous	Can be Broken Down	Has Multiple Atoms
Matter	+	+	+	+	−	−	+	+	+
Elements	+	+	+	+	+	+	−	−	+
Atom	+	+	+	−	−	−	−	−	−
Compound	+	+	−	−	−	−	−	+	+
Molecule	+	+	−	−	+	−	−	−	−
Pure Substance	+	+	+	+	+	−	−	+	+
Mixture	+	+	−	+	+	+	+	+	+

Summary Sentence: Pick any two words above and write a sentence comparing the two words. Write it below and be ready to share with the class. <u>Elements</u> and <u>pure substances</u> are alike since they have mass; can exist as solids, liquids, or gases; and can be seen with the naked eye, however, elements can't be broken down or their composition changed, but that can happen with <u>pure substances</u>.

ACTIVE PROCESSING THROUGH WRITING AND DISCUSSION

Effective vocabulary instruction encourages students to discuss and demonstrate meanings. The instructional strategies in this section focus on ways to expand definitions of words through reading, writing, and talking.

Vocabulary 245

Word Elaboration

Vocabulary is truly learned when it can be used accurately in speaking, listening, and writing. Word Elaboration involves three steps: talking, listening, and writing.

Introduction, Modeling, and Reflection

1. Select eight to ten words that relate to a single topic or concept students have studied. Write these words on the board. Ask students to record them in their learning logs.

2. Begin discussing the topic with the class using the listed words. In your model discussion, include context clues with the words.

   In this example, notice that each person offers new information about the terms when speaking. Not all of the words have to be used in one sentence.

Words:	*square, rhombus, rectangle, parallelogram*
Student 1:	I learned that a *square* is a four-sided geometric figure. All four sides are equal.
Student 2:	What you say is true, but a *rhombus* also has four sides of equal measure. What's the difference?
Student 1:	The difference is that the *square* has to have all four angles with the same measure—90 degrees. That is not required for a *rhombus*.
Student 2:	You know, that's kind of like the *parallelogram* and the *rectangle*. The *rectangle* has to have four right angles, but the *parallelgram* doesn't.
Student 1:	The *square* is a special *rectangle* with all sides equal and also a special *rhombus* with all angles of equal measure. The *rhombus* is a special *parallelogram* with all sides equal.

3. Pair students. Partners hold a conversation using as many words as they can. Each student keeps track of the words his or her partner uses correctly. Encourage students to use Student-Friendly Explanations.

4. Using the vocabulary words, each student writes a summary or brief paper on the topic. Explanations need to be in a student-friendly format.

Reflection

What does this strategy do to help you understand and learn new concepts? How does it include the elements of the CRISS Framework for Learning?

Support and Extensions

- Use Word Elaboration as a review of key vocabulary for a test and for foreign language practice.
- After students have read an assignment, have them list one or two key concepts from their reading and the vocabulary related to the concept. Follow through with the steps outlined above.
- Have students carry on their discussions digitally using e-mail or a blog.

Sentence and Word Expansion

Expansion is a brainstorming procedure that helps students elaborate on concepts and terms. Students can then use the expanded vocabulary in their speech and writing. Word Expansion works well as a revision procedure for incorporating more precise vocabulary in writing. It can also help students untangle difficult readings.

Introduction, Modeling, and Reflection

1. Take a concept from a text and use it in a simple sentence.
2. Decide upon a series of questions that make sense for the particular concept. Then answer the questions.

Concept in a Simple Sentence:	Plants photosynthesize.
What kind?	green trees, flowering plants, grass
When?	daytime, summer, when sun is out, some parts don't require sun, in artificial light
Where?	chloroplasts, leaves, chlorophyll
What is necessary?	sunlight, water, carbon dioxide, temperature
What is formed?	glucose, oxygen
Why?	to change light energy to chemical energy

3. Then ask students to expand the original sentence.

   Trees and flowering plants photosynthesize in the daytime. The chlorophyll in the chloroplasts located in the leaves combines with light, water, and carbon dioxide to form glucose and oxygen. The end result is that light energy changes into chemical energy.

Reflection

How might you use this strategy to write better explanations? How might you use it as a revision technique for your own writing?

Support and Extensions

- Expansion activities work well at the single word level, particularly when the expanded word is dull and overused. When a fourth grade teacher noticed that her students constantly used the word *said* in written dialogue, she decided to have a contest to get rid of the monotony. She divided her class into three teams and had each team find alternatives to *said*. Each team kept track of their words on a large sheet of paper. Each time a student thought of a new word for *said*, or came across one in their reading or conversation, they wrote it on the chart. The group that came up with the most words won.

Vocabulary 247

REPLACEMENT WORDS FOR *SAID*		
Group 1	**Group 2**	**Group 3**
asked	snorted	questioned
exclaimed	continued	guessed
replied	laughed	begged
muttered	yawned	grunted
yelled	screamed	suggested
explained	called	promised
groaned	screeched	demanded
whined	comforted	grumbled
wailed	squealed	mumbled
whispered	gulped	complained
cried	chuckled	begged
growled	gasped	commanded
boasted	requested	murmured
threatened	answered	refused
moaned	pleaded	decided
sighed		
giggled		

This activity with said or another word works best in cooperative teams. Students may use an online thesaurus or a hard copy. Display words on a large sheet of chart paper as a resource for writing.

- A middle school social studies teacher used the reverse form of Word Expansion to help her students untangle the meaning of the *Gettysburg Address*. She projected the *Gettysburg Address* on a whiteboard, then took students through the document line by line. They replaced complicated vocabulary with simpler, everyday language.

> **THE GETTYSBURG ADDRESS**
>
> Eighty— (4 × 20 = 80) ancestors started here in North America,
> ~~Fourscore~~ and seven years ago our ~~forefathers~~ brought forth, ~~upon this continent,~~ a new
> country, formed in freedom,   idea   people should be treated the same.
> ~~nation, conceived in Liberty,~~ and dedicated to the ~~proposition~~ that all ~~men are created equal.~~
>   involved   finding out if the United States,   country
> Now we are ~~engaged~~ in a great civil war, ~~testing whether that nation,~~ or any ~~nation so~~
> based on freedom, continue a long time.   Meeting   the Civil War.
> ~~conceived, and so dedicated,~~ can ~~long endure.~~ We are ~~met~~ here on a great battlefield of ~~that war.~~
>   piece   cemetery for the people who died
> We have come to dedicate a ~~portion~~ of it as a ~~final resting place for those who here gave their~~
> so   country continue. very good and acceptable
> ~~lives~~ that this ~~nation~~ might ~~live.~~ It is ~~altogether fitting and proper~~ that we should do this.
>   the bigger picture,   make special   bless
> But in ~~a larger sense,~~ we cannot dedicate—we cannot ~~consecrate~~—we cannot ~~hallow~~ this
> cemetery   made it special   beyond
> ~~ground.~~ The brave men, living and dead, who struggled, here, have ~~consecrated it~~ far ~~above~~ our
> ability to do more.   not   is said
> ~~poor power to add or detract.~~ The world will ~~little note, nor~~ long remember, what ~~we say~~ here,
>   the Civil War soldiers
> but can never forget what ~~they~~ did here……
>
> Sandy M., Grade 7

• 248   Chapter 9

After brainstorming the students rewrote the Gettysburg Address using the replacement words.

Student Revision

Eighty-seven years ago our ancestors started here in North America, a new country, formed in freedom, and dedicated to the idea that all people should be treated the same.

Now we are involved in a great civil war, finding out if the United States, or any country based on freedom, can continue a long time. We are meeting on a great battlefield of the Civil War. We have come to dedicate a piece of it as a cemetery for the people who died so that this country might continue. It is very good and acceptable that we should do this.

But in the bigger picture, we cannot dedicate—we cannot make special—we cannot bless this cemetery. The brave men, living and dead, who struggled here, have made it special far beyond our ability to do more. The world will not remember very long what is said here, but can never forget what the Civil War soldiers did here.

Sandy M., Grade 7

- A problem-solving strategy in mathematics is rewriting a word problem into simpler language and/or form.

  Original problem: *Find three positive, even consecutive integers such that the product of the two smallest integers is equal to two-thirds the product of the two largest integers.*

  Rewritten problem: *Find three even numbers all positive. They must be in a row, like 2-4-6 or 10-12-14. When you multiply the two smallest numbers, your answer should be the same as multiplying two-thirds times the answer you get when you multiply the two largest numbers.*

Word Combining

With Word Combining, students combine new words into original sentences and short paragraphs. Use it to reinforce vocabulary previously introduced. Students must have some familiarity with the words in order to use them successfully in their writing.

Introduction, Modeling, and Reflection

1. List three to five conceptually-related words on the board (or select words from the Academic Word Wall).
2. Review the words in a class discussion.
3. On the board, model one or two sentences using contextual clues to explain the words. If possible, show how the words relate to each other, as in the following mathematics and social studies examples.

Mathematics: Geometry unit on circles

Vocabulary words: *circle, center, diameter, radius, circumference*

The *diameter* of a *circle*, which is twice the length of the circle's *radius*, is the distance across the circle and through its *center*. The *circumference*, or distance around a *circle* is about three times the length of the *diameter* and about six times the length of the *radius*.

Social Studies: Civil War

Vocabulary words: *civilian, bounty, draft, habeas corpus*

By 1863, the Union gave *civilians*, those who had not joined the army, up to $300 in *bounties* or payments to join the Union forces. Because of the shortage of volunteers, the government passed a *draft* law requiring men between the ages of 20 and 45 to serve. To stop riots that broke out in protest of the draft, Lincoln suspended *habeas corpus*, the right to have a hearing before going to jail.

4. Using the same words (or other words from the Academic Word Wall), have students work in pairs to creat a summary paragraph about the concept.

Reflection

How does Word Combining help you to think metacognitively about your understanding of important concepts? How did this strategy help you become more actively involved in learning?

Support and Extensions

- Incorporate Word Combining with lectures. After lecturing for five to ten minutes, list key ideas from your lecture on the board. Using their journals, students quickly combine the words into a sentence or two. Take time to share.

- Use Word Combining to review Main Idea—Detail Notes (see page 137). Use the key words on the left, and have students combine them into one or two sentences.

- Possible Sentences. Ask students to do Word Combining as a way to determine their background knowledge about key concepts in a forthcoming reading assignment or lecture. Provide five or six words and ask students to use at least two in each sentence. Even if they are not sure about the meanings of all the words, they should try to predict the way they relate to one another. As they read, they can decide whether their sentences are correct. If not, they should revise them.

▲ ▲ ▲

Summary

We began this chapter with an overview of seven research principles about vocabulary learning and teaching: (1) Vocabulary knowledge relates to academic success, with those who achieve well in school having far more extensive vocabularies than those who achieve poorly. (2) A person's vocabulary development directly relates to how much one reads and (3) is strongly related to reading comprehension. (4) Pre-teaching key vocabulary before students read a selection leads to improved comprehension of the selection containing the pre-taught vocabulary. (5) One of the challenges to effective instruction is to be selective about the words to teach. Teach a few words well. (6) Effective vocabulary instruction involves rich instruction where students actively construct interrelationships among words and expand their understanding with writing and discussion. (7) Finally, we must make learning of new words transparent by helping students understand what it means to know a new word and by showing them strategies for attaining a deep understanding of essential concepts. These metacognitive skills are critical to vocabulary development.

We presented guidelines for selecting words to teach and have described ways to include Academic Word Walls and Vocabulary Journals as critical components of rich instruction. A key aspect of rich instruction is to help students understand how to learn words from inside out (Fisher & Frey, 2009). They must know how to use the surrounding context as well as the internal features of the words—morphemes and affixes—to figure out a word's meaning. We also explained ways to build personal definitions; initiate instruction with strategies for activating students' background knowledge and conclude instruction by generating Student-Friendly Explanations. We then stressed highly effective instructional strategies for helping students attain a deep understanding of content vocabulary. These included graphic organizers and charts and approaches for engaging students in active processing through writing and discussion. In the end, we want our students to be flexible and competent in a variety of procedures, so that they intuitively know the best approach for a particular learning situation.

CHAPTER 9 RESEARCH BASE

Research Conclusion	Reference
Vocabulary development is related to academic success. High school seniors achieving at the top of their class know about four times as many words as underachieving students. Longitudinal studies document that children who grow up in language rich households end up doing better in later reading achievement than do students from language poor families. The relationship between vocabulary and reading proficiency is so powerful that there is some evidence that vocabulary size in kindergarten is an effective predictor of reading comprehension and achievement in later school years.	Beck & McKeown, 2002 Beck, McKeown, & Kucan, 2002
Vocabulary development is positively related to wide reading—the more one reads, the richer one's vocabulary. Increasing the reading time is the most powerful thing we can do to increase vocabulary learning.	Gambrel & Headley, 2006
Learning an unfamiliar word requires repeated encounters in multiple contexts. Struggling readers typically do not read widely enough to have sufficient encounters with unfamiliar words. Individuals who read extensively have far more opportunities to construct meanings of words compared to students who read infrequently. Learning the nuances of words takes multiple exposures within rich contexts.	Gambrel & Headley, 2006
There is a significant relationship between reading comprehension and vocabulary knowledge. Students with a larger vocabulary do better in reading comprehension tasks than do students with poor vocabularies. This relationship is consistent across a variety of methodologies including factor analysis, correlation, and readability research.	Stahl & Fairbanks, 2006
Students do better comprehending a selection when pre-taught important vocabulary in the selection.	Nagy & Scott, 2006
When students study unfamiliar vocabulary in an upcoming reading selection, they do better than their control counterparts in comprehending the selection containing these words, but the effects do not generalize to vocabulary knowledge in general. In other words, learning key vocabulary in a reading selection helps one comprehend the selection containing the vocabulary words but does not necessarily transfer to other selections.	Nagy & Scott, 2006
Effective vocabulary instruction requires multiple exposures in varying contexts along with activities requiring deep processing. Most studies with positive effects involve methodologies where students do multiple "things" with vocabulary. Just looking up words in a dictionary, defining words parts, or analyzing contextual clues in and of themselves are insufficient.	Stahl & Fairbanks, 2006
Metacognitive skills are critical to vocabulary development. To be successful students must know how to learn new vocabulary.	Stahl & Fairbanks, 2006
While the evidence is inconclusive, it does appear that students who know how words are formed combining prefixes, suffixes, and roots tend to have larger vocabularies and better reading comprehension.	Kieffer & Lesaux, 2007

Program Implementation

10

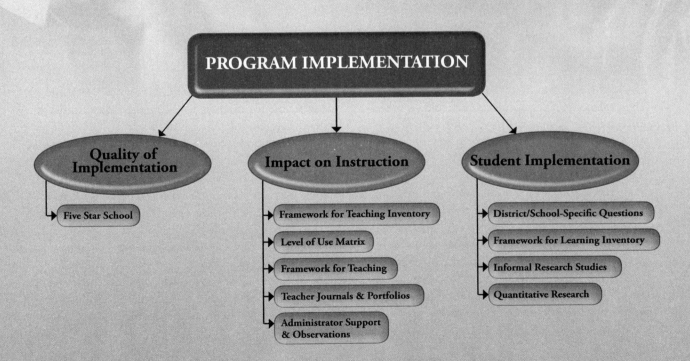

We are asked many questions about ways to evaluate the implementation of Project CRISS, including: How do I know if this project has helped students internalize the Framework for Learning? Do Project CRISS students have a better understanding of how to learn? Are students involved in Project CRISS able to read and learn from their classroom materials better than those who have not been involved? Have teachers changed the way they teach because of Project CRISS? How can we best evaluate whether or not CRISS has been effectively implemented in a district?

Before even considering issues of student or teacher change, the first area to examine is the depth of the Project CRISS implementation within a school. Has the implementation been broad-based, or have only a few teachers participated? If only three or four teachers in a school have attended a 12 to 18 hour CRISS workshop, you can't really look beyond the specific effects in a few individual classrooms. To expect changes within the broader school or district setting would not be reasonable.

One way to examine the depth of a CRISS implementation is to evaluate it in terms of an ideal benchmark. Our "gold standard" of implementation is the CRISS Five Star School. Schools reaching this standard have used the project for several years and have progressively embedded the program within multiple layers of their school setting. Analyzing your level of implementation provides a useful road map for how your school might progress toward becoming a CRISS Five Star School. Evaluating your implementation in terms of the Five Star criteria is the place to start.

QUALITY OF PROJECT CRISS IMPLEMENTATION

Take a moment to review the Project CRISS Five Star School Evaluation (see online reproducibles for Chapter 10). This form pulls together all the features of a Five Star School and provides space where schools can assess their level of implementation and plan for future growth.

The Five Star School

In the Five Star School at least 90 percent of the faculty have attended a Project CRISS Level I workshop. The *Project CRISS for Students* curricula (see page 283) are available for teachers to use in their classrooms. The Five Star School has a designated on-site CRISS Certified Trainer (teacher or administrator) who works with faculty and administrators to ensure continual implementation and follow-up. The CRISS Trainer plans Level I workshops for teachers and support staff including classroom aides, substitute teachers, and student teachers. He or she also facilitates follow-up sessions during or after school where teachers have opportunities to share ideas and learn more about the program. The trainer works in classrooms with teachers, conducts model lessons, and oversees the writing of an in-house newsletter of CRISS ideas. This person also helps plan annual *CRISS for Parents* workshops. The trainer oversees the collection of any teacher and student data and encourages teachers to conduct their own classroom research (see Chapter 11) and to share what they have learned with other faculty. He or she often organizes college classes as a way for teachers to earn credit for attending Level I workshops and follow-up sessions (including *CRISS Cornerstones*, see page 286). In general, the CRISS Trainer becomes the in-house knowledge broker who circulates professional articles, conducts workshops, encourages teacher collaboration, and generates professional energy within a school. Professional energy is vital for CRISS.

In a Five Star School, the principal and other key administrators have attended a Project CRISS Level I workshop and many of the follow-up sessions. Administrators encourage teachers to incorporate the CRISS Frameworks in lesson plans and classroom practices. CRISS becomes integral to being an instructional leader. Administrators include key features of CRISS as part of classroom walk-throughs (described later in this chapter). Because of their deep understanding of the CRISS Frameworks and instructional strategies, they know when teachers implement the project successfully and how to support them. These administrators also use CRISS strategies in the daily operation of the school, integrating them into meetings with staff, parents, and the community. They work closely with their CRISS facilitator to create opportunities for teachers to come together as a learning community. They also take an active role in CRISS parent workshops.

Use the Five Star School Evaluation and Plan (see the online reproducibles for Chapter 10) to determine where your school lies on the path to Five Star School status. The important consideration here is that Five Star Schools have a far greater chance of making a positive impact on student performance than schools where only a handful of teachers participate. If your school is striving to meet the criteria for a Five Star School, how might you move it in this direction? What steps need to be taken? Use the criteria summarized in the Evaluation and Plan to design your next steps. If your school is only in the beginning stages of implementation, you can't expect the same level of teacher growth and student achievement as schools which more closely align to the Five Star criteria.

IMPACT OF PROJECT CRISS ON INSTRUCTION

Project CRISS is a staff development program designed for improving instruction; therefore, it makes sense to begin by measuring the quality of teacher implementation. Only after teachers are effectively using CRISS does it make sense to examine the effects of the program on student achievement. Start the assessment of teacher implementation by posing questions: What are some ways that you and other participants in Project CRISS can evaluate your own lessons? What changes have you made in your teaching practices in light of the CRISS Framework for Teaching? Good teaching requires well thought out and strategic planning. Tools useful for guiding your self-assessment are the Framework for Teaching Inventory and the Level of Use Matrix (see the online reproducibles for Chapter 10). In addition, keep a journal and a portfolio of student samples.

Framework for Teaching Inventory

Think about these fundamental questions: How has Project CRISS changed your views about teaching? Do you think differently about what it means to teach because of your participation in the program? At the end of our workshop, we ask teachers to begin a process of self-reflection by completing the Framework for Teaching Inventory.

This inventory, which is usually completed several times during the first year of implementation, asks participants to evaluate their use of the key features of the project. For some, it serves as a positive confirmation, since many teachers already use some of the elements of CRISS in their teaching. The inventory also serves to remind teachers of key principles and strategies they might explore.

In any case, the inventory provides an opportunity to think about how we teach. Most of us don't take time to think about why we teach in a certain way, we just do it! By taking time for self-examination, we begin to see why some lessons work better than others. Usually, our more effective lessons reflect a well thought out Framework for Teaching where the Prepare, Engage, and Reflect strategies engage our students and guide them to successfully gain the targeted enduring understandings. Such reflection spurs us to use CRISS even more and to make changes in our teaching. We begin to "live" the teaching and learning frameworks. The inventory provides us with this metacognitive opportunity.

Use the Framework for Teaching Inventory periodically. Refer to it again three or four months after completing the workshop. What strategies have you added to your teaching repertoire over the last several months? Are you more aware of the principles that comprise the Framework for Learning? Compare your responses to those on your first inventory. Has your teaching changed? In what ways have you implemented the CRISS Framework for Teaching? Are there strategies listed on the inventory you haven't tried that might fit within future teaching plans? Are there others you want to know more about?

Results from the inventory are useful for planning follow-up sessions. After several months of implementing the project, participants can complete it again. Your local CRISS Trainer can tabulate the results to find out which strategies are used most and least frequently. Administering the inventory at the beginning of a follow-up session provides a review of Project CRISS, initiates professional conversations, and helps to formulate ideas for future follow-up sessions.

Level of Use Matrix

The Level of Use Matrix (see online reproducibles for Chapter 10) is structured such that the left-hand column contains the main components of the CRISS Framework for Learning and the next three columns contain descriptions of implementation levels ranging from "Ideal" to "Areas for Growth." The behaviors in the "Ideal" column portray components in terms of student ownership and knowledge. The teacher has succeeded in empowering students to use the Framework for Learning and strategy knowledge.

The difference between the "Ideal" column and the "Acceptable" column has to do with teacher control. The behaviors classified as acceptable remain in the hands of the teacher. The teacher is doing the majority of the work, not the student. Remember, teacher control is not all bad. We have to take some control in the beginning as we model and demonstrate strategies when material is particularly challenging. Control only becomes a problem if we never release power to the students even when they can do the work themselves. When the teacher continues to provide all of the explanations, connections, and transformations, we do the meaning making, not the student. Thus, we move back and forth from the ideal to the acceptable depending upon the difficulty of the material and where students are in their understanding of strategy use. Yet, we always strive for the ideal. Successful teachers make themselves progressively unnecessary.

In the "Areas for Growth" column, all the scenarios serve as reminders about things to watch out for in our own teaching. Except in the rarest of circumstances, we don't want to land here.

CRISS Framework for Teaching

We also recommend self-assessment based on the CRISS Framework for Teaching. The table on the following page reviews its components.

Think about a lesson or series of lessons you recently taught in your classroom. Reflect upon what you did to **plan** for instruction. Did your lesson teach students something important to learn and were these same understandings evaluated? Assessments must match essential content as well as the differing learning needs of our students. Was assessment information available to students before they began the lesson? When students know what they are expected to learn and how these content and learning processes will be assessed, they gain confidence and a sense of control over their own learning. Were the content materials appropriate for the students, and did they provide sufficient information to help students attain essential information?

CRISS Framework for Teaching: The CRISS Strategic Learning Plan (P-PER)	CRISS Framework for Learning: The Ingredients of Metacognition (PER)
PLAN *for instruction* • Determine Enduring Understandings • Create Assessments • Assess Student Needs • Select a variety of Content Materials	
PREPARE *for student learning* • Elicit Background Knowledge • Set Purposes for Student Learning • Determine Author's Craft Instruction	**PREPARE** *for student learning* • Think about Background Knowledge • Determine Purposes for Learning • Identify the Author's Craft
ENGAGE *with Content & Transform Information* • Identify Processes to Facilitate Involvement and Active Persistence • Identify and Facilitate Learning Activities with Writing, Discussion, Visualization, and Organization	**ENGAGE** *with Content & Transform Information* • Be Involved and Actively Persistent • Write, Discuss, Visualize, and Organize
REFLECT *on Teaching & Learning* • Facilitate Student Process and Content Discussions • Evaluate Student Learning • Analyze and Evaluate Planning and Instruction, including Modeling	**REFLECT** *on Teaching & Learning* • Evaluate the Effectiveness of Learning Processes • Assess Content Learning

How did you **prepare** students for learning? Did students have opportunities to talk about what they already knew about a topic, and did they know what they were going to learn from the lesson? Did you help them set clear purposes and targets for learning? Did they have opportunities to examine the Author's Craft as a tool for comprehending and learning content?

How did you **engage** students with content and guide them to transform information to help them understand the big ideas of the lesson or unit? Did these strategies help students actively persist after meaning? Did students have ample opportunities to talk, write, visualize, and transform information in meaningful ways? Did they self-monitor so they knew whether or not they understood the essential understandings of your lesson?

Did you give students sufficient time to **reflect** on their learning? Did they talk about the learning strategies that helped them understand and assess their learning? Examine your teaching. Lessons typically flounder because of insufficient modeling. Did you model enough for students to feel competent to take off on their own? If not, how could you have done it differently?

In short, the Framework for Teaching provides a way for you to plan and to examine your own teaching. Include several learning plans along with your reflections and student samples in a teaching portfolio.

Teacher Journals and Portfolios

A teaching journal can be an important data source. Too often, we forget not only what we have taught, but the details of our instruction. We can gain valuable insights about our teaching when taking time to think and write about our lessons. Teaching journals become invaluable tools. They create a place for analyzing the success of a particular lesson, keeping track of new ideas, thinking about specific students, and making plans for future lessons.

Another important data source is a teaching portfolio that might contain learning plans, student examples, and perhaps your journal. Keeping a collection of student work can be an excellent resource not only for yourself, but also for sharing ideas with colleagues either informally or as part of organized follow-up sessions. A teaching portfolio also comes in handy as a way to showcase your work as part of formal teaching evaluations.

Administrator Support and Observations

While these various tools for teacher implementation assessment (Framework for Teaching Inventory, Level of Use Matrix, Framework for Teaching plan, and teacher journals and portfolios) provide us with ways to examine our own practice, having others observe our lessons can also be helpful. In particular, we recommend that principals and other supervisors have opportunities to see how CRISS is working in classrooms. This not only helps principals and supervisors gain expertise, but their continual presence also supports us in becoming more effective with CRISS.

Some simple ways administrators can support implementation include attending a Level I workshop, participating in a number of follow-up sessions, and experiencing *CRISS for Administrators* (a guide and workshop for school leaders that addresses specific aspects of implementation planning, project monitoring and support, and reinforcing the CRISS Frameworks for Teaching and Learning). Once administrators feel fairly well versed in the project, they can provide valuable feedback to the teachers working directly with students.

We recommend classroom walk-throughs where principals, along with the curriculum specialist or reading coordinator, visit classrooms for short observations of Project CRISS in action. Their mission is to evaluate CRISS implementation (not the teacher) through questioning students and observing their learning behaviors. Brief, frequent visits are better than infrequent, longer visitations. Short observations lower teacher apprehension, make it feasible for administrators to fit visitations into their busy schedules, and provide opportunities for discerning patterns of CRISS behaviors. With continual access to classrooms, administrators become more effective instructional leaders who can offer support and determine staff needs.

To help with these walk-throughs, we have included three slightly different walk-through observation tools in our online reproducibles for Chapter 10. One guides the observer to attend to the level of student engagement, to examine whether or not the lesson aligns with district/state curriculum, and to note situations where students are using CRISS strategies and demonstrating their understanding of the CRISS Framework for Learning. In addition, the observer is asked to "walk the walls" or attend to any displays of student work. The other two reproducible walk-through tools provide some alternative options for guiding the walk-through process.

Over a number of visits, these observations generate a series of snapshots of student learning in a particular classroom. Administrators can readily use these as a basis for discussions with the teachers about implementation and for planning follow-up. Even more important, the administrator progressively gains more expertise about the variety of ways CRISS is being implemented in the school. Brief walk-throughs help them become more effective curriculum leaders, coaches, and change agents. They also provide administrators with a viable way to increase their visibility and credibility. The *CRISS for Administrators* manual and the accompanying workshop provide more details about walk-throughs as well as other information to ensure project effectiveness.

STUDENT IMPLEMENTATION

Our major goal with Project CRISS is to improve student learning. Are students learning more effectively, and are they more self-confident as learners because of their participation in CRISS? In this section, we offer a variety of suggestions for collecting information about the impact of Project CRISS on students.

District/School-Specific Questions

The most effective way to examine potential effects of Project CRISS is to evaluate program effectiveness with questions meaningful to your own context. For example, Elaine Buch, CRISS National Trainer and media specialist at Addison Trail High School in Addison, Illinois, shared with us how her school assessed the impact of CRISS on student achievement. She said school officials at Addison Trail talk about CRISS as being the "glue" for improving student achievement. Addison Trail meets the requirements for a Five Star CRISS School: All teachers have participated in at least one CRISS workshop, the staff has onsite CRISS Trainers, the Framework for Teaching is the model teachers use for organizing instruction, and the principal knows CRISS and is totally committed to on-going implementation and follow-up. They examined effectiveness based on questions relating to the following topics:

- Student failure rates in courses of study
- Changes in school organization
- Enrollment in Advanced Placement courses
- Changes in dropout rate
- Staff professionalism
- Instruction

Implementation of CRISS and other school organizational measures (double periods of math, teacher use of technology, expanded support systems for struggling students) resulted in decreased student failure rates in all areas of the curriculum. Moreover, enrollment in Advanced Placement courses increased over 50% and included over 900 students. Their dropout rate went from 4.9% to 1.6%. Students also improved on state achievement tests. School personnel credited Project CRISS with providing consistency of instruction across the content areas and grade levels, leading to improved student achievement.

In 2009, Addison Trail High School made *Newsweek*'s The Top of the Class list (June 8, 2009). Each year, *Newsweek* rates the country's top high schools based on a formula that combines Advanced Placement, International Baccalaureate, and/or Cambridge tests taken by all students at a school the previous year and divides that by the number of graduating seniors. The resulting list of 1500 schools is the top 6% of high schools nationwide.

Examining big issues such as dropout rate, achievement in courses, increased teacher professionalism, etc., by means of questions relevant to your own school context is often a more meaningful way to assess program effects than with any single measure. Just looking at student performance on standardized achievement tests often misses the bigger issues important to your school. Identify the important questions that need to be asked and examine how implementing Project CRISS can help answer these questions.

Framework for Learning Inventory

The Framework for Learning Inventory (FLI; see online reproducibles for Chapter 10) is a quick way to gather some data about student understanding and implementation of the CRISS Framework for Learning. It works well to administer the FLI to students before their teachers participate in a CRISS workshop and then administer it again several months later. In most cases, students respond quite differently, reflecting more knowledge about learning by the second administration. Teachers often assess students with the FLI several times during the year to monitor students' understanding and use of strategic learning practices over time.

Teachers also use the data diagnostically. Students who continually do poorly in school answer items on the FLI quite differently than students who do well. These data show that even after teachers have incorporated Project CRISS in their classrooms, students struggling academically still don't know how to employ strategic learning practices on their own and revert to less effective methods. An analysis of individual items provides insights about a student's specific needs. Information from the FLI becomes invaluable for instructional planning.

We have also used the FLI to collect comparison data on students in participating and non-participating CRISS classrooms. Again, the responses differ markedly between these groups. Students participating in CRISS classrooms show far more strategy use than those in non-CRISS classrooms. Consider using this inventory as part of your assessment program.

You may have noticed that questions on the Framework for Learning Inventory are identical to questions on the Framework for Teaching Inventory. Having similar questions between the teacher tool and the student tool allow you to compare teacher instruction with student ownership.

Informal Research Studies

Many CRISS teachers conduct informal research studies in their classrooms. This is a great way to convince both teachers and their students that application of CRISS theory and strategies makes a difference. Because we feel so strongly about teacher research, we have devoted a chapter in this book to it. For more in-depth information plus several sample studies, please look at Chapter 11.

Quantitative Research

Over the years we have collected considerable quantitative research data regarding the effects of CRISS on student learning. Evaluation reports are available at www.projectcriss.com. Because of these quantitative efforts, Project CRISS was recognized by the Department of Education Institute of Education Sciences in 2010 as an effective literacy program for adolescent students. Project CRISS is listed in the What Works Clearinghouse ("a central and trusted source of scientific evidence for what works in education" pre-K through high school) for its positive effects on achievement in reading comprehension. Having this federal stamp of approval adds further credence to project effectiveness.

Briefly, the evaluation design replicated what we used for national validation and funding by the National Diffusion Network of the U.S. Department of Education in 1986, 1992, and 1998. The evaluations involved multiple experimental and control sites; at least two classrooms were evaluated from grades 4, 6, 8, and 11. Each grade level had at least one experimental class and at least one control class. The teachers at the experimental sites were CRISS trained and kept a journal of the strategies they introduced in their classrooms. The control teachers did not participate in a CRISS workshop.

The evaluation involved two consecutive class days in the fall and two days in the spring (20-40 minutes each day). During the first class period, students at each grade level read age-appropriate selections (4 to 8 pages in length) on a science or history topic. The students read and studied the material any way they wanted. The next day, they took a free-recall test in which they wrote down everything they could remember from the selection, answered multiple-choice questions, and responded to a short, open-answer question. The same reading selections and tests were given in the spring. After the spring test, we asked students to write about how they learned the information in the selection. All scoring of data was done by an independent evaluator.

Districts with successful CRISS implementation found that their students learned and remembered more from the reading selections than students who had not participated in the project. In addition, an analysis of the written responses on strategy use indicated that CRISS students had a far richer repertoire of learning strategies than students in the control classrooms. (See the CRISS website for a summary of the most recent data and for copies of the "Evidence of Effectiveness" reports.)

If your district wants to participate as a data collection site, please contact the CRISS National Office. We will provide all of the testing materials and further details about conducting the evaluation.

▲ ▲ ▲

SUMMARY

In conclusion, CRISS offers districts a variety of ways to examine program implementation. Evaluation choices depend upon a school's or district's level of implementation and commitment.

If you or only a few teachers in your school implement the project, it doesn't make sense to do a broad-based evaluation. Examine effects based on how well students are implementing the project within these few classrooms. Consider using the Framework for Learning Inventory and doing some qualitative research similar to that conducted by teachers described in Chapter 11, "Project CRISS: A Story of Teachers and Students as Researchers." Design some of your own teacher-researcher studies. Are students performing better on your classroom assessments compared to last year? What happens to student performance when your students employ the Framework for Learning and a rich assortment of strategies as part of a unit of study? Can students talk and write about their own learning and strategy use? Such informal evaluations tend to be far more meaningful to you and your students than are the more formal measures.

If most teachers in your school are using CRISS, look for changes beyond individual classrooms. Evaluate the level of implementation by using the Five Star School Evaluation and Plan. If your school is not there yet, what are your next steps? Develop a multiple-year implementation plan with the goal of obtaining Five Star status. Administrators can play a critical role in this planning by assessing school implementation using the walk-through process (see the *CRISS for Administrators* materials). Have teachers self-assess by using the Framework for Teaching Inventory and the Level of Use Matrix. Work on getting an onsite CRISS Facilitator or Trainer to provide additional training and follow-up.

If your school is striving to meet the criteria for a Five Star School, look for changes in teaching (Framework for Teaching Inventory, evidence collected from walk-throughs, classroom research), and changes in students' knowledge about learning and studying (Framework for Learning Inventory). Identify changes in student achievement—has there been improvement in student performance on state assessments? Most importantly, design an approach to program evaluation that best fits within your school's or district's overall assessment plan.

CHAPTER 10 RESEARCH BASE

Research Conclusion	Reference
With successful implementation of CRISS, students comprehend more than students who do not participate in the project.	What Works Clearinghouse, 2010

Project CRISS: A Story of Teachers and Students as Researchers

11

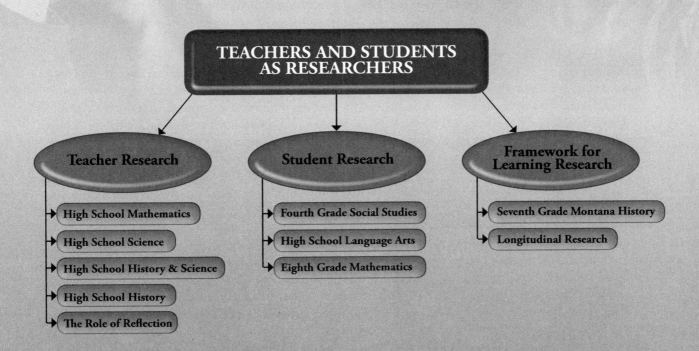

Project CRISS is an unending story of teacher research. It all started when Carol Santa landed in Kalispell in the early 80s. She and a group of high school teachers began investigating learning in the context of their high school classrooms. They began their examination by conducting informal studies in practically every content area. They spent time during lunch, planning periods, and after school sharing their informal data and talking about what they were learning. They wrote about their research in brief newsletters distributed to the rest of the high school faculty. Soon, other teachers became involved. Through this work, they slowly and systematically began to build a knowledge base which formed the foundation of Project CRISS. Probably even more important than their growing understanding of how students learn, was their emerging understanding of the power of teacher research. They learned what it meant to be teacher researchers. They took an investigative approach that became a process of self-examination, growth, and continuing change. Teacher research continues to be the basis for the on-going development of Project CRISS.

Proponents of teacher research argue it is the surest way to achieve school improvement and lasting change in education (Cochran-Smith, 2006). We could not agree more. Some of this research literature focuses on the effectiveness of teacher research as a way to create new products (such as curriculum), design a new staff plan, or, in our case, revise the CRISS manual. While we agree that the products and new understandings are an important result of teacher research, we see an even greater value in the *process* of doing research.

In the past 30 years of Project CRISS, we have been involved with literally hundreds of teacher researchers who have conducted informal experiments in their classrooms. Over these years, it became apparent that it is not enough to share the fruits of discovery. Successful CRISS teachers continually revise, assess, and refine their instruction as action research. It is an ongoing process. Some teachers become stagnant because they don't take on the attitude of a researcher. For example, they might discover in a research study that Main Idea—Detail Notes worked effectively with the first two chapters of their science textbook. From that day forward, they blindly use it for all note-taking experiences, no longer reviewing the outcomes of the process. Those who become stagnant also fail to engage both themselves and their students in the reflective process of inquiry.

Teacher research becomes a way of teaching, of never really finding the right answer, but continually seeking ways of doing the job even better. It involves maintaining a research attitude that encourages constant examination, growth, and continual change as opposed to finding the right solution to a single problem. Teacher research promotes a dynamic approach to the teaching profession as opposed to maintenance of the status quo. In looking back on these years, we now know that the real power of Project CRISS lies in its potential for fostering an investigative attitude among teachers and students.

TEACHER RESEARCH

We began the development of Project CRISS by setting up simple, short-term experiments in our classrooms. We did this in a natural way, where teachers used one of their class sections as an experimental group and another as a control, thus regulating teacher variability and allowing teachers and their students to determine for themselves the effectiveness of the variable studied. Teachers used regular classroom tests, typically short-answer quizzes, to assess the impact of using various elements of metacognition and/or strategies. They also made anecdotal observations of their students' behaviors and attitudes toward learning to see if using strategies for engagement and reflection had an affective impact. After completing their research, teachers shared the results with their students and then had them discuss and write about how the experimental strategies worked for them.

High School Mathematics

One of our first studies focused on the Prepare step of the Framework for Learning. Math teacher Cheryl Plettner felt that her students needed her to explain things to them and, consequently, she did most of the talking in her classes. Her research goal was to generate more student involvement. She also hoped to increase her students' motivation to read their math assignments. Cheryl decided to investigate whether or not it would be helpful to have her students briefly review the material and generate questions that might arise about the topic before whole group discussion.

In one of her three math classes, Cheryl had students pre-read their assignments in order to identify the concepts they did not understand and to formulate one or two questions concerning these difficult concepts. Then, she had students meet in pairs and talk about their questions. After these paired discussions, Cheryl listed all of the questions on the board. Students then read carefully and purposefully as they searched for the answers to their questions. All of this occurred before Cheryl explained any of the concepts. Her students seemed more engaged in the material with this approach. A brief quiz the following day confirmed her suspicions—the class that prepared by pre-reading, developing questions, and discussing outperformed the other two classes. She then shared the data with all of her classes and found the results initiated some lively discussion about why one class did better on the quiz than the others. Cheryl and her students began to understand the value of using questioning and discussion strategies to prepare for and engage in reading.

High School Science

Don Neu, a biology teacher, focused on metacognition through the use of Pre- and Post-Reading Learning Log Entries in one of his classes. Before students read a selection, he asked them to write about several key concepts to bring out their background knowledge. After they read, students checked their pre-reading entries for misconceptions and wrote post-reading journal entries. One week later, Don administered a quiz on the concepts students wrote about in their logs. More students in the experimental group exhibited an understanding of these concepts than did students in the control classes. Again, both students and teacher were able to see the value of the experimental strategy.

High School History and Science

In another series of experiments, history and science teachers focused on author's craft and engagement. They decided to study the effect of using Main Idea—Detail (MI-D) Notes with their reading assignments. They each taught two sections of the same class and designated one section as the experimental group and the other as the control. They taught their experimental students how to analyze their text, develop MI-D Notes, and study from their notes. The experimental biology and history classes that learned text analysis and note-taking procedures did far better on chapter tests than did the control classes. At the conclusion of the studies, the teachers showed students the results and facilitated a discussion about why the different results occurred.

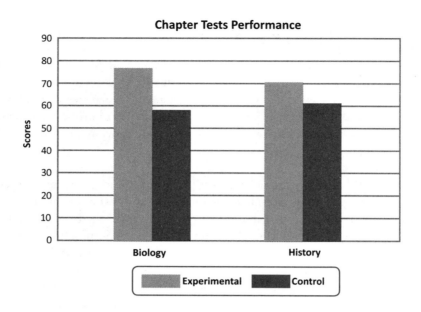

High School History

In another study, history teacher Jim Scalf, proved to his students that studying from their notes was essential. By this time, both of his classes were using Main Idea—Detail Notes (see page 137). He gave students in one class five minutes at the end of each class all week to study and learn the information in their MI-D Notes. He modeled how to study by covering the right-hand column and asking questions over the main ideas on the left. In the control class, he also allowed five minutes for studying, but did not give any directions or provide any modeling; most used their time to reread the textbook. Students who self-tested using the MI-D Notes did better on the chapter examinations than those not using their notes. Jim presented the data to convince the students to make better use of their notes.

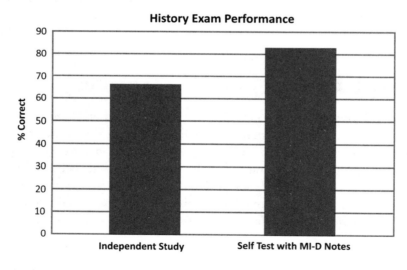

The Role of Reflection

An important aspect of these research efforts was the reflection and process conferencing. After completing a study, teachers and their students discussed and wrote about the research project. Students were encouraged to share their reactions. When asked to describe their study processes, students became metacognitively aware of what it takes to become effective learners.

The previous examples show how research provides teachers and students answers to specific learning and comprehension questions; more importantly, they demonstrate an investigative attitude of continual examination and reflection. Teaching becomes a process of ongoing research.

STUDENT RESEARCH

Involving students in the process of classroom research provides the same positive effect for students as it does for teachers. Students are empowered to ask questions about how they learn and to assume ownership of the learning process. As active participants in classroom research, students learn more. For both students and teachers, shifting the focus of learning from content to process promotes more involvement and builds life-long learning skills.

For example, teachers know why the principles comprising the CRISS Framework for Learning (e.g., metacognition, background knowledge, organization, discussion, etc.) are essential to student success; but do their students understand these principles and how they operate? Sandra Bradford, a fourth grade teacher; Jennifer Watson, a high school English teacher; Beverly Krusz, a middle school mathematics teacher; and Sue Dailey, a seventh grade social studies teacher, decided to address these issues directly by having students investigate their own learning.

Fourth Grade Social Studies

Sandra Bradford wanted her students to determine which organizational strategies worked best for them. She conducted her week-long study using the social studies curriculum. She divided a chapter from her social studies text into four sections. On Monday, the class collected baseline data by simply reading the first section of the chapter (without using any organizing strategies) and taking a test. On each of the following three days, using one of three comprehension strategies, students read and organized a section of the text before taking a test. On Tuesday, they used an adaptation of the K-W-L procedure (see page 112), in which they brainstormed what they knew about the topic, categorized information, and generated questions before beginning to read. On Wednesday, the children organized the material with Power Notes (see page 50). On Thursday, they constructed Concept Maps (see page 55) using the information they read. After reading and organizing each section, the students took a short quiz, graphed their individual tests results, and wrote personal reactions in their learning logs. Sandra then asked her students to examine their own learning results and determine which of the strategies worked best for them. As predicted, strategies worked differently for different people. The following is an example of one student's graph and journal.

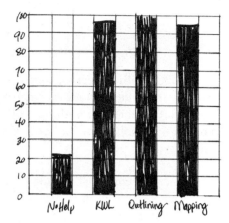

Sandra's study is a superb example of helping students begin to own strategies. Students did research on themselves and shared their results with one another. Practicing strategies, data collection, and talk about learning helped students come to their own conclusions.

High School Language Arts

Jennifer Pearson (Watson) and Carol Santa (1995) did a similar study with sophomore language arts students. As part of a unit on writing scientific papers, students examined their own performances and came to conclusions about which study strategies worked best for them.

Jennifer and Carol began by teaching students about the components of metacognition using an approach similar to what we currently use with teachers in the CRISS Level I workshop. They taught students, through lecture and demonstration, the elements comprising the Framework for Learning. Then students read a series of five articles, which provided them with background information for the next class novel, *To Kill a Mockingbird*. All of the selections were approximately one and a half pages long. The investigation included five learning procedures, one for each article. After reading and using the assigned strategy, students put aside the article and any notes they took and tested themselves by writing (on a blank sheet of paper) any and all information recalled from the article. They scored their own work by counting the number of correct ideas recalled and then charted the number on a graph. In this way, they compared their performance across the different strategies. They also discussed and wrote about each strategy based on their knowledge of learning principles, considering the value of each strategy in activating background knowledge, facilitating organization, and improving metacognitive skills. Next, they summarized their results in scientific papers and evaluated their papers according to a revision sheet. The experiment took about two weeks. The following is a sample of one student's scientific paper and the revision sheet.

Researching My Own Learning

Introduction. For many years, researchers have been trying to find the most effective study methods. They have found that using background knowledge, organizing, active learning, and metacognition are useful and effective study and learning methods. Metacognition is being aware of which information you know and which information you don't know. Based on my experiences with studying and preparing for tests and quizzes, using organizing strategies helps me learn best.

Methods and Procedures. Our class read five articles about the years during the Depression, each time using one or more study methods. We graphed the number of facts that we remembered for each article, so we could visually see which methods worked the best for each one of us.

1. On day one, we read an article about Eleanor Roosevelt. We read this article only once and then tested ourselves. We graphed the results of how much we could remember. This experiment was our control experiment.

2. For the next procedure, we read an article about Franklin Roosevelt. First, we brainstormed existing knowledge on this subject. Then, we skimmed through the article and we brainstormed facts that we had just read. Last, we read through the article and tested ourselves to see how much we could remember. Then we graphed the results on our graph.

3. For the next study, we had an article on the Great Depression. First, we brainstormed background knowledge and skimmed through the article. Next, we read the article, underlining the major points. Then we wrote study questions from the underlined phrases. Last, we wrote down the number of facts we remembered and graphed them.

4. Our next strategy involved brainstorming what we knew about African Americans during the Depression. We read the article, underlined, and then did a Concept Map. As before, we wrote down the facts and graphed our results.

5. For the last study, we read an article about the author of *To Kill a Mockingbird*, Harper Lee. First, we skimmed the article; then, we reread it and underlined key words and phrases. From the underlined information we made a Concept Map and then discussed the information with a partner. Again, we wrote down the facts we remembered and graphed the results.

Results and Discussion. After using different study methods, we took a blank sheet of paper and wrote down everything we remembered. Then we counted up the number of facts and graphed our results in a notebook. My results are as follows:

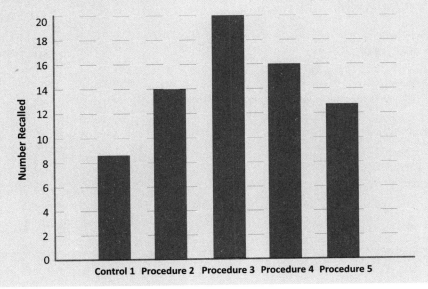

Project CRISS: A Story of Teachers and Students as Researchers

I remembered the most facts about the Great Depression article. I think the reason I did the best was because I knew something about the Depression before I read the article. Another reason why I believe I did better on this article is because we wrote out our study questions for it and that organization technique helped me remember facts better.

The article I did the worst on (except for the control, procedure 1) was the one about Harper Lee. During this experiment we made a Concept Map for organization. I think it made the information harder for me to remember because the Concept Map was too cluttered and disorganized. I didn't know anything about Harper Lee before reading the article. I also like working alone better than working with a partner.

By performing these experiments and being able to visually see the results, I discovered that having background knowledge on the subject helped me remember more facts. Another thing that helped me was to have my information organized by using two-column notes or another organizational technique. In the future, I will try to brainstorm all of the facts I previously know about the subject to get my brain thinking on the right path. I will also try to be more organized with my studying and always be an active listener.

Revision sheet for student use in writing a scientific paper

Writer _____

Point Count
Rough draft editing sheet (25) _____
Final draft (125) _____
Total Points _____

Introduction (25 points)
1. Thesis statement _____
2. Theory: Metacognition _____
   Background Knowledge _____
   Organizing Information _____
   Active Learning _____
   Relate ideas to self _____
   Glimpse of upcoming study _____   Points _____

Methods and materials (25 points)
   Clear presentation of four conditions   Points _____

Results and discussion (25 points)
1. Graph _____
2. Explanation of results _____
3. Discussion of why results occurred _____   Points _____

Implications (25 points)
   Explanation of how results might influence future learning   Points _____

Conventions (25 points)
1. Spelling _____
2. Punctuation _____
3. Sentences _____
   Fragments _____
   Run-ons _____
4. Grammar _____   Points _____

Having students investigate and write about their own learning helped them to internalize personal learning systems. Most found they recalled more when they had opportunities not only to organize information but also to discuss what they were learning with other students. Students experimented with a variety of strategies, kept track of their performances, analyzed their results, and then wrote scientific papers presenting their data. As with Sandra Bradford's fourth grade study, students responded differently to different strategies.

Eighth Grade Mathematics

Beverly Krusz decided to help her algebra, pre-algebra, and eighth grade math students incorporate metacognition—especially identifying mistakes—into their test-taking routine. Typically, Beverly gave her students a 20-question test. She graded all problems and gave partial credit when appropriate. She returned the tests and modeled for students the correct way to solve any of the problems with which they had difficulties. For her metacognition study, she gave the same test, but put an answer box numbered 1-20 in the margin. When she graded the tests she merely looked at the answer box. Answers were either right or wrong. Each student received a percent score, e.g., a student having five incorrect responses would receive a score of 75%.

The next day she returned the papers and allowed students to work in cooperative groups to determine what they did wrong. To get partial credit for the problems they missed, they were required to do the following:

- Circle the specific error(s) in red.
- Write in words what they did wrong. For example, *I copied the numbers from question 8, but actually solved the problem that was question 9. I was in a hurry and reversed the numbers before dividing.*
- Redo the problem (using numbers and variables) to get the correct answer.

Once students completed their corrections, she asked if anyone needed her to demonstrate a solution. In most cases, students solved their own problems and didn't need to have her model. She reviewed their corrected tests and gave partial credit (not full credit) for correct responses. She then had students journal about how this process worked for them.

> **PARAGRAPH**
> I like the way we do it now. You have to look back into the problem and see what you did wrong. Many times I see my mistakes (many times dumb ones) and I try to be more aware of those kind of problems or things in upcoming problems. I think people will learn more with the way we do it now.

> **Algebra test Write about Tests**
> I like the new way of doing the tests, even though it takes a little longer. I like that we can redo the problem and learn how to do it and what I did wrong. The old way I really didn't know how to do it any better for the next time, nor do I get any better grade.

Through this process, students discovered the types of mistakes they tended to make and then looked for them prior to handing in an assignment or test. Being part of their teacher's research study helped them see the importance of metacognition for learning—and for earning a better grade!

▲ ▲ ▲

These self-explorations, both at the elementary and secondary levels, helped students discover for themselves effective strategies for a variety of different contexts and provided a way to evaluate whether or not CRISS had become part of their learning lives. Even more important, students became researchers; they became problem solvers as they tested out their own theories of learning.

FRAMEWORK FOR LEARNING RESEARCH

With most of our studies, teachers pick one strategy or principle of learning to research. In the following study, a teacher investigated the power of teaching her students the full Framework for Learning. She not only studied the impact her instruction has on how her students learn in her classroom, but she did a follow-up study to see if students' knowledge of the Framework for Learning will help them achieve in the following school years.

Seventh Grade Montana History

Sue Dailey, a CRISS National Trainer, taught a variety of CRISS strategies to the students in her seventh grade Montana history class. During this instruction, she stressed the CRISS Framework for Learning by having her students discuss when and why to use certain techniques. But, did they really get it? She decided to hit this question head-on while her students were studying about early pioneers traveling on the Oregon Trail. She asked her students to respond to a series of questions as they progressed through the unit.

She began by dividing her class into small groups of three and four students. Students kept all their work in folders and responded to questions in their learning logs. After discussing a question in their groups and performing a specific task, they wrote in their logs.

PREPARE Question 1: *What are you going to do to activate your background knowledge before reading?*

Most groups decided to organize their discussions using an adaptation of the K-W-L strategy. As they talked about what they knew and what they wanted to learn about the Oregon Trail, one person in each group took notes, which students then used as a guide for their own journal responses.

> *My group decided to find out the definitions of the vocabulary words because we want to understand what the words are when we read the chapter later on. We decided to read the introduction because we thought it would help to set us up for what we are going to read and learn. Then we put our ideas on a K-W-L sheet.*

What do I Know?	What do I Want to Learn?
• covered wagons	• who went
• very little in Montana	• where they came from
• a lot of people got sick	• about their lives
• looking for gold – mad rush of pioneers	• where they traveled
• after trapping was famous	• what was it like in a wagon
	• why they went there

• 272   Chapter 11

Sue didn't stop here. She wanted them to think hard about their particular strategy choices and to begin analyzing their own thinking.

PREPARE Question 2: *Why were your PREPARE strategies helpful? Talk about this question in your group and then write about your own thinking.*

After their group discussion, they again wrote in their journals.

Doing these things before we read helped me to gain some background knowledge. If you know a little bit about what you're going to read, you can understand it a little better. Also knowing the vocabulary words will help me understand what I'm reading. If you know the vocabulary and how the facts fit together you can remember longer and understand what you're reading.

Next, the groups made decisions about strategies for processing the information during reading.

Sue prompted:

How are you going to read actively and begin organizing the information? Just reading it through once isn't enough! Talk about this in your groups and develop a reading plan.

After each group spent some time discussing these issues, they responded to the next question in their journals:

ENGAGE Question 3: *What active strategies did your group decide to use to keep you engaged, and why did you choose them?*

My group decided to underline and take margin notes while we read. We thought that it would help to underline, but some things are kind of confusing and you don't know for sure what to underline, but you understand what it means, so you just have to jot down the facts on the side.

After students in each group made their "strategy" decisions, they used them to complete their homework. The next day, groups discussed their learning from the assignment and how well a particular approach worked for them. They concluded with written reflections.

ENGAGE Question 4: *How did your ENGAGE strategies help you understand the material? Why is this an effective approach for you?*

We discussed what we underlined. This helped me understand the material because I had to think about what I read, so it stuck in my head more. This is a good strategy for me because it's easy to re-read over for a test or when I need quick information.

Next, Sue reminded her students about the importance of processing and transforming information in order to make knowledge personally meaningful. She prompted:

TRANSFORM Question 5: *You have to do more with information than just read or read and underline. You have to change it, to transform it so that it becomes your own. How will you do that?*

Sue challenged each group to come up with their own transforming or organizing strategies. The groups decided how to organize the information to make it personally meaningful. Groups selected different ways to do this. One group chose to do a timeline.

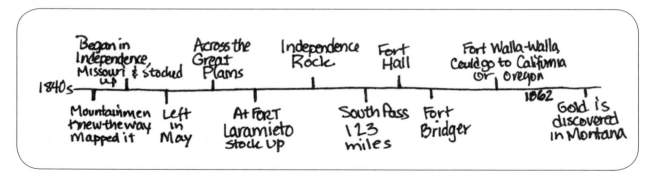

Another group chose to do a concept map.

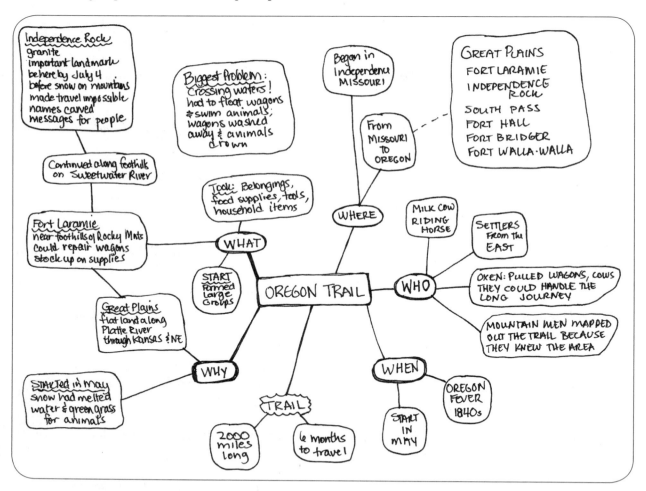

A third group created Picture Notes.

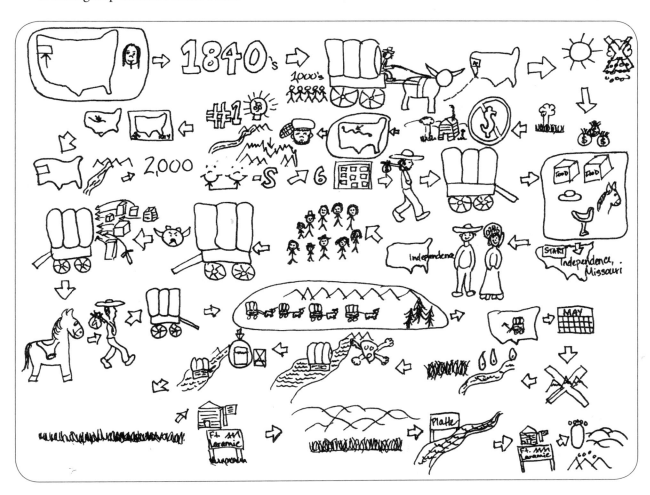

Upon completing their transforming strategies and talking about the information, they responded to Sue's next question.

TRANSFORM Question 6: *Explain how you TRANSFORMED the information in your group.*

> *My group made Picture Notes to process the information. This really helps me to understand because while I am drawing, the information goes into my memory and stays there because I am drawing the facts the way I see them which helps me to remember them.*

Next, Sue asked them to think about how they would study for a test.

STUDYING TO LEARN Question 7: *How are you going to study for your test? What do you have to do to make sure you understand and know the information? The only way you really know if you understand is to check your own comprehension. How are you going to do this? I want each group to come up with a way to self-test.*

After the groups discussed these questions, they came up with a plan. Most decided to convert their transformation strategies (Concept Maps, Picture Notes, Timelines) into Main Idea—Detail Notes for self-testing. Each group developed key questions they thought might be on the test which then became the focus of a whole class discussion.

After students developed their plans for studying, they wrote about their ideas in their journals:

Now we are going to take Main Idea—Detail Notes to organize the data the way I understand it so I can quiz myself.

Oregon Trail	Lucy
1. When & Why did the Oregon trail start?	1. The first wagon train left in 1843. People wanted to go to Oregon to farm, because of climate and free land.
2. How did they prepare for the journey?	2. They met in Independence, Missouri with all their wagons. They put food staples in their wagons & left in groups. 2,000 miles
3. When did the wagons leave & why?	3. Left in May because there was plenty of water & green grass. Took 6 months.
4. Where did they go first?	4. across the great plains to Fort Laramie where they stocked

The next the day, Sue led a discussion reviewing major concepts about the Oregon Trail. She told the students about items that would definitely be on the test so they could add them to their self-testing plans. Sue doesn't believe in surprises. Everyone has the right to do well! When students felt ready, she gave them the test. After finishing, students responded to one final question in their journals.

REFLECT Question 8: *Think about all of the strategies you used to learn about the Oregon Trail. Where do you think real learning takes place?*

With all the strategies that I used, I think they really helped me. I think these strategies don't really help unless you know what your purpose for doing all this work is for. You could just copy right out of the text and hand in your work and when test time comes you'd be clueless. I did as much as I could to learn metacognitively about the Oregon Trail. The strategy that helps me most with all this information is a Picture Map or a Concept Map. I understand the Oregon Trail very well now. I also think Two-Column Notes and self-testing helped me a lot, too.

Longitudinal Research

Sue Dailey continued to do similar lesson sequences (see pages 272-276) with her students throughout their seventh grade year. Yet, she wondered whether or not they would continue to live and breathe CRISS as they progressed through school. She decided to find out by writing to this group of students when they were eighth graders and then again as sophomores.

Dear Blue Team Eighth Graders!

Guess what—I am really missing you and wondering how you are doing this year in eighth grade. I hope you are all having a great year.

I keep thinking about all of the things we did last year. While I was teaching you about Montana history, I was also teaching you about how to become a better learner. We talked a lot about metacognition, and I showed you many ways to become more metacognitive while you were learning history. For example, you learned how to stop and fix up your comprehension when you came to a "clunk" or something you didn't understand in your reading. We also spent tons of time thinking about how important it is to use your background knowledge when reading and how essential it is to set a purpose for your learning. You learned many ways to become actively engaged while you were reading (sticky notes, stopping and asking a question, rereading). Do you remember how hard you worked in your small groups to plan different ways to organize and transform information about Montana history?

I am interested in finding out how you are doing this year and in hearing about any learning strategies you use in your eighth grade classes. Please write to me and let me know how you are and whether or not what we did in seventh grade is helping you be a better learner. Thank you so much. Your input helps me be a better teacher!

Sincerely,
Mrs. Dailey

An eighth grader's response:

Dear Mrs. Dailey,

How's school going this year? It's doing pretty good here. I want to thank you for helping me with these skills last year. They have already helped me with eighth grade, and I know they will help me even into college. I have found myself using any kind of map to help process science and social studies information. I also use Two-Column Notes. These help me get the most important information to stick in my head by reading it a few times. Yes, Two-Column Notes are expected from us. Thanks to you I know and understand how to do them and use them. I can also tell when I'm understanding information better than I could before. When I hit a "clunk," I reread the sentence or paragraph to see if I missed something or go to an adult or older brother. These things have helped me tons in my short eighth grade experience. Thanks again. I hope to see you around, and I'll try to visit as often as I can.

Sincerely,
Becky

Sue wrote to them again as sophomores.

Dear Blue Team Sophomores!

Surprise! I haven't forgotten you. I am still teaching 7th graders lots of CRISS strategies and am still doing CRISS workshops for teachers. I want to learn how students continue to use CRISS strategies as they go through the grades. I am interested in the following things:

1. *Are you a metacognitive learner? Do you know when you come to something in your reading that you don't understand and do you use fix-up strategies? Do your teachers encourage you to really learn the material by using lots of discussion, writing, and active learning strategies?*

2. *What CRISS strategies are you encouraged or required to use by your teachers? This could include Power Thinking and Outlining, K-W-L Sheets, Concept Maps, summarizing, Two-Column Notes, Spool Papers, RAFT, discussion, journaling, etc.*

3. *What CRISS strategies do you use independently?*

Thank you for taking the time to do this for me. I still miss you. The year you were here was still my best ever!

Sincerely,
Mrs. Dailey

Here is an example of one of her student's responses

Dear Mrs. Dailey,

Hi, how are you? Your letter was quite a surprise. Yes, I do feel that I am a metacognitive learner. I can usually tell pretty quickly when I do and don't understand something. This has been a very important skill this year. The responsibility to make sure I'm on track and understanding the material has been shifted almost completely to my shoulders.

The only techniques I've been encouraged to use in most classes are Two-Column Notes and discussion. Of course in English we still use all the techniques.

In general, I use discussion and journaling on my own. I still need to put things in my own words either verbally or by writing them out.

I hope this helps you out. It's nice to know you're keeping track of us.

Sincerely,
Julian

Sue's longitudinal study provided her clear evidence that her students had incorporated the CRISS Framework for Learning and strategies into of their learning lives. Her research methodology became a lesson in itself about how to lead students through a process of internalizing ways of learning. Including discussion and writing about learning as part of content instruction gave her students an opportunity to internalize strategy use. Students don't really get it unless strategy processing occurs as part of regular course instruction over time. For Sue, talking and writing about learning started as a daily exercise in her class, but her data showed that for most of her students that habit expanded to a multi-year process.

▲ ▲ ▲

Summary

These examples demonstrate different ways effective CRISS teachers use research as part of their day-to-day teaching. Over the years, teachers continue to share their own teacher-researcher studies with us. Many of these appear in CRISS newsletters and are posted on our website.

While the results of these studies have served to build the knowledge base of CRISS, the outcome is not as important as the process of continual examination. It is the on-going clinical process of exploring how to teach and how students learn. Teachers and students who engage in research about learning come to trust their own abilities to construct knowledge and improve their practice. Therefore, we must continually challenge ourselves and our students to become better clinicians of teaching and learning.

CHAPTER 11 RESEARCH BASE

Research Conclusion	Reference
Teacher research is an effective way to ensure school improvement and lasting change in schools.	Cochran-Smith, 2007

Beyond the CRISS Workshop

12

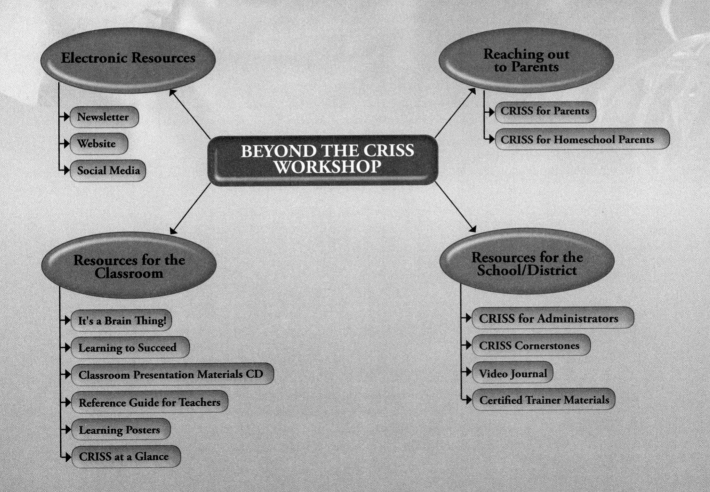

Learning Forward, the organization formerly known as the National Staff Development Council, released a technical report, *Professional Learning in the Learning Profession: A Status Report on Teacher Development in the U.S. and Abroad* (Darling-Hammond et al, 2009) that summarized key elements of highly effective professional development. This report highlights the need for professional development to (1) focus on concrete, practical implementation of instruction and content with "hands-on" training; (2) implement coherent, sustained, and job-embedded learning of over 40 hours over six to twelve months; and (3) provide opportunities for focused, structured, collaborative work amongst professional colleagues within a school (as Professional Learning Communities, for example). Each of these is integral to ensuring professional development has a lasting and positive impact on student achievement.

This report, pulling from a multitude of studies, validates what we have known about Project CRISS for years: professional learning cannot stop with the completion of a single workshop. Schools implementing CRISS, or any other professional development for that matter, need to place the introductory workshop within a long-term plan, ideally of three or more years. We know CRISS can have a significant impact on students from all socio-economic and geographic origins. Teachers in classrooms across the United States, Canada, Europe, and beyond have implemented CRISS to great effect. Student-owned and directed learning is the ultimate goal, but it takes time, patience, and trial and error for each individual instructor. It is the work of collaborative educators that takes student achievement further, faster. And it is this knowledge that has informed the development of a variety of support options for Project CRISS implementation.

Leadership is invaluable to effective implementation, as is the identification of a CRISS practitioner who has time and energy dedicated to facilitating school or district-wide implementation. Ideally, each implementing district will develop and maintain at least one individual as a certified CRISS Trainer. Having on-site expertise informs and adapts CRISS to the local context, while maintaining the integrity of what works. Specific information about growing a District CRISS Trainer via the CRISS Level II Training of Trainers workshop and apprenticeship is available on the Project CRISS website, http://www.projectcriss.com.

A menu of CRISS follow-up workshops is available which includes subject-specific implementation sessions, CRISS Framework for Teaching lesson design, *CRISS for Administrators* sessions, *CRISS for Parents* workshops, Professional Learning Community facilitation sessions, and others. Master and National Trainers can work with teachers at the local level through classroom observations and coaching, teaching model lessons, analyzing school data, etc. to ensure effective implementation that results in student achievement.

▲ ▲ ▲

Beyond workshops and on-the-ground support, CRISS provides a variety of other resources to support implementation at the school and classroom levels.

Electronic Resources

One benefit of participation in a CRISS workshop is a subscription to the *Comments from CRISS* national newsletter. Posted on our website and available via email three times per year, this newsletter provides teachers with specific examples of CRISS implementation, often including student examples and teacher-created handouts. Many of the articles are written by teachers currently implementing CRISS in their classrooms, so they are practical and realistic for today's schools. Keep in mind, CRISS is always looking for authors to share their experiences with CRISS. Contact the CRISS office if you have an idea to share.

The Project CRISS website, http://www.projectcriss.com, has a variety of resources for teachers, including lesson plans; archived newsletter articles with practical ideas for the classroom sorted by subject, grade, and strategy; a blog that addresses current education initiatives and provides resources; and research reports and articles. In the months and years ahead, we expect our web resources to expand to include student examples, videos, online workshops, and more reproducibles to save you time. Some of these resources will be available by subscription—the first year of which is free to CRISS training participants. At the time of publication, CRISS is also an active participant in social media venues, including Facebook and Twitter, sharing links to quality resources, announcements, and the occasional commentary on the state of education.

▲ ▲ ▲

The certified teaching staff in the CRISS National Office, as well as trainers from many states and provinces, have created a number of supplementary products to help you implement CRISS at your school. Development of new tools continues, and we encourage you to visit our website often to learn about the latest.

Resources for the Classroom

Project CRISS for Students I: It's a Brain Thing ~ Learning How to Learn!
Project CRISS for Students I: It's a Brain Thing ~ Learning How to Learn! is a semester curriculum appropriate for grades 5-9 that is designed to teach the CRISS principles and strategies directly to students. Great for an advisory or study skills class, this curriculum can also be used to supplement English language arts or science classes. Using the tradebook, *Tough Terminators*, written by award-winning author Sneed B. Collard III, students are guided through learning activities that promote metacognitive thinking and active engagement with content.

The classroom set consists of a teacher's manual, a *Critterman* DVD, 31 copies of *Tough Terminators*, and 30 student workbooks (materials are also available in sets of 10). A set of transparencies and reproducibles is available. Visit our website for the latest samples.

Project CRISS for Students II: LEARNING To Succeed

Project CRISS for Students II: LEARNING To Succeed is a flexible curriculum designed to teach the CRISS principles and strategies directly to students. Half of the lessons in the student workbook are based on the CRISS Keys to Learning - principles aligned with the Framework for Learning, derived from cognitive psychology and brain research. To be independent, successful learners, it's critical that students understand and can use these principles: metacognition, building on background knowledge, setting purposes for reading and learning, identifying an author's craft and style, staying actively engaged while learning, and transforming information. Alternating with these lessons, students apply strategies to untangle the issue of global warming as presented by award-winning science author Sneed B. Collard III in his book, *Global Warming: A Personal Guide to Causes and Solutions*.

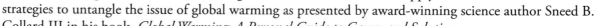

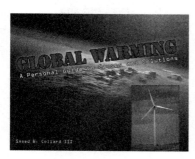

As they work through the lessons, students' learning is guided by the CRISS Framework for Learning, a four-step plan that incorporates learning strategies to help students "Prepare" for reading, "Engage" with the text, "Organize" the newly learned information, and "Apply" or use it in meaningful ways. After each lesson students reflect on the content learned and the processes used for learning; they identify strategies that worked for them and write about how they can use those strategies in their other classes; finally, they collect applications of successful strategy use to put into their *LEARNING To Succeed* portfolios.

LEARNING To Succeed may be adapted to a variety of situations with all student populations. Teachers may use all chapters or focus on those that make the most sense for their students. For example, reading teachers may choose to target the chapters dealing with Keys to Learning. Science teachers might prefer to use the lessons devoted to global warming. The curriculum may be used effectively as a stand-alone study skills, advisory, or reading curriculum, a science unit dealing with global warming, a summer school unit, or to supplement traditional classroom instruction. The target audience for this program is high school students, but it can be used with advanced middle school students as well. Within the teacher's wraparound edition, we've provided guidelines for differentiation—lesson modifications for high and intermediate ability students and for struggling and English language learners.

Project CRISS Classroom Presentation Materials

CD is a time-saving instructional tool which includes PowerPoint® Slides and reproducibles for all CRISS Strategies. Reproducibles are in two formats: MS Word, for easy adaptation, and as static pdf files. Site licensing is available so contents can be shared in a school's internal online resource center.

Project CRISS Reference Guide for Teachers: Strategies for Successful Teaching and Learning

While the Project CRISS training manual is a valuable resource, sometimes teachers can benefit from a quick and easy reminder. This full-color flipbook includes an overview of the CRISS Principles and Philosophy, explanations, examples, and adaptations of our most popular strategies, and a description of the CRISS Framework for Teaching.

CRISS Learning Posters
Student ownership and self-directed learning requires multiple models and exposures to effective learning strategies. The CRISS Learning Posters provide visual representations of key tools to help students remember the strategies they learned in class. The full set includes 36 posters (22" x 18"). The four-color posters are divided into six categories or topics, with six posters in each topic: Basics, Discussion, Strategies for Learning, Organizing for Learning, Writing, and Vocabulary.

CRISS at a Glance Poster/Desk Mat
This 17" x 22" ivory, heavyweight poster with blue ink displays 21 CRISS strategy prompts "at a glance." This poster resource is a great classroom reference and is ready to laminate.

CRISS at a Glance for Students
This 8 1/2" x 11" laminated card-stock resource is three-hole punched for easy organization in student binders. The card displays 21 CRISS strategy "prompts," plus three guidelines for good study habits. It is available in packs of ten or with a limited license to print.

Resources for the School/District

CRISS for Administrators
This administrator booklet comes with a leadership DVD and a video on CD-ROM which reviews the CRISS Level I training and shows real classroom applications. This tool provides guidance to administrators and CRISS implementation teams on how to plan, implement, and sustain Project CRISS in a school or district. It is available in Elementary and Secondary versions.

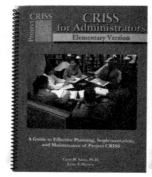

CRISS Cornerstones
The Cornerstones booklet and accompanying video on CD-ROM provide on-going support for Project CRISS implementation. Available for Elementary or Secondary levels, this tool is an excellent guide for independent study or professional learning community implementation of CRISS. The materials review key elements of CRISS, guide users through classroom implementation and reflection, and provide video clips of real teachers using CRISS in their classrooms.

Reading in the Content Areas with Dr. Carol Santa
Produced by the School Improvement Network (Video Journal of Education), this resource guides users through the elements of a CRISS workshop and it includes clips of classroom implementation. Available for Elementary or Secondary, this DVD (or VHS) is for individual use only.

Project CRISS Certified Trainer Materials
Educators who complete all certification requirements, including the Level II Training of Trainers workshop, receive a binder containing the necessary materials for facilitating a CRISS Level I workshop. Included with the binder is a CD-Rom with PowerPoint slides for training and awareness sessions and reproducibles for the training handouts. All certified trainers also have access to trainer resources on the CRISS website.

Reaching out to Parents

CRISS for Parents

It is difficult for most parents to stay engaged with their students' learning as the children progress through the grades and the curriculum becomes increasingly complex. *CRISS for Parents* provides parents with some practical tools to assist their students' learning of content. Instead of worrying about the content, parents can learn to help their children choose tools to help themselves access new information. The *CRISS for Parents* flipbook and corresponding workshop acquaint parents with the learning principles and several of the strategies their students are using in school. This full color flipbook includes an overview of the CRISS Keys to Learning (elements of metacognition), explanations, examples, and adaptations of over 16 of our most popular strategies for organizing information, formal and informal writing, and learning vocabulary. The flipbook is a great help for parents working with their students—especially those using CRISS strategies in the classroom. This resource is available in both English and Spanish.

Project CRISS for Homeschool Parents

This booklet provides guidance to parent educators who homeschool their children by helping them incorporate the CRISS principles and strategies into their children's learning experiences. *Project CRISS for Homeschool Parents* is designed to introduce parents and their children to the Project CRISS principles along with some key learning strategies. Strategy overviews and examples will help children incorporate the learning principles as they read, write, view, and experience curricular information. These will help children incorporate the learning principles as they read, write, view, and experience curricular information. If learning is to happen effectively, children must apply these principles to all learning situations—they are critical to learning and remembering information for learners of all ages. A workshop is also available for Homeschool parents.

Beyond the CRISS Workshop 287

CHAPTER 12 RESEARCH BASE

Research Conclusion	Reference
Effective professional development focuses on practical implementation of instruction and content with hands-on training; is coherent, sustained for over 40 hours over the course of a year, and job-embedded; and provides opportunities for structured, collaborative work amongst professional colleagues within a school.	Wei, Darling-Hammond, Andree, Richardson, & Orphanos, 2009

References Cited

Adler, M., Rougle, E., & Caughlan, S. (2004). Closing the gap between concept and practice: Toward more dialogic discussion in the language arts classroom. *Journal of Adolescent and Adult Literacy, 47* (4), 312-322.

Almasi, J. (2008). Using questioning strategies to promote students' active discussion and comprehension of content area material. In D. Lapp, J. Flood & N. Farnnam (Eds.), *Content area reading and learning* (pp. 487-513). Hillsdale, NJ: Lawrence Earlbaum.

Alvermann, D. (1991). The discussion web: A graphic aid for learning across the curriculum. *The Reading Teacher*, 45, 92-99.

Armbruster, B. (1984). The problem of "inconsiderate text." In G. Duffy, L. Roehler, & J. Mason (Eds.), *Comprehension instruction: Perspectives and suggestions* (pp. 202-217). New York: Longman.

Armbruster, B. (2008). Matching readers and texts: the continuing quest. In D. Lapp, J. Flood, & N. Farnam (Eds.), *Content area reading and learning* (pp. 35-52). Hillsdale, NJ: Lawrence Earlbaum.

Anders, P., & Bos, D. (1986). Semantic feature analysis: An interactive strategy for vocabulary development and text comprehension. *Journal of Reading, 29* (7), 610-616.

Anders, P., & Spitler, E. (2007). Reinventing comprehension instruction for adolescents. In J. Lewis & G. Moorman (Eds.), *Adolescent literacy instruction: Policies and promising practices.* (pp. 167-191). Newark, DE: International Reading Association.

Anderson, L. W., & Krathwohl, D.R. (Eds.). (2001). *A taxonomy for learning, teaching and assessing: A revision of Bloom's Taxonomy of educational objectives.* New York: Longman.

Atwell, N. (1998). *In the middle: New understanding about writing, reading and learning.* Portsmouth, NH: Boynton/Cook Publishers.

Atwell, N. (2007). *Lessons That Change Writers.* Portsmouth, NH: Heinemann.

Baker, L. (2002). Metacognition in comprehension instruction. In C. Block & M. Pressley (Eds.), *Comprehension instruction: Research-based practices* (pp. 77-95). New York: Guilford Press.

Baker, L. (2008). Metacognition in comprehension instruction. What we have learned since NRP. In C. Block & S. Paris (Eds.), *Comprehension instruction: Research-based best practices*, (pp. 65-79). New York: Guilford Press.

Baumann, J. F. (1986). Effect of rewritten content textbook selections on middle grade students' comprehension of main ideas: Making the inconsiderate considerate. *Journal of Reading Behavior, 18*, 1-22.

Baumann, J. F., Ware, D., & Edwards, E. C. (2007). Bumping into spicy, tasty words that catch your tongue: A formative experiment on vocabulary instruction. *The Reading Teacher, 62,* 108-122.

Beck, I. L., & McKeown, M. G. (2002). Questioning the author: Making sense of social studies. *Educational Leadership, 60,* 44-47.

Beck, I. L., McKeown, M. G., Hamilton, R.L., & Kucan, L. (1997). *Questioning the author: An approach for enhancing student engagement with text.* Newark, DE: International Reading Association.

Beck, I. L., McKeown, M. G., & Kucan, L. (2002). *Bringing words to life: Robust vocabulary instruction.* New York: Guilford Press.

Beck, I. L., McKeown, M. G., & Kucan, L. (2008). *Creating robust vocabulary: Frequently asked questions & extended examples.* New York: Guilford Press.

Beck, I. L., McKeown, M. G., Sinatra, G. M., & Loxterman, J. A. (1991). Revising social studies text from a text-processing perspective: Evidence of improved comprehensibility. *Reading Research Quarterly, 26* (3), 251-276.

Beck, I. L., McKeown, M. G., & Worthy, J. (1995). Giving a text voice can improve students' understanding. *Reading Research Quarterly, 30* (2), 220-238.

Blachowicz, C., & Fisher, P. (2006). *Teaching vocabulary in all classrooms* (3rd ed.). Upper Saddle River, NJ: Merrill Prentice-Hall.

Bloodgood, J., & Pacifici, L. (2004). Bringing word study to intermediate classrooms. *The Reading Teacher, 58* (3), 250-263.

Bloom, B., Engelhart, M., Furst, E., Hill, W., & Krathwohl, D. R. (1956). *Taxonomy of educational objectives: The classification of educational goals. Handbook 1:Cognitive Domain.* New York: Longman.

Bransford, J. D., Brown, A. L., & Cocking, R.R. (2000). *How people learn: Brain, mind, experience, and school.* Washington, DC: National Academy Press.

Bromley, K. (2007). Nine things every teacher should know about words and vocabulary instruction. *Journal of Adolescent and Adult Literacy, 50* (7), 528-539.

Brozo, W. (2010). Response to intervention or responsive instruction: Challenges and possibilities of response to intervention for adolescent literacy. *Journal of Adolescent & Adult Literacy, 54* (4), 277-281.

Buehl, D. (2008). *Insider questions: Building inquiring minds around classroom texts.* Presentation at the Project CRISS Trainers Workshop, Orlando, Florida.

Buehl, D. (2009). *Classroom Strategies for Interactive Learning.* Newark, DE: International Reading Association.

Calkins, L. (1994). *The Art of Teaching Writing.* Portsmouth, NH: Heinemann.

Calkins, L., Hartman, A., & White, Z. (2005). *One to One: The Art of Conferring with Young Writers.* Portsmouth, NH: Heinemann.

Carr, E., & Ogle, D. (1987). K-W-L Plus: A strategy for comprehension and summarization. *Journal of Reading, 30,* 626-631.

Cazden, C. B. (1988). *Classroom discourse: The language of teaching and learning.* Portsmouth, NH: Heinemann.

Cochran-Smith, M., (2006). *Policy, practice & politics in teacher Education: Editorials for the Journal of Teacher Education.* Thousand Oaks, CA: Corwin Press.

Conley, M. (2008). Cognitive strategy instruction for adolescents: What we know about the promise, what we don't know about the potential. *Harvard Educational Review, 78* (1), 84-106.

Connolly B., & Smith, M. (2002). Teachers and students talk about talk: Class discussion and the way it should be. *Journal of Adolescent and Adult Literacy, 46,* 18-26.

Cope, K., Kalschuer, d., & l. Karges. (1991). Facilitating metacognition during lecturing and note-taking: Strategies for secondary teachers and students. Presentation at the International Reading Association Conference, Las Vegas, NV.

Copeland, M. (2005). *Socratic Circles: Fostering critical and creative thinking in middle and high school.* Portland, ME: Stenhouse.

Culham, R. (2003). *6 + 1 Traits of Writing: The Complete Guide (Grades 3 and Up).* New York: Scholastic.

Culham, R. (2010). *Traits of Writing.* New York: Scholastic Books.

Dale, E. (1965). Vocabulary measurement: Techniques and major findings. *Elementary English, 62* (5), 895-901, 948.

Daniels, H. (1994). *Literature circles: Voice and choice in the student-centered classroom.* Portland, ME: Stenhouse.

Daniels, H., & Steineke, N. (2004). *Mini-lessons for literature circles.* Portsmouth, NH: Heinemann.

Darling-Hammond, L. (2008) Knowledge for teaching: What do we know? In M. Cochran-Smith, S. Feiman-Nemser & D. J. McIntyre (Eds.), *Handbook of Research on Teacher Education, 3rd edition* (pp. 1316-1323). New York: Routledge.

Darling-Hammond, L., Wei, R.C., Andree, A., Richardson, N., & S. Orphanos. (2009). *Professional Learning in the Learning Profession: A Status Report on Teacher Development in the United States and Abroad.* Standford, CA: NSDC.

Donovan, M. S., Bransford, J., & Pellegrino, J. (2000). *How people learn: Brain, mind, experience, and School.* Washington, D.C: National Academy Press.

Duffy, G. (2002). The case for direct explanation of strategies. In C. Block & M. Pressley (Eds.). *Comprehension instruction: Research-based practices* (pp. 28-41). New York: Guilford Press.

Duke, N., & Pearson, P.D. (2002). Effective practices for developing reading comprehension. In A. Farstrup & J. Samuels (Eds.) *What Research has to say about reading instruction* (pp. 205-242). Newark, DE: International Reading Association.

Durkin, D. (1978-1979). What classroom observations reveal about reading comprehension instruction. *Reading Research Quarterly, 14*, 481-533.

Farnan, N., & Fearn, L. (2008). Writing in the disciplines: More than writing across the curriculum. In Lapp, D., & Flood, J. & Farnan, N. (Eds.). *Content Reading and Learning* (pp. 403-423). New York: Lawrence Earlbaum.

Felton, M., & Herko, S. (2004). From dialogue to two-side argument: scaffolding adolescent persuasive writing. *Journal of Adolescent and Adult Literacy, 47* (8), 672-683.

Fisher, D., & Frey, N. (2008). *Wordwise content rich: Five essential steps to teaching academic vocabulary*. Portsmouth, NH: Heinemann.

Fisher, D., Frey, N., & Lapp, D. (2009). *Reading state of mind: Brain research, teacher modeling and comprehension instruction*. Newark, DE.: International Reading Association.

Flanigan, K., & Greenwood. S. (2007). Effective content instruction in the middle: Matching students, purposes, words, and strategies. *Journal of Adolescent Literacy, 51* (3), 226-238.

Fletcher, R. (2010). *Pyrotechnics: Playful craft that sparks writing*. Portland, ME: Stenhouse.

Frayer, D., Fredrick, W., & Klausmeier, H. (1969). *A Schema for testing the level of cognitive mastery*. Madison, WI: Center for Education Research.

Fry, E. (1977). *Elementary Reading Instruction*. Columbus, OH: McGraw-Hill.

Gallagher, K. (2006). *Teaching adolescent writers*. Portland, ME: Stenhouse.

Gambrell, L. (1996). What research reveals about discussion. In L. B. Gambrell & J. F. Almasi (Eds.), *Lively Discussion: Fostering engaged reading* (pp. 25-38). Newark, DE: International Reading Association.

Gambrell, L., & Headley, K. (2006). Developing vocabulary by learning words through context. In C. Block & J. Mangieri (Eds.), *The vocabulary-enriched classroom* (pp. 18-35). New York: Scholastic.

Gambrell. L., & Koskinen, P. (2002). Imagery: A strategy for enhancing comprehension. In C. Block and M. Pressley, *Comprehension Instruction: Research-based practices* (pp. 305-318). New York: Guilford Press.

Gilmore, B. (2006). *Speaking volumes: How to get students discussing books–and much more*. Portsmouth, NH: Heinemann.

Goldman S., & Rakestraw, J. (2000). Structural aspects of constructing meaning from text. In M. Kamil, P. Mosenthal, P. D. Pearson & R. Barr (Eds.), *Handbook of Reading Research* Vol. III (pp. 311-335). New York: Longman.

Graham, S., & Hebert, M. (2010). Writing to read: Evidence for how writing can improve reading. *Carnegie Corporation Time to Act Report*. Washington, DC: Alliance for Excellent Education.

Graham, S., & Perin, D. (2007). *Writing next: Effective strategies to improve writing of adolescents in middle and high schools*. New York: Carnegie Corporation of New York.

Granat, K. (2004, July). *Walking through a painting*. Presentation at the Project CRISS National Conference, Kalispell, Montana.

Graves, D. (1994). *A Fresh Look at Writing*. Portsmouth, NH: Heinemann.

Harmon, J., Wood, K., Hedrick, W., Vintinner, J., & Willeford, T. (2009). Interactive word walls: More than just reading the writing on the walls. *Journal of Adolescent and Adult Literacy, 52* (5), 398-408.

Heller, R., & Greenleaf, C. (2007). *Literacy instruction in the content areas: Getting to the core of middle and high school improvement*. Washington, D C: Alliance for Excellent Education.

Herber, H. (1978). *Teaching reading in content areas* (2nd ed.). Englewood Cliffs, NJ: Prentice Hall.

Herman, P.A. (1984). *Incidental Learning of Word Meanings from Expository Texts that Systematically Vary Text Features*. Paper presented at the National Reading Conference, St. Petersburg, Florida.

Holliday, W. (1991). Helping students learn effectively from text. In C. Santa & D. Alvermann (Eds.), *Science learning: processes and applications*. Newark: DE: International Reading Association.

Jensen, E. (2005). *Teaching with the brain in mind*. Alexandria, VA: ASCD.

Johnson D., & Pearson. P. (1984). *Teaching reading vocabulary* (2nd ed.). New York: Holt, Rinehart and Winston.

Kagan, S. (1989). The structural approach to cooperative learning. *Educational Leadership, 40* (4), 12-3.

Keene, E., & Zimmermann, S. (2007). *Mosaic of Thought: Teaching Comprehension in a Reader's Workshop*. Portsmouth, NH: Heinemann.

Kieffer, M., & Lesaux, N. (2007). Breaking down words to build meaning: Morphology, vocabulary and reading comprehension in the urban classroom. *The Reading Teacher, 61* (2), 134-144.

Kintsch, W. (2009). Learning and constructivism. In S. Tobias & T. M. Duffy (Eds.) *Constructivist Instruction: Success or failure?* (pp. 223-241). New York: Routledge.

Kletzien, S. (2009). Paraphrasing: An effective comprehension strategy. *The Reading Teacher, 63* (1), 73-77.

Kletzien, S., & Baloche, L (1994). The shifting muffled sound of the pick: Facilitating student-to-student discussions. *Journal of Reading. 37* (7), 540-545.

Langer, J. (2009). Contexts for adolescent literacy. In L. Christenbury, R. Bomer & P. Smagorinsky (Eds.), *Handbook of Adolescent Literacy Research* (pp.49-64). New York: Guilford Press.

Larson, L.C. (2009). e-Reading and e-responding: New tools for the next generation of readers. *Journal of Adolescent & Adult Literacy, 53* (3), 255–258.

Laverick, C. (2002). B-D-A strategy: Reinventing the wheel can be a good thing. *Journal of Adolescent & Adult Literacy, 46* (2), 144-147.

Liang, L., & Dole, J.A. (2006). Help With Teaching Reading Comprehension: Comprehension Instructional Frameworks. *The Reading Teacher, 59* (8), 742–753.

Lorch, R. F. (1989). Text signaling devices and their effects on reading and memory processes. *Educational Psychology Review, 1,* 209-234.

Lorch, R. F., Lorch, E. P., Ritchey, K., McGovern, L., & Coleman, D. (2001). Effects of headings on text summarization. *Contemporary Educational Psychology, 26,* 171-191.

Marzano, R. (2004). *Building background knowledge for academic achievement: Research on what words in schools.* Alexandria, VA: ASCD.

Marzano, R. (2010). Summarizing to comprehend. *Educational Leadership, 67* (6), 83-84.

Marzano, R. J., Frontier, T., & Livingston, D. (2011). *Effective supervision: supporting the art and science of teaching.* Alexandria, VA: ASCD.

Marzano, R., Pickering, D., & Pollock J. (2001). *Classroom instruction that works: Research-based strategies for increasing student achievement.* Alexandria, VA: ASCD.

Mason, L., Benedek-Wood, E., & Valasa, L. (2010). Teaching low-achieving students to self-regulate persuasive quick write responses. *Journal of Adolescent & Adult Literacy, 53,* 303-312.

McIntosh, M., & Draper R. (1995). Applying the question-answer relationship strategy in mathematics. *Journal of Adolescent & Adult Literacy, 39* (2), 120-129.

McKeown, M., & Beck, I. (2008). Issues in the advancement of vocabulary instruction. In K. D. Stahl & M. C. McKenna (Eds.) *Reading research at work: Foundations of effective practice* (pp. 262-271). New York: Guilford Press.

McKeown, M.G., Beck, I.L., & Blake, R.K. (2009). Rethinking reading comprehension Instruction: A Comparison of instruction for strategies and content approaches. *Reading Research Quarterly, 44* (3), 218–253.

McKeown, M. G., & Curtis, M. E. (Eds.). (1987). *The nature of vocabulary acquisition.* Mahwah, NJ: Lawrence Earlbaum.

Miller, G. (1956). The magical number seven, plus or minus two: Some limits on our capacity for processing information. *Psychological Review, 63,* 81-97.

Moje, E. B., Stockdill, D., Kim, K., & Kim, H. (2011). The role of text in disciplinary learning. In M. Kamil, P. D. Pearson, P. Mosenthal, P. Afflerback, & E. B. Moje (Eds.), *Handbook of Reading Research*, Vol. IV, pp. 453-486. Mahwah, NJ: Erlbaum/Taylor & Francis.

Moje, E. (2007). Developing socially just subject-matter instruction: A review of the literacy on disciplinary literacy teaching. *Review of Research in Education, 31,* 1-44.

Morrow, L., & Gambrell, L. (2000). Literature-based reading instruction. In M. Kamil, P. Mosenthal, P. D. Pearson & R. Barr (Eds.), *Handbook of Reading Research* Vol. III, (pp.563-586). Mahwah, NJ: Lawrence Earlbaum.

Nagy, W., & Scott, J. (2006). The state of vocabulary research in the mid-1980s. In K. Stahl & M. McKenna (Eds.), *Reading research at work: Foundations of effective practice* (pp. 217-225.) New York: Guilford Press.

Narvaez, D. (2002). Individual differences that influence reading comprehension. In C. Block & M. Pressley (Eds.), *Comprehension Instruction: Research-based practices* (pp. 158-175). New York: Guilford Press.

Nash, R. J. and D. A. Shipman. 1974. The English teacher as questioner. *English Journal,* 63:42-45.

National Governors Association Center for Best Practices & Council of Chief State School Officers. (2010). *Common Core State Standards*. Retrieved from http://www.corestandards.org.

National Governors Association Center for Best Practices and the Council of Chief State Officers. (2010). *Common Core Standards*. Retrieved from the Common Core Standards Initiative website: http://www.corestandards.org/assets/CCSSI_ELA%20Standards.pdf.

National Reading Panel (2000). *Teaching children to read: An evidence-based assessment of the scientific research literature on reading and its implications for reading instruction*. Washington, DC: U.S. Department of Health and Human Services.

Nystrand, M. (2006). Research on the role of classroom discourse as it affects reading comprehension. *Research in the Teaching of English*. 40, 393-412.

Ogle, D. (1986). K-W-L: A teaching method that develops action reading of expository text. *Reading Teacher*. 40: 464-570.

Ogle, D., & Blachowicz, C. (2002). Beyond literature circles: helping students comprehend informational texts. In C. Block & M. Pressley (Eds.), *Comprehension instruction: Research-based practices* (pp. 259-271). New York: Guilford Press.

Palincsar, A., & Brown, A. (1984). Reciprocal teaching of comprehension-fostering and comprehension-monitoring activities. *Cognition and Instruction, 2*, 117-175.

Palincsar, A., & Brown, A. (1986). Interactive teaching to promote independent learning from text. *Reading Teacher, 39*, 772-777.

Paris, S., Wasik, B., & Turner, J. (1991). The development of strategic readers. In R. Barr, M Kamil, P. Mosenthal & P. David Pearson (Eds.), *Handbook of Reading Research*, Vol. II, 609-640. New York: Longman.

Pearson, J. W., & Santa, C. M. (1995). Students as researchers of their own learning. *Journal of Reading, 38* (6), 462-469.

Pearson, P. D., & Fielding, L. (1991). Comprehension instruction. In R. Barr, M. Kamil, P. Mosenthal & P. David Pearson (Eds.), *Handbook of Reading Research*, Vol. II, 815-860. New York: Longman.

Pickert, J. W., & Anderson, R. C. (1977). Taking different perspectives on story. *Journal of Educational Psychology, 69* (4), 309-315.

Pressley, M. (2002). Comprehension strategy instruction: A turn-of-the-century status report. In C. Block & M. Pressley (Eds.), *Comprehension Instruction: Research-based practices* (pp 11-27). New York: Guilford Press.

Pressley, M. (2000). What should comprehension instruction be the instruction of? In M. Kamil, P. Mosenthal, P. D. Pearson & R. Barr (Eds.), *Handbook of Reading Research* Vol. III, (545-561). Mahwah, NJ: Lawrence Earlbaum.

Pressley, M., Disney, L., & Anderson, K. (2007). Landmark vocabulary instructional research and the vocabulary instructional research that makes sense now. In R. Wagner, A. Muse & K. Tannenbaum (Eds.). *Vocabulary acquisition: Implications for reading comprehension* (pp. 205-232). New York: Guilford Press.

RAND Reading Study Group. (2002). Reading for understanding: Toward an R&D program in reading comprehension. Santa Monica, CA: RAND. Retrieved from http://nces.ed.gov/pubsearch/pubsinfo.

Raphael, T. (1986). Teaching question answer relationships, revisited. *The Reading Teacher, 39* (6), 516-522.

Raphael, T., & Au, K. (2005). QAR: Enhancing comprehension and test taking across grades and content areas. *The Reading Teacher, 59* (3), 206-221.

Raphael, T., & Au, K. (2010). QAR: Enhancing comprehension and test taking across grades and content areas. In Afflerbach, P. (Ed.), *Essential Readings on Assessment* (pp. 73-88). Newark, DE: International Reading Association.

Raphael, T., & McKinney, J. (1983). An examination of 5th and 8th grade children's question-answering behavior: An instructional study in metacognition. *Journal of Reading Behavior, 15*, 67-86.

Raphael, T., & Wonnocott, C. (1985). Heightening fourth grade students' sensitivity to sources of information for answering comprehension questions. *Reading Research Quarterly, 30*, 206-282.

Richek, M. (2005). Words are wonderful: interactive, time-efficient strategies to teach meaning vocabulary. *The Reading Teacher, 58* (5), 414-423.

Rief, L. (2007). *Writer's-Reader's Notebook*. Portsmouth, NH: Heinemann.

Robb, L. (2010). *Teaching middle school writers: What every English teacher needs to know*. Portsmouth, NH: Heinemann.

Roe, B.D., Smith, S. H., & Burns, P. C. (2005). *Teaching reading in today's elementary schools* (9th ed.). Boston: Houghton Mifflin.

Romano, T. K. (1987). *Clearing the way: Working with teenage writers*. Portsmouth, NH: Heinemann.

Romano, T. K (1995). *Writing with passion: Life stories, multiple genres.* Portsmouth, NH: Heinemann.

Romano, T. K. (2004), *Crafting authentic voice.* Portsmouth, NH: Heinemann.

Rosenshine, B., & Meister, C. (1994). Reciprocal teaching: A review of the research. *Review of Educational Research, 64* (4), 479-530.

Saunders, W., & Goldenberg, C. (1999). The effects of instructional conversations and literature logs on limited and fluent English proficient students' story comprehension and thematic understanding. *The Elementary School Journal, 99*, 277-301.

Santa, C. M., Havens, L., & Harrison, S. (2008). Teaching secondary science through reading, writing, studying and problem solving. In D. Lapp, J. Flood & N. Farnan (Eds.). *Content Reading and Learning* (pp. 237-256). New York: Lawrence Earlbaum.

Santa, C., Dailey, S., & Nelson, M. (1985). Free response and opinion proof: A reading and writing strategy for middle and secondary teachers. *Journal of Reading, 28* (4), 346-352.

Schmidt, P., Gillen, S., Zolo, T., & Stone, R. (2002). Literacy learning and scientific inquiry: children respond. *The Reading Teacher. 55* (6), 534-548.

Schwartz, R. (1988). Learning to learn vocabulary in content area textbooks. *Journal of Reading, 32* (2), 108-118.

Schwartz, R., & Raphael T. (1985). Concept of definition: A key to improving students' vocabulary. *The Reading Teacher, 39*, 198-205.

Seglem, R., & Witte, S. (2009). You gotta see it to believe it: Teaching visual literacy in the English Classroom. *Journal of Adolescent and Adult Literacy. 53* (3) 216-226.

Shanahan, T., & Shanahan, C. (2008). Teaching disciplinary literacy to adolescents: Rethinking content-area literacy. *Harvard Educational Review, 78* (1), 40-59.

Simpson, M., & Nist, S. (2002). Encouraging active reading at the college level. In C. Block and M. Pressley. *Comprehension Instruction: Research-based practices* (pp. 365-379). New York: Guilford Press.

Spandel, V., & Stiggins, R. (1997). *Creating Writers*, New York: Longman.

Sparks. J. E. (1982). *Write for Power.* Los Angeles: Communication Associates.

Spielvogel, J. J., & Zike, D. (2010). *World History.* USA: Glencoe/McGraw-Hill.

Stahl, S., & Fairbanks, M. (2006). The effects of vocabulary instruction. A model-based meta-analysis. In K. D. Stahl & M. C. McKenna (Eds.), *Reading Research at Work: Foundations of effective practice* (pp. 226-261). New York: Guilford Press.

Stahl, S. A., Jacobson, M. G., Davis, C. E., & Davis, R. L. (2006). Prior knowledge and difficult vocabulary in the comprehension of unfamiliar text. In K. D. Stahl & M. C. McKenna (Eds.), *Reading Research at Work: Foundations of effective practice* (pp. 284-302). New York: Guilford Press.

Stahl, S. A., & McKenna, M. (Eds.). (2003). *Reading Research at work: Foundations of effective practice* (pp. 262-271). New York: Guilford Press.

Stanovich, K. E. (1986). Matthew effects in reading: Some consequences of individual differences in the acquisition of literacy. *Reading Research Quarterly, 21*, 360-407.

Stein, D., & Beed, P. (2004). Bridging the gap between fiction and nonfiction in the literature circle setting. *The Reading Teacher, 57* (6), 510-518.

Stiggins, R., Arter, J., Chappuis, J., & Chappuis, S. (2007). *Classroom Assessment for student learning: Doing it right-doing it well.* Upper Saddle River, NJ: Pearson Education.

Stiggins, R., & McTighe, J. (2006). *Understanding by Design* (2nd ed.). Upper Saddle River, NJ: Pearson Education.

Sweigart, W. (1991). Classroom talk, knowledge, development, and writing. *Research in the Teaching of English, 25* (4), 469-496.

Taylor, B. (1982a). A Summarizing Strategy to Improve Middle Grade Students' Reading and Writing Skills. *The Reading Teacher, 36* (2), 202-205.

Taylor, B. (1982b). Text structure and children's comprehension and memory for expository material. *Journal of Educational Psychology, 74*, 323-340.

Tovani, C. (2000). *I read it, but I don't get it: Comprehension strategies for adolescent readers.* Portland, ME: Stenhouse.

Tovani, C. (2004). *Do I really have to teach reading?* Portland, ME: Stenhouse.

Townsend, D. (2009). Building academic vocabulary in after-school settings: Games for growth with middle school English-language learners. *Journal of Adolescent and Adult Literacy, 53* (3), 242-251.

Trabasso, T., & Bouchard, E. (2002). Teaching readers how to comprehend text strategically. In C. Block & M. Pressley (Eds.). *Comprehension Instruction: Research-based practices* (pp. 176-200). New York: Guilford Press.

Tylka, P. (2010). *The ACT Writing Test*. Presented at the 35th Day of Reading Conference of the Secondary Reading League, Illinois. http://www.dayofreading.org/DOR10HO/Tylka-ACTWritin.pdf.

U. S. Department of Education, Institute of Education Sciences, What Works Clearinghouse. (2010). *Intervention Report: Project CRISS (CReating Independence through Student-owned Strategies)*. Retrieved from ies.ed.gov/wwc/pdf/wwc_projectcriss>061510.pdf.

Vacca, R., Vacca, J. K., & Mraz, M. (2010). *Content Area Reading: Literacy and Learning Across the Curriculum* (10th ed.). Boston: Allyn & Bacon.

Villaume, S. K., Worden, T., Williams, S., Hopkins, L., & Rosenblatt, C. (1994). Five teachers in search of a discussion. *The Reading Teacher, 47* (6), 480-487.

Wade, S. E., Schraw, G., Buxton, W. M., & Hayes, M. T. (1993). Seduction of the strategic reader: Effects of interest on strategies and recall. *Reading Research Quarterly, 28*, 93-114.

Wiggins, G., & McTighe, J. (2005). *Understanding by Design*. Alexandria, VA: ASCD.

Wilfong, L. (2009). Textmasters: Bringing literature circles to textbook reading across the curriculum. *Journal of Adolescent & Adult Literacy, 53* (2), 164-171.

Wilkinson, I. A. G. & Son, E. H. (2011). A dialogic turn in research on learning and teaching to comprehend. In M. L. Kamil, P. D. Pearson, E. B. Moje & P. Afflerbach (Eds.), *Handbook of Reading Research*, Vol. III, (pp.359-387). New York: Taylor & Francis.

Wilson, N., Grisham, D., & Smetana, L. (2009). Investigating content area teaches understanding of a content literacy framework: A yearlong professional development initiative. *Journal of Adolescent and Adult Literacy, 52* (8), 708-718.

Wittrock, M. (1992). Generative learning processes of the brain. *Educational Psychologist, 27* (4), 531-541.

Zoss, M. (2009). Visual arts and literacy. In L. Christenbury, R. Bomer & P. Smagorinsky (Eds.). *Handbook of Adolescent Literacy Research* (pp. 183-196). New York: Guilford Press.

Index

A

ABC Brainstorming, 77–78
Academic Word Walls, 223–224
Active persistence and transformation, 4-5
Active processing through writing and discussion *see* Vocabulary
Active strategies for learning (Chapter 5), 111–134
    about, 112
    combined strategies, 131–133
        Reciprocal Teaching, 132–133
    paraphrasing strategies, 123–124
        In My Own Words, 123–124
    pre/post strategies, 112–119
        Anticipation Guides, 117–119
        Know—Want to Learn—Learned Plus (K-W-L+), 112–116
    Research Base for, 112, 134
    summarizing strategies, 124–129
        Magnet Summaries, 127–129
        One-Sentence Summaries, 129–131
        Read-Recall-Check-Organize-Summarize, 127
        Summarizing Nonfiction Text, 125–127
    visualizing strategies, 119–123
        Mental Imagery, 120–121
        Picture Notes, 121–123
Addison Trail High School (Addison, Illinois), 259
Adler, M., 73, 109
Administrator support/observations, 258–259
Advantages-Disadvantages, 145–146
Almasi, J., 73, 94, 109
Alvermann, D., 82
Analyzing and applying basic patterns and structures (Chapter 3), 43–69
    about, 44–45
    analyzing author's craft and perspective, 46–50
        Analyzing Author's Craft, 46–47
        Analyzing the Author's Perspective, 47–50
    comparison organizers, 58–63
        Venn Diagrams, 58–63
            Contrast and Compare Chart, 62
            Differences and Similarities Chart, 63
            Triangular Comparison Diagram, 63
            V-Diagram, 61-62
    main idea—detail organizers, 50–58
        Concept Maps, 55–58
            Pre- and Post-Reading Concept Maps, 58
        Power Thinking, 50–53
            Power Writing, 53
            Selective Underlining and Highlighting, 54
    pattern organizers, 64–68
        Pattern Puzzles, 66–68
        Sequence Organizers, 64–66
    Research Base for, 69
Anders, P., 4, 21
Anderson, K., 220, 228
Anderson, L. W., 102, 103
Anderson, R. C., 4, 21
Andree, A., 288
Anticipation Guides, 117–119
Armbruster, B., 24–25, 26, 29, 41
Arter, J., 10
Art examples, 63, 64, 101, 116, 184, 187, 212, 224
Assessments
    creating, 10
    student needs 10–11
Atwell, N., 194, 216
Au, K., 97, 100, 102, 109
Authentic Questions, 95–96
    chart, 95
Author's craft
    Analyzing Author's Craft, 46–47
    analyzing author's craft and perspective, 46–50
    Analyzing the Author's Perspective, 47–50
    organization of CRISS manual, 40
    text complexity and, 23–41

B

Background knowledge, 3, 5, 8, 11–12, 18, 257
Baker, L., 3, 5, 21
Baloche, L., 79
Baumann, J. F., 25, 41, 220
Beck, I. L., 9, 21, 25, 27, 29, 41, 44, 69, 105, 220, 221, 222, 228, 231
Beed, P., 89
Benedek-Wood, E., 142
Beyond the CRISS Workshop (Chapter 12), 281–288
    classroom resources, 283–286
    electronic resources, 282–283
    parent resources, 287
    school/district resources, 286

Blachowicz, C., 112
Blake, R. K., 9, 21, 44, 69
Bloom, B., 102
Bloom's taxonomy, 102, 105
    chart, 103
    revised, 103
Bouchard, E., 55, 69, 94, 109, 124, 132
Bradford, S., 267–268, 271
Bransford, J. D., 3, 136, 167
Bromley, K., 228
Brown, A. L., 3, 132, 134, 136, 167
Brozo, W., 112
Buch, E., 259
Buehl, D., 27, 50, 76, 78, 82, 95, 104, 117, 120, 127, 146, 153, 181, 231
Burns, P. C., 97
Buxton, W. M., 29, 41

C

Calkins, L., 194, 216
Carousel Brainstorming, 86–87
Carr, E., 112
Caughlan, S., 73, 109
Cause-Effect (or Because-Effect), 153
Cazden, C. B., 72
Chappuis, J., 10
Chappuis, S., 10
Character Map, 57
Clark, J., 208
Classroom resources, 283–285
Cochran-Smith, M., 264, 279
Cocking, R. R., 3, 134, 136, 167
Coleman, D., 25, 41
Collard, S. B., 283–284
Combined strategies, 131–133
    Reciprocal Teaching, 132–133
Comments from CRISS (newsletter), 282
Common Core Standards, 27–28
Common writing patterns, 27–28
Comparison organizers, 58–63
Concentric Circle Discussions, 79
Concept development *see* Frayer Model
Concept Maps, 55–58
Concept of Definition Map, 235–238
Concession/Refutation Templates, 200
Conclusion-Support Notes, 142–149
    Advantages-Disadvantages, 145–146
    charts, 143
    Conclusion-Support-Interpretation Notes, 143–145
    Hypothesis-Evidence, 148–149
    Proposition-Support, 146–147
Conley, M., 112, 134
Connolly, B., 73, 109
Content domain variables, 30–32
Content Enduring Understandings, 9
Content Frames, 158–161
Content materials, selecting, 11
Content textbook assessment rubric, 33–37
Context, figuring out new words from, 226–227
Contrast and Compare Chart, 62
Conway, M., 151
Cope, K., 130

Copeland, M., 74, 80
CRISS at a Glance for Students, 285
CRISS at a Glance Poster/Desk Mat, 285
CRISS Cornerstones, 286
CRISS for Administrators, 282, 286
CRISS for Parents, 282, 287
CRISS Framework for Learning *see* Framework for Learning
CRISS Framework for Teaching *see* Framework for Teaching
CRISS Learning Posters, 285
Culham, R., 194, 216
Curtis, M. E., 220

D

Dailey, S., 142, 267, 272–278
Dale, F., 231
Daniels, H., 89
Darling-Hammond, L., 288
Devine, J., 157
Dialogue Journals, 176–178
Differences and Similarities Chart, 63
Discussion: the conversation of learning (Chapter 4), 71–109
    about, 72–74
    active persistence and transformation, 4–5
    guidelines, 74
    questioning strategies, 94–107
        Authentic Questions, 95–96
        Higher Level Thinking Questions, 102–105
        Question-Answer Relationships, 97–102
            Question Starters, 100
        Questioning the Author (QtA), 105–107
    Research Base for, 72–74, 109
    small group discussion strategies, 75–93
        ABC Brainstorming, 77–78
        Carousel Brainstorming, 86–87
        Concentric Circle Discussions, 79
            Fishbowl, 79
        Discussion Web, 82–84
        Mind Streaming, 76
            Paired Verbal Fluency, 76
        Read and Explain, 81–82
        Read-and-Say-Something, 81
        Roles within Cooperative Teams, 89–94
        Seed Discussions, 87–88
        Socratic Circles, 80–81
        Sticky-Note Discussions, 84–86
            React to the Fact, 86
        Think-Pair-Share, 75–76
        Three-Minute Pause, 78–79
Discussion Roles, 89, 90–93
Discussion Web, 82–84
Disney, L., 220, 228
District/school-specific questions to guide implementation, 259
Dole, J. A., 7
Double-Entry Reflective Journals, 174–176
Draper, R., 102
Duffy, G., 15, 21
Duke, N., 3, 4, 21, 46, 69
Durkin, D., 112, 134
Duval, D., 78, 127, 177, 183

E

Edwards, E. C., 220
Electronic resources, 282–283
Elementary school examples, 52, 85, 156, 162, 238, 247-248, 267-268
ENGAGE with content and transform information, 8, 13-15, 18
    chart (P-PER, PER), 8, 257
    discussion, 8, 14, 18, see also Chapter 4
    organization, 8, 14–15, 18, see also Chapters 3, 5, 6, and 9
    visualization, 8, 14, 18, 119–123
    writing, 8, 13–14, 18, see also Chapters 7 and 8
Engelhart, M., 102
English see English language arts examples
English language arts examples, 62, 77, 83, 85, 91, 92, 93, 96, 105, 129, 144, 145-146, 151, 162, 163, 172, 177, 178, 198, 199, 201-202, 205, 210, 212, 225, 238, 239, 247-248, 268-271
English as a second or other language examples, 208–209
Essay examination, 213–216
    preparing for, 213
Essential questions, 9
Evaluating journals and learning logs, 189–190
Examining author's perspective, 31-32
Explanation Entries, 186–189
Explanatory writing, 27–28

F

Fact-Opinion Notes, 140–141
Fact-Reason Notes, 140
Fairbanks, M., 220, 221
Felton, M., 143
Ferwerda, J., 210
Fielding, L., 3, 21
Figuring Out New Words from Context, 226-227
Fishbowl, 79
Fisher, D., 2, 228
Five Star School, 254–255
Flanagan, K., 222–223
Fletcher, R., 194, 216
Fogle, B. J., 140
Foreign language examples, 59, 231, 239, 246
Formal writing to learn: writing reports and essays (Chapter 8), 193–218
    about, 194–195
    essay examination, 213–216
    RAFT, 206–212
        Multi-Genre Report, 212
    Research Base for, 194-195, 218
    Spool Papers, 200–206
    Writing Templates, 195–200
Foster, J., 63
Four-level-framework (word identification), 222–223
Fourth grade social studies, student research, 267–268
Framework for Learning, 17-18
    diagram, 8, 257
    questions to consider chart, 18
Framework for Learning Inventory, 260
Framework for Learning Questions to Consider, 18
Framework for Teaching, 9–15
    diagram, 8, 257
Framework for Teaching Inventory, 255–256
PLAN for instruction, 9–11
Frayer, D., 240
Frayer Model, 240–243
Frederick, W., 240
Free-Write Entries, 170–174, 171
Frey, N., 2, 228
Fry, E., 24
Furst, E., 102

G

Gallagher, K., 194, 216
Gambrell, L., 4, 21, 73, 109, 119, 134, 220
Gillen, S., 116
Gilmore, B., 79
Global Warming: A Personal Guide to Causes and Solutions (Collard), 284
Goldenberg, C., 73, 109
Goldman, S., 4, 21, 29, 32, 41, 46, 55, 69
Graham, S., 4, 21, 170, 191, 194, 218
Granat, K., 184
Graphic organizers and charts, 235–238
    Concept of Definition Map, 235–238
    Vocabulary Maps, 238–240
Graves, D., 194, 216
Greenleaf, C., 30, 41
Greenwood, S., 222–223
Grisham, D., 97, 109
Guided practice see modeling and guided practice
Guide Templates, 174

H

Harmon, J., 224
Hayes, M. T., 29, 41
Headley, K., 220
Health examples, 58, 113-114, 120, 147, 152
Hebert, M., 4, 21, 170, 191, 194, 218
Hedrick, W., 224
Heller, R., 30, 41
Herber, H., 117
Herko, S., 143
Herman, P. A., 26
Higher Level Thinking Questions, 102–105
High school examples, 52, 53, 57, 58, 59, 60, 61, 62, 63, 64, 65, 66, 67, 77, 78, 83, 85, 91, 92-93, 96, 101, 102, 105, 106, 107, 114, 115, 116, 118, 119, 120, 121, 122, 123, 127, 129, 130, 131, 138, 140, 141, 144, 147, 148-149, 150, 151, 153, 155, 156, 157, 159, 160, 163, 164, 165, 166, 172, 175, 175-176, 178, 179, 180-181, 181, 182-183, 184, 185, 185-186, 186-187, 187, 188, 189, 196-197, 198, 199, 205, 206, 208-209, 210, 211, 212, 224, 230, 234, 237, 239, 242, 243, 244, 245, 246, 247, 248-249, 249, 250, 268-271, 271, see also secondary school examples
Hill, W., 102
History examples see social studies examples
History-Change Frame, 153–154
Hocker, K., 131
Holliday, B., 26, 27, 221
Hopkins, L., 82
Hypothesis-Evidence, 148–149

I

Impact of Project CRISS on instruction, 255-259, *see also* program implementation
Informal research studies, 260
Informal writing to learn (Chapter 7), 169–191
    about, 170
    Dialogue Journals, 176–178
    Double-Entry Reflective Journals, 174–176
    Explanation Entries, 186–189
    Free-Write Entries, 170–174
        Stop-and-Think, 171
    managing and evaluating journals and learning logs, 189–190
    Observation Entries, 180–181
    Perspective Entries, 184–186
    Pre- and Post-Reading Entries, 178–180
    Research Base for, 170, 191
    You Ought to Be in Pictures, 181–184
        Walking Through a Painting, 184
In My Own Words, 123–124
Institute of Education Sciences (U.S. Department of Education), 260
Introduction, Modeling, and Reflection, 15-16, 44–45
Introduction, of strategies, 15

J

Jensen, E., 3, 4, 21
Jensen, S., 115
Johnson, J., 159
Journals *see* informal writing to learn

K

K-W-L + *see* Know—Want to Learn—Learned Plus
Kagan, S., 75
Keene, E., 4, 21
Kerby, K., 77
Kieffer, M., 228
Kim, H., 30
Kim, K., 30
Kintsch, W., 2, 3, 4, 5, 21, 28–29, 41
Klausmeier, H., 240
Kletzien, S., 79, 123–124, 134
Know—Want to Learn—Learned Plus (K-W-L+), 112–116
    chart, 113
Koskinen, P., 4, 21, 119, 134
Krathwohl, D. R., 102, 103
Krusz, B., 267, 271
Kucan, L., 27, 41, 105, 220, 221, 222, 228

L

Langer, J., 72, 109
Language arts examples *see* English language arts examples
Lapp, D., 2
Larson, L. C., 176
Laverick, C., 116
Learning *see* active strategies for learning; Frameworks for Learning; organizing for learning
Learning Forward, 282
Learning logs, *see* informal writing to learn
Lesaux, N., 228
Level of Use Matrix, 256

Liang, L., 7
Literature Study Guidelines for Younger Students, 85
Long, D., 212
Longitudinal research, 276–278
Lorch, E. P., 25, 41
Lorch, R. F., 25, 41
Loxterman, J. A., 25, 41
Luberda, J., 144

M

Magnet Summaries, 127–129
Main Idea—Detail Notes, 137-141
    12-Minute Study, 139–140
    Fact-Opinion, 140–141
    Fact-Reason, 140
    Main Events—Significance, 141
    Three-Column Notes, 141
Main Idea—Detail Organizers, 50–58
    Concept Maps, 55–58
        Pre- and Post-Reading Concept Maps, 58
    Power Thinking, 50–53
        Power Writing, 53
    Selective Underlining and Highlighting, 54–55
Managing journals and learning logs, 189–190
Marshall, B., 140
Marzano, R., 55, 69, 94, 109, 124, 125, 134, 223
Mason, L., 142
Mathematics examples, 60, 62, 66, 67, 75, 92, 102, 107, 119, 130, 155, 156, 157, 158, 160, 165, 186-187, 188, 189, 198, 210-211, 234, 237, 243, 246, 249, 271
Mathematics textbook rubric, 39
McGovern, L., 25, 41
McIntosh, M., 102
McKeown, M. G., 9, 21, 25, 27, 29, 41, 44, 69, 105, 220, 221, 222, 228
McKinney, J., 97
McTighe, J., 9, 21
Meister, C., 132, 134
Mental Imagery, 120–121
Metacognition
    as Project CRISS foundational element, 2–3
    elements of, 3–7
    helping students understand (vignette), 6–7
    importance of, 6
    ingredients of (PER), 8, 257
    instructional frameworks for, 7–8, *see also* Framework for Learning; Framework for Teaching
    model of metacognitive teaching (vignette), 19
    vocabulary and, 221, 241
Meyer, J., 57
Middle school examples, 58, 60, 75, 85, 102, 120, 152, 157, 159, 162, 173, 177, 189, 198, 225, 237, 248-249, 272-276
Miller, G., 5
Miller, J. 50
Mind Streaming, 76
Mitchel, K., 144
Modeling and guided practice, 15–17
Moje, E., 30, 41
Montana History, 272–276
Montana Writing Project, 206–207
Morpheme and context clue analysis chart, 230

Morphemic analysis, 228–231
Morrow, L., 73, 109
Mraz, M., 97
Multi-Genre Report, 212
Music examples, 56, 101

N

Nagy, W., 220, 221
Narvaez, D., 4, 21
Nash, R.J., 94
National Assessment of Educational Progress, 112
National Diffusion Network, U.S. Department of Education, 260
National Reading Panel, 97, 220
National Staff Development Council, 282
Nelson, M., 142
News Article Power Writing Guide, 53
Nist, S., 124
Nystrand, M., 72, 94, 109

O

Observation Entries, 180–181
Ogle, D., 112
One-Sentence Summaries, 129–131
Organization of CRISS manual, 40
Organizing, *see also* organizing for learning
    Problem-Solving Organizer, 157–158
    for vocabulary instruction, 222–225
Organizing for learning (Chapter 6), 135–167
    about, 136
    Content Frames, 158–161
    Research Base for, 136, 167
    Story Plans, 161–166
    Two-Column Notes, 137–158
        Conclusion-Support Notes, 142–149
        Main Idea—Detail Notes, 137–141
            12 Minute Study, 139
            Fact-Opinion, 140–141
            Fact-Reason, 140
            Main Events—Significance, 141
            Three-Column Notes, 141
        Problem-Solution Notes, 149–154
            Cause-Effect (or Because-Effect), 153
            History-Change Frame, 153–154
            Problem-Analysis Notes, 153
            Problem-Solution Graphic Structure, 152
        Process Notes, 154–158
Orphanos, S., 288

P

Paired Verbal Fluency, 76
Palinscar, A. M., 132, 134
Paraphrasing strategies, 123–124
    In My Own Words, 123–124
Parents, resources for reaching out to, 287
Pattern organizers, 64–68. *see also* analyzing *and* applying basic patterns *and* structures
    Pattern Puzzles, 66–68
    Sequence Organizers, 64–66
Pattern Puzzles, 66–68
Pearson, P. D., 3, 4, 21, 41, 46, 69

Peck, R., 96
Perin, D., 194, 218
Personal definitions, 231–234
    Rate Your Knowledge, 231–232
    Student-Friendly Explanations, 233–234
Perspective Entries, 184–186
Physical education examples, 50-51
Pickering, D., 94, 109
Pickert, J. W., 4, 21
Picture Notes, 121–123, 136
PLAN for instruction, 8, 9-11
    assessment, 10-11
    chart (P-PER), 8, 257
    content materials selection, 11
    enduring understandings, 9–10
Plettner, C., 265
Poetry, discussion roles for, 92-93
Pollock, J., 94, 109
Power Notes, 52, 136
Power Thinking, 50–53
Power Writing, 53
Pre- and Post-Concept Maps, 58
Pre- and Post-Reading Entries, 178–180
Prefixes chart, 229
PREPARE for student learning, 8, 11-13, 257
    author's craft, 12-13, 18
    background knowledge, 11–12, 18
    chart (PER), 8, 257
    purpose setting, 12, 18
Pre/post strategies, 112–119
    Anticipation Guides, 117–119
    Know—Want to Learn—Learned Plus (K-W-L+), 112–116
Pressley, M., 3, 21, 112, 134, 220, 228
Problem-Analysis Notes, 153
Problem-Solution Notes, 149–154
    Cause-Effect (or Because-Effect), 153
    framework for fiction, 151
    History-Change Frame, 153–154
    Problem-Analysis Notes, 153
    Problem-Solution Graphic Structure, 152
Problem-Solving Organizer, 157–158
Process conference, 5, 6, 16, 45, 112, 113, *see also* reflection *and* REFLECT on teaching and learning
Process Enduring Understandings, 9–10
Process Notes, 154–158
Professional Learning in the Learning Profession: A Status Report on Teacher Development in the U.S. and Abroad (Learning Forward), 282, 282
Program implementation (Chapter 10), 253–262
    about, 253–254
    impact of Project CRISS on instruction, 255–259
        administrator support and observations, 258–259
        CRISS Framework for Teaching, 256–257
        Framework for Teaching Inventory, 255–256
        Level of Use Matrix, 256
        teacher journals and portfolios, 258
    quality of Project CRISS implementation, 254–255
        Five Star School, 254–255
    Research Base for, 262
    student implementation, 259–261
        district/school-specific questions, 259
        informal research studies, 260

quantitative research, 260–261
    Student Framework for Learning Inventory, 260
Project CRISS, defined, 2–3
Project CRISS: teachers/students as researchers (Chapter 11), 263–279
    about, 264
    Framework for Learning research, 272–278
    longitudinal research, 276–278
    Research Base for, 279
    student research, 267–272
    teacher research, 264–267
Project CRISS Certified Trainer Materials, 286
Project CRISS Classroom Presentation Materials CD, 284
Project CRISS for Homeschool Parents, 287
Project CRISS for Students I: It's a Brain Thing - Learning How to Learn!, 283
Project CRISS for Students II: LEARNING To Succeed, 284
Project CRISS Reference Guide for Teachers: Strategies for Successful Teaching and Learning, 284
Project CRISS website, 282–283
Proposition-Support, 146–147
Purpose setting, 3-4, 5, 8, 12

Q

Qualitative measures defining considerate text, 25–27
Quantitative measures of text difficulty, 24–25
Quantitative research, 260–261
Question-Answer Relationships, 97–102
    4 types of questions, 97
    book vs. brain, 100
Questioning strategies, 94–107
    Authentic Questions, 95–96
    Question-Answer Relationships, 97–102
    Questioning the Author (QtA), 105–107
Question Starters, 100
Question Starters & Frames for Higher-Level Questions table, 104
Questions for Critical Analysis of Author's Perspective, 49

R

RAFT, 206–212
    formats chart, 208
    Multi-genre Reports, 212
    strong verbs chart, 208
Rakestraw, J., 4, 21, 29, 32, 46, 55, 69
RAND Reading Study Group, 97
Raphael, T., 97, 100, 102, 109, 235
Rate Your Knowledge, 231-232
React to the Fact, 86
Read and Explain, 81–82
Read-and-Say-Something, 81
Reading in the Content Areas with Dr. Carol Santa, 286
Reading Research Quarterly, 112
Read-Recall-Check-Organize-Summarize, 127
Reciprocal Teaching, 132–133
Reflection, 5–6, 7, *see also* REFLECT on teaching and learning *and* process conference
    as part of instructional sequence, 16, 44–45
    role of (in teacher research), 266
REFLECT on teaching and learning, 3, 5–6, 7, 8, 15, 16, 18, 44–45
    chart (PER), 8, 257

Research *see also* Project CRISS: teachers/students as researchers
    informal studies, 260
    quantitative, 260–261
Research Base (annotated charts)
    Chapter 1: Teaching for Understanding, 21
    Chapter 2: Text Complexity, 41
    Chapter 3: Patterns and Structures, 69
    Chapter 4: Discussion, 109
    Chapter 5: Active Strategies for Learning, 134
    Chapter 6: Organizing for Learning, 167
    Chapter 7: Informal Writing, 169
    Chapter 8: Formal Writing, 218
    Chapter 9: Vocabulary, 252
    Chapter 10: Program Implementation, 262
    Chapter 11: Teachers and Students as Researchers, 279
    Chapter 12: Beyond the CRISS Workshop, 296
Resources *see* Beyond the CRISS Workshop
Review a Book in an Hour, 123
Revised Bloom's taxonomy, 102-103
Richardson, N., 288
Rief, L., 194, 216
Ritchey, K., 25, 41
Robb, L., 194, 216
Roe, B. D., 97
Roles within Cooperative Teams, 89–93
Romano, T., 194, 212, 216
Rosenblatt, C., 87
Rosenshine, B., 132, 134
Rougle, E., 73, 109
Rusnak, G., 153

S

Sample subject-specific rubrics, 37–39
Santa, C., 142, 264, 268
Saunders, W., 73, 109
Scalf, J., 266
Schmidt, P., 116
School/district resources, 286
Schraw, G., 29, 41
Schwartz, R., 235
Science examples, 60, 61-62, 65, 101, 105, 120, 121, 122, 131, 138, 140, 144, 146, 148-149, 150, 156, 159, 166, 173, 175, 179, 180-181, 185-186, 188, 196-197, 199-200, 206, 209-210, 212, 214-215, 230, 234, 238, 243, 244, 245, 247
Scientific Inquiry Grid, 116
Scott, J., 220, 221
Secondary school examples, 52, 53, 57, 58, 59, 60, 61, 62, 63, 64, 65, 66, 67, 77, 78, 83, 85, 91, 92-93, 96, 101, 102, 105, 106, 107, 114, 115, 116, 118, 119, 120, 121, 122, 123, 127, 129, 130, 131, 138, 140, 141, 144, 147, 148-149, 150, 151, 153, 155, 156, 157, 159, 160, 162, 163, 164, 165, 166, 172, 173, 175, 175-176, 177, 178, 179, 180-181, 181, 182-183, 184, 185, 185-186, 186-187, 187, 188, 189, 196-197, 198, 199, 205, 206, 208-209, 210, 211, 212, 224, 225, 230, 234, 237, 239, 242, 243, 244, 245, 246, 247, 248-249, 249, 250, 268-271, 271, 272-276
Seed Discussion Roles, 88
Seed Discussions, 87–88

Seglem, R., 119
Selective Underlining/Highlighting, 53–55
Semantic Feature Analysis, 244–245
Sentence and Word Expansion, 247–249
Sequence Organizers, 64–66
Shanahan, C., 30–31, 41
Shanahan, T., 30–31, 41
Shipman, D.A., 94
Simpson, M., 124
Sinatra, G. M., 25, 41
Skoog, J., 243
Small group discussion strategies, 75–93
    ABC Brainstorming, 77–78
    Carousel Brainstorming, 86–87
    Concentric Circle Discussions, 79
        Fishbowl, 79
    Discussion Web, 82–84
    Mind Streaming, 76
        Paired Verbal Fluency, 76
    Read and Explain, 81–82
    Read-and-Say-Something, 81
    Roles within Cooperative Teams, 89–93
    Seed Discussions, 87–88
    Socratic Circles, 80–81
    Sticky-Note Discussions, 84–86
        React to the Fact, 86
    Think-Pair-Share, 75–76
    Three-Minute Pause, 78–79
Smetana, L., 97, 109
Smith, M., 73, 109
Smith, S. H., 97
Sobota, T., 210
Social studies examples, 52, 53, 57, 78, 83, 105, 106, 115, 118, 123, 127, 140, 141, 141, 144, 153, 154, 160, 164, 172, 175-176, 179, 182-183, 185, 197, 198, 199, 205, 206, 211, 212, 215, 237, 238, 242, 248-249, 250, 272-276
Socratic Circles, 80–81
Sonderegger, M., 211
Spandel, V., 194
Sparks, J. E., 50
Spitler, E., 4, 21
Spool Paper Outline, 203
Spool Papers, 200–206
    editing checklist, 204
Stahl, S., 220, 221
Stanovich, K. E., 220
Stein, D., 89
Steineke, N., 89
Stern, R., 116, 145
Stevens, R., 72
Sticky-Note Discussions, 84–86
Sticky-Note Guidelines, 85
Stiggins, R., 10, 194
Stockdill, D., 30
Stone, J., 116
Stone, R., 116
Stop-and-Think, 171
Story Plan Map, 163
Story Plans, 161–166
Strong Verbs Chart, 208
Structures *see* analyzing and applying basic patterns and structures

Student-Friendly Explanations guide, 233
Student implementation, 259–261
    district/school-specific questions, 259
    Framework for Learning Inventory, 260
    informal research studies, 260
    quantitative research, 260–261
Student/text variables, 28–30
Suffixes, 229
Summarizing Nonfiction Text, 125–127
Summarizing strategies, 124–131
    Magnet Summaries, 127–129
    One-Sentence Summaries, 129–131
    Read-Recall-Check-Organize-Summarize, 127
    Summarizing Nonfiction Text, 125–127
Support and Extensions sequences, explained, 16, 45
Survival word attack skills, 225–231
Sweigart, W., 73, 109

T

Taylor, B., 125
Teacher journals and portfolios, 258
Teachers, as researchers, 263–279
Teaching *see* Frameworks for Teaching; teaching for understanding
Teaching for understanding (Chapter 1), 1–21
    about, 2–3
    background knowledge, eliciting, 11–12
    elements of metacognition, 3–7
        active persistence and transformation, 4–5
        author's craft, 4, 12–13
        background knowledge, 3, 11–12
        purpose setting, 3–4, 12
        reflection, 5–7, 15
    Framework for Learning, 7–8, 17–18
        questions to consider, 18
    Framework for Teaching, 7–11
        ENGAGE with content and transform information, 13–15
        PLAN for instruction, 9-11
        PREPARE for student learning, 11–13
        REFLECT on teaching and learning, 15
    Frameworks for teaching and learning, 7-18
        chart, 8
    modeling and guided practice, 15–17
    Research Base for, 2-3, 21
Ten Concession/Refutation Templates, 200
Text complexity: identifying the author's craft and design (Chapter 2), 23–41
    examining text complexity, 24–32
        common writing patterns, 27–28
        content domain variables, 30–32
        qualitative measures defining considerate text, 25–27
        quantitative measures of text difficulty, 24–25
        student and text variables, 28–30
        student knowledge of text structure, 32
    organization of CRISS manual, 40
    Research Base for, 41
    tools for examining text, 33–39
        content textbook assessment rubric, 33–37
        sample subject-specific rubrics, 37–39
Text Features Two-Column Notes, 47
Theis, K., 115

Thiessen, E., 212
Think-Pair-Share, 75–76
Thorndike, E. L., 220
Three-Column Notes, 141
Three-Minute Pause, 78–79
Todnem, G., 118
Tools for examining text, 33–39
Tovani, C., 140, 174
Trabasso, T., 55, 69, 94, 109, 124, 132, 134, 161, 167
Transform information *see* ENGAGE with content and transform information
Transition signal words, 196
Triangular Comparison Diagram, 63
12-Minute Study, 139
Two-Column Notes, 137–158
    Conclusion-Support Notes, 142–149
        Advantages-Disadvantages, 145–146
        Conclusion-Support-Interpretation Notes, 143
        Hypothesis-Evidence, 148–149
        Proposition-Support, 146–147
    Main Idea—Detail Notes 137–141
        Fact-Opinion, 140–141
        Fact-Reason, 140
        Main Events—Significance, 141
        Three-Column Notes, 141
        12-Minute Study, 139–140
    Problem-Solution Notes, 149–154
        Cause-Effect (Because-Effect), 153
        History-Change Frame, 153–154
        Problem-Analysis Notes, 153
        Problem-Solution Graphic Structure, 152
    Process Notes 154–158
        Problem-Solving Organizer, 157–158
Tylka, P., 200

U
Understanding by Design (Wiggins, McTighe), 9
U.S. Department of Education, 260

V
Vacca, J. K., 97
Vacca, R., 97
Valasa, L., 142
Vandevanter, N., 206–207
V-Diagrams, 61–62
Venn Diagrams, 58–63
    blank diagram, 59
    contrast and compare charts, 62
    differences and similarities charts, 63
    triangular comparison diagrams, 63
    V-Diagrams, 61–62
Vignettes
    I. Helping students understand metacognition, 6-7
    II. A model of metacognitive teaching, 19-20
Villaume, S. K., 82
Vintinner, J., 224
Visualizing strategies, 119–123
    Mental Imagery, 120–121
    Picture Notes, 121–123
Vocabulary (Chapter 9), 219–252
    about, 220-222

    active processing through writing and discussion, 245–250
        Sentence and Word Expansion, 247–249
        Word Combining, 249–250
            Possible Sentences, 250
        Word Elaboration, 246
    building personal definitions, 231–234
        Rate Your Knowledge, 231–232
        Vocabulary Knowledge Chart, 232
        Student-Friendly Explanations, 233–234
    graphic organizers and charts, 235–245
        Concept of Definition Map, 235–238
        Frayer Model, 240–243
        Semantic Feature Analysis, 244–245
        Vocabulary Maps, 238–240
        Vocabulary Flash Cards, 240
    organizing for vocabulary instruction, 222–225
        Academic Word Walls, 223–224
        identifying words worthy of rich instruction, 222–223
        Vocabulary Learning Logs, 224–225
    Research Base for, 220–222, 252
    survival word attack skills, 225–231
        figuring out new words from context, 226–227
        morphemic analysis, 228–231
    Vocabulary Maps, 238–240
Vocabulary Flash Cards, 238–240
Vocabulary Knowledge Chart, 232
Vocabulary Learning Logs, 224–225
Vocabulary Maps, 238–240

W
Wade, S. E., 29, 41
Walking Through a Painting, 184
Ware, D., 220
Watson, J., 267, 268
Wiggins, G., 9, 21
Wilfong, L., 89
Willeford, T., 224
Williams, S., 82
Wilson, N., 97, 109
Witte, S., 119
Wittrock, M., 136, 167
Wood, K., 224
Word attack skills, 225–231
Word Combining, 249–250
Word Elaboration, 246
Word problem process notes, 154-155
Worden, T., 82
Word roots, 228
World language examples *see* Foreign language examples
Worthy, J., 29, 41
Writing. *see also* informal writing to learn *and* formal writing to learn
    common writing patterns, 27–28
    component of active persistence and transformation, 4
    creating opportunities for (ENGAGE), 13–14
    research supporting, 170, 191, 194, 218
Writing Templates, 195–200

Y
You Ought to Be in Pictures, 181–184

Z
Zimmermann, S., 4, 21
Zolo, T., 116
Zoss, M., 5, 29, 41